Landmarks in Science

LANDMARKS IN SCIENCE
Hippocrates to Carson

ROBERT B. DOWNS

LIBRARIES UNLIMITED, INC.
Littleton, Colorado
1982

LIBRARIES UNLIMITED, INC.
P.O. Box 263
Littleton, Colorado 80160

Library of Congress Cataloging in Publication Data

Main entry under title:

Landmarks in science.

    Bibliography: p. 291
    Includes index.
    1. Science--History. 2. Scientists--Biography.
I. Downs, Robert Bingham, 1903-
Q125.L29   500   82-154
ISBN 0-87287-295-5   AACR2

Table of Contents

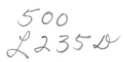
5

Acknowledgments

Various chapters appearing in the present work in revised form have been taken over from earlier works.

By permission of The Macmillan Company, the following authors from my *Books That Changed America* are incorporated herein: William Beaumont, Oliver Wendell Holmes, and Rachel Carson.

Appreciation should be expressed also to McGraw-Hill Book Company for permission to include, from my *Famous American Books*, essays in revised form on Benjamin Franklin, Nathaniel Bowditch, John James Audubon, Asa Gray, Matthew Fontaine Maury, William James, and Alfred Kinsey.

From *Books That Changed the World* (American Library Association and New American Library), modified discussions have been added of the writings of Nicolaus Copernicus, William Harvey, Isaac Newton, Charles Darwin, Sigmund Freud, and Albert Einstein.

Chief responsibility for the preparation of the manuscript, as frequently in the past, was in the highly capable hands of Deloris Holiman. She was assisted by Robert F. Delzell and Jytte Millan, to all of whom I am grateful. Their help was indispensable.

Introduction

In undertaking to survey the great landmarks, milestones, or masterworks in science from ancient to modern times, selection is a primary factor. The extent of the literature is simply overwhelming. For example, the catalog of the great history of science collection at the University of Oklahoma (London: Mansell, 1976. 2v.) contains 39,000 entries, describing 50,000 separate volumes. For a more limited period, Margaret Stillwell's *The Awakening Interest in Science during the First Century of Printing, 1450-1550* (New York: Bibliographical Society of America, 1970) lists 900 works.

Three highly selective sources were the chief guides used in choosing books to be discussed in the present work:

> Dibner, Bern. *Heralds of Science, as Represented by Two Hundred Epochal Books and Pamphlets Selected from the Burndy Library* (Norwalk, CT: Burndy Library, 1955). (Collection now in the Smithsonian Institution.)

> Horblit, Harrison D. *One Hundred Books Famous In Science, Based on an Exhibition Held at the Grolier Club* (New York: Grolier Club, 1964).

> Buffalo Society of Natural History Library. *Milestones of Science, Epochal Books in the History of Science as Represented in the Library of the Buffalo Society of Natural History, Catalog Compiled by Ruth A. Sparrow* (Buffalo, NY: The Society, 1972).

Numerous standard histories of science were also consulted and proved useful in deciding among outstanding figures and titles. Of particular value, especially for the early centuries, were George Sarton's renowned five-volume *Introduction to the History of Science* and his other important works in the field.

A. R. Hall's *The Scientific Revolution, 1500-1800* examined the state of scientific books before 1500. He notes that "the printed literature of science at the beginning of the sixteenth century was in the main dominated by the established traditions." As evidence, he cites A. C. Klebs' *Incunabula Scientifica et Medica* (1938), which lists more than 3,000 editions of 1,044 titles by about 650 authors. Among these are 95 editions and collections of works attributed to Aristotle, eighteen editions of Pliny's *Natural History*, seven of Ptolemy's *Cosmographia*, two of Euclid, and five of Lucretius. Of ancient medical writers, Dioscorides' *De Materia Medica* was printed twice and Galen once, but Hippocrates and Galen were included in numerous collections of medical authorities. Celsus' *De Medica* was printed four times. In addition, translations from the Arabic were often printed, including fourteen editions of Avicenna's *Canon of Medicine.*

Hall states that the proportion of scientific books printed in vernacular languages was relatively small. Latin was still the predominant language of science in Europe. German was best represented, followed by French and Italian. Herbals were available to the vernacular reader, as were treatises on anatomy. H. S. Bennett, in *English Books and Readers, 1475-1557*, found several surgical and anatomical texts in English, but he concluded that "they contributed little or nothing that was new. Their compilers were content to reproduce knowledge that had been current for centuries."

From these facts, Hall points out that "those texts which had been most in demand before the invention of printing were the very ones that became most widely disseminated after it. Printing, therefore, had comparatively little immediate effect on the literature of science in the way of substituting novelties for traditions."

This situation could be attributed to at least two factors. First, readers were assumed to prefer the familiar, and second, anything new or revolutionary might have been dangerous to the health of the authors and printers. Self-preservation provided a strong motive not to depart from traditional tenets and beliefs, no matter how little based on demonstrated facts.

Tragic examples fill pages in science history. Roger Bacon in the thirteenth century was condemned by his Franciscan order for what it regarded as heretical doctrine, and spent his last years under house arrest. Nicolaus Copernicus was deterred for years from publication of his *Revolutions of the Celestial Spheres* because of the potential disapproval of the Church, and did not see the book until a few hours before his death. Giordano Bruno rejected the idea that the earth is the center of the universe and held that the universe is infinite, for which beliefs he was burned at the stake. The same fate was suffered by Michael Servetus, at the hands of John Calvin, for his heretical views, including a belief in the circulation of the blood. William Harvey was subjected to prolonged hostility by the University of Paris medical school faculty for his writings on blood circulation. Andreas Vesalius was roundly condemned because his findings on the structure of the human body ran contrary to the teachings of the ancient Galen, and he narrowly escaped trial by the Inquisition. Galileo was less fortunate; for his advocacy of the Copernican theories he was tried by the Inquisition and forced to spend his last years under house arrest. Controversies raging around Charles Darwin and the theory of evolution have persisted into the twentieth century, though burnings at the stake have gone out of fashion.

Science in the present work is broadly interpreted to include several branches of technology. The original plan was to treat the field of medicine separately, but interrelationships with other sciences, especially in early periods, made separation inadvisable.

The arrangement of titles calls for a brief explanation. Throughout, the order is by birth dates of the authors. The aim is to illustrate the development of scientific ideas and their interaction over the centuries. As one reviews the list as a whole, the continuity of knowledge is obvious. Isaac Newton, for example, built upon the work begun by Copernicus and carried forward by Brahe, Kepler, and Galileo. "If I have seen farther than other men," Newton remarked, "it is by standing on the shoulders of giants."

At the same time, it is virtually impossible to determine the beginning of any idea, scientific or otherwise. Modern thinkers striking out alone on what they believe are untrodden paths are likely to discover that some ancient Greek, Assyrian, Egyptian, or Roman has preceded them on the same journey. This view is well expressed by a leading historian of science, Duane H. D. Roller:

> I happen to believe that history is continuous, and as a consequence I disagree wholeheartedly with the idea that this list of books, or perhaps any other, represents "the pioneer and the trail-blazer" or that these books are the ones which first presented ideas. The mere fact that most of these books are actually summaries of many years of work done before their publication, by the author and/or others, points up how difficult it is to find the beginning of anything ... if I may illustrate with a few examples: Harvey's book represents research that builds upon that of sixteenth-century anatomists and physiologists. Yet it is through the book of Harvey that the idea has its impact. The book of Linneaus is the culmination of some two centuries of explanation of systems of classifying, particularly plants, and cannot by any means be said to represent really the beginning of anything. It is important because of its impact.[1]

A period-by-period summary or synthesis reveals the major trends of science over the more than two millennia dealt with in the present work.

We begin with the notable advances in science and mathematics, during the fourth and third centuries, B.C., by Hippocrates, Archimedes, Euclid, Theophrastus, Dioscorides, and the supreme genius Aristotle, among the Greeks. Less spectacularly, the Roman era produced a few outstanding figures, such as Galen, a native of Asia Minor who practiced medicine in Rome; Pliny in natural history; and Lucretius, philosophical poet.

The Middle Ages were indeed the dark ages for science in general. Except for a few Arabic writers, there are no great names in all these centuries that can compare with those of the philosophers of ancient Greece and Alexandria. The first impressive figures to emerge from the darkness were Albertus Magnus, writing on the physical sciences, and Roger Bacon, both in the thirteenth century, and Leonardo da Vinci in the fifteenth century. Previously, scientific progress had been hopelessly held back by the stultifying atmosphere of medieval theology, religious dogma, and superstition. Christian thought became antagonistic to secular learning, identifying it with heathenism.

During this interval of nearly a thousand years, such interest in science as was shown took the form of philosophical inquiry, rather than laboratory experiments or direct observations of nature. Dampier-Whetham in his *History of Science* observed, "With the Greeks natural science became merged in metaphysics; with the Roman Stoics it faded into the need to support the morality of the human will. So in the early Christian atmosphere natural knowledge was valued only as a means of edification, or as an illustration of the doctrines of the Church or the passages of Scripture."

The Renaissance was essentially a revival of the humanities. In educated circles the natural sciences were largely ignored or scorned. Even Erasmus disliked scientific study, as is shown by the passages in *The Praise of Folly* holding up to ridicule the "natural philosophers" and mathematicians. The

Reformation was marked by a still more direct and aggressive hostility to the scientific spirit. Poets and painters far outnumbered great scientific names between 1500 and 1690. Nevertheless, the resurrection of classical learning represented by the Renaissance and the questioning of established beliefs inevitably accompanying the Reformation created an intellectual climate favorable to science. The works of Archimedes, Aristarchus, Hippocrates, Galen, Euclid, Ptolemy, and other ancients enabled early modern scientists to take up where like-minded men had left off centuries before. The results of the scientific revolution of the sixteenth and seventeenth centuries, according to one historian of science, Herbert Butterfield, "outshine everything since the rise of Christianity and reduce the Renaissance and Reformation to the rank of mere episodes, mere internal displacements, within the system of medieval Christendom."

The new advance of science ignored national boundaries. Of the five geniuses who laid the foundations for modern astronomy, Copernicus was a Pole, Brahe a Dane, Kepler a German, Galileo an Italian, and Newton an Englishman.

By common agreement, modern science dates its birth from the publication of Copernicus' epochal *Concerning the Revolutions of the Heavenly Spheres*, in which the earth and the planets were conceived as revolving around the sun; the disturbing effect of the theory upon man's faith and philosophy can scarcely be overestimated. In the same year (1543) was published Vesalius' *The Structure of the Human Body*, equally revolutionary in its field and likewise indicative of a new spirit in scientific investigation. There followed in succession Brahe's accumulation of an immense body of astronomical data, systematically collected over a period of years; Kepler's formulation of three laws of the solar system, based upon Brahe's observations; Galileo's invention of the telescope and fundamental discoveries in dynamics and mechanics; and the work of the most universal genius of all, Sir Isaac Newton's mathematical proof of the discovery and establishment of the physical law by which the whole universe is governed.

In other branches of scientific effort, Sir William Gilbert was describing and experimenting with magnets and magnetism; William Harvey was establishing modern experimental medicine through his discovery of the circulation of the blood; Robert Boyle's laboratory experiments were beginning to separate medieval alchemy from modern chemistry; and Robert Hooke was carrying on pioneer research in microscopy. Two other thinkers, Francis Bacon in England and René Descartes in France, were making theoretical rather than practical contributions to science through their emphasis on scientific method and research. Bacon's enthusiasm for planned experimentation and his proposal for a cooperative research institute had immense influence in bringing about the establishment of scientific societies and of scientific research as a recognized profession. Descartes' great historical achievement was his teaching that, through proper and systematic use of his intelligence, divorced from myth, magic, and superstition, man could penetrate the most hidden secrets of the universe.

Thus did the Renaissance, the Reformation, and the rise of modern science set the stage for the century of enlightenment and reason to follow.

Scientific progress vastly increased the faith of the men of the Enlightenment in nature and reason. Notably, Newton's perfection of the calculus and his mathematical formulation of a "system of the world," showing the relationship of the planets to the laws of gravity, appeared to his contemporaries to explain, or at least to point the way to an explanation of, all natural phenomena. Instead of a dark, malevolent power to be feared and placated, as in earlier eras, nature to the Enlightenment became a benign concept. The working of the universe was seen to be orderly and simple. If the same principles operative in nature could be applied to human affairs, mankind's happiness would be assured. Such "unnatural" social phenomena as class distinctions, special privileges of clergy and royalty, and the distressing contrast between the rich and the poor would disappear.

The understanding of nature and of its bearing on human behavior, according to the Enlightenment, can be achieved through reason, represented in its purest form by the science of mathematics. As aptly phrased by Crane Brinton, "Reason applied to human relations will show us that kings are not fathers of their people, that if meat is good to eat on Thursdays it is good to eat on Fridays, that if pork is nourishing to a Gentile it is nourishing to a Jew." Reason enables man to differentiate between "natural" and "unnatural" human institutions and thus to eliminate error, injustice, and superstitions. A dominant theme running throughout the Enlightenment, consequently, is the desire to extend to man and society the methods and laws of the natural scientists. Reason, if logically followed, it was believed, is opposed to tradition, authority, and revelation. Voltaire called it "the light of common sense."

Growing out of their unlimited confidence in the omnipotence of controlled nature and science is the somewhat naive faith in progress universally held by the *philosophes* of the Enlightenment. One historian, Franklin Le Van Baumer, notes that "the Enlightenment represents European civilization at its cockiest." With no distrust of human nature or of machine technology, there was an almost mystical trust in the future, and solutions were believed imminent for all the great political and social problems inherited from the past. This view was typified by Condorcet, writing toward the end of the eighteenth century, when he asserted that "we are approaching one of the grand revolutions of the human race."

Scientific achievement in the eighteenth century fell below the spectacular advances of the seventeenth century. But progress was far from negligible. New fields were entered. Scientists were busy gathering, describing, and classifying the infinity of things to be found in the world. Diderot noted in his *Encyclopédie* that "men's minds seem caught in a general movement towards natural history, anatomy, chemistry, and experimental physics." Amateurs like Voltaire collected specimens of plants, birds, fossils, and rocks. Buffon, author of the celebrated *Natural History, General and Particular*; Lamarck, pre-Darwinian evolutionist; Cuvier, founder of the science of paleontology; and Linnaeus, the great systematizer of botany, were all diligent in collecting, classifying, and preserving specimens. The foundations of experimental chemistry were being laid by Cavendish's discovery of hydrogen and of the synthetic production of water, Rutherford's isolation of nitrogen, Priestley's discovery of oxygen, and Lavoisier's establishment of the science of quantitative chemistry. James Hutton and William Smith opened up a new science of geology by insisting upon a vastly greater age for the earth than the five or six thousand years allowed by biblical chronology, offering as incontrovertible evidence the stratification of rocks and the study of fossils.

The march of scientific progress continued uninterrupted throughout the nineteenth century. Astronomy had dominated the thinking of scientists in the sixteenth and seventeenth centuries, and the eighteenth was outstanding for pioneer investigations in chemistry. Important beginnings had also been made earlier in biological research, notably by Vesalius, Harvey, Leeuwenhoek, Linnaeus, Buffon, Cuvier, Lamarck, and others. But it is the nineteenth century that may properly be entitled the Age of Biology, especially if the term is interpreted broadly to include medicine. A field closely related in many of its aspects, geology, also came of age and firmly established itself as a major science.

By 1800 a foundation had been laid for the biological sciences in the classification of plants and animals (taxonomy) and their form and structure (morphology). Biology, however, rated below older branches of science, as is evidenced, for example, by Auguste Comte's priority listing of the sciences. Mathematics and astronomy were held to be most perfect and complete, followed in descending order by physics, chemistry, biology, and psychology. The life sciences, according to Comte, had yet to prove themselves.

Among the distinguished biologists of the nineteenth century, Charles Darwin unquestionably ranks first. For several generations a long line of workers had been developing the idea for which Darwin is most celebrated—the theory of organic evolution. Charles Lyell and his predecessors in geological research found incontrovertible evidence that life on the earth had existed for millions of years. Furthermore, fossil remains indicated a progression from simple to complex forms of life. It was Darwin's masterly achievement to bring the mass of facts and theories derived from studies by himself and others into a coherent whole. Darwin acknowledged particular indebtedness to Lyell for his conclusions on ancient life forms and to Malthus' view that population tended to increase faster than food supply. Seeking an explanation of why some species survive and others perish, Darwin formulated the principle of natural selection, theorizing that those individuals would survive and perpetuate the species which were best adapted to live in their particular natural environment. Evolution occurred chiefly, it was held, through minute variations among individuals.

Though Darwin conceded that man is evolution's major triumph, the theory still made man a descendant from lower forms and a member of the animal kingdom. Inevitably, therefore, the Darwinian hypothesis was an object of bitter theological attack, on the grounds that it contradicted the Bible and degraded man. Nevertheless, with the enthusiastic support of such aggressive and able advocates as Huxley and Spencer, the general concept of evolutionary progress rapidly invaded all fields of thought.

Medical science was also making phenomenal advances. After the work of William Harvey in the seventeenth century, the next great landmarks were Edward Jenner's discovery, in 1796, of vaccination as a preventive of smallpox, and Louis Pasteur's development of the germ theory in the mid-nineteenth century. Subsequently, the British surgeon Joseph Lister applied Pasteur's bacterial discoveries to antiseptic surgery, with remarkable success, and Robert Koch in Germany used them as a basis for pioneer researches in preventive medicine.

Great names in other divisions of science dot the period. Pierre Simon Laplace carried forward Newton's work, with his *Treatise on Celestial Mechanics*, exploring the origin and development of the solar system into its present form and proposing the nebular hypothesis. John Dalton placed the atomic theory upon a definite mathematical basis, setting the stage for modern chemical investigation. Michael Faraday ushered in the electrical age by discovering and formulating the laws of electrostatics and electromagnetism and with brilliant insight conceived the idea of an electromagnetic field—later developed mathematically by Clerk Maxwell. Successive editions of Charles Lyell's *Principles of Geology* presented a comprehensive synthesis of the field, and a special aspect was given almost definitive treatment in Louis Agassiz's studies on glaciers.

Numerous forces and movements have reshaped the world since 1750, and any attempt to summarize them necessarily tends toward oversimplification. Continued faith in the idea of progress led to constant stress on scientific research and on the practical applications of science to human affairs. By the end of the era, virtually all the elements that were to mold the twentieth century were present, at least in embryo form.

Previous reference has been made to the scientific and technological advances of the past two hundred years and their bearing upon contemporary events. Among the constructive workers was an obscure Austrian monk named Gregor Mendel, whose experiments led to the formulation of the laws of normal heredity. A noted American scientist, Josiah Willard Gibbs, working in similar obscurity, discovered general principles upon which physical chemistry, with all of its implications for modern industry, is based. And researches of four scientists, Roentgen, Becquerel, Pierre Curie, and Marie Curie, culminated in the epoch-making discovery of X-rays and the new element, radium.

In the public mind, the name that best represents the scientific revolution of the first half of the twentieth century is that of Albert Einstein. The work of great physicists and mathematicians like Einstein, Max Planck, and Niels Bohr produced, in quantum mechanics, researches in atomic structure, and the theory of relativity, new master-theorems about the physical universe, leading directly to the Atomic Age.

Perhaps less spectacular, but of profound significance for the human race, were the investigations of certain psychologists—Havelock Ellis, Sigmund Freud, and Ivan Petrovitch Pavlov—all trained originally in medicine.

By helping to remove puritan restrictions upon the scientific investigation of sexual phenomena, Ellis facilitated acceptance of Freud and Jung in psychological theory, encouraged further studies in sex by such scientists as Alfred Kinsey, and in literature inspired development of the psychological novel by Joyce, Proust, and other writers.

Pavlov's most noteworthy contribution was the idea of conditioned reflexes, demonstrated through years of experiments on canine subjects. Human symptoms of neurosis, or even psychosis, could be produced in the laboratory animals by certain kinds of frustrations and induced mental confusion. Social scientists are in general agreement that the concept of conditioned reflexes developed by Pavlov goes far toward explaining habit formation and apparently irrational behavior in human beings under given sets of conditions.

Sigmund Freud has been characterized as one of the most complex figures in the intellectual history of the West, the subject of innumerable controversies. Whether supported or rejected, however, Freud has continued to exert a powerful influence not only on psychology and psychiatry, but on twentieth-century art, literature, biographical writing, and religious thought. In the medical field, the impact of his teachings has been felt particularly in the treatment of psychoneurotic personality disorders and the coordination of information about psychological and bodily functions known as psychosomatic medicine. It is perhaps appropriate that one of the final choices of titles considered in the present work to have shaped the Western scientific world should be *Civilization and Its Discontents*, a product of Freud's later years. In this searching analysis, Freud presents a general view of the nature of man and calculates his chances for happiness.

A pressing concern of the world during the second half of the twentieth century is ecology and environmental problems—the conservation of natural resources, the rescue of endangered species of wildlife, and halting the ravages committed by mankind on a small planet. An exemplar of the extensive literature on these matters is Rachel Carson's *Silent Spring*.

1

Great Physician

Hippocrates (c.460-377 B.C.)

Aphorisms

Like many ancient writers, exact facts concerning Hippocrates, often described as the "Father of Medicine," are hard to come by. He remains an obscure figure, about whom little of a specific nature is known. There are passing references to him in Plato's *Phaedrus* and Aristotle's *Politics*. He was venerated by Aristotle as the "Great Physician." Five centuries later, the Greek physician Soranus wrote a life of Hippocrates, based partly on tradition and in part on imagination. It is generally assumed that Hippocrates was the son of a physician, descendant of a long line of physicians, and was born about 460 B.C. on the island of Cos. He traveled widely in Greece and Asia Minor, practicing and teaching medicine. Among other places, he frequently taught at the medical school at Cos. His death is believed to have occurred about 377 B.C., at Larissa.

A period of not less than one hundred centuries in the history of mankind elapsed before the man of medicine prevailed over the medicine man. Among both primitive tribes and advanced civilizations, disease was fought by exorcising and propitiating spirits, ghosts, and demons. Illness was attributed to attacks by supernatural beings, or to their actual entry into the body of the sufferer—an affliction sent as a punishment for sin. Hag-ridden and god-ridden, men fought with shadows. The priests were the doctors. Imhetep, with his magic, became the god of healing in Egypt.

Before the time of Hippocrates, Greek medicine, too, was a strange mixture of religion, necromancy, and mysticism. Temples were erected to the god of medicine, Aesculapius, and ill persons were carried to the temples, where suitable offerings were made to the gods. Belief in the supernatural was supplemented by many drugs and healing lotions. Greek physicians were reputed to be skillful in dressing wounds and bandaging, while at the same time reciting appropriate prayers and incantations.

Anything approaching a rational system of medicine was not established until the coming of Hippocrates. In an age contemporary with Phidias, Lysias, Herodotus, Sophocles, Euripides, Aristophanes, Socrates, Plato, and Thucydides, it was quite natural for medicine to produce a leader who would rise above superstitious dogmas and lay the foundation for a true medical science. With the emergence of Hippocrates in the fifth century, practical medicine for the first time began to be separated from religion and philosophy, and the belief became established that all diseases are due to natural causes—not to the wrath of the gods. The school of medicine represented by Hippocrates had an approach to the art far in advance of anything preceding it and similar in spirit to modern medical theory and practice. There are few traces of superstition and hardly any reference to religion in the Hippocratic writings. His method was to ignore all the gods and to hold instead that disease is a natural phenomenon governed by natural laws.

About eighty-seven works, now called the "Hippocratic Collection" or "Hippocratic Corpus," are attributed to Hippocrates, but it has long been realized that not all of these writings, which differ greatly in length, style, and intended use, are by Hippocrates himself. It is probable, in fact, that the collection constituted the medical library of the school at Cos. Critics have concluded that no less than nineteen authors are represented, some of whom lived after Hippocrates' time. As a whole, the diverse works deal with the following subjects: anatomy, clinical topics, diseases of women and children, prognosis, treatment by diet and drugs, surgery, and medical ethics.

Although Hippocrates has been called "a symbol rather than a doctor, a name more than a man," the knowledge that the medical profession has accumulated since his time has been gained by the basic principle established by him—precise observation. He urged a clear differentiation between speculation and guesses on the one hand and exact knowledge obtained from observation on the other. "To know is one thing," he stated, "merely to believe one knows is another. To know is science, but merely to believe one knows is ignorance."

In attempting to discover the true causes of disease, Hippocrates believed that the four elements, earth, air, fire, and water—or, as sometimes described, heat, cold, dryness, and moisture—are represented in the body by four body fluids or "humors": blood, phlegm, black bile, and yellow bile. When a person is in sound health, the fluids exist in his body in harmonious proportions. The fundamental condition of life is the innate heat, greatest in youth and gradually declining with age. These fanciful notions remained the accepted doctrine among physicians as to the causes of diseases as late as the mid-nineteenth century.

According to the Hippocratic view, diseases were to be cured by restoring the disturbed harmony in the relation of the elements and humors. In actual treatment, however, Hippocrates departed from beautiful theories and depended upon common sense. Primarily, he believed in the healing power of nature. He considered health as a normal state, disease as an abnormal condition. Therefore, if the disease is not too serious, he held, nature will assert itself and health will be promptly regained. The main duty of the physician is to stand by and to help nature, to relieve pain whenever possible, and to strengthen the patient's body and spirit.

The therapeutic means at Hippocrates' disposal were few and weak. He advised moderation in all things—working, eating, drinking, exercising, sleeping—as preventive of disease. He used emetics, purges and enemas, bloodletting, starvation diets to evacuate the body, warm baths, applications of cold water, frictions and massage. Drugs used, some of which have a known value today, included asafetida, myrrh, alum, niter, dried ox-gall, hydromel (honey with water), oxymel (honey with vinegar), wine, barley water and barley gruel, and probably opium.

But more valuable than drugs, Hippocrates taught, are diet and exercise. His diets were prescribed according to certain sensible rules. The age of the patient was to be considered: "Old people use less nutriment than young." The seasons: "In winter abundant nourishment is wholesome; in summer a more frugal diet." The physical state of the person: "Lean persons should take little food, but this little should be fat; fat persons, on the other hand, should take much food, but it should be lean." Digestibility of the food: "White meat is more digestible than dark." The best guarantee of health is a moderate amount of nourishment with a moderate amount of exercise. Sedentary persons are advised to walk.

Hippocrates was one of the first to note that different diseases have distinctive symptoms, thus differentiating one disease from another. From a clinical standpoint, the most famous of all Hippocratic writings are his records of actual cases. Some forty-two have survived, all short and clear. Here are to be found classical descriptions of gout, arthritis, puerperal septicemia, tuberculosis, mumps, hysteria, epilepsy, and different types of malaria. Also described by Hippocrates are acute inflammation of the throat, pneumonia, tetanus, erysipelas, inflammatory diseases of many organs, apoplexy, and infantile paralysis. As Lambert and Goodwin comment in their *Medical Leaders*, "These descriptions with a few changes would be appropriate for a modern text-book." Often cited is the appearance of the face at the point of death in many acute diseases: "Nose sharp, eyes hollow, temples sunken, ears cold and contracted with their lobes turned outwards, the skin about the face hard and tense and parched, the color of the face as a whole being yellow or black" — observations used by Shakespeare in describing the death of Falstaff.

Hippocrates was less concerned with diagnosis than with prognosis, i.e., predicting the course of a disease and the possibility of cure or of death. Through prognosis the doctor could recognize, and eventually foretell, different stages that occur in every disease. For this purpose, the clinical records of previous cases were essential. Hippocrates paid close attention to variations in the appearance of the eyes, the color of the skin, the prominence of the veins, pulsations in the arteries, the existence of fevers, chills, tremors, and sweating, frequency of respiration, the position of the patient in bed, the condition of the tongue, and the influence of environment on health and disease.

The Hippocratic doctors' knowledge of anatomy was rudimentary, except for the structure and arrangement of the bones. Contributions relating to fractures and dislocations were accurate. On the other hand, knowledge of the internal organs, arteries, veins, and nerves was practically nonexistent, because among the Greeks dissection of the human body was forbidden by the prejudice of religion and custom. Hippocrates knew that the heart is divided into four cavities, but held the curious notion that two contain blood and the others air.

An aspect of Hippocratic medicine with a modern ring is his belief in psychologic healing. In addition to allowing the patient to rest as much as possible, confined in bed and kept on a light diet, the surroundings should be kept quiet and the patient be invigorated by good cheer and hope. The physician must have a good "bedside manner," dealing very gently with his patients.

Hippocrates was meticulous in his directions to physicians, including such details as preparation of the operating room, the employment of artificial and natural light, scrupulous cleanliness of the hands, the care and use of implements, method of bandaging, placing of the patient, use of splints, and the necessity for general tidiness, order, and cleanliness. He held that the physician himself should be a man of honor, in good health, sympathetic and friendly, personally clean and properly dressed, careful to avoid notoriety and self-seeking, temperate in eating and drinking, and a philosopher in outlook.

Out of these high standards for the physician came the "Hippocratic Oath"—in a modern form administered to candidates for the Doctor of Medicine degree. As revised, the oath reads:

> I do solemnly swear by that which I hold most sacred: That I will be loyal to the profession of medicine and just and generous to its members; that I will lead my life and practice my art in uprightness and honor; that into whatsoever house I shall enter, it shall be for the good of the sick to the utmost of my power, I holding myself aloof from wrong, from corruption, from the tempting of others to vice; that I will exercise my art solely for the cure of my patients, and I will give no drug, perform no operation for a criminal purpose, even if solicited, far less suggest it; that whatsoever I shall see or hear of the lives of men which is not fitted to be spoken, I will keep inviolably secret; these things I do promise and in proportion as I am faithful to this my oath may happiness and good repute be ever mine—the opposite if I shall be forsworn.

Most widely circulated and best-known of the works ascribed to Hippocrates is his *Aphorisms*, consisting of precepts, observations, and summations drawn from his medical treatises, mainly *The Prognostics, On the Articulations*, and *On Airs, Waters, and Places*.

With Hippocrates, we come, as Sir William Osler phrases it, "out of the murky night of the East, heavy with phantoms, into the bright daylight of the West." To which George Sarton adds, "The main achievement of Hippocrates was the introduction of a scientific point of view and scientific method in the cure of diseases, and the beginning of scientific medical literature and clinical archives. The importance of this can hardly be exaggerated. Hippocrates' personality, however shadowy, symbolizes one of the greatest initiatives in the history of mankind."

Rebelling against the ancient myths and superstitions prevalent among the physicians of his day and against the intrusions of philosophy into medical doctrine, Hippocrates laid a solid foundation for the study and practice of the healing arts.

2

Father of Natural History
Aristotle (384-322 B.C.)

History of Animals

Aristotle was unquestionably the greatest collector and systematizer of knowledge produced by the ancient world. Prior to the Renaissance in modern Europe, he was the first to undertake a systematic survey of all existing knowledge in all fields of science. His works are an encyclopedia of the learning of the ancient world, and except in physics and astronomy, he made important contributions in practically every subject touched.

Aristotle was one of the true founders of modern biology. He recorded the main facts of biological life (as he saw them) in his *History of Animals*, supplemented with a series of specialized treatises: *On the Parts of Animals, Generation of Animals, Movement of Animals,* and *Progression of Animals*. "For all his faults," notes William Wightman in *The Growth of Scientific Ideas*, "Aristotle is the fountain-head of more ideas in the science of biology than anyone before or since." The greatest of modern biologists, Charles Darwin, offers another tribute: "From quotations which I had seen, I had a high notion of Aristotle's merits, but I had not the most remote notion what a wonderful man he was. Linnaeus and Cuvier have been my two gods, though in very different ways, but they were mere schoolboys to old Aristotle."

Aristotle's researches were aided by his use of the inductive method, of which he was one of the founders, and he was the first to conceive the idea of organized research. These techniques enabled him to make major advances in exact knowledge of biological facts. Adopting a broad approach and bringing a wealth of detail to his investigations, Aristotle pioneered in the main branches of biologic inquiry: comparative anatomy and physiology, embryology, ethnology (habits of animals), geographic distribution, and ecology (relation between organisms and their environment). Life was defined by him as "the power of self-nourishment and of independent growth and decay." Zoology is divided into three parts: 1) the general phenomena of animal life, that is, natural history; 2) the parts of animals, i.e., organs and their functions; 3) animal reproduction and embryology.

Approximately 540 different animals are mentioned by Aristotle, often with an accuracy and detail that show personal observation, and 50 with exact knowledge that could only have been gained by dissection. In some instances, his accounts are based on information supplied by fishermen, hunters, herdsmen, bird catchers, and travelers, and legendary lore.

Because of religious taboos, Aristotle probably never dissected the human body, and was therefore seriously handicapped in this branch of biologic observation and experimentation. The restriction accounts for a number of errors doubtless founded on mere hypotheses. That he made a careful and thorough investigation wherever feasible, however, is apparent throughout Aristotle's zoological treatises. Among the direct results of his inductive-deductive methods were such notable original discoveries as the mammalian character of the cetaceans (whales, dolphins, porpoises, etc.), differences between cartilaginous and bony fishes, the morphology of the four-chambered stomachs of ruminants, the development of the embryo chick (including the presence of the beating heart after the fourth day), the viviparous (producing living young instead of eggs) character of the dogfish shark, the close similarities in structure between birds and reptiles, the place of the monkey's form midway between quadrupeds and man, the fact that as species become more highly developed and specialized they produce fewer offspring.

Further, Aristotle propounded various biological problems whose solutions were not found until recent times, e.g., the breeding of eels, the anatomy of the hyena, questions of heredity (resolved by Gregor Mendel's experiments in the nineteenth century), the reproduction of bees (a phenomenon not yet fully explained), and the influence of diet on animal habits.

On the other hand, because he was exploring new worlds and blazing new trails, Aristotle was frequently misled into erroneous theories and conclusions. The lapses may be attributed to a total lack of scientific instruments and reliable reference sources, to the want of opportunity for vivisection and dissection, and on occasion to preconceived notions. Thus, Aristotle states such propositions—absurd to us—as these: the heart is the seat of intelligence and the brain's function is to cool the heart; man has only eight ribs on each side; woman has fewer teeth than man; the male element in reproduction merely stimulates and quickens; plants do not reproduce sexually; the egg or cell is not a living thing; the lowest forms of life are "spontaneously generated" (i.e., such highly developed organisms as worms, insects, and some fishes could come into being from mud); the lungs serve to temper the body heat by means of the inhaled air; there is no essential difference between arteries and veins; some viviparous quadrupeds lack gall bladders; and female offspring are the result of the failure of form to dominate matter, i.e., they are imperfect or incomplete men.

Of particular interest in the development of the biological sciences is Aristotle's efforts to classify animal species—a field in which his contributions were the most significant up to the time of Linnaeus, more than two thousand years later. The practice of naming and classifying plants and animals has an ancient history. In the beginning, it is likely that man divided animal and plant life on the basis of usefulness: first, that which provided food or could be used for clothing and shelters, and, second, that which was unfit for use, poisonous, unclean, or dangerous. In the biblical story of the Flood, animals are classified into more or less natural groups, according to their habits. Listed are aquatic animals, birds, and land animals. A further division places land animals in three groups: wild beasts, domestic animals, and creeping creatures. For purposes of religious rituals, certain animals, such as sheep, goats, and bullocks, were acceptable for sacrifices, while the pig, for example, was tabooed both for sacrifice and human consumption.

Aristotle's classification begins with a fundamental division of the animal kingdom into two parts: those with blood and those without blood — corresponding approximately to the modern groupings of vertebrates and invertebrates. He believed that all life forms one continuous link, each variety shading into the next. Proceeding from the lowest to the highest organisms, there are infinitesimal gradations in structure, manner of life, methods of reproduction and rearing, sensation, and feeling. "Nature makes so gradual a transition from the inanimate to the animate kingdom," declares Aristotle, "that the boundary lines which separate them are indistinct and doubtful." The correlation is direct, he holds, between intelligence and complexity of structure and mobility of form.

In his system of classification, Aristotle rejected an earlier theory that animals could be placed in contrasting groups, e.g., land and water animals, and those with or without wings; he noted, for example, the existence of winged and wingless ants. Three kinds of likeness, according to Aristotle, are to be found in the animal kingdom: complete identity of type within a given species, though with minor variations between individuals; likeness between species of the same "greatest genus" possessing the same bodily parts, but these parts differing in such characteristics as number, size, softness or hardness, smoothness or roughness; and, finally, likeness by analogy between the "greatest genera." Concerning the last, Aristotle warns against mistaking apparent similarities due to homology (e.g., bone and fish spine, scales and feathers, nail and hoof, and arm, foreleg, wing, and fin) for real relationships.

Applying all criteria available to him, Aristotle's classification scheme, or "Ladder of Nature" as it came to be called by later naturalists, comprises six major groups of vertebrates, in descending order: man, hairy quadrupeds (land animals), sea mammals, birds, reptiles and amphibia, and fishes. The invertebrates were reduced to five principal classes — cephalopods (squids, cuttlefishes, octopuses, etc.); crustacea (lobsters, shrimps, crabs, etc.); insects; mollusks other than cephaloids; and zoophytes (corals, sea anemones, hydroids, sponges, etc.) — the last presumed to be produced by spontaneous generation.

The breadth of Aristotle's approach to the whole field of biology is revealed by examining the ten "books" in which the *History of Animals* is divided:

I.   Book I begins with a general review of the animal kingdom, ideas for a natural arrangement of animals in groups, according to their external form or their way of life, a comparison of animals among themselves, with a description of some of their habits. Then the human form is introduced, as a basis for comparison, with a description of the several parts of the human body, external and internal.

II.   The second book describes the different parts of animals with red blood, arranged in groups: viviparous and oviparous quadrupeds, fish, serpents, and birds. Special note is taken of a few animals: the ape, elephant, and chameleon.

III.   Book III begins with a description of the internal organs, especially the generative system, and the course of the veins is discussed. The constituent parts of the body are reviewed: sinews, fibres, bone, marrow, cartilage, nails, hoofs, claws, horns, and beaks of birds, hair, scales, membranes, flesh, fat, blood, marrow, milk, and the spermatic fluid.

IV.   Here animals without blood, starting with the cephaloids, are described, followed by the crustaceans, hermit crabs, insects, etc. Toward the end, the organs of sense are considered and afterwards the voice, sleep, age, and differences in sexes.

V-VI.   In the fifth and sixth books, animals' modes of reproduction are treated in detail, concluding with a long description of bees and their habits in book V. Aristotle then proceeds to consider the seasons, climates, and ages of animals and how far these influence their reproduction.

VII.   The seventh book is almost entirely devoted to reproduction in man, tracing humans from birth to death.

VIII.   In a broad sweep, Aristotle summarizes the character and habits of the whole animal world. Among other topics, he deals with the food of animals, their migrations, their health and diseases, and climatic influences.

IX.   Particular attention is paid in book IX to animals' relations with each other, and especially the friendship and hostility of different species.

The tenth book, of doubtful authorship, is a treatise on the causes of barrenness in the human species.

The catholicity of Aristotle's biologic interests is also displayed in his writings on the geographic distribution of plants and animals. He dwells at length on the migration of animals, biological geography, the relation between living things and their physical environment, the ways in which each animal is affected by other animals and plants, the incredible prolificness of certain animals (such as mice), observations of the fact that some animals prey on others or are preyed upon, and the disappearance of some species because of unfavorable environmental factors.

The culminating section of Aristotle's zoological works is the *Generation of Animals*, treating of the organs of reproduction and the reproductive functions. This work made important contributions to the science of embryology, notably in such steps as the introduction of the comparative method, the classification of animals according to their manner of embryonic development; the conclusion that sex is determined at the very beginning of embryonic growth; and establishment of the correct functions of the placenta and the umbilical cord.

A distinctive feature of Aristotelian biology is a profound belief in teleology, the doctrine that "nature never makes anything that is superfluous." As opposed to mechanical explanations of life, teleology holds that every species or individual is being directed toward an end or shaped for a purpose; all parts work for the greatest good of the whole; every organ or part of the body has its distinctive function. This concept is closely allied to Aristotle's idea of the soul. "As every instrument and every bodily member serves some partial end, some special action," he declares, "so the whole body must be destined to minister to some fuller, some completer, some greater sphere of action. The body must somehow be made for the soul and each part thereof for some separate function to which it is adapted." For Aristotle, living things are intelligible only in relation to the idea of the soul. Aristotle is thus a "vitalist," and as Charles Singer observes, "the division between *vitalist* and mechanist extends throughout the history of science and still separates students of living things."

Summing up the magnitude of Aristotle's biologic genius, George Sarton comments, "He was not only the first great one in his field, somewhat like Hippocrates in medicine, but he remained the greatest for two thousand years."

3

First Scientific Botanist
Theophrastus (c.370-287 B.C.)

On the History of Plants
and
On the Causes of Plants

Theophrastus was the logical successor to Aristotle in carrying on research in natural history, as well as in other respects. Born Tyrtamus of Eresus in Lesbos, he received the nickname Theophrastus ("divine of speech") from Aristotle. At an early age, Theophrastus traveled to Athens and there became a member of the Platonic circle, a fellow student with Aristotle, though about fifteen years the latter's junior. After Plato's death, he attached himself to Aristotle.

In his writings, Theophrastus was as prolific and versatile as Aristotle. He is credited with 227 treatises on subjects as diverse as religion, mathematics, astronomy, logic, meteorology, music, poetry, love, epilepsy, water, fire, odors, dreams, inventions, and natural history. Of his literary writings, the most popular is *Characters*, thirty sketches of moral weaknesses, e.g., arrogance, backbiting, superstition, boorishness, and buffoonery, which subsequently exerted considerable influence on drama and other branches of literature.

In his will, Aristotle made Theophrastus guardian of his children, bequeathed to him his library and garden and the originals of his works, and named him as his successor at the Lyceum. Theophrastus presided over the Peripatetic school for thirty-five years, until his death at age eighty-five.

Theophrastus was the great popularizer of science during his era. His major contributions were two large botanical works: *On the History of Plants* and *On the Causes of Plants*. Combined, these treatises represent the most important contribution to botanical science from ancient times through the Middle Ages. It has been noted that there was not a single new discovery in the science of botany for more than eighteen hundred years after Theophrastus' death in 287 B.C.

What Aristotle did for the animal kingdom his pupil Theophrastus did in large measure for the vegetable or plant kingdom. The latter, however, was much less a classifier than Aristotle, and his writings pay comparatively little attention to theoretical questions. Theophrastus' approach is highly practical, dealing, for example, with the making of charcoal, of pitch, and of resin, and the effects of various plants on the animal organism when taken as food or medicine.

The realism of Theophrastus' writings on botany clearly shows that they are the work of a gardener rather than a philosopher or medical man. He had, for instance, an exact knowledge of germination, making a distinction between seed and fruit. His expert knowledge of grafting and propagation of cuttings is revealed by his famous saying, "A plant has the power of growth in all its parts, inasmuch as it has life in all its parts." For a working classification, his divisions are trees, shrubs, under-shrubs, and herbs. Theophrastus attempted to establish a natural classification, based on essential similarities of form, habit, and habitat. He urged the use of a variety of types as the basis of comparative studies: wild and cultivated, aquatic and terrestrial, fruit-bearing and fruitless, flowering and flowerless, evergreen and deciduous. Of special significance was his work on plant reproduction, by seed, root, and slip. His examination of seeds led him to make an important distinction between cereals and legumes. Still of interest also is his account of the sex life of the palm.

George Sarton, in his great *History of Science*, comments that "Theophrastus (as well as Aristotle) wrote the synthesis and did most of the work, but his facts were gathered not only by himself but by many other men. Among his two thousand disciples, he must have obtained the collaboration of many." A particular debt was owed by Theophrastus to his friend and patron Alexander the Great. Alexander took with him to the East scientifically trained observers, and their observations were sent back for Theophrastus' use. Consequently, his descriptions of plants are not limited to the flora of Greece and the Levant. His accounts of such plants as cotton, banyan, pepper, cinnamon, coconut, myrrh, and frankincense he owed to reports received from Alexander's followers. Nearer home, it appears that "traveling students" were employed to gather facts and material. Facts and fancies were also drawn from such diverse sources as philosophers, drug collectors, root diggers, farmers, woodmen, and charcoal burners.

In any case, as Sarton observed, "Theophrastus' accumulation of botanic knowledge is as wonderful as Aristotle's accumulation of biologic knowledge; both are almost unbelievable."

In the course of his collecting activities, Theophrastus learned of much curious folklore and superstitions associated with plants, about most of which he was skeptical but recorded because he thought it too interesting to omit. The root diggers' calling, he found, was governed by various strange beliefs, such as the following: if taboos were broken, the herbs collected lost their efficacy; it was necessary to eat garlic before going to gather certain plants; some had to be collected by day and others only by night; in given instances, the best quality of drugs could be obtained by approaching on the windward side; with others, top-quality material required the digger to face east while lifting the roots; one had to beware, too, of the woodpecker, buzzard hawk, and eagle, respectively, while plucking peony, feverwort, and black hellebore, taking the precaution of drawing circles around the plant with a sword or placing fruit and cakes in the hole in the ground from which the plant had been uprooted.

Altogether, Theophrastus treats of nearly 550 different plants. For each of these plants he attempted to identify and describe the features which distinguish it from other plants, and to indicate its individual "nature" or peculiar characteristics. He was handicapped by a lack of botanical terms, then largely nonexistent, and on occasion he was impelled to give special technical meanings to words in more or less current use, a method common to modern scientific nomenclature.

A matter of special importance and one of Theophrastus' original contributions is his firm insistence on differences between the animal and the vegetable kingdom. Aristotle, in his *The Parts of Animals*, advanced the theory that animals were descended from man and plants were derived from animals. It was a theory of degeneration, not evolution, from man through animals to plants. No clear distinction is drawn between animals and plants, and too close a parallel was drawn between the parts of animals and of plants. Theophrastus clears up this confusion in the first chapter of his *History of Plants*. In animals, he notes, a part is permanent unless lost by disease, age, or injury, while in plants many parts (flower, catkin, leaf, and fruit) are renewed and die every year. In Theophrastus' view, "It is a waste of time to force comparisons where they do not exist and constitutes an obstacle to our special branch of knowledge."

On the History of Plants is chiefly concerned with descriptions, discussions of structural parts of plants, and differences between plants. The nine books cover the following topics: parts of plants and their nature and classification; propagation, especially of trees; wild trees; trees and plants special to particular districts and situations, i.e., geographic botany; timber of various trees and its uses; undershrubs; herbaceous plants, other than coronary, potherbs, and similar wild herbs; herbaceous plants, cereals, pulses, and "summer crops"; juices of plants and medicinal properties of herbs.

In treating of trees, Theophrastus enumerates such external parts as roots, stems, branches, buds, leaves, flowers, and fruits, and refers to the sap, fibres, vessels, flesh, wood, bark, and pith. In addition to distinguishing woody from herbaceous plants, land from aquatic plants, and permanent organs from the deciduous ones, the *History* also considers the lack of seed in elms and willows, the dissemination of seeds by rain and floods, the bleeding of turpentine from the stems of needle-leaved trees, and the use of roses for the manufacture of attar. Theophrastus recognizes fungi, algae, and lichens in plants, and he divides the plant world into the two subkingdoms of flowering and flowerless plants. Another plant classification that he found useful was based on duration: annual, biennial, and perennial.

On the Causes of Plants, Theophrastus' second major botanical work, is divided into six books: generation and propagation of plants, fructification and maturity of fruits; effects of the environment and of agriculture; plantation of shrubs and preparation of the soil, viticulture; goodness of seeds and their degeneration and culture of legumes; diseases and other causes of failure; savors and odors of plants.

Of the 500 to 550 species and varieties of plants dealt with by Theophrastus, most were cultivated. He states that wild plants were largely unknown, and he assumed that certain wild plants could not be domesticated.

Theophrastus dwells at length on the various modes of plant reproduction. He states that "the manner of generation of trees and plants are these: spontaneous, from a seed, from a root, from a piece torn off, from a branch or twig, from the trunk itself, or from pieces of the wood cut up small." Theophrastus, like Aristotle, was fascinated by the miracle of germination, and comments in detail on closely observed behavior of germinating seeds—wheat, barley, beans, chick peas, lupines, etc. A clear distinction is drawn between plants having single or multiple seed leaves: monocotyledon and dicotyledon, in modern botanical terminology.

One of the most remarkable passages in Theophrastus' *History* deals with plant sexuality. Explaining the fecundation of palm trees, he states, "With dates it is helpful to bring the male to the female; for it is the male which causes the fruit to persist and ripen." The process of pollination is then described, with specific directions for pollinating by hand. Theophrastus' discovery was almost completely forgotten until its reintroduction more than two thousand years later. Ignorance on the subject is demonstrated as late as the seventeenth century, when the English herbalist Parkinson, in his *Theatre of Plants*, scoffed at Theophrastus' theory: "The ancient writers have set down many things of dates," he wrote, "but I pray you account this among the rest of their fables."

Both the *History* and *Causes* contain a considerable discussion of phytopathology — damage to plants, especially farm crops, by insects, worms, and other parasites. Theophrastus describes flea beetles, caterpillars, "horned worms" (a beetle), pea weevils, red spiders, codling moths, and other destructive insects that made life difficult for the Greek farmer. The particular plants attacked by each pest are noted, and control measures recommended.

Though Theophrastus does not treat of ecology (relations between organisms and their environment) in modern terms, he deals with wild plants in what are in effect ecological groups — e.g., marine herbs (algae), submerged marine trees (chiefly corals), marine shore plants, and plants found in deep fresh water, shallow lake shores, river banks, and marshes. Charles Singer, historian of medicine, concludes that "Theophrastus has a perfectly clear idea of plant distribution as dependent on soil and climate, and at times seems to be on the point of passing from a statement of climatic distribution into one of real geographical regions."

Book nine of the *History* is largely medical. Therein, Theophrastus discusses the medical juices of plants, the cutting of roots for medicinal purposes (and certain superstitions connected therewith), the medical uses of different parts of plants, various kinds of "all-heal" herbs, localities which specially produce medicinal herbs, how use diminishes the efficacy of drugs, and many related topics.

It is extraordinary that so much botanic knowledge should have been accumulated by the end of the fourth century, B.C., and even stranger that nothing significant was added to it in ancient times. Theophrastus had Greek followers, but their chief interest appears to have been in herbs. The main contributions of such Roman writers as Cato, Varro, and Pliny related to agriculture. As Sarton emphasizes, "the botany of Theophrastus and the zoology of Aristotle represent the climax of natural history in antiquity."

4

Master Mathematician
Euclid (c.330-275 B.C.)

Elements of Geometry

Euclid is frequently referred to as the originator or father of geometry, a misleading conception, for Egyptian and Babylonian writings in the same field precede him by more than a thousand years. He must be credited, however, with synthesizing all mathematical knowledge up to his time and with placing all known propositions in a strong, logical order.

It is equally erroneous to consider Euclid as a mere textbook author, with no original ideas, who simply assembled in good order discoveries made by other people. Many propositions in the *Elements* can be traced back to earlier geometers. An impressive number, on the other hand, apparently originated with Euclid himself. Furthermore, the arrangement of the *Elements* can be ascribed to Euclid alone. George Sarton comments admiringly, "he created a monument that is as marvelous in its symmetry, inner beauty, and clearness as the Parthenon, but incomparably more complex and more durable."

Sir James Jeans has suggested that Euclid's *Elements of Geometry* may have been designed for any one of three purposes: to be a textbook for students, a compendium of existing geometrical knowledge, or "a scholar's effort to demonstrate that the facts of geometry are inevitable truths which can be deduced from axioms of indisputable validity."

Regardless of the intent, all three possible aims have been admirably served by the book for more than two millennia. Euclid may rightly be termed a master of masters, not only giving training in exact reasoning to the youth of sixty generations throughout the civilized world, but deeply influencing the writings of Archimedes, Apollonius, Galileo, Newton, Huygens, and a host of other mathematicians, ancient and modern.

There is little certain knowledge about Euclid himself. Even the places and dates of his birth and death are unknown. He is called Euclid of Alexandria, the only city with which he can be definitely connected. It is likely that his mathematical training was received at the Academy in Athens, the outstanding mathematical school of the fourth century. His patron was Ptolemy I, Pharaoh of Egypt, and he may have been "the first professor of geometry" in a university, the Museum, founded by Ptolemy to compete with the Lyceum in Athens. Primarily, in any event, Euclid is known by his works.

The long period of slow development in the science of geometry was marked by perhaps the first textbook in the field, the *Elements* of Hippocrates of Chios (not to be confused with Hippocrates, the "Father of Medicine"), written about 440 B.C., which introduced to the Greeks the fascinating and insoluble problem of "squaring the circle." Other famous predecessors included Thales and the Pythagoreans; Eudoxus (c.408-355 B.C.), who discovered the theory of proportion and originated the idea of "proof of exhaustion"; Archytas of Tarentum (c.430-360 B.C.), who greatly advanced the study of three-dimensional geometry; Menaechmus (fl. 350 B.C.), who shares with Plato credit for discovery of the three conic sections; Theudios of Magnesia; Theatetus; and others.

As previously noted, however, Euclid was a creative mathematician in his own right. His early Greek editor, Proclus, points out that Euclid "put together the *Elements*, collecting many of Eudorus' theorems, perfecting many of Theatetus; and also bringing to irrefragable demonstration the things which were only somewhat loosely proved by his predecessors." In short, Euclid linked together in his *Elements* as a united whole the works of earlier mathematicians. The book may thus be considered a kind of history of geometry up to the author's time.

The *Elements* is divided into thirteen books. The first two are on the geometry of the straight line, probably derived from the Pythagoreans; the next two, on the circle, may have been taken from Hippocrates of Chios; the fifth and sixth, on the theory of proportion, are believed to have been based on Eudoxus' method. It is these first six books that have constituted a classic textbook for generation after generation of students. But to them, the *Elements* added books VII to IX, introducing arithmetic, reviewing the Pythagorean theory of numbers, and proving that the number of primes is infinite. Book X, the longest of all, is devoted to the study of incommensurable magnitudes, or "irrational lines." The fifth and last part, books XI-XIII, deal with solid geometry.

Any logical system must start, mathematicians agree, with undefined concepts or assumptions. Some matters must be taken for granted as common sense or common knowledge, not requiring concrete proof. Thus, Euclid founded his geometry on a few simple declarations of self-evident truths, postulates and axioms, none of which was seriously questioned until the mid-nineteenth century. In summary, the twelve Euclidean axioms state that: 1) equal quantities added, subtracted, multiplied, or divided by equal quantities remain equal; 2) a point has only position, not extension; 3) a moving point generates a plane, or flat surface; 4) a moving plane generates a solid having three dimensions — length, breadth, and thickness; and 5) through a given point only one straight line can be drawn parallel to a given straight line.

Although Euclid's work is commonly referred to as the *Elements of Geometry*, its scope extends far beyond what is now regarded as geometry proper. Specifically, arithmetic and algebra figure prominently in the subject matter. The second book is, in substance, a treatise on geometric algebra (the only kind of algebra known to the Greeks), with algebraic problems solved by geometric methods. Three of the thirteen books are devoted to arithmetic and to the theory of numbers, and one to irrational quantities. (In another work, Euclid also wrote on optics and the reflection of light.)

Euclid appears to have been unconcerned with practical applications of his geometric theories and teaching. A familiar anecdote relates that a student, when he had learned the first theorem, asked Euclid, "Can you tell me what practical advantage there is in learning these things?" Euclid called his slave and said,

"Give him an obol [a Greek coin], since he must gain from what he learns." A similar story is told by Noah Fehl about an English lad who expressed deep feelings about the study of geometry by young gentlemen at the public schools and later at Cambridge and Oxford: "Why," he asked, "can't we just accept Euclid's theorems on his word as a gentleman without all this nasty proof?"

Reservations were held among some of Euclid's contemporaries. His patron Ptolemy once expressed his impatience at Euclid's elaborate manner of explaining his theorems: "Isn't there a shorter way of learning geometry than through your method?" asked the king. Euclid replied, "In the country there are two kinds of roads—the hard road for the common people and the easy road for the royal family, but in geometry all must go the same way. There is no royal road to learning." Some agreed with Socrates, who, according to Xenophon, "disapproved of the study of geometry when carried the length of its most difficult problems. For though himself not inconversant with these, he did not perceive of what utility they could be, calculated as they were to consume the life of a man and to turn him away from many other and important acquirements."

On occasion, however, Euclid could demonstrate a practical application of his theories. When his fellow scholars at Alexandria maintained that there was no human way to measure the height of the Great Pyramid, Euclid proceeded to measure it as follows: He waited for the hour of the day when the length of his shadow was exactly equal to the height of his person, and then he measured the length of the pyramid's shadow. "That," he informed his colleagues, "is the exact height of the Great Pyramid."

Few scholars and scientists have disputed the majority of Euclid's axioms. Nevertheless, mathematicians have continually examined them for possible fallacies. By basing their reasoning on different assumptions from Euclid's and even denying the validity of some of them, experimental geometers, led by Nikolai Lobachevski in Russia and Bernhard Riemann in Germany, began during the nineteenth century to develop non-Euclidean geometries. In particular, the tenth axiom (two straight lines cannot enclose a space) and the twelfth (through a given point only one straight line can be drawn parallel to another straight line) were proven to be inadequate explanations of the physical universe.

Euclidean geometry is essentially two-dimensional. In terms of the spherical geometry used by astronomers and navigators, it is seriously erroneous. Euclid apparently proceeded on the assumption that the earth is flat. Over very small areas the difference between Euclidean and non-Euclidean geometry is insignificant, but over large areas there are enormous divergences. In navigation, for example, an ocean is not a flat surface. It is part of the surface of a sphere, and the shortest distance between two points is not a straight line but an arc (a curve technically known as a geodesic). Similarly, the shortest path between two points around the brow of a hill is the arc of a circle. On a sphere, furthermore, any two geodesics always intersect in precisely two points, and only two geodesics always enclose a space.

When Einstein began to work out his theory of relativity, introducing time as a fourth dimension, he adopted the non-Euclidean system of geometry conceived by Riemann. In the geometry of the theory of relativity the paths of light rays in space-time are the geodesics, corresponding to straight lines, but generally not straight because distorted by such masses as the sun.

Euclid's *Elements* is undoubtedly the most famous mathematical treatise of all time. It was widely used by the Arabs and by medieval Latin scholars. The number of printed editions is estimated to be in excess of a thousand—probably more than any other book except the Bible. "As far as elementary geometry is concerned," George Sarton points out, "the *Elements* of Euclid is the only example of a textbook that has remained serviceable until our own day.... Twenty-two centuries of changes, wars, revolution, catastrophes of every kind, yet it still is profitable to study geometry in Euclid."

5

Mechanical Wizard
Archimedes (287?-212 B.C.)

On the Sphere and the Cylinder

The consensus among historians of science is that Archimedes was the greatest mathematician of antiquity and conceivably the greatest mathematical genius of all time. Both in theories and in practical applications, his achievements are phenomenal.

Archimedes, a native of Syracuse, Sicily, was probably too young to have studied under Euclid. His instructors in mathematics at Alexandria, where he went to study, however, were students and followers of Euclid. Despite the fact that his versatile mind touched many fields, Archimedes always considered himself, like Euclid, a geometer. By his own choice he would most likely have devoted his entire time to the study of geometrical problems. His mechanical inventions, as he saw them, were simply "the diversions of geometry at play."

But his patron, King Hiero of Syracuse, had discovered that his protégé had extraordinary mechanical ingenuity and fully recognized his abilities. Under the kind's urging, Archimedes invented a variety of mechanical contrivances, a total of more than forty different machines.

The discoveries with which the name of Archimedes is most intimately associated are in hydrostatics and statics, of which sciences he is generally acknowledged to be the founder. According to an often-told story, the fundamental concept of hydrostatics came to Archimedes while bathing. King Hiero had ordered a pure gold crown. When it was delivered, he suspected the artisan had used silver as well as gold in its making. Archimedes was assigned the task of finding the facts without destroying the crown. Noticing the buoyancy and loss of weight of his own body in the bath water, he suddenly realized that here was the solution: "Any body immersed in a liquid must lose weight equal to the weight of the liquid displaced." He knew that a pound of silver occupies nearly twice as much space as a pound of gold. Using a piece of silver and a piece of gold, each of equal weight to that of the crown, and a full vessel, he measured how much water ran over, and thereby ascertained by mathematics exactly how much silver had been alloyed with the gold.

Thus was established the "Archimedes Principle" that every substance has a characteristic density or specific gravity. Briefly described, the principle is that a solid body, when surrounded by a fluid, will be buoyed up by a force equal to the weight of the fluid it displaces. When bodies lighter than water are forced down into it, they displace an amount of water of greater weight than their own, so that, when let free, they rise to the surface of the water and float. Only as much of their bulk remains submerged as will displace a quantity of water of exactly equal weight. Bodies having the same density as water have no tendency to rise or sink, since their weights are identical. The principle applies also to bodies surrounded by other liquids, gases, and the air. An example of Archimedes' theory is the buoyancy of balloons.

Subsequently, Archimedes worked out methods for calculating the stability of floating bodies, a practical application of which was to design ships that would not turn over — introducing the basic idea of equilibrium.

Scarcely less celebrated than Archimedes' discovery of the first law of hydrostatics is his theoretical and practical approach to laws of the lever. His axioms, easily verified by simple experiments, state: "weights which balance at equal distances are equal, unequal weights at equal distance will not balance, and unequal weights at unequal distances will balance, the greater weight being at the lesser distance." These laws are the basis of operation, for example, of elevators and steam cranes. In brief, make the lever long enough, push the long end down far enough, and any weight can be lifted at the short end.

Out of his experiments with levers came another traditional tale about Archimedes. "Give me a place to stand on and I will move the earth," he stated to King Hiero. Impressed but skeptical, Hiero asked for a demonstration. As Plutarch relates the episode, the king possessed a large ship, a vessel which could be drawn out of the dock only with the labor of many men. "Loading her with many passengers and a full freight, sitting himself the while off, with no great endeavor, but only holding the head of the pulley in his hand and drawing the cord by degrees, Archimedes drew the ship in a straight line, as smoothly and evenly as if she had been at sea." Archimedes had devised for the experiment a combination of pulleys now known as a pulley-block or a block-and-tackle.

Most spectacular of Archimedes' inventions were those designed to defend Syracuse against invading Roman forces. Again as told by Plutarch, a colossal catapult hurled "immense masses of stone" that "came down with incredible noise and violence, against which no man could stand." Cranes caught ships that ventured in too close and up-ended them or hoisted them high in the air and then flung them back into the sea. Iron beaks seized other ships and smashed them into jutting cliffs or held them fast while giant boulders were dropped on them. The Roman legions fled in panic from the devastation wrought by Archimedes' war machines. Syracuse was saved until three years later, when the Roman general Marcellus took it from the rear while the inhabitants were sleeping.

Though Archimedes' great mechanical ingenuity had to serve mainly military ends, he devised several important contrivances for peaceful purposes. One of the best known is a form of pump, called the "Screw of Archimedes," a device for raising water, seeming to make water run uphill, and long used in irrigation and water pumping. This seemingly simple device was in effect a pipe twisted in the form of a corkscrew, confined within a cylinder; as it revolved about its axis, the "screw" drew the water up until it came out at the top. Also invented by Archimedes was a sphere for demonstrating the motions of the planets. This orrery, the first "planetarium," was actually seen by Cicero, according to whom it represented the motions of sun and moon so well that eclipses could be demonstrated.

Nevertheless, Archimedes held his inventions in low esteem. He had been taught at Syracuse that a scientist was above practical affairs and everyday problems. Plutarch wrote, "Although they [the inventions] had obtained for him the reputation of more than human sagacity, he did not deign to leave behind him any written work on such subject, but, regarding as ignoble and sordid the business of mechanics and every sort of art which is directed to use and profit, he placed his whole ambition in those speculations the beauty and subtlety of which are untainted by any admixture of the common needs of life." Like that of other great Greek mathematicians before him—Thales, Pythagoras, Eudoxus, Euclid—such an attitude reflected intellectual snobbery, a contempt for practical applications, considered fit only for merchants and slaves. Yet, the practical problems fascinated Archimedes throughout his career.

Archimedes was correct, in a sense, in viewing his "speculations" as of first importance. Nearly two thousand years before Isaac Newton and Leibniz devised the modern calculus, Archimedes invented the integral calculus and in one of his problems anticipated the invention of the differential calculus. His chief interest was in pure geometry, and he regarded his discovery of the ratio of the volume of a cylinder to that of a sphere inscribed on it as his greatest achievement. In fact, he attached so much value to this finding that he ordered the diagram relative to it to be engraved on his tombstone. He deduced the centers of gravity of many figures, including parabolic areas. He showed *pi*, the ratio of the circumference of a circle to its diameter, to be almost exactly the figure used in modern mathematics. Many of the common formulas of geometry are attributed to him. He has also been credited by recent writers on the history of mathematics with fundamental developments in trigonometry. In short, his work in mathematics was of immense range and variety.

Archimedes was no mere compiler. Nearly all his writings are accounts of his own discoveries. Apparently a majority of his works have survived. The longest of his writings is a treatise *On the Sphere and the Cylinder.* Others are entitled *On Plane Equilibrium, On Spirals, On Conoids and Spheroids, On Floating Bodies, The Measurement of a Circle,* and *The Sand Reckoner.* The last developed a system of notation which allowed Archimedes to express a number that would require 800 million cyphers in modern notation. The pretext for this exercise was to find the number of grains of sand contained in the universe and, incidentally, to give a succinct account of the astronomical system of Aristarchus of Samos, who in the third century B.C. held that the earth rotates on its own axis and revolves about the sun—foreshadowing Copernicus by eighteen centuries.

Of Archimedes, George Sarton comments, "When one bears in mind that he had formulated and solved a good many abstruse problems without having any of the analytic instruments that we have, his genius fills us with awe." To which Bell, in his *Men of Mathematics*, adds: "Archimedes, the greatest intellect of antiquity, is modern to the core. He and Newton would have understood each other perfectly, and it is just possible that Archimedes, could he come to life long enough to take a post-graduate course in mathematics and physics, would understand Einstein, Bohr, Heisenberg, and Dirac better than they understand themselves."

Archimedes met his end like a true scientist. Again according to our chief authority, Plutarch, when the Romans finally conquered Syracuse in 212 B.C., the Roman general Marcellus gave orders that Archimedes' life was to be spared. Archimedes refused to surrender, however, until he had completed a mathematical design on which he was engaged, and was slain by an irate soldier.

6

Poet of Science
Lucretius (99-55 B.C.)

On the Nature of Things

Of all the great figures of ancient literature, Lucretius is a rare, perhaps a unique, example of a writer who is known by a single composition — a work upon which he spent his life, and even so, left unfinished. His *De Rerum Natura*, "On the Nature of Things," has the epic qualities of the *Iliad* and the *Aeneid*, but differs radically from them in being an epic, in poetical form, of scientific philosophy.

Lucretius was born into a Roman world in which fear and superstition were rampant. It was a period of great disturbance — a society demoralized by war and civil strife, with a government characterized by greed, corruption, inefficiency, and injustice. While Caesar and Pompey were carrying on their imperial conquests abroad, the republican system at home was breaking down. For such a society Lucretius aspired to be an apostle of freedom, aiming to bring an intelligent understanding of the world in place of the darkness of fear and doubt.

Lucretius lived in an age of famous personalities. Cicero, Caesar, Catullus, and Vergil were his Roman contemporaries. Little reliable information is known about Lucretius' own life. A reference in the works of St. Jerome based on a lost work of Suetonius, written two centuries after the death of Lucretius, states that Lucretius lived during the period 95 to 52 B.C., he was driven mad by taking a love philter, he composed his books in periods of lucidity, and committed suicide at age forty-four. All these claims have been questioned; they were possibly based on gossip, and are suspect because St. Jerome may have felt the antagonism of a churchman for an iconoclast who appeared to deny all religion. From more reliable evidence, deduced from Lucretius' own writings, it seems probable that he was of urban Roman origin and belonged to an aristocratic family.

On the Nature of Things is a long and complex work. It is at once a scientific treatise, a gospel of salvation, and an epic of nature and man. Every important facet of the work drew upon and was inspired by the speculative thinkers and poets of Greece. Lucretius' science, generally speaking, was the creation of Democritus; his gospel of salvation was the work of Epicurus, and several centuries earlier Empedocles, Greek philosopher and statesman, had composed a celebrated poem on the nature of things.

Early in life, Lucretius apparently became an ardent convert to Epicurean philosophy, a system which he regarded as the final and complete solution of "the riddle of this painful earth." In *De Rerum Natura*, he represents himself as a disciple of the great master, Epicurus (c.342-270 B.C.). Since only fragments of Epicurus' own writings have survived, Lucretius' magnificent epic poem, extending to 7,415 lines, is the most complete and systematic statement in existence of Epicurean thought.

The popular conception of Epicureanism is of a philosophy preaching pleasure and self-indulgence as the highest good, emphasizing sensual enjoyment and even debauchery. According to the moral teachings of Epicurus and his followers, such as Lucretius, however, man's true happiness is derived through freedom from superstition, fear, the renunciation of excessive ambition, and of the pursuit of wealth, and delight in the simpler forms of pleasure, especially those of the mind.

Lucretius' poem is divided into six books. After an invocation to Venus, goddess of creation, the author expresses his main purpose. He wishes to describe "the nature of things," their beginning, evolution, and dissolution—in short, to explain the universe in physical terms. The approach is two-pronged: to defend science and to attack superstition. The fundamental fact is assumed to be the permanence of matter; nothing can come of nothing and at the same time nothing can vanish. Matter consists of particles separated by empty space. Neither particles or vacuum are visible, but they exist. Lucretius held that the vacuum is boundless, the universe is infinite, and the particles or atoms are numberless.

The second book begins with the praise of philosophy and of science. It continues with the study of atomic motions, various atomic shapes, and the effect of the shapes on the compounds formed from them. Atoms are totally lacking in color, temperature, sound, taste, or odor. All bodies, living and dead, are made up of atoms. There are many worlds in the infinite universe, and each world passes through four stages: birth, growth, decay, and death.

Book three seeks to explain the nature of the soul and to destroy the fear of death. Body and soul are mortal. Death is no more to be feared than a dreamless sleep. The mind or soul is treated further in the fourth book, which explains the nature of sensation, especially sight and thought, considers some of the functions of the body, and concludes with an attack on the passion of love.

In the fifth book, the longest, Lucretius describes how the world came into existence out of atoms moving in infinite space, and goes on to discuss the sun, the moon, and the stars. Back on the earth, he considers the beginning of life and traces the development of living creatures, of men, and of human civilization. Thus this section is mainly concerned with astronomy, organic evolution, anthropology, and the history of culture. In similar fashion, the final book deals with meteorology, geography, and medicine: thunder, lightning, hurricanes, clouds, rain and rainbow, earthquakes, and volcanoes—for all of which, Lucretius contends, there is a physical explanation. The poem ends with a description of the pestilence that devastated Athens in the early years of the Peloponnesian War.

The chief purpose of *De Rerum Natura* is to show clearly the way to the ideal life, to the tranquility of spirit and soul which was Epicurus' aim. As viewed by Lucretius, mankind is confronted by two major obstacles in its search for happiness and peace of mind: fear of the gods and fear of death. These impediments can be overcome, he maintains, by an understanding of the true nature of things. A rational approach will show that everything can be explained in natural, nothing in supernatural, terms. Hence, Lucretius' exposition of natural science was designed first of all to remove fear. We will cease to fear the gods, he believed, when we learn the laws of natural science, and we will no longer fear death when we learn the nature of the soul.

Lucretius was a bitter enemy of superstition and of religion in all its forms, repudiating the concept of a divine providence watching over the ways and fates of man. He also condemns the idea of unseen powers hostile to man and capable of doing him evil as gross superstition, disproved by all nature. Because of their ignorance of natural phenomena and of the great forces of nature, men had come to believe that the gods were responsible for them and that these gods lived in the sky. Lucretius does not deny the existence of the gods; instead, he concludes that they dwell outside the world, in a state of untroubled bliss; that they have no control over nature; and that they are totally unconcerned with the affairs of the world. Also, despite his opposition to the religion of his time, Lucretius shows a devout reverence for the powers of nature, which he in effect deifies.

The atomic theory was adopted by Lucretius to explain the universe in rational terms and to dispel miracles and superstitions. An atomic theory had been invented by Leucippus (fl. 475 B.C.), and formulated more specifically by Democritus (c.460-370 B.C.), who used the term "atom" to define a fundamental particle of matter so small and firm that it could not be further divided or smashed. The theory reached Lucretius several centuries later through the writings of Epicurus.

Foreshadowing Mendelian principles of heredity, Lucretius notes that germ seeds descend from parent to offspring, reproducing characteristics even of remote ancestors. The idea of organic evolution appears in book five. Prefiguring the "survival of the fittest" doctrine is Lucretius' observation that many plants and animals have disappeared from the earth because they failed to adapt to changing conditions.

In the evolution of man himself, Lucretius shows himself in harmony with modern anthropology. The fifth book traces the origin of life and the gradual advance of man from the most primitive cave dweller—the speechless subhuman prowler—to the most civilized Roman citizen. It tells how, step by step, man began social life, originated language, discovered fire, learned the use of metals, developed the art of war (next to religion the most detestable of practices in Lucretius' eyes), and as civilization progressed developed clothing, horticulture, music, and writing. According to his account, nothing has a divine origin; everything evolves and grows from the operation of natural causes. Lucretius was thus the first to advance the idea of human progress.

Even grander in concept are Lucretius' theories of the cosmos. He considers possible processes by which the earth, the sky, sun, moon, and stars are formed. Since there is an infinite number of universes, he holds, there are infinite potentialities for differences in natural phenomena.

Man's fear of death and his efforts to shut out thoughts of it from his mind are responsible, according to Lucretius, for avarice, uncontrolled ambition, war, murder, and even suicide. To Lucretius, the extinction of life is not a sad thing; it is a blessing, a relief, an emancipation. The endless chain of life-death-life must continue. From a universal view, the individual is insignificant.

To a great majority of mankind, the Epicurean philosophy as thus propounded by Lucretius is unconvincing and unsatisfying. Except for Vergil, on whose writings the Lucretian influence is clear and profound, *De Rerum Natura* received slight attention from ancient authors. In fact, there is little to show that the work received any considerable notice prior to the Renaissance. Curiously, despite its antireligious bias, the poem was carefully preserved in the Christian monastic libraries of the Middle Ages—possibly because it attacks the heathen gods. Beginning with the rationalist thought of the sixteenth century, however, Lucretius was a seminal influence. Giordano Bruno (1548-1600) was one of the first to be deeply attracted to him and to discuss the atomic theory. Sir Isaac Newton (1642-1727) was a convinced atomist, and his ideas of the atom closely resemble those of Lucretius. Under the influence of Newton, John Dalton (1766-1844) revived the atomic theory and used it to explain his observations on the action of gases—laying the foundation for modern chemistry. In the nineteenth century, Clerk Maxwell and Lord Kelvin, and in the twentieth, Albert Einstein are among the great scientists who have paid tribute to Lucretius. Though our knowledge of atomic science and of other fields for scientific inquiry explored by Lucretius has vastly expanded and changed since his era, his teachings have had a direct and beneficial influence upon the development of modern science.

Summing up a critical review of Lucretius and his work, the historian Thomas Macaulay writes, "In energy, perspicuity, variety of illustration, knowledge of life and manners, talent for description, sense of the beauty of the external world, and elevation and dignity of moral feeling, Lucretius has hardly ever an equal." Another critic, Kenneth Rexroth, in his *Classics Revisited*, concludes that "no sounder view of nature was to appear for almost two thousand years. We should understand that the atom of Lucretius is not our atom, much less our molecule, but ... today it is the foundation of our physics of ultimate particles. So with his anthropology and pre-history, archeology and the discovery of pre-civilized peoples have substantiated the general outline of his history of human society."

7

First Medical Historian
Celsus (c.25 B.C.-A.D. 50)

De Medicina

To a Roman, born two thousand years ago, we are indebted for the first reasonably complete history of medicine and summary of medical lore at the beginning of the Christian era. Practically nothing is known of the author. Doubts exist about the correct form of his name, whether he was a practicing physician or simply a well-informed layman, and whether his book is an original treatise or a translation from the Greek.

The consensus among the authorities is that: first, a work so complete and so accurate as *De Medicina* must have come from the pen of a man with professional experience; second, though the author was obviously familiar with and drew upon the writings of Hippocrates and other early medical men, *De Medicina* is essentially an original contribution; and, third, the book was probably one part of an encyclopedia-like compilation, but the remaining parts — on agriculture, military arts, rhetoric, philosophy, and jurisprudence — are lost.

In any event, Celsus' *De Medicina* and Dioscorides' *Materia Medica*, both of the first century A.D., are the only books of any magnitude in medical literature between the time of Hippocrates in the fourth century B.C. and Galen in the second century A.D. During the Middle Ages, the Celsus manuscript disappeared. In the fifteenth century, it was rediscovered by Pope Nicholas V, and through his influence was the first book on general medicine to be printed (Florence, 1478). To the men of the Renaissance, it revealed the amazing extent of the medical knowledge possessed by the ancient Greeks and Romans. Sixty editions were issued in the two centuries following the first printing. The works of seventy-two authors mentioned by Celsus have been lost, and his book is the only source of information concerning them.

De Medicina is divided into eight parts or "books." In a lengthy preface, Celsus presents a history of medical progress from the days of Homer to his own time, dealing fully with the dogmatic, the methodic, and the empiric schools. Of the two main contemporary medical schools of thought, the empiricists claimed to be able to cure all diseases by the use of drugs; the methodists, on the other hand, maintained that disease could be combated only by diet and exercise. Such inflexible approaches to medical science were unacceptable to Celsus. As a whole, his work emphasizes the importance of anatomy in the study and practice of medicine, and (following the lead of Hippocrates) of diagnosis and prognosis as preliminary to treatment. He frequently recommends the use of drugs, and recognizes the value of general hygiene and physical exercise.

Analyzing *De Medicina* in more specific detail, we find that the first two books relate to diet and hygiene, discussing the digestibility and effects of many forms of food and drink; describing exercises beneficial to the maintenance of health; and giving detailed consideration to the causes and symptoms of diseases. The third book is concerned with the treatment of disease, in particular fevers (probably malarial), insanity, cardiac disorders, lethargy, dropsy, tuberculosis, jaundice, and palsy. Also mentioned are the familiar signs of inflammation: heat, redness, swelling, and pain. The prime interest of the fourth book is internal diseases, from head to foot, including the throat, thorax, abdomen, and various bodily organs.

Book five takes up two main topics: first, drugs and their uses; second, wounds and their treatment. Celsus classifies substances according to their effect on the body, following this analysis with prescriptions for poultices, plasters, ointments, gargles, antidotes, liniments, draughts, pills, anesthetics, etc. The second section, on lesions, deals with a great diversity of wounds, e.g., injuries to various parts of the body inflicted by weapons, by the bites of animals, serpents, or insects, by burns, and by ulcerations and abscesses. Book six is devoted to skin diseases, diseases of the eye, ear, nose, teeth, and tonsils, and to other "special subjects," including venereal diseases.

It has been surmised that the preference for external remedies shown in *De Medicina* can be attributed to the ban on dissection, which limited knowledge of anatomy and internal conditions. The ancient Egyptians, through their embalming practices, were familiar with internal anatomy, but the Greeks rejected the use of dead bodies for purposes of study and investigation. The prejudice continued during the succeeding centuries. In fact, it was not until the Renaissance, under the influence of painters and sculptures, that dissection and vivisection began to form the basis for medical training. Celsus, fifteen hundred or more years earlier, wrote without any real knowledge of internal conditions. He could treat the symptoms, not the disease.

The two last books of *De Medicina* deal largely with surgery. Book seven is concerned with operative procedures, such as the removal of foreign bodies: operations for goiter, hernia, stones in the bladder, and cataracts; and tonsillectomies. It is in this book that Celsus describes some characteristics of the successful surgeon: "He should be youthful or at any rate nearer youth than age; with a strong and steady hand which never trembles, and ready to use the left hand as well as the right; with vision sharp and clear, and spirit undaunted; filled with pity, so that he wishes to cure his patient, yet is not moved by his cries, to go too fast, or cut less than is necessary; but he does everything just as if the cries of pain cause him no emotion." The eighth and last book gives precise directions for the treatment of fractures and dislocations. Celsus recommends wooden splints, fixed by bandages stiffened with starch or by casts of wax.

A number of medical procedures are mentioned by Celsus earlier than any other writer. Among these are the use of nutrient enemata, the operation on the eye for cataract, the operation for cure of hernia, and a classical description of the operation for bladder or kidney stones. Celsus advocates the use of ligotures to control hemorrhage, a device rediscovered by Ambrose Paré in the sixteenth century.

The physicians of Celsus' time knew little or nothing of the actual causes of disease. Nevertheless, *De Medicina* described accurately the symptoms of many recognized diseases and their orthodox treatments. Among the diseases and conditions reviewed are pneumonia, arthritis, dysentery, tonsillitis, cancer, kidney and liver diseases, tuberculosis, hemorrhoids, diabetes, malaria, epilepsy, and such mental illnesses as paranoia. For the treatment of these and other ailments, a surprisingly large number of medicines were available in Celsus' time, both for internal and external use. A mere listing, with brief notes, fills forty-five pages of the standard translation of *De Medicina*. The ingredients were mainly derived from herbs and vegetables (some had been used medicinally from the earliest time), but many others came from animal organic and inorganic substances. Comparisons with a modern materia medica show a substantial number still in use.

Astonishing also is the number of surgical instruments developed and used by Roman medical men. Celsus describes more than a hundred different types, many of them similar in shape or design to their modern counterparts, such as saws for amputations, drills, sutures, scalpels, clamps, trepans, and forceps. The instruments noted by Celsus correspond to those found in the house of a surgeon at Pompeii (destroyed A.D. 79), now on view in the Naples museum.

Celsus endorses the view that physicians should not be bound by hard and fast rules. Instead, treatment should vary according to climate and other conditions, and must be based on experience.

The development of modern medicine owes much to Celsus' pioneering work. His book, one of the few great works in its field during ancient times, was written in a truly scientific spirit. Rejecting the false, narrow doctrines and beliefs widely prevailing among medical practitioners of his era, he reported solely what he conceived to be factual and important. His admirable ability to select what was accurate and worth recording and his extensive knowledge of existing medical literature enabled him to summarize in a clear and practical fashion the ideas and discoveries of the art of medicine from his own and preceding centuries and from all portions of the known world. By Latinizing Greek medical terminology, Celsus gave substantial aid to establishing and standardizing scientific medical terms. Finally, the early appearance of *De Medicina* in printed form came at a strategic moment in the history of Western Europe, playing a vital part during the course of the Renaissance in awakening interest in a science and art which had been long neglected.

8

The Great Compiler
Pliny the Elder (23-79)

Natural History

To Gaius Plinius Secundus, usually called Pliny the Elder (to distinguish him from his famous nephew and protégé of the same name), we are indebted for the preservation of excerpts from hundreds of ancient writers whose works would otherwise have vanished completely. According to a list appended by Pliny to the first book of his *Natural History*, he consulted some two thousand works by 147 Latin and 327 foreign authors in the preparation of this encyclopedic treatise.

Writing was more of an avocation than a vocation for Pliny. Following his birth in northern Italy and a period of study in Rome, he began, in his early twenties, an active military and governmental career that occupied him for the remainder of his life. Before completing his formal education, he had become interested in the study of plants. Shortly thereafter, under Seneca's influence, he had turned to philosophy and rhetoric and had begun the practice of law. On official missions, he traveled in Germany, Spain, Gaul, Africa, and possibly in Judea and Syria.

Despite multiple demands made on his time as soldier, lawyer, governor of provinces, and adviser to the Roman court, Pliny was a prolific author. A record left by the younger Pliny notes that he wrote on the use of the javelin by cavalry, on the training of the orator, a history of the German wars, a treatise on grammar, a history of Rome, and finally the *Natural History*, largest and most important of his works, and the only one that has survived. To account for such extraordinary literary productivity, Pliny the Younger describes his uncle's working habits. The elder Pliny was accustomed to reading or having books read to him at meals, in the bath, while traveling, or taking exercise—in brief, during every available minute. As he read or listened, he made notes or extracts from the material at hand, and when traveling he was accompanied by a corps of secretaries to take down his words in shorthand. By these methodical practices, he gradually amassed a vast store of data for subsequent use.

In his preface, Pliny claims to deal with no less than 20,000 subjects—to elucidate which he draws principally upon 100 selected authors. In the main, therefore, the *Natural History* is a secondhand compilation from the works of others, though Pliny intersperses many observations of his own. Critics agree that he showed little judgment or discrimination in his selections, mixed the true and the false in hodgepodge fashion, neglected to arrange the mass of material by any intelligible method, and often failed to understand his authorities.

Natural history, as interpreted by Pliny, encompassed considerably more than does the modern definition of the term. In his work, he attempted to give a comprehensive survey of all contemporary knowledge of the physical universe, and of this world in particular as well as all of its constituents — animal, vegetable, and mineral. The compilation is thus an encyclopedia of astronomy, meteorology, geography, mineralogy, zoology, and botany. But, in addition, it treats of the fine arts, painting and sculpture, human inventions and institutions, and the author's views on religion, ethics, and literature.

The thirty-seven books of the *Natural History* are logically arranged, even though the contents are unsystematic. They are distributed as follows: mathematical and physical description of the world; geography and ethnography of Europe, Africa, and Asia; anthropology and human physiology; zoology of land animals, sea creatures, birds, and insects; botany, including agriculture and materia medica; medical zoology; mineralogy; history of ancient art, silver chasing, bronze statuary, painting, marble statuary, and precious stones. The portions relating to the fine arts, painting, and sculpture, while irrelevant from the point of view of natural history proper, are now regarded as among the most important parts of the work.

The main theme running through Pliny's *Natural History* is that nature is designed to serve the human race. Natural objects are usually described, therefore, only in their relation to man, for Pliny believed that all things were intended for some useful purpose. "Nature and Earth fill us with admiration," writes Pliny, "as we contemplate the great variety of plants and find that they are created for the wants or enjoyments of mankind." In his view, every plant has some special medicinal value, if it can be discovered, and for every disease there is a curative plant. It was this belief in an omniscient and omnipotent nature that won great favor for the non-Christian Pliny and his works among the early Christians.

Through his writings on medical botany and materia medica, Pliny influenced the progress of medicine for the next fifteen hundred years. He offered a vast collection of remedies based on what he had heard or what he himself believed, though naturally without foundation in scientific experiment. His credulity is attested, for example, by the statement: "The herb dittany has power to extract arrows. This was proved by stags who had been struck by these missiles, which were loosened when they fed on this plant." Obviously, this is folklore, as were many of the current superstitions and notions Pliny subscribes to about the medicinal properties of various waters and of fishes and other aquatic creatures.

In writing on zoology, Pliny listed animals without regard to likenesses in structure, but usually with the largest and most remarkable described first. As with botany, each animal was considered in its relation to man, whether it was beneficial or harmful, and especially its use for medical purposes. For example, here are two of hundreds of "cures" offered:

> A tooth stops aching when worms are taken
> from a certain prickly plant, put with some
> bread in a pill-box and bound on the arm on the
> same side of the body as the aching tooth.

> Two bed-bugs bound to the left arm in wool
> stolen from shepherds are a charm against
> nocturnal fevers, against diurnal fevers if
> wrapped in russet cloth instead.

Bed bugs are also listed as a cure for snake bites.

It is characteristic of Pliny that he accepted uncritically almost everything that he heard or read, without attempting to verify his facts by trial or observation. The marvelous and the monstrous held a special fascination for him. Thus, in writing about faraway places, he told of men whose feet were turned the wrong way, of mouthless men who fed upon the fragrance of flowers and fruit, of men whose feet were so large that they could hold them over their heads as parasols to protect them from the sun, of winged horses, unicorns, mermaids, near-human dolphins, and many other prodigies. Some of these yarns may be found later scattered through the *Arabian Nights* and the folk tales of Europe. On the other hand, Pliny rejected the prevailing belief in the astrological influences of the stars upon the human race, including the superstition that each falling star marked the death of the particular human to whom fate had attached it.

Influenced by Pliny, all sorts of romantic and extraordinary beliefs about animals and plants continued to be held by even educated persons for centuries afterwards, and by some common folk today. The medical historian Charles Seizer notes that the spells recited by gypsy fortunetellers are inaccurate formulas taken from Pliny and handed down by word of mouth through the centuries.

For such reasons, the *Natural History* has been called a "repository of all the errors of antiquity." Pliny's editor and translator, Harris Rackham, points out, "nevertheless, it is a mistake to underrate the value of his work. He is diligent, accurate and free from prejudice. Though he had no considerable first-hand knowledge of the sciences and was not himself a systematic observer, he had a naturally scientific mind, and an unaffected and absorbing interest in his subjects. If he gives us much attention to what is merely curious as to what has an essential importance, this curiosity has incidentally preserved much valuable detail."

From a scientific point of view, Pliny's most useful contribution is in the field of botany. Sixteen of the thirty-seven books of his *Natural History* deal with plants as follows: on trees and their products, such as fruit, gums, perfumes, etc.; on the grape and the making of wine; on the olive, fig, apple, and other fruits; on forest trees and timber and on their culture, diseases, pruning, training, etc.; on farming and cereals; on horticulture; on the medicinal properties of garden plants; on flowers, bees, honey, and plant anatomy; on herbs used in medicine and in cookery; on the medicinal properties of cultivated and forest trees; and on the medicinal properties of wild herbaceous plants. Nearly a thousand plants are mentioned. Like Theophrastus, Pliny recognized the existence of sex in all plants, herbs, and trees, using the date palm as a specific instance.

In religion, Pliny tended to be a Stoic. The *Natural History* contains numerous digressions on human morals and puritanical tirades. The author is critical of luxury and artificiality and urges simplicity in living. In general, he has a low estimate of human ability, deplores human wickedness, and mistrusts the wisdom of Providence.

Literature also receives Pliny's attention. His evaluation of great literary figures placed Homer and Cicero at the summit, with Vergil ranking only slightly below them.

Scientific curiosity cost Pliny his life. In A.D. 79, at fifty-six years of age, he was in command of a Roman fleet in the Bay of Naples. The volcano Vesuvius began to erupt, and Pliny landed to get a closer view. While he was on shore, a terrific eruption, which buried the city of Pompeii, occurred, and Pliny was suffocated by sulphur fumes. A vivid account of this disaster is furnished by Pliny the Younger.

After Pliny's time, the *Natural History* was copied and recopied. For fifty generations it was the paramount authority in its field among medieval and Renaissance scholars. At least two hundred manuscript copies prior to the invention of printing are in existence, and it is significant that Pliny's *Natural History* was the first scientific work to be printed (Venice, 1469). Before the end of the fifteenth century, six more editions appeared in Italy alone.

Pliny's great storehouse of not very well digested information has been described as the earliest example of a popular natural history book. The progress of modern science has made virtually all of his knowledge obsolete, and the work is read today principally for its historical and antiquarian interest. In the *Natural History*, however, we have an encyclopedic mine of classical data, even though often inaccurate, on the natural sciences; and the compilation marks an important stage in the development of scientific knowledge. Further, the sections on sculpture, painting, and ancient culture in general contain valuable information available in no other extant writings of the period. Lynn Thorndike, in his *History of Magic and Experimental Science*, states that *Natural History* "is perhaps the most important single source extant for the history of ancient civilization."

9

First Herbalist
Dioscorides (c.40-80)

Materia Medica

A Greek surgeon in the army of the Roman emperor Nero, Pedacius Dioscorides, was the originator of the branch of medical science known as *materia medica*, the materials of medicine. Dioscorides' pioneer treatise is the ancestor of the voluminous pharmacopaoeias of modern medicine and the chief authority on the materia medica of antiquity.

Little is known of the life of Dioscorides, a contemporary of Pliny the Elder. He was born in Anazarba, Cilicia, in Asia Minor, about A.D. 40. According to tradition, he joined Nero's army in order to be able to study the flora and fauna of different countries. In the course of his military career, he traveled through Italy, Greece, Spain, France, and Asia Minor, collecting a vast number of botanical, mineralogical, and biologic specimens. Wherever he went, Dioscorides questioned the natives of the area about the medicinal values and practical uses of the specimens he was gathering. The data thus acquired, together with information obtained from the extant texts of other writers on natural history, formed the basis of his famous herbal.

As Theophrastus had been the first scientific botanist, so Dioscorides was the first to write on medical botany as an applied science. His work is divided into five books: first, aromatics, oils, ointments, trees; second, animal products of dietetic and medicinal value, cereals, and garden herbs; third and fourth, roots, juices, and other medicinal plants; and fifth, vines, wines, and metallic ores.

Some six hundred plants and plant products are described by Dioscorides — at least a hundred more than were listed by Theophrastus. Hippocrates and other Greek physicians of his time had known about 150 of the herbs recorded by Dioscorides, and approximately 90 are still used in the practice of medicine. Dioscorides set the pattern for later works on materia medica by a qualitative rather than a botanical classification; he lists plants under the diseases for which they were reputed to be beneficial. For each plant a short account was given of habitat, appearance, and use as a remedy, insofar as Dioscorides possessed the information. Latin, Dacian, Gallic, Punic, and Egyptian synonyms are listed for some of the plants. Like Theophrastus earlier and such later writers as Linnaeus, he recognized natural families of plants. His descriptions, as could be anticipated for a first attempt in a new field, are often extremely meager, or even altogether lacking. The bulk of the descriptions are made on the authority of others, notably Theophrastus and Nicander.

In a prefatory note of dedication, Dioscorides emphasizes the importance of the task to which he has set himself: "Now it is obvious to everybody that a treatise on medicine is necessary, for it is conjoined to the whole art of healing, and by itself yields a mighty assistance to every part. And because its scope may be enlarged both in the direction of methods of preparation, and of mixtures, and of experiments on diseases and because a knowledge of each separate medicine contributes much hereunto, we will include matter that is familiar and closely allied, that the book may be complete."

Examples of the specific virtues and uses of various plants described by Dioscorides illustrate his methods, as well as the contemporary state of medical science. Acacia is recommended as an astringent gum in hemorrhage; agaric in the treatment of gastric disorders; brine for the cleansing of ulcers; aloe for hemorrhoids and ulcers; ammoniacal substances obtained from plants for the treatment of asthma; dill, anise, bitter almond, and juniper as diuretics; bitter almond as a laxative and soporific, and, when compounded in rose-oil poultices, for the relief of headaches; dill for cases of nausea and as a hip bath for hysterical women; licorice for sore throats, ulceration of the bladder, and, when mixed with wine, for diarrhea; balsam for sores; wormwood for the treatment of dropsy and toothache; lichens for inflammatory conditions; gentian for diseases of the liver and stomach; pennyroyal as an aid in obstetric cases; hemlock in the treatment of erysipelas and other inflammations of the skin; mint in vinegar for eliminating roundworms, for the relief of coughing and vomiting, and as an aphrodisiac; lettuce for a mild sedative; a plaster of bird lime and caustic lye for tumorous growths; verdigris for the treatment of trachoma and other eye diseases; fish glue for the removal of wrinkles from the face; cardamon for intestinal worms and stones in the bladder; and buckthorn for the cure of various intestinal conditions.

As an anesthetic, Dioscorides prepared an alcoholic extract of the root of the mandrake, a concoction also used in diseases of the eye, in insomnia, and as a soporific in surgery. Dioscorides was the first to recognize its value as another soporific. He notes that the best variety has a heavy, stupefying odor, and refers to the lethargic state induced by an overdose of the drug.

Among other significant contributions made by Dioscorides to medicine and general science were tests for recognizing adulterated drugs; methods for the preparation of white lead and artificial calamine; and the identification of a surprising number of metallic oxides, sulphates, and sulphides.

Dioscorides offers detailed directions for the gathering and storing of herbs. The effectiveness or ineffectiveness of the materials for medical purposes will depend, he says, upon whether his instructions are heeded or neglected. For example, "We ought to gather herbs when the weather is clear, for there is a great difference whether it be dry or rainy when the gathering is made": medicinal plants found growing in high altitudes, exposed to the wind, in cold, dry areas are stronger than those growing on plains, in the shade, and protected from the wind. The degree of maturity must also be taken into account, to avoid gathering plants when they are either too young or are beginning to fade. The skilled herbalist will collect his material only at the height of maturity.

"Herbs which are full of branches," Dioscorides further directs, "should be gathered whilst they are great with seed; flowers ought to be gathered before they fall; fruits when they are ripe, and seeds when they begin to be dry, and before they fall out." Roots should be collected when the herbs are beginning to lose their leaves. Dioscorides then goes on to recommend various types of containers and vessels for the storage and proper preservation of the medicinal herbs. With few exceptions, such as the hellebore, herbs deteriorate and generally will not be effective for a longer period than three years from the time they are gathered.

Translated into many languages, Dioscorides' herbal continued in use for more than fifteen hundred years. It was one of the principal sources of scientific knowledge throughout the medieval era and well into the Renaissance. The book is said to have been more attentively studied by learned men than any other botanical work. In his *History of Medicine*, F. M. Garrison observes that "up to the beginning of the seventeenth century the best books on medical botany were still simply commentaries on the treatise of Dioscorides, which is the historic source of most of our herbal therapy."

Unfortunately, such utter dependence upon an authority whose work was necessarily incomplete and somewhat inaccurate had a severely repressive effect upon further progress. For centuries, no drug was considered genuine that did not agree with Dioscorides' description. Northern European botanists, unaware of the geographical limitation of species, wasted an infinite amount of labor trying to identify the plants of their region with those described by Dioscorides from the Mediterranean area. Thus, the minds of botanists were diverted from the first-hand study of plants. As Richard Pulteney, English botanist, cogently remarked in 1790, "the descriptions of plants in the ancient authors were, at best, short, vague, and insufficient; and with this inconvenience, the study of nature herself was neglected."

10

Beginning of Scientific Cartography
Ptolemaeus (c.100-170)

Geography

The fame of Claudius Ptolemaeus, more commonly known as Ptolemy, Greco-Egyptian astronomer, geographer, and geometer, rests upon two works: the *Geography* and the *Almagest*, the latter an astronomical compilation. Ptolemy and Hipparchus are the outstanding astronomers of antiquity, despite serious defects in their theories of the solar system. The Ptolemaic system was geocentric, i.e., earth-centered, and for fourteen centuries, as presented in the *Almagest*, it was almost universally accepted. Not until Nicolaus Copernicus, in the sixteenth century, revived the work of the Greek philosopher Aristarchus (c.310-230 B.C.) and developed the idea of a heliocentric (sun-centered) cosmos, was the Ptolemaic system finally and reluctantly discarded.

Though less celebrated, Ptolemy's *Geography* has been of greater permanent significance than his erroneous assumptions in astronomy. Ptolemy was the first to attempt to place the study of geography on a scientific basis, and he easily holds first rank among ancient writers on the subject. One authority, Edward Luther Stevenson, concludes that "the whole of modern cartography has developed from Ptolemy's *Atlas*."

Scarcely anything is known with certainty about Ptolemy himself. He was a native of Egypt, probably of Greek parentage, and lived and wrote at Alexandria about the middle of the second century A.D. His *Geography* is assigned to the period 150-160. Otherwise, there are only legends.

In the *Geography*, Ptolemy set himself the extremely ambitious task of describing and mapping the then known world. The book which resulted remained the standard work in its field for fourteen centuries, until its theories were disproved by Columbus' discovery of America and the ensuing great age of navigation. Covered by Ptolemy's maps were countries as far apart as India, China, Norway, and England (or "Albion").

The *Geography* was divided by Ptolemy into eight books or sections. The first treats of the principles of mathematical geography and map projection, with consideration of the length and breadth of the inhabited world. There follow six books listing the latitude and longitude of some eight thousand places shown on the maps, and outlining the boundaries of the countries. The last book is concerned more with astronomy than with geography, estimating the length of the longest day in different latitudes and longitudes and the course of the sun in tropical areas.

Ptolemy was the first geographer to designate length and breadth as longitude and latitude. He calculated according to rules laid down by Eratosthenes (c.276-294 B.C.), and by Hipparchus (fl. 140 B.C.), who had conceived the idea that a map should be based upon points of which the latitude and longitude are known. Ptolemy's immediate predecessor, Marinus, had followed the same principle.

Unfortunately, as modern commentators have pointed out, Ptolemy's theoretical science outstripped his power of applying it practically. In his time exact data were exceedingly scarce. He studied itineraries of Roman officials and merchants. He estimated distances by the averages of time required for journeys or voyages between certain points. He compared authorities. But in the end, such vague sources could produce only rough approximations, and the farther removed the localities were from known places, the more unreliable the figures became.

Ptolemy held to the theory of a fixed earth, without revolution or rotation. He accepted the measurement of its circumference stated by Poseidonius (c.130-50 B.C.)—18,000 geographical miles, an estimate having an error of one-sixth. He also adopted Hipparchus' division of the equator into 360 parts or degrees, each degree equivalent to fifty, rather than the correct sixty, miles. An early notion that the world was surrounded by the ocean was rejected by Ptolemy as it had been by Hipparchus and Herodotus.

To represent the curved surface of the earth on a plane surface, Ptolemy developed a scheme to indicate the parallels of latitude by arcs of concentric circles, the centers of which are at the North Pole. The meridians of longitude are shown by straight lines which converge to the Pole.

The boundaries of the world known to, or imagined by, Ptolemy and delineated by him are: on the north the ocean which surrounds the British Isles, the northern parts of Europe, and the unknown land in the northern region of Asia; on the south, the unknown land which encloses the Indian Sea, and the unknown land to the south of Libya and Ethiopia; on the east, the unknown land which adjoins the eastern nations of Asia, including the Chinese; on the west, the Western Ocean and unknown parts of Libya. In essence, this was a summary of contemporary Roman knowledge of the earth's surface. Among the major errors were assumptions of a land connection between southeastern Africa and southeastern Asia, and of the Indian Ocean as an enclosed sea. On the other hand, there was a realization, perhaps for the first time, of the tremendous bulk—though not the form or shape—of the earth's land surface. Robert E. Dickinson and O. J. R. Howarth, in their *The Making of Geography*, suggest that "Ptolemy's belief in a far eastern extension of Asia helped Christopher Columbus to believe both that he could reach Asia by sailing westward across the Atlantic, and, subsequently, that he had done so."

Ptolemy's atlas comprised three maps of the ancient world and a large number of country or province maps. The world maps were drawn with the middle meridian and the middle parallel as straight lines, and with all other meridians and parallels curved. Curvatures were omitted from the numerous country and province maps; the parallels were straight lines east and west, and the meridians straight lines converging to the north. Individual cities, islands, and other points were then introduced into the network at the longitudes and latitudes derived from Ptolemy's calculations. The completeness of the Ptolemaic system and the carefully drawn maps enhanced the prestige of the *Geography* and gave it an appearance of final authority which it could not possibly have possessed.

Ptolemy has had a lasting influence on the science of geography. Progress in geographical studies during the Middle Ages was virtually nil, but the coming of the Renaissance brought an upsurge of revived interest. Latin translations of Ptolemy multiplied rapidly, first in manuscript and later in printed form. Discoveries of new continents, countries, coasts, and islands led quickly, of course, to supersedure of the Ptolemaic maps. Though obsolete and fallen into oblivion, however, Ptolemy's *Geography* had established the principles upon which any valid representation of the earth's surface must be based: scientific observation and mathematical exactness. Ptolemy himself lacked the tools for such an approach. The ever-increasing accumulation of geographical facts and a vast improvement in the instruments, methods, and materials available for map construction have enabled his modern successors to accomplish what Ptolemy essayed but was incapable of performing.

11

Dictator of Medieval Medicine

Galen (c.130-200)

On the Natural Faculties

By the beginning of the Christian era, medicine as a profession had sadly degenerated. Most practitioners were charlatans who pretended to possess supernatural insight in methods of treating various diseases. They included gatherers and peddlers of herbs, dealers in salves, venders of amulets, love-philters and abortifacients, astrologers, midwives, attendants and masseurs from the baths, and quack specialists, particularly for diseases of the eye. Most of the physicians were Greeks or of Grecian education, and many were slaves or freedmen.

For virtually all his contemporaries in the medical field, Galen, who after Hippocrates ranks as the greatest physician of antiquity, had the utmost contempt and was highly critical. A Greek physician and writer, he dominated European medical thought for nearly fifteen hundred years. Even in his own lifetime, "full of ambition and overriding pride, energetic and violent, given to intrigue and anxious to impress the world," as René Taton, historian of science, describes him, Galen was a controversial figure.

A just appraisal of Galen in relation to medical progress is exceedingly difficult. Historians are inclined to view him as a false prophet, in contrast to Hippocrates, the true prophet. On balance, Galen's teachings may have been more harmful than beneficial. Yet, he has been called the first experimental physiologist, he made significant contributions to the previously neglected science of anatomy, and his encyclopedic treatises preserved much of the classical knowledge of medicine throughout the Dark Ages in Europe. Today the Galenic writings are our chief source for the history of Greek medicine.

Galen, born about A.D. 130, began his professional career as surgeon to the gladiators at Pergamum, his native town in Asia Minor. Subsequently, at the height of the empire, he became the foremost medical practitioner in Rome, personal physician to Emperor Marcus Aurelius and to several succeeding emperors. Meanwhile, he was constantly busy with his dissections and studies, and his prolific pen was producing scores of books on all phases of medicine, medical history, and medical philosophy. His treatise *On the Natural Faculties* contains his most basic theories, and forms an excellent introduction to his more specialized works.

Galen pays frequent tribute to his illustrious forerunner Hippocrates, and follows the latter closely in his belief in the workings of nature. Among all physicians and philosophers, wrote Galen, "Hippocrates was the first to recognize what nature does." The essence of Galen's teaching is summarized in the sentence, "We say that animals are governed at once by their soul and by their nature and plants by their nature alone, and that growth and nutrition are the effects of nature, not of soul."

Galen's notions of what occurred in the process of nutrition and assimilation, however, were highly fanciful. He theorized that the "blood-making faculty" of the portal vein changes food into blood. Three spirits then take over. On reaching the liver, the blood receives the "natural spirit"; in the heart, mixed with air from the lungs, it becomes the "vital spirit"; and the part which goes to the brain, bringing about movement and the higher functions of the body, is the "animal spirit." Galen exploded the prevailing doctrine that the arteries are filled with air, by opening the pulmonary artery of a live dog, but he was convinced that air was absorbed by the arteries and exhausted through the lungs.

Galen was in accord with Hippocratic methods of observing the natural course of disease, including a belief in the four humors. He divided diseases into three classes: those affecting such simple tissues as muscles, ligaments, and nerves; those affecting compound tissues, such as the heart and lungs; and those affecting tissues generally. In treating patients, diagnoses could be made, Galen claimed, by noting alterations or disturbances in the tissues. For example, he showed that inflammation of a part or organ was marked by heat, redness, swelling, and tenderness. He was able to differentiate between pneumonia and pleurisy, and he gave an accurate description of pulmonary tuberculosis. He also described gout and noted its frequent connection with kidney stones.

From his accounts, we learn that Galen was familiar with many drugs, that he collected medicinal plants in distant places, and that he used opium, colocynth, hyoscyamus, and numerous other drugs with full understanding of their effects on his patients. Combining opium and some seventy other drugs, he developed a universal remedy or panacea called theriaca, a compound highly esteemed by Marcus Aurelius. A remedy he compounded for toothache contained black pepper, saffron, carrot seeds, aniseed, and parsley seeds. A remedy for colic, highly recommended by him, contained black pepper, saffron, opium, and several other plant products. Galen's writings show that herbs were extensively used during his era. Their popularity continued long afterwards. The number of plants supposed to have medicinal value increased as new countries were explored. Spices from the East brought high prices because of their supposed medicinal value.

Galen was preeminent as an anatomist. There is no certain evidence that he ever dissected a human cadaver (Greek and Roman religious beliefs forbade such abuses of the human body, as has been noted previously), although in his *History of Medicine*, M. Neuberger states that Galen on two occasions obtained through accident two human skeletons, one the body of a corpse washed out of its grave by a river flood and the other the body of an executed robber. In any case, for his research efforts Galen started with the anatomical knowledge handed down by the Alexandrian school and enlarged upon this knowledge with his own contributions. Lacking human materials, Galen was forced to resort to the dissection and vivisection of many mammals, especially the pig, cow, sheep, dog, bear, and monkey. He assumed that man's internal organs were similar in form and arrangement to those of hogs and apes — an assumption with an unfortunate impact on medical theory and practice for centuries to come.

Galen's most valuable anatomical investigations related to the central nervous system. By cutting through the spinal cord at various points (an investigation which George Sarton classes as one of the two most notable experiments of ancient times), he showed that the powers of sense and motion of different parts of the body are vitally dependent upon the maintenance of nervous connection with the brain. He observed that nerves of sensation originated in the brain, and motor nerves in the spinal cord. Further, he described the coverings of the brain, gave permanent names to several parts of the brain, and named seven of the twelve pairs of cranial nerves. He made skillful dissections of many of the muscles. Galen was fascinated by the brain's influence over the body as a whole, and he was fully persuaded that the soul was centered in the brain.

From the point of view of clinical medicine, as noted, Galen adhered to the Hippocratic school, preferred dietetic and prophylactic to therapeutic measures whenever possible, and held that the most important aim should be to maintain the body in good health rather than to restore it from illness. He prescribed baths and massages, changes of climate and moderate physical exercise, and bloodletting and purges. When these methods failed, he turned to his vast array of natural remedies.

In studying medical history, weighing Galen's accomplishments pro and con, one realizes that his work had baneful effects, persisting for centuries. All the theories and speculations evolved since the time of Hippocrates were lumped into Galen's "system" of medicine. Because they were based upon animal dissections, his anatomical findings, as applied to human beings, were frequently erroneous. For example, he contended that pus formation, "laudable pus," is necessary to the healing of wounds. The medical profession had to wait until the sixteenth century for Andreas Vesalius to demonstrate Galen's mistakes in anatomy, the seventeenth century for William Harvey to correct his theories of blood circulation, and the nineteenth century for Joseph Lister to reveal the dire consequences of infections.

On the other hand, Galen should be blamed only in part for retarding medical advances. After Galen, science went into a decline from which it failed to recover until the Renaissance. Galen's successors stopped experimentation, discontinued making their own investigations, even ceased using their eyes, and chose instead to regard Galen as an unchallengeable authority — an attitude close to idolatry. Along with the proven facts Galen had discovered by first-hand research, they accepted with the same lack of question or skepticism his useless theories and foolish systems. Galen's doctrine thus became far more important in men's minds than the free spirit of inquiry which had guided Galen himself.

What was the secret of Galen's vast and prolonged influence? Critics agree on three basic reasons. First, Galen was extremely positive in his statements and had a plausible explanation for every contingency. His complete egotism is revealed in the statement, "Never as yet have I gone astray, whether in treatment or in prognosis, as have so many other physicians of great reputation. If anyone wishes to gain fame ... all that he needs is to accept what I have been able to establish." Second, nearly all the world's knowledge of biology, physiology, anatomy, and botany was comprised in Galen's voluminous writings. Through repeated copying and translations, they saturated the intellectual life of the Middle Ages. Strongest of all was a third factor. Galen was a teleologist; that is, he believed that everything is made for a particular and recognizable purpose, therefore that every feature, structure, or function of the human body has been created according to a divine plan. "It was the Creator's infinite wisdom," asserts Galen, "which selected the best means to attain his beneficent ends, and it is proof of his omnipotence that he created every good thing according to his design, and thereby fulfilled his will." Such a concept fitted perfectly the prevailing theological doctrines of the Middle Ages—Christian, Moslem, and Jewish.

In his prolific career as a writer, Galen composed some five hundred treatises on diverse subjects. In the medical area, there have survived six books on anatomy, seventeen on physiology, six on pathology, fourteen on therapeutics, thirty on materia medica, and sixteen on the pulse. He was also the author of several introductions to medicine and numerous works on hygiene. The fourteen books on therapeutic method remained the medical bible for many centuries to come. The first printed edition of Galen's works in Greek came from the press of Alduz Manutius in 1475. A Latin edition was printed in Venice by Pintium in 1490.

Dr. Arthur J. Brock, leading twentieth-century Galen translator and commentator, concludes that "despite his personal foibles—his imperious temper and tendency to self-glorification—Galen was undoubtedly one of the great men of history. He belonged to the same type as Leonardo da Vinci and Goethe—men who to an extraordinary breadth and clarity of outlook, which took in the whole civilization of their times together with its historical origins, united a perfervid will and moral force which imposed upon them the task not only of themselves assimilating this material, but of handing it on to the people of their generation." Other jurors have returned different verdicts.

12

Prince of Physicians

Avicenna (Abu Ali a-Husain ibn Abdallah ibn Sina) (980-1037)

Canon of Medicine

The versatility so much admired by men of the Renaissance was personified by the Arabian-Persian physician ibn-Sina, or Avicenna as he is known in the West. A youthful prodigy, at ten he knew the Koran by heart and was well read in the classical authors. Next he turned to the study of philosophy, jurisprudence, and mathematics, and at sixteen to medicine. At eighteen he was famous as a physician, and was called into consultation in the illness of the ruling emir.

An amazingly prolific and many-sided writer, Avicenna is estimated to have produced as many as 160 books on such diverse subjects as medicine, philosophy, all the sciences, mathematics, physics, music, astronomy, alchemy, theology, and philology. He was dominated by an insatiable thirst for knowledge. In his own words, "At home of nights, by lamplight, I read and I wrote, and when I grew so sleepy that I felt my powers of work were failing me I drank a glass of wine to restore my energies and resumed my labors. When at length I fell asleep, I was still so full of my studies, that often on waking I found that problems which had perplexed me had been solved during slumber. Thus I continued my studies until I had attained to a complete knowledge of dialectics, physics, and mathematics. Then I turned to theology and metaphysics."

In fitting recognition of such prodigious productivity, the Moslem world has accorded Avicenna the laudatory titles of Prince of All Learning, Prince of Physicians, and Father of Geology (for a book on the formation of mountains).

Avicenna's medical contributions, which have survived to modern times, are comprised in a monumental treatise called *The Canon*, a work that served as the chief guide to medical science in the West from the twelfth to the seventeenth centuries and is still occasionally consulted in the Moslem East. *The Canon* borrows much from the learning of the ancients (notably the writings of Galen, Hippocrates, and Aristotle), to which Avicenna added the contemporary Arabian knowledge of medicine and his own observations. Essentially, the work is a summary of Greco-Arabic medicine, containing Avicenna's own interpretation of the prevailing Galenic system.

The Canon contains good descriptions of diabetes and anthrax and the first description of the guinea worm, a parasite which burrows and causes an abcess.

Avicenna advocated the Hippocratic method of reducing spinal deformities by forcible reduction.

Since Galen was his chief authority, Avicenna's work has similar defects. Like Galen, he wished to make medicine an exact science for treating disease — as precise as mathematics. The wide acceptance of *The Canon* among physicians was facilitated by Avicenna's extraordinary skill as a classifier and encyclopedist. For example, he distinguishes fifteen qualities of pain. The section on materia medica, based in part on Dioscorides, includes descriptions of some 700 drugs.

As a whole, *The Canon* is divided into five books, devoted to the theory of medicine, the simpler drugs, special pathology and therapeutics, general diseases, and the pharmacopoeia, including the composition and preparation of remedies. Each section is further arranged into subsections, and these in turn are split up into smaller divisions. The enumeration of symptoms of disease is extensive, but the work is inferior in practical medicine and surgery, and it shows slight knowledge of natural history and botany. In Avicenna's hands, Henry Sigerist comments in his *The Great Doctors*, "medicine became a huge, unified, circumscribed, logical edifice, embracing the whole of Greek and Arabian knowledge."

Avicenna's attitude toward surgery was characteristic of his era. Because of their religious beliefs, none of the Arabian physicians dissected bodies. Hence, surgery was regarded by Avicenna as an inferior art, to be carried on by men of lower social rank. The distinction between the superior physician and the inferior surgeon was subsequently transmitted to Europe and persisted as late as the eighteenth century. Consequently, surgery was left to barbers, executioners, and bathhouse keepers.

When the physician was called upon to direct a surgical operation, Avicenna advocated the use of the cautery, a red-hot iron, instead of the knife. The fire was, of course, extremely painful, but it killed bacteria, thus preventing infection. Nothing was known in Avicenna's day of the connection between putrefaction and disease or of the use of antiseptics against infection. It is ironical that when cautery was generally discarded in the sixteenth century as a cruel and brutal practice, deaths from infections multiplied.

After Avicenna, the medicine of Europe became largely his system, superseding all preceding ones. *The Canon* was translated into Latin in the twelfth century, and was the chief medical textbook in European universities down to the seventeenth century. Following the invention of printing, some thirty Latin editions were published. Avicenna's influence, unfortunately, was often harmful, simply because his work was so widely received as canonical. Physicians were thereby led to philosophize upon existing knowledge, instead of hunting for and discovering facts.

13

Admirable Doctor
Roger Bacon (1214?-1294)

Opus Majus

Comparisons between the intellectual ideas of Roger Bacon in the thirteenth century and Francis Bacon in the seventeenth have long intrigued scholars. Though these two celebrated personalities were unrelated and separated by several centuries, striking similarities may be found in their recorded thoughts on science and philosophy. The environments in which the two Bacons operated were strikingly different. Francis was at the peak of his career in the Elizabethan age, when the English Renaissance was in full flower, an era whose intellectual vigor has scarcely ever been surpassed. In contrast, the dead hand of the past was heavy on Roger Bacon in thirteenth-century England.

All Europe, in fact, was cursed with a blind reverence for dead things in Roger Bacon's time. Aristotle was regarded as infallible, and to question Galen was highly heretical. Fixed dogmas about the heavens and the earth were passed on from generation to generation without any scientific experimentation to determine whether such doctrines were true. It was thought that Aristotle had solved all problems in metaphysics and natural history and that Galen had discovered all that could be known about the human body and medical science; hence, further research and experimentation were regarded as little short of sacrilegious. The Church, the supreme influence of the time, looked askance at the practice of the "magical arts," i.e., science; yet to lead an intellectual life outside the Church was a virtual impossibility. Such science as was permitted to exist was based upon authority, revelation, and superstition. A sterile scholasticism dominated the universities.

It was against this state of affairs that Roger Bacon, one of the greatest minds of the Middle Ages, rebelled; his revolt inevitably brought him into constant conflict with the Church authorities.

Bacon's unorthodox ideas were first developed while he was a student at Oxford. There he came under the influence of two men: Adam Smith, a mathematician, and Robert Grosseteste, Chancellor of Oxford and afterward Bishop of Lincoln. The young student soon turned against the unscientific attitudes of his teachers at Oxford.

Bacon was convinced, first of all, that true science would strengthen instead of weaken the Church and religion. "The surest method of extirpating all heresies, and of destroying the Kingdom of Antichrist, and of establishing true religion in the hearts of man," he writes, "is by perfecting a true system of natural philosophy." He viewed the sciences as supporters and pillars of scriptural revelation, destroyers of the faith of infidels, and prime contributors to the unity and solidarity of Christianity.

After taking orders at Oxford in 1233, Bacon transferred to the University of Paris, the preeminent university of its time, where he became a doctor of theology and is reputed to have been a brilliant teacher, attracting numerous students by his lecturing and gaining for himself the title of "Doctor Mirabilis." While in Paris, he became acquainted with the writings of two great Arab scientists, Alhazen and Avicenna, whose works thereafter strongly influenced his life.

The study of languages was highly prized by Bacon. He was impressed by the importance of the study of the original language of Aristotle and the New Testament. Especially he commended the study of Hebrew, Greek, and Arabic, in an age when Latin was considered the only ancient language worth knowing. The prevailing ignorance of the original tongues, he constantly reiterated, produced atrocious, misleading, and corrupt translations. The Church fathers often adapted their translations to the prejudices of their age.

About 1250, Bacon returned to Oxford to lecture and to carry on scientific experiments. His lectures dealt with education and science rather than religious matters. He experimented with burning glasses, gunpowder, the magnet, Greek fire, artificial gold, magic mirrors, and the philosopher's stone. In this respect a true child of his age, which considered everything linked with supernatural causes, he regarded astrology and alchemy as valuable scientific studies.

The mysterious experiments carried on by Bacon in his laboratory, his heretical teachings, and his outspoken criticisms of both ancient and contemporary scholars soon created suspicion among his superiors in the Franciscan order. Bonaventura, general of the Franciscans, directed Bacon to cease his blasphemous lecturing and to go to Paris, where for ten years he was kept in close confinement, denied all opportunity to write, and deprived of books and instruments.

Relief for the prisoner came from a new pope, Clement IV, who in 1265 sent a letter to Bacon instructing him to forward secretly and privately any writing he could prepare, notwithstanding all injunctions to the contrary of his superiors. Accepting this mandate, Bacon immediately began the preparation of his greatest work, the *Opus Majus*, in part an encyclopedia of medieval knowledge and in part a criticism of existing scholarship and scientific methodology, the whole composed in an eighteen-month period.

The *Opus Majus* is divided into seven parts. Part 1 deals with the causes of error, as seen by Bacon: authority, long-established custom, the opinion of the untutored many, i.e., popular prejudice, and the concealment of real ignorance with pretense of knowledge, the last the most dangerous of all. The second part treats of the relation between philosophy and religion, maintaining that all wisdom is contained in the Scriptures, at least implicitly. In the third part, Bacon emphasizes the importance of language study as a basis for accurate translations.

The fourth part of *Opus Majus* is devoted to one of Bacon's favorite themes, a treatise on mathematics, "the alphabet of philosophy," holding that all the sciences rest ultimately on mathematics, knowledge that was also essential in theology. This section is concerned, too, with geography and astronomy. Christopher Columbus is reputed to have been strongly influenced by Bacon's reasoning on geographical matters.

Next, in part 5, Bacon goes on to deal with the subject of perspective, the anatomy of the eye, the laws of reflection and refraction, the construction of mirrors and lenses, and other aspects of physiological optics. In part 6, Bacon is concerned with experimental science. He points out that there are two methods of acquiring knowledge, one by argument, the other by experience. Mere argument is never sufficient. Experimental methods alone produce truth in science, for "without experiment nothing can be adequately known." Further, "the strongest argument proves nothing so long as the conclusions are unverified by experience. Experimental science is the queen of science and the goal of all speculation." Experimental science, it is noted, accomplishes three purposes: confirms conclusions to which other methods point, adds to the sum of human knowledge through discovery, and creates new departments of science. In this connection, Bacon again stresses the need for mathematical knowledge, without which other sciences are unintelligible and fundamental scientific precepts cannot be adequately expressed. In reaction against the excessive argumentation characteristic of the university instruction of his time, Bacon insisted that mathematics is a more basic discipline than logic.

The final section of the *Opus Majus*, the seventh, relates to moral philosophy.

Bacon's curiosity, which appears to have been insatiable, led him to the discovery of many practical facts as well as to profound far-reaching theories. He noted the extreme inaccuracy of the calendar of his day, demonstrated the characteristics of the magnetic field, knew more of optics and of optical laws than any other man of his time, suggested the practicability of constructing eyeglasses, observed a spiral nebula through a primitive type of telescope, and peered at cells through a forerunner of the microscope. He also speculated on the possibilities of gunpowder, airplanes, armored cars, mechanically propelled boats, and of reaching India by sailing west across the Atlantic—the notion that caught Columbus' fancy.

Nevertheless, Bacon's viewpoints were restricted by the medieval frame of mind existing in his time. He believed, for example, that the universe is bounded by the sphere of the fixed stars with the earth at the center; he accepted the ultimate authority of the Scriptures, if accurately translated; and agreed that the purpose of all science and philosophy was to elucidate and adorn theology.

How Pope Clement IV reacted to the *Opus Majus* is unknown, for he died soon after its receipt. Bacon was permitted to return to Oxford for a few years, but deprived of Clement's protection he suffered, with no possibility of appeal, a sentence of imprisonment passed in 1277 by Pope Nicholas IV. The charge was "certain suspected heresies and novelties." For the next fourteen years, probably until after Nicholas' death, following conviction for these crimes, Bacon remained in jail. He lived only two years after being released. His last written work, composed near the end, was a tract entitled *Compendium Theologiae*.

Roger Bacon's influence in his own day was limited. The entire *Opus Majus* was printed for the first time in 1733, nearly five hundred years after it was written. Bacon's criticism of scholasticism was out of harmony with the prevailing spirit of the period and consequently produced little effect.

Dampier-Whetham, historian of science, concluded, "it is clear that Friar Bacon himself was in spirit a man of science and a scientific philosopher, born out of due time and chafing unconsciously against the external obstacles at which he rails so openly and so often; a true harbinger of the ages of experiment." Of all medieval minds, Bacon's is most closely akin to our own.

14

Universal Genius
Leonardo da Vinci (1452-1519)

Notebooks

The ideal of the Renaissance was the universal man, one who knew everything and could do anything. John Milton and Francis Bacon, among others, aspired in their minds to encompass all knowledge. Of the many creative geniuses who came out of the Italian Renaissance, probably the most versatile, an incarnation of the universal man, was Leonardo da Vinci — artist, musician, engineer, and natural scientist. The present account will concentrate on the latter two aspects of his career.

The beginnings were unpromising. Leonardo was the illegitimate son of a peasant girl and a local official of Vinci, a village between Florence and Pisa. He never received a formal or standard classical education, but benefited greatly from years spent in the studio of Andrea Verrochio, a leading painter, goldsmith, and all-round versatile character. Early on, Leonardo was irresistibly drawn toward scientific and technical investigations of every sort, and began to develop as an engineer. Presently, he left Florence to move to Milan to join the court of Duke Ludovico Sforza as a civil and military engineer, pageant mater, sculptor, painter, and architect. In that capacity, he superintended important hydraulic works and continued his various scientific experiments and researches. This mutually satisfactory arrangement was broken up in 1500, when Milan was conquered by the French. During the years that followed, Leonardo returned to Florence and remained there until 1513, spent two unhappy years at the papal court in Rome, and ended his career in the service of the young king of France, Francis I.

Leonardo had an insatiable curiosity about everything in science and technology. His work as a practical engineer led him into the field of geology, as he observed the various layers of sand and clay while cutting a canal and tried to explain the fossils that he found imbedded in rocks. He ridiculed the idea that the fossils were "freaks of nature" or the remians of Noah's flood, and concluded that the shells had once lived in the sea. According to his calculations, the Po River's alluvial deposits were two hundred thousand years old. He also understood the geological action of water and its meteorological cycle.

Further, Leonardo's work as a military engineer led him to study metallurgy — the smelting and casting of bronze and the rolling, drawing, planning, and drilling of iron. In northern Italy, he undertook extensive hydraulic work, particularly digging of canals, for which he devised a range of excavating machines and tools, built sluices, water wheels, and pipes. There are frequent references in the notes to his study of hydrodynamics.

Leonardo's manuscripts also contain a great number of architectural drawings of churches and other buildings, including such technical matters as the proportion of arches, construction of bridges and staircases, repairing breaks in walls, and methods for moving houses and churches. A number of schemes were proposed by him to improve public sanitation.

While on Ludovico's staff, Leonardo devoted major attention to military engineering, devising all sorts of arms and armor, offensive and defensive appliances, plans for fortifications, portable bridges, mining, liquid fire, poison gases, and even tanks and submarines.

Leonardo appears to have been a born mechanic. As Sarton points out, "He devised machines for almost every purpose which could be thought of in his day ... various types of lathes; machines to shear cloth; automatic file-cutting machines; sprocket wheels and chains for power transmission; machines to saw marble, to raise water, to grind plane and concave mirrors, to dive under water, to lift up, to heat, to light; paddle wheels to move boats."

A problem that fascinated Leonardo throughout his lifetime was flying, a subject on which he made exhaustive studies. The only thing lacking in his designs was a suitable motor. He first investigated the natural flying of birds and bats, especially the structure and function of their wings. He noted that birds took advantage of the wind and used their wings, tails, and heads as propellers, balancers, and rudders. These researches were followed with mechanical studies on artificial wings and apparatus for moving them. Elaborate drawings showed every detail of importance in machines invented by Leonardo, practically in the nature of blueprints, so precise that some of the machines have been reconstructed in modern times.

In Leonardo's case, he was more the philosopher than the practical inventor, who not only conceives of a machine but proceeds to construct it and to make it operational. He was totally preoccupied with theories on weight, gravitation, force and motion, impetus and impact, with no desire actually to build the machine that he had conceived. The discovery of basic principles was foremost in Leonardo's mind. Thus he recognized the principle of inertia, afterward demonstrated by Galileo. "Nothing perceptible by the senses is able to move itself," wrote Leonardo. "Every body has a weight in the direction of movement." He knew that the speed of a falling body increases with the time, and clearly understood the experimental impossibility of "perpetual motion" as a source of power. Also dealt with were theories of waves — in water, in the air, and in sound.

The catholicity of Leonardo's interests is demonstrated in two other branches of science, astronomy and botany. In astronomy, he viewed the universe as a celestial machine conforming to definite laws — a significant change from the Aristotelian concept of the heavenly bodies as divine and incorruptible, not subject, like the world, to change and decay. He calls the earth a star, like others, and believed that it reflected light, like the moon.

Leonardo's attention was frequently turned to botany, and his notes contain many references to the life of plants, the mathematical distribution of leaves on a stem, and the characteristics of various species.

Historians of science are in general agreement that Leonardo's most brilliant and original contributions were in the field of anatomy, perhaps because of his need for precise knowledge as a painter and sculptor. Anatomy was not completely neglected in the Middle Ages, despite religious prejudices, but there were few dissections and these were handicapped by inability to observe properly and without prejudice. Physicians were dominated by Galen and Avicenna, as Sarton comments, "to such an unbelievable extent that they were unable to see with their own eyes." If what they observed was contrary to Galen, it was obviously unreal and false.

In the course of his career, Leonardo dissected the bodies of some thirty individuals, including young and old, male and female, and in one case a woman with an unborn child in her womb. He left a large number of anatomical drawings, themselves works of art never surpassed in exact detail and artistry.

From anatomy, Leonardo went on to study physiology. He describes how blood affects the body of man, bringing energy to the organs and carrying off waste parts. He studied the muscles of the heart and made drawings of the valves. He compared the flow of blood with the circulation of water from the hills to the rivers and the sea, from the sea to the clouds and back to the hills as rain. It thus appears that Leonardo understood the general principle of the circulation of the blood a century or more before William Harvey revealed the facts to the world. Leonardo also investigated the structure and manner of operation of the eye, and made a model of the optical parts.

Leonardo was an untrammeled spirit in another respect, his attitude toward the many superstitions believed in by even the most educated minds of his day. The terrible madness of the witch mania began in Europe during his time and prevailed for more than two centuries after his death. Leonardo's contempt for astrologers and alchemists, believers in ghosts, medical quacks, and necromancers was repeatedly expressed.

Of first significance from the point of view of science was Leonardo's method. As stated by him:

> To me it seems that those sciences are vain and full of errors which are not born of experience, the mother of all certainty, and which do not end in experience observed, that is, whose origin or middle or end do not come to us through any of the five senses.... But the true sciences are those in which experience has penetrated through the senses and has imposed silence on the tongues of all disputants, and which do not feed their investigators with dreams, but always proceed successively and with true implications from first truths and self-evident principles to the end; as occurs in first mathematics, that is, with number and measure, the sciences called arithmetic and geometry, which treat with highest truth of quantity, both discrete and continuous.

Leonardo's influence was negligible in his own time, simply because he printed nothing and revealed nothing except to a few close associates. He is accepted as one of the greatest men of science in history, but only his art was known to his contemporaries. He was not discovered as a man of science until centuries after his death. He himself was to blame for this fact; he did nothing to publish his discoveries, though the art of printing was flourishing in his lifetime.

Practically the only record we have of Leonardo's achievements, ideas, and discoveries is contained in his notebooks. Until about 1880 he was remembered for and judged by his paintings. Since then, the voluminous notebooks that he began to keep after 1482 have come to light, been explored, and partially published in *The Notebooks of Leonardo da Vinci.* The notebooks are difficult to use. Leonardo wrote from right to left (mirror script), perhaps because he was left-handed. His comments, memoranda, diagrams, and drawings are lacking any orderly arrangement: the same page may contain remarks on dynamics, on astronomy, an anatomical sketch, and perhaps calculations for a machine. Most impressive are Leonardo's anatomical drawings, observations on flight, military machines, projects for canals, and beautiful botanical and geological drawings. Despite the fact that his investigations are buried in these notebooks, modern historians rate Leonardo as a great natural scientist.

15

Sun-Centered Universe

Copernicus (1473-1543)

De Revolutionibus Orbium Coelestium
(Concerning the Revolutions of the Heavenly Spheres)

For more than fourteen centuries, a system devised by Claudius Ptolemy, second-century Egyptian astronomer, was accepted as the true conception of the universe. Ptolemy held that the world is a fixed and immovable sphere, situated at the center of the universe, about which all celestial bodies, including the sun and fixed stars, revolve. Thus the Ptolemaic system relegated the sun and the stars to the position of the earth's satellites.

The Ptolemaic system held sway for fifteen hundred years and seemed destined to maintain its grip forever. Learned philosophers maintained that the scheme was based upon the infallible evidence of the senses. As stated by them, the sky is an inverted bowl and the earth occupies the center of the bowl. Starting from this "obvious fact," astronomers insisted that the earth stands firmly in its place and all the heavenly bodies pay homage to it. Their view was that the sun travels over the earth by day and under the earth at night, while the stars travel under the earth by day and over the earth by night. In short, the universe was considered to be a perfect sphere making a complete revolution around the earth every twenty-four hours.

But early on it was observed that some facts were not explained by the Ptolemaic theory. Some stars kept changing places in relation to other stars. These "wandering stars" appeared to have a motion of their own. For example, Venus seemed to follow the setting sun and at other times to precede the rising sun. Jupiter's leisurely journey over the sky took twelve years, Mars two years, and Saturn thirty years. The moon made its revolution of the sky in about twenty-eight days.

Nevertheless, the Ptolemaic structure remained substantially intact until the coming of the great era of intellectual awakening in Europe, the Renaissance. Its destruction was the work of a Polish astronomer and churchman, Nicolaus Copernicus, the Latinized form of Niklas Kopernik.

After a careful study of Ptolemy's theory of the heavens, Copernicus rejected it in favor of a theory advanced by Pythagoras and Aristarchus nearly two thousand years earlier—that the sun was the center of the universe around which all the planets, including the earth, moved. Ptolemy had argued that the earth could not be whirling around on its axis every twenty-four hours; otherwise bodies on its surface would be instantly thrown off. Copernicus insisted that this fear was quite imaginary, for the atmosphere and all loose objects were carried with the earth in its rotation. He noted further that if all the stars were fixed in a gigantic globe, as Ptolemy believed, they must all be equidistant from the earth, a most unlikely situation.

Copernicus' investigations were carried on quietly and alone, without help or consultation. For an observatory, Copernicus used a turret, a protective wall built around the cathedral at Frauenberg. Astronomical instruments available to him were crude and primitive. For example, his work was done nearly a century prior to the invention of the telescope. For measuring purposes, he used a sundial; a triquetrum, a three-sided wooden instrument which he devised to obtain the altitudes of the stars and planets; and an astrolabe, a sphere within vertical and horizontal rings. The climate was unfavorable to astronomical observations; proximity to the the Baltic Sea and rivers brought fogs and clouds, and clear days and nights were rare. Nevertheless, on every possible occasion, year after year, Copernicus labored over his calculations.

The revolutionary theory which Copernicus was attempting to prove through his prolonged studies went directly contrary to the time-honored and revered Ptolemaic system. In short, as noted, he was attempting to demonstrate that the earth is not stationary but rotates on its axis once daily and travels around the sun once each year. So fantastic was such a concept in the sixteenth century that Copernicus did not dare to announce it until he was convinced his data were irrefutable. Consequently, thirty years elapsed before the Copernican system was revealed to the world.

It is conceivable that Copernicus' masterpiece, on which he had toiled for so many years, might never have reached the printing press and therefore would have been lost to posterity except for the efforts of a young German scholar, George Joachim Rheticus. Hearing of Copernicus and his experiments, Rheticus paid him a lengthy visit and was immensely impressed with the aging astronomer's discoveries. In 1540, at Danzig, Rheticus printed the *Narratio prima* (First Account), the first published statement of Copernicus' world-shaking theories.

Previously, Copernicus had been extremely reluctant to permit publication of his complete work. He was a perfectionist who felt that every observation had to be checked and rechecked. Furthermore, it is possible that the potential disapproval of the Church may have deterred him. The Protestant Reformation and the intellectual ferment of the Renaissance were making religious authorities suspicious of revolutionary theories, especially of any thoughts that might upset orthodox teachings. Finally, however, responding to the urgent pleas of Rheticus and other admirers, Copernicus yielded. The manuscript was entrusted to Rheticus to take to Nuremberg for printing. While the book was still in press the author suffered a severe stroke. He died a few hours after the first copy of *De Revolutionibus Orbium Coelestium* had been placed in his hands.

Diplomatically, Copernicus dedicated his work to Pope Paul III, stating in part:

> I hesitated for a long time as to whether I should publish that which I have written to demonstrate the earth's motion, or whether it would not be better to follow the example of the Pythagoreans, who used to hand down the secrets of philosophy to their relatives and friends in

oral form.... I was almost impelled to put the finished work wholly aside, through the scorn I had reason to anticipate on account of the newness and apparent contrariness to reason of my theory.

De Revolutionibus is divided into six "books" or main sections. In the beginning, Copernicus presents his views of the universe, arguments in favor of the heliocentric or sun-centered theory (including the idea that the earth, like other planets, revolves around the sun), and a discussion of the seasons. The second section deals with the motions of the celestial bodies, measured mathematically, and closes with a catalog of stars, showing the position of each in the sky. The last four "books" present detailed descriptions of the motions of the earth, the moon, and the other planets. In each instance, explanation of the motions is accompanied by a geometrical diagram showing the course followed by the sphere on the basis of Copernicus' calculations.

For Copernicus, the sun was inert and passive, stationary amid revolving planets. Its only functions were to supply light and heat. The universe was strictly limited. Outside the sphere of the stars, as Ptolemy had taught, space ceased to exist. Neither did Copernicus abandon Ptolemy's system of epicycles, reaffirming the ancient astronomer's assertion that for each of the orbits there was a different center. These features of the Copernican system were to be corrected by later astronomers.

Acceptance of the Copernican theories was slow, both among scientists and the general populace. With a few exceptions, expressions of contemporary opinion were in violent opposition. Martin Luther severely criticized Copernicus, and John Calvin was equally emphatic in his condemnation. Not until 1615, however, was the book placed on the Catholic *Index Librorum Prohibitorum*, and there it remained for over two centuries.

In the light of numerous modifications made by scientists in later centuries, the question may reasonably be asked: Is the Copernican theory true? Undeniably, Copernicus left his system incomplete and inaccurate at various points. His conception of the perfectly circular motion of celestial bodies, of a universe with finite limitations, and of other details does not conform to present-day knowledge. But in its essential feature, the choice of the sun as the center of our planetary system, Copernicus discovered a fundamental truth and provided a foundation for modern scientific astronomy.

Copernicus' place in the history of science is permanently established. His influence on his contemporaries and on all subsequent thought entitles him to a preeminent position. Harold C. Urey, one of the great scientists of our own day, agrees:

> All superlatives fail when describing the work of Nicolaus Copernicus. He broke with a conception of the solar system that had stood for one thousand years, and introduced an entirely new concept of the relation of the planets to the sun. In so doing he initiated the whole modern method of scientific thought, and modified our thinking on all phases of human life.[2]

It is scarcely surprising that contemporary doubts and misgivings arose about the Copernican system. Religious dissent was rife in the sixteenth century, but there was no difference among the contending factions in the conviction that the world had been created for man's express benefit. This belief was easy to accept because it fed the human ego. Instead of being a speck in space, the earth was the center of the heavens, with the planets and stars revolving about it. The whole universe seemed to be made for man. Now, according to Copernicus, the earth was just one, and not the largest, of the planets. It is little wonder that Giordano Bruno was burned at the stake in 1600 for his active support of these ideas, and that Galileo was tried by the Inquisition, forced to recant his belief that the sun is the central body about which earth and planets revolve, and suffered house arrest for the last ten years of his life.

16

Father of Mineralogy
Agricola (1490-1555)

De Re Metallica

In the Middle Ages, Germany lead all of Europe in mining and metallurgy and the technology there reached a high state of development. Ores and metals were much sought after and brought high prices. In the famous Rammelsberg, German miners have been digging for silver for a thousand years. The silver mines of Freiberg opened in the twelfth century. Mining for copper began in Mansfield in the thirteenth century, and copper ores were soon found in the Alps and in Silesia. Lead, tin, and gold were discovered in other German localities. Iron ores were, of course, particularly important for industrial purposes, and were being mined in many parts of Germany at the time.

Given these rich resources, mining and metallurgy and trading in their products dominated the German economy in the fifteenth and sixteenth centuries. By 1525, an estimated one hundred thousand people were employed in German mining and smelting. Other European countries, seeking to develop their own mineral resources, called on the expertise of German engineers and technologists.

Printed literature relating to mining, however, was limited, except for numerous small mining and assaying manuals. No systematic scientific work on the whole process of extracting minerals existed. The lack and the need were observed by a city physician of a mining town, Georgius Agricola, who thereafter spent years studying the metallic arts.

Agricola was another example of the universal man produced by the Renaissance. Amazingly precocious and versatile, he was born in Saxony, and early in his career taught Greek and Latin and studied medicine, physics, and chemistry. For his doctor's degree he went to Italy. While in Italy, he studied at Bologna and Padua, spent two years in Venice to learn printing, picked up much information about industry, and gained most of his extraordinary knowledge of the scientific, medical, and philosophical works of ancient and medieval writers. Following his return to Germany, he settled as a practicing physician in the Joachimstal, a center of mining and smelting works. There on the basis of careful observation of ores and the methods of their treatment, he began to write about mineralogy.

In 1530, Agricola migrated to Chemnitz, one of the centers of the mining industry, where he spent the remainder of his active career. His writing and research on mineralogy were continued, but in addition he produced published works on physical geology, and medical, mathematical, theological, and historical subjects.

As early as 1529, Agricola began his greatest work, *De Re Metallica.* It was completed in 1550, but not published until 1556, four months after the author's death. The delay was caused by the preparation of numerous woodcuts. In a long introduction, Agricola explains the purpose of the book and outlines the history of mining and metallurgy, pursuits which he claims are as ancient as the agricultural arts. His earliest source was Pliny's *Natural History*, and he drew upon extensive alchemical literature, despite his contempt for alchemists. His principal sources, however, were observations made with his own eyes in Germany and Italy and oral traditions collected from his many associates.

De Re Metallica is a complete and systematic treatise on mining and metallurgy, decorated with 273 woodcuts, also of great historical value. The work is divided into twelve "books," described by Agricola as follows:

> The first contains all that can be said against the art, and against mines and miners by their opponents; the second instructs the miner concerning the sort of man he is to be, and goes on to discuss the discovery of veins; the third deals with veins and faults, and their distortion. The fourth describes the method of following the veins, and also describes the various offices of the mining community. The fifth describes the getting of the ore, and the art of separating the values. The sixth describes mining tools and machinery. The seventh deals with the testing of ores. The eighth gives instruction in firing the ore, pulverizing it, washing it, and roasting it. The ninth describes the art of smelting the ores. The tenth gives an account of separating silver from gold, and lead from the latter and silver. The eleventh shows how silver is to be separated from copper. The twelfth gives recipes for preparing salt, soda, alum, vitriol, sulphur, mineral wax, bitumen, and glass.

Agricola goes on to state that illustrations are included in order to make his printed words more understandable. He adds, "I have omitted all those things which I have not myself seen, or have read or heard of from persons upon whom I can rely. That which I have neither seen, nor carefully considered after reading or hearing of, I have not written about." He was a firm believer in observation as opposed to inductive speculation — the favorite method of the bigoted scholastics of his time. In Agricola's own words, "Those things which we see with our eyes and understand by means of our senses are more clearly to be demonstrated than if learned by means of reasoning."

In his published work, Agricola showed a grasp of wider aspects of geological phenomena. His is the first adequate description of the part played by erosion in mountain sculpture. His theoretical views on the origin of ore deposits are of special interest, since he had unusual opportunities for observation and experience. The treatment of mineralogy by Agricola was the first systematic attempt, though erroneous in some respects in the light of modern knowledge. He was the first to assert that bismuth and antimony are true primary metals, and he added twenty actual mineral species to some sixty that had been described previous to his time.

Concerning the contributions made to the sciences of mining and metallurgy in *De Re Metallica*, Agricola describes scores of methods and processes, but he does not claim that these were discoveries or inventions of his own. They represent, on the contrary, the accumulation of generations of experience and lore. It was Agricola, however, who for the first time, in clear, detailed, and intelligent exposition, presented virtually all existing knowledge. His long association with workingmen, miners, metallurgists, and smiths enabled him to be practical, factual, and down to earth, without engaging in philosophical theories.

It is paradoxical, as historians of science have noted, that the first noteworthy treatise on mining and metallurgy was written by a man who was neither a miner nor a metal-worker, but a physician. While teaching Greek and Latin, Agricola's scientific curiosity was aroused by his study of classical authors, however, and his proximity to problems of geology and metallurgy naturally turned his attention and energies in that direction.

De Re Metallica remained a standard work for two centuries, and went through many editions in Latin, German, and Italian. The first English edition, translated from the Latin by Herbert Hoover and his wife, was published in 1912. George Sarton remarks that "Mr. Hoover is no doubt the only chief of state who ever translated one of the great scientific classics." The task of translation, Hoover wrote, was made doubly difficult and complicated because the classical Latin in which the original text is written contains no words for many technical terms; consequently, Agricola coined several hundred Latin expressions to meet his needs.

The preface to the Hoover translation concedes that *De Re Metallica* is no longer a work of practical value. "The methods and processes have long since been superseded; yet such a milestone on the road of development of one of the two most basic of human industrial activities is more worthy of preservation than the thousands of volumes devoted to records of human destruction."

Unquestionably, Agricola played a considerable role in the great awakening of learning. Beyond the confines of the particular science to which he applied himself, he was the first to found any of the natural sciences upon research and observation, in place of sterile speculation. *De Re Metallica* is rated today as the classic text of the metallic arts, the most famous engineering book of the late Renaissance, and one of the most influential works in all engineering literature. It is valuable as a historical document, also, because it is the main source of information about metals production at the beginning of the modern era. Agricola brings to bear on metals technology in the sixteenth century everything available from mathematics, surveying, applied mechanics, and chemistry, as well as pragmatic intelligence. In the Hall of Fame of the German Museum in Munich, there is a portrait of Agricola with the inscription: "Georg Agricola, famous as investigator and physician, became herald of the great achievements of German technology, a great experimenter, and expounder of medieval mining and smelting."

Agricola's last years were unhappy. He remained to the end a staunch Catholic, while the community of Chemnitz had gone over completely to the Lutheran cause. So violent was the theological feeling against him that when he died, burial was not permitted in the local cemetery but his body was carried to Zeitz, seven miles away, for interment.

17

Complete Skeptic

Paracelsus (1493-1541)

Selected Writings

The first strong challenge to Galenic medicine and to medieval science in general came from one of the most versatile and controversial names in the history of scientific thought: Theophrastus Bombostus von Hohenheim, better known as Paracelsus, a Swiss born at Einsieden. Early in the sixteenth century, Paracelsus undertook the task of exposing all the humbug and fraud that characterized the medical practice of the day and fighting for common sense in the treatment of disease.

The range of Paracelsus' interests and research efforts is astounding. He has been called the first modern medical scientist, the precursor of microchemistry, antisepsis, modern wound surgery, and homeopathy. He originated and developed the theory of protoplasm and anticipated the germ theory of disease and something of the cell theory in biology. He was the first chemist to differentiate between gases and air in general. The basic ideas of chemotherapy appear in his writings. He held that chemicals used for medical treatment should be specific in kind and amount, and that almost any substance may be beneficial or harmful depending on the amount used and the way it is combined with other substances. It was Paracelsus who introduced arsenic, mercury, sulfur, and other chemicals into medical practice. Also, he preceded Ambroise Paré in emphasizing asepsis in treating wounds and in surgery, and urged the conservative use of surgery. Other achievements included the first accurate description of syphilis and the introduction of mercury therapy for the disease, and recognition of gynecology as a medical specialty. Paracelsus was the first to observe the influence of heredity, occupation, and environment on disease; the first to write an accurate clinical description of mental illness (especially hysteria and epilepsy); the first to describe tartaric diseases, such as arthritis.

For such a variety of reasons, Paracelsus has been called by medical historians the founder of gynecology, internal medicine, occupational medicine, chemotherapy, scientific pharmacology, biochemistry, and other specialties. Paracelsus broke with the monks and alchemists, assailed the physicians who treated chicken-pox with a soup made of the hearts and livers of vipers, and laid the foundation of modern medical chemistry.

Paracelsus came upon the scene at a highly propitious moment in European history. It was the period of the late Renaissance and the Protestant Reformation. The bonds of tradition and authority were being broken and the accepted dogmas of centuries rejected. New leaders in art, literature, philosophy, politics, and theology were emerging. The invention of printing in the mid-fifteenth century broke the medieval church's monopoly on letters and learning, insuring the rapid spread of the printed word. At the same time, there was a remarkable growth of universities, old and new. The discovery of America, a year prior to Paracelsus' birth, and other world explorations also were operating to break down traditional conservatism and to provide a world view. Among Paracelsus' contemporaries were Michelangelo, Machiavelli, Leonardo da Vinci, Columbus, Copernicus, Erasmus, Luther, Rabelais, and Vesalius.

Paracelsus led a stormy life, leading his professional opponents to characterize him as an ignorant egotist, a charlatan, a drunken braggart, and a superstitious visionary. The principal facts are reasonably clear. Paracelsus learned botany, chemistry, medicine, and mineralogy from his father, a physician. He attended the universities of Tübingen, Vienna, and possibly Ferrara. After obtaining his medical degree, he traveled throughout Europe, the Near East, and the Orient, accumulating a wide range of knowledge of medical folklore and of such subjects as astronomy and alchemy. During those years, from 1511 to about 1526, he often served as military physician and surgeon.

In 1527, Paracelsus was appointed to the medical faculty at Basel and became town physician. Immediately thereafter he started a series of lectures and simultaneously began to make enemies. He showed respect for Hippocrates, but spoke contemptuously of Galen and the Arab physicians. Under his inspiration, his students burned the works of Galen in the marketplace. To the medical profession as a whole, whose knowledge was based on Galenic teachings, this was little short of sacrilege. Furthermore, Paracelsus delivered his lectures in German instead of Latin, the universal language of the profession at the time, and based them on his own writings and research. To add further insult, he referred to his colleagues as "whited sepulchres," unworthy "to loosen the latchets of his shoes," and antagonized pharmacists by denouncing their concoctions as worthless. The fundamental principles of medicine, as currently understood, were rejected and replaced by his own concepts and terminology. His critics began to refer to him sarcastically as "Paracelsus" (greater than Celsus), a nickname which caught his fancy and was therefore adopted.

Naturally, Paracelsus' attacks on the medical practitioners of his time and his exposure of their practical ignorance, pomposity, and greed brought on retaliation. As a result of the antagonism created by him, he was forced after two years to resign his position as professor of medicine and city physician, and to flee Basel to avoid arrest. Thenceforward, Paracelsus was an itinerant physician, moving from place to place, never holding a permanent position. He died in Salzburg at age 48, the cause of his death uncertain. According to one version, he died from a stroke; another suggested that he was murdered by agents of the physicians and apothecaries he had offended.

Despite holding many views in advance of his time, ideas now regarded as modern, Paracelsus was unable to rid himself of some medieval notions. He believed in and experimented for years with alchemy, aiming to transmute base metals into gold. A good physician, he wrote, should have a knowledge of astronomy because certain stars caused diseases by their inhalations, and it was difficult to cure certain diseases while certain stars were in their ascendancy.

Medical problems can be mastered only by virtuous physicians. In anatomy, he maintained that the body is composed basically of three substances: salt, sulfur, and mercury.

The Hippocratic theory that the four humors were the cause of disease was discarded by Paracelsus, who theorized that there are five different agencies which act to produce disease: cosmic influence from the stars; pathologic poisons, such as from food; natural causes resulting from organic defects; psychic causes from spirits and demons; and causes of divine origin.

More rationally, Paracelsus was the first to record that individuals in certain types of work were susceptible to occupational diseases. In particular, he described a lung condition among miners caused by inhaling dust. Discussing the dreadful effects of their trades on miners and metal workers, the asthmas, consumption, and vomitings, he comments that medical science had found no remedy for these conditions. In explaining joint diseases and the formation of stones in the bladder, Paracelsus stated that the stomach acts to destroy poisons and that other organs excrete those not destroyed. If a poison is not destroyed or excreted, it is deposited in the teeth, in the joints, or as "tartar" in the bladder.

Lambert and Goodwin, in their *Medical Leaders*, pointed out that Paracelsus combined mysticism with the practical use of drugs. Illustrating the former was a strange "weapon salve" concocted by Paracelsus, composed of the moss grown on a skull exposed to the weather, human blood and human fat, a drug from dried Egyptian mummy, armeniac, oil of roses, and linseed oil. In case of injury, the weapon causing the injury or a splinter of wood dipped in the blood of the wound was anointed with the salve. Nothing was applied to the wound itself except a dressing of clean lint. Presumably the ointment exerted a magnetic influence to withdraw poison from the wound.

On the other hand, Paracelsus had some common-sense advice for physicians, including a return to Hippocratic methods of treating diseases, depending upon the body to cure disease, without too much interference, and advising that the patient should receive every assistance in maintaining his vitality in order to overcome and survive the course of the disease.

Several new drugs, or drugs previously little used, as noted, were introduced by Paracelsus: mercury, lead, sulfur, iron, arsenic, and copper sulphate. He had a strong preference for alcoholic extracts, i.e., tinctures. A prevailing theory that pus was necessary to the healing of wounds he completely rejected and denounced.

The chief influence that Paracelsus had on chemistry was his contention that the main business of this branch of science was the preparation and purification of chemical substances for use as drugs. After him, chemistry became an essential part of medical training, though for a long while afterward physicians were divided into two camps: those who believed in the new chemically produced drugs, and the herbalists, who were faithful to the old herbal drugs.

Aside from his lasting contribution to medicine by way of introducing new drugs, Paracelsus rendered medical science a major service by refusing to submit to ancient authority and maintaining that it should not be bound by clerical restrictions. Rejecting medieval conceptions, he was among the first to view nature as an entity whose laws dominate all living things, plants, animals, and man alike.

Three hundred years after his death, a monument was erected to Paracelsus' memory at Basel, the city from which he was driven in the early part of his career.

Paracelsus' prolific writings dealt with a multitude of subjects, a majority issued after his death. Fourteen works were published during his lifetime, and 234 are known to have appeared between 1542 and 1845. Several collected editions have been published, the earliest in 1589-91.

From available evidence, Paracelsus' attitude toward medicine and the teachings of Galen made little impact on his contemporaries. Only in modern times has the importance of his work been fully recognized. In part, as one commentator observed, "It is a problem how to reconcile his ignorance, his weakness, his superstition, his crude notions, his erroneous observations, his ridiculous influences and theories, with his grasp of method, his lofty views of the true scope of medicine, his lucid statements, his incisive and epigrammatic criticisms of men and motives." On balance, in any event, it came to be acknowledged by the mid-twentieth century that Paracelsus was among the most original and powerful influences on the development of modern science.

18

Great Herbalist

Leonhard Fuchs (1501-1566)

De Historia Stirpium Commentarii Insignes
(Important Commentaries Concerning the History of Plants)

In the Middle Ages, plants were classified according to their uses: medicinal, edible, or poisonous. During the same period there began to be produced botanical books called herbals, describing plants considered to have medicinal value. With the coming of printing in the mid-fifteenth century, such works started to appear in printed form, often illustrated with woodcuts.

The Age of Herbals, as it is sometimes called, lasted for nearly two centuries, from about 1470 to 1670. Under its impetus, the study of botany, especially from a practical point of view, made steady and rapid progress. Nevertheless, it remained an age when superstitions persisted. For example, there was wide belief in what was known as the "Doctrine of Signatures," which held that the medicinal plant was stamped with some clear indication (i.e., signature) of its specific remedial power. As an instance, plants with yellow sap were supposed to cure jaundice.

Actually, manuscript herbals preceded printed works by many centuries. The Chinese have a compilation of about one thousand ancient herbals, and hundreds of medicinal plants were known to India prior to the Christian era. Manuscript herbals based largely on Dioscorides and Pliny were numerous in medieval Europe. Konrad von Megenberg's "Book of Nature," printed in 1475, included the first known woodcuts for botanical illustrations.

A number of famous herbals were produced during the first half of the sixteenth century. Otto Brunfels, a German physician and botanist, brought out his *Herbarium Vivae Eicones* in the 1630s, containing excellent and accurate wood engravings and describing for the first time the native plants of Germany.

The most notable herbal of all was the work of another German physician and botanist, Leonhard Fuchs, most of whose professional career was spent in the practice or teaching of medicine in various locations. Fuchs was an advocate of the Galenic school of medicine and published several Latin translations of treatises by Galen and Hippocrates. He is chiefly remembered, however, for his *De Historia Stirpium Commentarii Insignes*, printed at Basel in 1542, a work illustrated with more than five hundred full-page drawings. Included for the first time were figures of the common foxglove and of another species of the genus digitalis, which was so named by Fuchs. Some four hundred German and one hundred foreign plants are treated. Many new plants from America, e.g., Indian corn and the pumpkin, are presented. The introduction contains the first vocabulary of botanical terms. From the point of view of text, as well as illustrations, the Fuchs herbal is excellent. The author was generous in acknowledging assistance; his book carries not only his own portrait but that of three collaborators, including the woodcut maker.

Fuchs apparently had opportunities to botanize over wide areas, and the satisfaction of such close contacts with nature is well described by him:

> There is no reason why I should expatiate on the pleasure and delight
> of acquiring knowledge of plants, since there is no one who does not
> know that there is nothing in this life more pleasant and delightful
> than to wander over mountains, woods and fields garlanded and
> adorned with exquisite little flowers and plants of various sorts.... But
> it increases the pleasure and delight not a little, if there be added an
> acquaintance with the virtues and powers of these plants.

By an odd coincidence, explained perhaps by the intellectual ferment prevailing in the Europe of their time, three masterpieces of scientific literature appeared within a year of each other: Leonhard Fuchs' great herbal (1542), and Nicolaus Copernicus' *On the Revolutions of the Celestial Spheres* and Andreas Vesalius' *On the Structure of the Human Body*, both in 1543.

19

Founder of Modern Anatomy
Andreas Vesalius (1514-1564)

De Humani Corporis Fabrica
(On the Structure of the Human Body)

It is an amazing coincidence, testimony to the intellectual ferment prevailing in the Renaissance era, that Nicolaus Copernicus' *De Revolutionibus Orbium Coelestium*, Andreas Vesalius' *De Humani Corporis Fabrica*, and Leonhard Fuchs' monumental herbal *De Historia Stirpium Commentarii Insignes* were all issued within a year of each other. In fact, the works of Copernicus and Vesalius came off the press within a week of each other, in 1543. Historians of science agree that, as such events can be traced, the two latter works represent the end of the medieval age and the birth of modern science. There was a striking difference between the ages of the authors: Copernicus was seventy and Vesalius only twenty-eight when their books appeared.

Vesalius came from a Belgian family that had produced five generations of physicians, and he was determined from the outset to follow in their footsteps. His specific interest in anatomy began early. As a boy, he became fascinated by the physical characteristics of animals, and he dissected hundreds of them — moles, toads, rats, pigs, cats, dogs, and monkeys. After a preliminary education at Louvain, he chose to go to Paris to study anatomy. The chief attraction there appears to have been a renowned teacher, Jacobus Sylvius. But Vesalius was destined to be bitterly disappointed in Sylvius' lectures and demonstrations.

The teaching of anatomy and the sciences in general was, at the time, highly formalized, a practice handed down from the Middle Ages. The professor of anatomy sat on a raised platform, high above the class, reading appropriately sanctioned passages from Galen, the second-century Greek physician. At his feet was a body, usually of an animal, and beside it a barber-surgeon, who dissected the specimen in crude fashion and pointed out the parts described by the physician.

In the preface to his celebrated book, Vesalius referred contemptuously to "the detestable procedure now in vogue, that one man should carry out the dissection of the body, and another give the description of the parts." He continued:

These latter are perched up aloft in a pulpit like jackdaws, and with a notable air of disdain they drone out information about facts they have never approached at first hand, but which they merely commit to memory from the books of others, or of which they have descriptions before their eyes; the former are so ignorant of languages that they are unable to explain their dissections to the onlookers and botch what ought to be exhibited in accordance with the instruction of the physician, who never applies his hand to the dissection, and contemptuously steers the ship out of the manual. Thus everything is wrongly taught, days are wasted in absurd questions, and in the confusion less is offered to the onlooker than a butcher in his stall could teach a doctor.

It was customary for teachers of anatomy to pay attention to the organs of the abdomen and chest and to the brain and omit any particular demonstration of the muscles, joints, and skeleton. As Roger Bacon, Leonardo da Vinci, and other rebels had found, Galen's writings were read with almost idolatrous reverence. His treatise was the final authority on everything related to anatomy, physiology, diagnosis, therapy, and medical theory. To doubt him might well lead to death for heresy. In dissection, if any specimen differed in any particular from Galen's descriptions, the explanation was that the human body had changed since the master's time. A crushing blow to Galenical tradition in anatomy was destined to be delivered by Andreas Vesalius.

On leaving Paris, Vesalius returned to Louvain and began lecturing in anatomy. At the age of twenty-three he accepted a professorship of anatomy at Padua and also lectured frequently at Bologna and Pisa, where he was free to pursue his anatomical investigations as he pleased.

Reflecting his dissatisfaction with the type of instruction he had encountered at Paris, Vesalius did away with the barber prosector and undertook to do the dissecting himself. Furthermore, he concluded that anatomy could be learned only through first-hand dissection of human bodies. Cadavers, however, were extremely difficult to come by. His search for material led him at considerable personal risk to go on body-snatching expeditions. On one occasion, he stole a corpse from the gallows outside the Louvain city walls, the body being that of a criminal who had been left hanging as a warning to other malefactors.

At Padua, Vesalius lectured to overflow classes of students, personally performing all operations and demonstrating by his own hand not only the organs of the body but the muscles, joints and bones, nerves, and blood vessels. He unhesitatingly corrected Galen when his own dissections showed Galen in error. Meanwhile, work continued on his great anatomical treatise, conceived several years earlier.

By late summer 1542, Vesalius had ready the text and illustrations for *De Humani Corporis Fabrica*, "On the Structure of the Human Body." The magnificent drawings are believed to have been done under Vesalius' direction by Jan Stephan van Calcar, a pupil of Titian. The *Fabrica*, as one commentator wrote, "is more than a milestone in the history of medicine; it is a great work of creative art." The woodcuts combine scientific exactness and artistic beauty, while the printing is a superb example of the typography of Oporinus of Basel, the Swiss city where the book was produced.

The subject matter in the *Fabrica* was arranged in the same order of topics as Vesalius' lectures: the bones, the muscles, blood vessels and nerves, the internal organs, and the brain. Though Vesalius' anatomical descriptions have great merit, chief interest centers in the plates, frequently described as the finest anatomical drawings ever made. Even the initial letters are works of art, showing cherubs engaged in dissection and other activities. In the frontispiece, Vesalius himself is shown standing beside the dissecting table, on which a body lies, with a panoramic view of the dissection theatre as a background. Here is depicted the birth of scientific anatomy, man's first clear and accurate knowledge of the foundation stone of medical science and of the whole science of the human body.

Vesalius' *Fabrica* blazed new trails in the making of medical books. It is a large volume of 690 pages. The skeleton and dissection of the muscles are presented in detail but also as a portrayal of the whole body. The drawings depict a man standing in the foreground, with a background representing a landscape including trees and buildings and distant hills. The initial letters, as noted, have figures of cherubs grouped around them performing various acts associated with the study of anatomy or the practice of medicine. The *Fabrica* is not limited to anatomical demonstrations but treats also of various phases of surgery and medicine. Despite his extensive knowledge of anatomy, there is no evidence that Vesalius had any conception of blood circulation.

The effect of such a radical publication as the *Fabrica* on a superstitious age was explosive. Because it denied concepts of the structure of the human body accepted for centuries and attacked the sacred writings of Galen himself, Vesalius was uncompromisingly condemned by the stubborn forces of tradition. Leading the attack was Sylvius, Vesalius' old teacher at Paris, who spoke of Vesalius as a madman, and added:

> I implore his Majesty the Emperor to punish severely as he deserves, this monster, born and reared in his own home, this most pernicious exemplar of ignorance, ingratitude, arrogance, and impiety: and to suppress him completely lest he poison the rest of Europe with his pestilential breath.

The book also drew venomous criticisms from other Galenists, all of whom denied the truth of Vesalius' statements. Even more dangerous for Vesalius personally, the *Fabrica* incurred the extreme displeasure of ecclesiastical authorities, who became alarmed by Vesalius' insistence that man, although a descendant of Adam, did not have a rib less on one side than on the other, as stated in Genesis. He also exploded the myth that somewhere in the vertebral column there was a "resurrection bone," from which the body was to be reconstructed after death.

Vesalius, fearful that charges of heresy might be made against him, resigned his professorship at Padua and burned all his notebooks, his proposed book on Rhazes which he had edited, and also his copies of Galen's books which he had used as a student. In 1544, he moved to Spain to become personal physician to Charles V, and then to his son, Philip II. His career in anatomical research was finished.

Vesalius' reputation followed him, however, as new editions of his book appeared. Only royal favor saved him from the criticisms and attacks of the Church and the Spanish Inquisition. According to one charge, he had started a dissection too early, when the body was still alive. In 1563, Vesalius was convicted of heresy and condemned to death by the Inquisition. His patron, Philip II, commuted his sentence on condition that he undertake a pilgrimage to Jerusalem as an expiation for his scientific sins. On his way to the Holy Land, or on his way back, he stopped in Cyprus, where he received an offer from the Venetian senate to return to his professorship in Padua. He sailed back, but on the return voyage his ship was wrecked off the Ionian island of Zante, and he died of exposure, not quite fifty years of age.

Vesalius was fortunate that his great folio volume was completed at this point in history. Printing had been invented nearly a century earlier. Johann Oporinus was a master printer, and Vesalius spent a year overseeing personally the printing and publication of his book. The graphic arts had also reached a high state of development by Vesalius' time. Though Jan Stephan was the artist, Vesalius was the directing mind, and the combination of drawings and text constituted a revolution in scientific method.

Vesalius was more than the founder of a real science of anatomy; along with Harvey, he was instrumental in establishing sound principles of scientific research—science based on fact rather than tradition. Sir William Osler, the noted Canadian authority, called the *Fabrica* "the greatest medical book ever written—from which modern medicine starts." The famous British physiologist, Sir Michael Foster, concurred:

> This book is the beginning, not only of modern anatomy, but of modern physiology.... Upon the publication of the "Fabrica" the pall of authority was once and for ever removed. It ended, for all time, the long reign of fourteen centuries of precedent; it began in a true sense the renaissance of medicine.

Vesalius placed Italian medicine, and especially the university at Padua, in the first rank. Young medical men were attracted there from throughout Europe, later to return home and spread the revolt against the Galenical tradition.

It was many years after Vesalius that anatomical investigations became at all common. Much of the opposition to his book rose from objections to the dissection of the human body. The problem was referred by the Emperor Charles V to the theological faculty at Salamanca in 1556. These representatives of the Church agreed that dissection by physicians for the benefit and teaching of medicine was acceptable. But a century and a half after Vesalius' masterpiece, William Cowper's *Anatomy of Human Bodies* (Oxford, 1698) aroused bitter controversy in England.

20

Start of Modern Zoology
Conrad Gesner (1516-1565)

Historia Animalium

At the beginning of the sixteenth century, laboratory experimentation in the field of biology was rare, though there was increasing interest in living animals and plants. For information, chief reliance was still placed on the writings of ancient authors and innumerable commentaries on them. Highly popular, too, were large encyclopedic works, such as those by Conrad Gesner and Ulisse Androvandi.

Gesner, a Swiss, was born in Zurich, and studied in Basel, Paris, and Montpellier. Subsequently, he served as professor of Greek at the newly founded academy of Lausanne, took a degree at the famous medical university of Montpellier, and settled down to practice at Zurich. Throughout his career he found time for scientific studies, especially botany. Annual summer botanical excursions were made in his native land. In fact, his contemporaries knew him best as a botanist, though his manuscripts in that field were not published until about two centuries after his death.

Modern critics are in general agreement that Gesner was the most learned naturalist of his period and perhaps the best zoologist to have appeared since Aristotle. His reputation was based chiefly on his monumental *Historia Animalium*, "History of Animals," in five volumes, published at Zurich from 1551 to 1587 — which represents the high point in zoology between Aristotle and Linnaeus. An English version is reputed to have been Shakespeare's source book.

The *Historia Animalium* described and pictured every animal then known to Europe. Besides naming and describing each animal, Gesner discussed its natural functions, the quality of its soul, its use to man in general and as food or medicine in particular, and gave a concordance of literary references to it. There was little effort to classify animals beyond Aristotle's scheme. In the group of oviparous quadrupeds, for example, Gesner had only a few divisions: frogs, lizards, tortoises, and he knew only three or four different kinds in each group. The five volumes on the history of animals were divided among quadrupeds, birds, fishes, and snakes.

To make his encyclopedia easier to use, Gesner arranged the animals in alphabetical order within the groups. All known names of each animal were given, including names in different languages. Many accurate observations of his own were reported by the author, but at the same time he carried over much inaccurate information from earlier writers, especially Aristotle and Pliny. Included were descriptions and drawings of animals that Gesner had been told existed in America, though actually they often were found only in the imaginations of travelers and explorers. Much of his data were ancient, medieval, or fabulous. A good deal of dependence was placed on accounts received from travelers, sailors, whalers, and hunters, who had observed the birds, fishes, insects, and animals of newly discovered lands. Among real animals and birds noticed for the first time were turkeys, peccaries, llamas, tapirs, armadillos, vampires, and various species of parrots.

George Sarton calls Gesner's *Historia Animalium* "a summary of Renaissance zoology," and noted further that "the influence of the abundant illustrations was even stronger than that of the texts, for the latter reached only the humanists, while the pictures could reach every thinking person."

The development of the art of printing from movable type, which began about seventy years before Gesner's birth, was of inestimable importance to the international spread of scientific knowledge. It was a prime belief of Gesner's that science belonged to everyone. Consequently, his encyclopedic treatise on animals was designed to educate the world, not merely other scientists.

In a major unpublished work, *Historia Plantarum*, Gesner was the first to recognize generic status, writing, "We may hold this for certain that there are hardly any plants that constitute a genus which may not be divided into two or more species. The ancients describe one species of gentian; I know of ten or more." Gesner recognized species as falling into groups or genera, and as varying in character. He maintained that flower, fruit, and seed are better evidences of affinity than habitat or foliage.

At his death, Gesner left some 1,500 drawings of plants, for the most part original. Many were used later in works by other writers, especially herbalists.

Gesner's scientific contributions led him into other areas as well. His *De Rerum Fossilium* was the first extensively illustrated work showing fossils. He also produced numerous minor publications on medicine, mineralogy, linguistics, and mountain climbing.

Comparable in size to his massive treatise on animals was Gesner's work in an entirely different field, the *Bibliotheca Universalis*, "Universal Book Catalog," issued in four volumes from 1545 to 1555, an undertaking that has earned for him the title of father of bibliography. Therein Gesner set out to list all known books in Greek, Latin, and Hebrew, a faithful record of the first century of printing. The aim was to catalog all writers who had ever lived, along with the titles of their works, and other information. Predictably, such an ambitious enterprise was only partially successful, even so soon after the invention of printing.

Few writers in the history of science have been as prolific or as versatile as Conrad Gesner.

21

Classic of Experimental Science
William Gilbert (1540-1603)

De Magnete, Magneticisque Corporibus,
et De Magno Magnete Tellure
(On the Loadstone, Magnetic Bodies, and on the
Great Magnet the Earth)

Dr. William Gilbert has been accorded such laudatory titles as "the father of electricity," "the father of experimental science in England," "the founder of magnetic and electrical sciences," and "the first great man of science in England since Roger Bacon." It is hardly an overstatement to refer to him, as did the German philosopher Kurd Lasswitz, as "the first real physicist and the first trustworthy methodical experimenter," and his *De Magnete* as the first great work of physical science to be published in England.

Gilbert held degrees from St. John's College, Cambridge, after which he began the study of medicine. His M.D. degree was obtained at Cambridge in 1569. There followed a period of postgraduate work in Italy, where it is probable that he studied under the famous Italian physician Fabricius at Padua. Upon his return to England he became chief physician to Queen Elizabeth and for a short time James I. Another honor in 1600 was to be elected president of the Royal College of Physicians.

With such prestigious connections and being a man of substance, Gilbert was able to conduct expensive magnetic experiments and to attract around him the leading men of science of his time.

The intellectual climate of his day was propitious for Gilbert. Fielding H. Garrison, a leading science historian, points out that "the seventeenth century, the age of Shakespeare and Milton, Valesquez and Rembrandt, Bach and Purcell, Cervantes and Molière, Newton and Leibnitz, Bacon and Descartes, Spinoza and Locke, was preeminently a period of intense individualism, intellectual and spiritual." The very first year of the century is made memorable for us by the appearance of Gilbert's epoch-making *De Magnete.*

Medieval superstition still flourished, however, and perhaps nowhere with more damaging effect than in Gilbert's field of interest—magnetism and electricity. Gilbert, an avid reader of books ancient and modern, complained that "the shops of the booksellers are crammed" with scientifically valueless works replete with false ideas handed down from ancient times on alchemy, astrology, and magic.

In the introduction to *De Magnete*, Gilbert reviews some of the innumerable writings on magnetism since the times of Plato and Aristotle, enumerating the manifold errors and exploding the wornout theories. In particular, Gilbert reviewed the exaggerated fables surrounding the properties of the loadstone and proceeded to destroy the myths through direct and demonstrable scientific data. Prevailing beliefs held that the loadstone's magnetic power, dulled at night, could be restored by a bath in goat's blood; that its power, extending to the area of domesticity, could reconcile husbands to wives and wives to husbands; that it could detect faithlessness of women; that if pickled in the salt of a sucking fish the loadstone gained additional power to pick up gold from the deepest wells; and that if rubbed with garlic, or placed where there was a diamond nearby, it could not attract iron. Applying experimental methods to each of these absurd but accepted beliefs, Gilbert proved them to be without foundation.

Gilbert vehemently attacked alchemists and their obscure language. He likewise rejected the explanation of electric and magnetic attraction by means of sympathy, as had been theorized by Fracastro in 1530. On the other hand, he believed in horoscopes, like most of his contemporaries, comparing the magnetizing effect of the earth on pieces of iron being forged in a smithy with the influence of the stars on a child during its birth.

Gilbert had little hope of converting his opponents in his rejection of many superstitious notions. In the preface to his *De Magnete*, he pays his respects to the priggish doctrinaire believers and the anti-intellectuals devoted to their ignorance:

> Why should I submit this noble science and this new philosophy to the judgment of men who have taken oath to follow the opinions of others, to the most senseless corrupters of the arts, to lettered clowns, grammatists, sophists, spouters, and the wrongheaded rabble, to be denounced, torn to tatters, and heaped with contumely! To you alone, true philosophers, ingenuous minds, who not only in books but in things themselves look for knowledge, have I dedicated these foundations of magnetic science.

The last sentence supplies the key to Gilbert's basic principle: scientific knowledge is valid only if founded on the bases of practical experiment and observation. Idle speculations and theories are worthless unless they are supported by demonstrable evidence. In the modern world, the practice of scientific experimentation has become so commonplace that it is difficult to realize how revolutionary was the concept of experimental evidence in 1600.

De Magnete consists of six sections or "books." In the main body of the volume, Gilbert describes his own experimental work on magnetism. One of the principal pieces of apparatus he used was a large spherical loadstone, which he called a *terrella* — a miniature earth; its magnetic poles were found by using a minute compass needle. Here Gilbert introduced what most historians of science regard as his greatest contribution: his view of the earth itself as one great magnet. He proved that the magnetic nature of the earth accounts for the behavior of the mariner's compass. "There resides, therefore," he says, "a Magnetick force in the earth just as in the terrella." By his theory and experiments on the magnetic nature of the earth, Gilbert created the science of terrestrial magnetism.

Through the study of terrestrial magnetism, Gilbert then became a strong advocate, the first in England, of the Copernican system, lending support which required considerable courage during that intolerant era. In the same year, *De Magnete* was published, Giordano Bruno was burned at the stake in Italy for promoting Copernicus' theory, and Galileo was shortly to be condemned by the Inquisition. Copies of *De Magnete* reaching Italy were so censored that all mention of the heretical doctrine was effaced.

Most of Gilbert's work is concerned with magnetism, but one section is devoted to the phenomena of electrical attraction. Gilbert was the first scientist to differentiate between electrical and magnetic attraction. Prior to his time, it was thought that only amber could be electrified by friction. Gilbert's experiments revealed that the same phenomena could be observed to take place in more than a score of substances, including glass, sulphur, resin, and such precious stones as the diamond and sapphire, all of which on vigorous rubbing acquired similar properties to those of amber. His proof came with the help of a delicately mounted needle, called a "versorium," now known as an electroscope. Substances showing positive magnetic attraction were classed as "electrics"; those on which the versorium had a negative effect were called "non-electrics"—the equivalents of modern-day conductors and insulators.

De Magnete is well illustrated with ninety woodcuts of diagrams and pictures of loadstones and apparatuses used in Gilbert's experiments. An unusual feature of the text is the use of stars along the margins to indicate the importance of the discoveries described. Twenty-one large stars and nearly two hundred small ones show Gilbert's estimation of the relative value of his experiments.

Also included in the original edition is a glossary of new scientific terms invented by Gilbert, another significant contribution. It was he who introduced the word *electricity* into the language (from the Greek word meaning amber), and the words *axis* and *equator* (of a magnet), *magnetic meridians* (of the earth), and *armature*.

Among Gilbert's warmest contemporary admirers were Kepler and Galileo. No better estimate of his career has been expressed than that by Galileo, who, after reading *De Magnete*, wrote:

> I think him worthy of the greatest praise for the many new and true observations which he had made, to the disgrace of so many vain and fabling authors, who write not from their own knowledge only, but repeat everything they hear from the foolish and vulgar, without attempting to satisfy themselves of the same by experiment.

De Magnete not only demonstrated the value and importance of experiment, but also established magnetism and electricity as sciences, paving the way for further investigations down to the time of Michael Faraday.

Gilbert's book was the first great scientific work by an Englishman. The second, appearing only a generation later, was William Harvey's on blood circulation. Both were in Latin.

22

Astronomical Observer Supreme
Tycho Brahe (1546-1601)

Astronomiae Instauratae Progymnasmata
(Studies in the New Astronomy)

Three years after the death of Copernicus there was born a Danish astronomer, Tycho Brahe, destined to make major contributions to the Copernican theory and to astronomical science in general. Copernicus had hoped that future observers would be able to calculate more exactly the position of the planets, for the purpose of testing the correctness of his findings regarding the paths of the heavenly bodies: Erasmus Reinhold (1511-1553) designed astronomical tables which were considerably more accurate, but far greater progress was made by Brahe, who paved the way for important new discoveries.

Astronomy is probably the oldest and most exact of the sciences, and its predictions, such as those for solar and lunar eclipses, have attained amazing accuracy. It was not until the mid-sixteenth century, however, when astronomers were suddenly faced with the question of deciding between the old Ptolemaic and the new Copernican systems of the world, that the need for precise facts on celestial motions was realized. Brahe may have been the first to become fully aware of the problem. Observational astronomy in the modern sense began with him.

Brahe was of noble family. He was adopted by an uncle, who sent him at an early age to Copenhagen to study philosophy and rhetoric. When Brahe witnessed a total solar eclipse, at age fourteen, however, he came to regard astronomy as something divine and remained fascinated with the subject for the rest of his life. As a law student in Leipzig, he continued to make observations with a globe, a pair of compasses, and a "cross-staff." Later, at Augsburg, he spent two years in the study of chemistry.

A maternal uncle permitted Brahe to install a laboratory in his castle of Herritzvad. There he caught sight of a new star, measured its position, observed its gradual changes of magnitude during the sixteen months of its appearance, and showed that it was a real star, not a meteor. Brahe wrote and published an account of his observations. His first recorded observation was made in 1563, at age seventeen, noting the close approach of Jupiter and Saturn; he was shocked to find that the prediction based on the Alphonsine Tables was a month in error, and that the Prussian Tables were wrong by many days.

When only sixteen, according to his biographer, J. L. E. Dreyer, Brahe's eyes were opened to the great fact, which seems to us so simple to grasp but which had escaped the attention of all European astronomers before him, that only through a steadily pursued course of observations would it be possible to obtain a better insight into the motions of the planets and decide which system of the world was the true one.

Brahe's plan to leave Denmark and to settle in Basel was changed by Frederick II, King of Denmark, who recognized his extraordinary ability and bestowed upon him for life the island of Hveen in the Sound, together with a generous pension, a canonry in the cathedral of Roskilde, the income of an estate in Norway, and funds for constructing and equipping a magnificent new observatory. In the observatory of Uraniborg (Castle of the Heavens), Brahe spent the next twenty-one years. There the greater part of his work was done and a mass of data collected, to be published long afterwards as the Rudolphine Tables. Uraniborg became a scientific center, and astronomers, statesmen, philosophers, and students flocked there to observe and learn, or simply to sightsee.

By modern standards, Brahe's instruments were crude in the extreme. The telescope was yet to be invented. The equipment provided was mainly devised by Brahe himself, and was the work of the most skilled German craftsmen. He invented a new form of sight and a sort of diagonal scale for reading fractions of a degree. In measuring the longitude of a star or its right ascension, an accurate measure of time is needed, and for that purpose Brahe devised a technique by which observations were referred to the position of the sun. He was the first astronomer in Europe to use the modern celestial coordinates, reckoning star positions with reference to the celestial equator. Also innovative was Brahe's practice of observing planetary positions not simply at a few isolated spots but at frequent intervals so that the whole orbit could be plotted.

The most astonishing fact is that despite all the instruments he could devise or invent, Brahe's observations, which were remarkably precise, were made with the naked eye without lenses of any kind. Nevertheless, as George Sarton notes, "the organization of every modern observatory derives from Uraniborg, though the instruments used there have been developed far beyond Brahe's possibilities and even his conceptions."

Brahe's observations and research were directed toward fulfilling one prime ambition. When he made his first observations with a home-made quadrant, he found that the places given in star catalogs were wrong, and that such events as eclipses occurred as much as two or three days from the predicted times. Copernicus' tables had made little improvement. Brahe therefore untertook to plot the positions of the brightest stars, and thereafter, with a fundamental map of the sky established, to observe the motions of the sun, moon, and planets, so that their orbits could be calculated without mistake. Brahe recognized the necessity for continuous observations, as noted, and with royal support he was able to employ regular assistants for this task.

A large number of stars were observed by Brahe, and he began to prepare a catalog, to be published as the first volume of a great astronomical treatise entitled *Astronomiae Instauratae Progymnasmata* (Studies in the New Astronomy). The work was begun in 1588 and much of it was printed in 1592, but it was still incomplete at the time of Brahe's death. The complete catalog of 777 stars was edited and published by Johann Kepler in two volumes, 1602-1603.

The precision of Brahe's observations is shown by the fact that for his nine fundamental stars the error was less than one degree. His estimate of the length of the tropical year was only a small fraction too small. He determined the precession of the equinoxes exactly. Further, he established that the parallax of a new star was too small for it to be as near as the planets and that it must accordingly belong to the sphere of the stars whose unchangeability had been a basic principle of astronomy since ancient times. Another illusion was destroyed when Brahe proved that a comet must have passed through the material of the spheres, if in fact they existed. He concluded that comets are very distant heavenly bodies, rather than being luminous formations in the earth's atmosphere, as previously thought. It was also found from the motions of the planets that their paths varied from far away to near the sun, showing that the space of the heavens allows for free motion between all these orbits of the planets.

Brahe was a far greater observer than an interpreter. He was never willing to accept the Copernican theory that the sun and not the earth is the center of the universe, and that the earth and planets revolve around it. The reasons for his non-acceptance of the heliocentric system, Brahe stated, were that the earth is too sluggish to move; if the world is spinning in space, it would be felt and objects would be swept off its surface; and the whole doctrine was contrary to Scripture. The Copernican system was a stumbling block for Brahe, it appears, because of its unorthodoxy and its conflict with what he regarded as common sense.

In place of the heliocentric concept, Brahe adopted a hypothesis that can be traced back to the Egyptians — that the planets revolve around the sun, which in turn revolves around the fixed earth. The idea is in accord with the Aristotelian opinion that it is the nature of the earth to stay where it is. Meanwhile, the mass of observations being accumulated by Brahe was actually proving the validity of the Copernican system. The Tychonic system which he devised died with Brahe.

In other respects, too, Brahe was a creature of his time, at the crossroads between the medieval era and the enlightened Renaissance. He was, for example, a firm believer in astrology and in alchemy, the turning of base metals into gold. He had superstitious notions about comets, believing, as he wrote: "They are formed by the ascending from the earth of human sins and wickedness, formed into a gas, and ignited by the anger of God. This poisonous stuff falls down again on peoples' heads, and causes all kinds of mischief, such as pestilence, Frenchmen, sudden death, and bad weather."

In an address defending astrology, delivered at the University of Copenhagen in 1574, Brahe considered the conclusions concerning human destiny which can be drawn from celestial movements. Unless the stars and planets affect human lives, he said, they have no purpose, and this would deny the wisdom and goodness of God. The influence of the moon on the tides is well known, and ancient writers noted a connection between the weather and the rise and setting of certain stars and the configuration of the planets. Projecting these ideas, if the heavenly bodies affect the course of nature, they must affect mankind. Brahe also held that there is a similarity between certain parts of the body and particular planets.

Because of a most cantankerous disposition, Brahe was his own worst enemy. His arrogance and rudeness antagonized powerful and influential persons, from the royal family on down. Against the opposition of his family and friends, he married a peasant girl (a marriage that seemed to turn out happily). At age twenty, his nose was cut off in a duel. Instead of showing gratitude to his royal protector, and ingratiating himself with government officials and his own subordinates, he made himself disliked by various abuses and bad manners. He has been described as arrogant, self-willed, irritable, intolerant, contemptuous of others, narrow-minded, chockful of prejudices, revengeful, and timorous.

Because of these personality conflicts, Brahe's work at Uraniborg came to an end in 1597. Following the death of King Frederick in 1588, his son Christian IV came to the throne. The hostility of the young king and his advisers made life increasingly difficult for Brahe. His privileges were taken away from him, and he moved to Copenhagen. His instruments were gradually dismantled, and the observatory itself was eventually destroyed. In further wanderings, Brahe left Denmark, spent short periods in Rostock and Wandsbeck (near Hamburg), Germany, and arrived in Prague in 1599. While in Wandsbeck, Brahe published an album, *Astronomiae Instauratae Mechanica* (Mechanics of the New Astronomy), describing and illustrating his old observatory and its instruments.

In Bohemia, where he spent his last days, Brahe was fortunate in two respects. Rudolf II received him with the greatest honors and turned over to him the castle of Benarky, about twenty miles from Prague. There Brahe established a new observatory, set up his instruments, some of which had been sent on to him from Uraniborg, and continued his work.

The second highly favorable circumstance was the arrival in January 1600 of Johann Kepler as Brahe's assistant. Kepler was himself an exile, driven out of his native province of Styria, Austria, by Archduke Ferdinand for being a heretic and a Protestant. The collaboration lasted only a short time, for Brahe died the following year. By then, however, Kepler had become well acquainted with Brahe's methods, could easily use his accumulated notes, and was able to carry on his activities. It was Kepler who saved Brahe's most important writings from oblivion.

Brahe was an important link in the chain of great astronomers which began with Copernicus and continued with Kepler, Galileo, and Newton. Dreyer sums up the case for him by stating: "He not only conceived the necessity of supplying materials for discovery of the true motions of the heavenly bodies, and by his improvement of instruments and accumulation of observations, made it possible for Kepler to reach his goal, but in almost all the branches of practical and spherical astronomy he opened new paths, and made the first serious advance since the days of the Alexandrian school.... Considering the extent, accuracy and importance of Tycho Brahe's observations, and the results to which they led, we can conclude that there is no observer, ancient or modern, whose labors have produced a more marked influence on the progress of astronomy."

Brahe rated his own accomplishments at Hveen, writing in his *Astronomiae Instauratae Mechanica* (Mechanics of the New Astronomy), published in 1598 at Wandsbeck. As listed, these were "the improved elements of the solar orbit, the discovery of a new inequality in the moon's motion, the variability of the inclination of the lunar orbit and the motion of the modes, the observation of accurate positions of a thousand fixed stars, the explosion of the time-honored error about the irregularity in the precession of the equinoxes, the accumulation of a vast mass of carefully planned observations of the planets, in order to have new tables of their motions constructed, and the observations of comets, proving them to be much farther from the earth than the moon." Perhaps no astronomer in history could justly claim more or greater achievements.

23

Pursuit of Knowledge
Francis Bacon (1561-1626)

Of the Proficience and Advancement of Learning,
Divine and Human

Hardly less controversial than the theory that Sir Francis Bacon wrote the Shakespearean plays is the question of the nature and extent of his contribution, if any, to modern scientific research methods. On one side his defenders, who call him "the Columbus of experimental science," claim that he "did much to usher into the world the present scientific age" and believe, along with Macaulay, that Bacon "moved the intellects which have moved the world." On the opposite side, his attackers voice their unanimity in arguing that "the result reached by Bacon's method is always zero" and that "the overthrow of scholasticism by Bacon was the warfare of the famous knight with windmills." As is usually the case in such debates, there is a measure of truth in both arguments.

Whichever view we adopt, it will be worth noting the judgment of a leading historian of science, Florian Cajori, who asserts: " ... one thing is clear, Bacon ranks as the earliest prominent methodologist of scientific inquiry. He represents an effort to proceed beyond the crude and slovenly inductive procedure of a simple enumeration of affirmative observations. Bacon insists that men should mark when they miss as well as when they hit; they should observe many cases — the more the better."

The Baconian doctrines were first set forth in detail in *Of the Proficience and Advancement of Learning, Divine and Human* (1605), and developed further in the author's *Novum Organum* (1620). The former was the only philosophical work published by Bacon in a language other than Latin, the universal scholarly language of the day.

Bacon's originality of thought and breadth of view, as well as his limitations, can best be understood by examining the state of the sciences in his time. The scientific world in general was still in a rudimentary stage. The fundamental science of dynamics was yet to be established by Galileo, who invented the telescope and made major astronomical discoveries. In astronomy, despite Copernicus, Brahe, Kepler, and their adherents, it was still generally held that the earth was the fixed center of the universe and that the stars and the sun revolved about it. The three fundamental laws of planetary motion were discovered by Kepler in Bacon's lifetime, but had little immediate effect on contemporary thinking. Not long after Bacon's death, Newton produced his theory, based on the Keplerian laws, of the phenomenon of falling bodies and universal gravitation. A Bacon contemporary, William Gilbert, discovered elementary facts about natural magnets, but the existence of electricity and its connection with magnetism were unknown. The emergence of chemistry, as distinct from alchemy, as a true science was still a century and a half away. Finally, the Aristotelian notion that all earthly bodies are composed of four elements (earth, air, fire, and water), while heavenly bodies are fundamentally different, was commonly accepted by scholars.

Corresponding to the prevailing shortage of accurate scientific knowledge was a lack of power over nature. Man had made little progress toward harnessing nature for his own comfort and convenience. The only available devices for obtaining mechanical energy, for example, were clockwork, waterwheels, and windmills. Land transport was by foot or by horse, and rowing and sailing were the only ways to cross water. The population was frequently struck by catastrophes and uncontrolled epidemics of the plague. Food shortages often caused acute problems.

Scientific progress for the solution of any of these dilemmas, Bacon noted, had been glacially slow. He was convinced that this situation could be changed, that man could overcome his ignorance of nature and, by improved methods, make it serve him. Given the right method, he believed that there would be no limit to the growth of human knowledge and human power over nature.

The reasons for the lack of advancement up to his time were analyzed by Bacon. The chief fault was that theories had not been followed up by observation, experience, and practical applications.

Bacon begins his work by attacking the sterile scholasticism inherited from the Middle Ages. Aristotelian logic served only to foster debates and controversy, while the empirical method led to general conclusions based on limited and emotionally biased experiments. Bacon insists that men ought to "throw aside all thought of philosophy, or at least to expect but little and poor fruit from it, until an approved and careful natural and experimental history be prepared and constructed." The medieval schoolmen and logicians are compared by Bacon to spiders, which "bring forth indeed cobwebs of learning, admirable for the fineness of thread and work, but of no substance or profit." For what purpose, he asks, "are these braincreations and idle displays of power?" Scientific investigation had been continually handicapped because of its entanglement with the philosophical search for final causes. Bacon firmly asserts that the right method of scientific research, that is, the inductive method, could give mankind sovereignty over nature. The tendency to make general statements on the basis of preconceived ideas led him to regard "the present method of experiment," mainly in the hands of charlatans and misguided zealots, as "blind and stupid." The charlatans and quacks had carried on their experiments for material gain, for such purposes as turning lead into gold or discovering a panacea for all diseases. Further, such discoveries as they made were kept secret and not shared.

In order "to extend more widely the limits of the power and greatness of man," Bacon outlined steps by which progress towards a mastery over nature might be made more certain. The proper procedure, he wrote, is to record all available facts, make all possible observations, perform all practical experiments, then collect and tabulate the results to determine the connections between different phenomena, from which general laws could be formulated.

Bacon places great stress on the study of natural history. In the past, he states, in *The Advancement of Learning*, natural history had scarcely gone beyond "nature in course" or the "history of creatures," especially the history of marvels.

Bacon was realist enough to know that to collect the vast amount of data from which the laws of nature were to be extracted, the use of his methods would require a huge research organization. A large staff would have to be employed at various levels, and expensive equipment and buildings would be needed. Only the government had the resources to support such an ambitious undertaking.

The *Advancement of Learning* is divided into two books. In the first, Bacon undertakes a defense of knowledge, the pursuit of which is recommended as a vocation suitable for kings and statesmen. Of greater interest to modern readers is the second book. Here Bacon includes all branches of learning within his domain. Reviewing each major field of study in an effort to reveal the limitations of existing knowledge, he then proceeds to show how men might make further progress. This section contains Bacon's famous classification of the sciences, the value of which was attested by Diderot, the encyclopedist, who wrote in his *Prospectus*:

> If we come out successful from this vast undertaking, we shall owe it mainly to Chancellor Bacon, who sketched the plan of a universal dictionary of sciences and arts at a time when there were not, so to speak, either arts or sciences. This extraordinary genius, when it was impossible to write a history of what men knew, wrote one of what they had to learn.

Learning is divided by Bacon into three categories: history, which corresponds to memory; poetry, which corresponds to imagination; and philosophy, which corresponds to reason. There follow divisions and subdivisions of each branch of knowledge.

Bacon, impatient with the metaphysical search for final causes, believed that true knowledge must be materially applicable to practical life so that men might live as commodiously as possible. As he puts it, "men must know that in this theatre of man's life it is reserved only for God and the angels to be lookers-on."

Limitations in Bacon's scientific method have been cited by various critics. The weakness chiefly mentioned is his failure to provide for the use of preliminary hypotheses to be tested against known facts or to be demonstrated by special experiments—a method that has accelerated immensely the development of modern scientific theories. That Bacon neglected to recognize the vast importance of mathematics in the study of natural phenomena is another failure for which opponents seek to inculpate him. Nevertheless, the Baconian principles were predominant in the work of such later scientists as Linnaeus, Cuvier, Agassiz, Darwin, and Alexander von Humboldt. Their application to astronomy, physics, and other sciences making extensive use of mathematics is less noticeable.

Bacon has been criticized severely for his unsympathetic attitude toward such contemporary scientists as Copernicus, Galileo, Kepler, and Harvey. Because he rejected the theory of blood circulation, refused to accept the Copernican theory, and was contemptuous of the microscope and telescope, it has even been argued that Bacon obstructed scientific progress.

One Bacon biographer, Mary Sturt, comments, "It is hard to say what anyone ever learnt direct from Bacon. He was no scientist, he made no great discoveries, he lived and died an amateur, and yet his general ideas accord so exactly with the course that history has taken, that every laboratory might be decorated with his texts and every international society turn to him for a motto."

C. D. Broad, of Cambridge University, adds that Bacon's "service to science was to criticize the existing bad methods, to try to formulate the methods which should be substituted for them, and to paint a glowing picture of the power which men might acquire by such means over nature"; and, finally, Cajori concludes: "The facts support the statement that Sir Francis Bacon was a herald of the dawn of experimental research, that his method does not fully describe the processes usually followed by men engaged in actual research, but represents as a rule only the preliminary stages, and that in some instances the exclusive use of his method has led to far-reaching results."[3] Bacon's enthusiasm for planned experimentation and his proposal for a cooperative research institute had immense influence in bringing about the establishment of scientific societies and of scientific research as a recognized profession.

Bacon's last years were tragic. Many honors came to him from Queen Elizabeth and James I, but he was careless in money matters and led an extravagant life. He was accused and pleaded guilty to accepting bribes, was heavily fined, and banished from the royal court.

24

Explorer of Outer Space
Galileo (1564-1642)

Dialogo ... sopra i Due Massimi Sistemi del Mondo Tolemaico, e Copernicano
(Dialogue on the Two Chief Systems of the World, the Ptolemaic and the Copernican)

By a curious coincidence, the birth of the brilliant Italian astronomer, Galileo Galilei, occurred in the same year, 1564, as Shakespeare's, and Michelangelo died on the identical day that Galileo was born. Further, Sir Isaac Newton, who was to place a capstone on many of Galileo's discoveries, was born the year Galileo died. Between them, Galileo and Newton's lifespans covered the entire seventeenth century.

Galileo, son of a Pisan nobleman, was an early convert to Copernicus' theory of a sun-centered universe. Mathematics held a particular fascination for him, specifically in its application to the investigation of bodies in motion. His experiments and demonstrations dealing with the phenomena of movement proved to be of extraordinary significance in the study of mechanics, and provided a basis for research on the vaster problems of the movement of celestial bodies.

Prior to Galileo, Copernican ideas had had little impact on European thought. The theories advanced by Copernicus some seventy-five years earlier were viewed as mere hypotheses, a fact that led the church authorities to regard the Copernican discoveries as too inconsequential to ban. Galileo, however, soon changed the attitude from indifference to one of intense concern.

The first known telescope, a refractor, was designed and built by Hans Lippershey of Holland in 1608. Two years later, Galileo was the first to improve and use the new invention for observing the heavenly bodies and to make a major contribution to astronomy. As he related:

> About ten months ago probably in 1609 a rumor came to our ears that an optical instrument had been elaborated by a Dutchman, Johannes Lippershey, by the aid of which visible objects, even though far distant from the eye of the observer, were distinctly seen as if near at hand.... I applied myself entirely to seeking out the theory and discovering the means by which I might arrive at the invention of a

similar instrument, an end which I attained a little later, from considerations of the theory of refraction; and I first prepared a tube of lead, in the ends of which I fitted two glass lenses, both plane on one side, one being spherically convex, the other concave, on the other side.

Never before had anyone viewed the skies except with the naked eye. Naturally, startling new facts were discovered. The ancient antronomers had described the moon as a smooth, perfect sphere. Galileo's telescope revealed contradictory evidence: "It is full of inequalities, uneven, full of hollows and protuberances, just like the surface of the Earth itself, which is varied everywhere by lofty mountains and deep valleys."

Continuing his observations, Galileo discovered sunspots, and by watching their changing positions calculated that the sun revolves on its axis every twenty-four days. He found that the Milky Way was "nothing else but a mass of innumerable stars planted together in clusters." But in Galileo's own opinion, most amazing was his discovery that there were four moons revolving around the planet Jupiter. Further observations revealed the phases of Venus and the rings surrounding the planet Saturn. "We are absolutely compelled to say," asserted Galileo, "that Venus and Mercury also revolve around the sun, as do also all the rest of the planets—a truth believed indeed by the Pythagorean school, by Copernicus, and by Kepler, but never proved by the evidence of our senses as is now proved in the case of Venus and Mercury."

Here was irrefutable argument, Galileo was convinced, validating the truth of the Copernican theory. "I am filled with infinite astonishment and also infinite gratitude to God," he wrote, "that it has pleased Him to make me alone the first observer of such wonderful things, which have been hidden in all past centuries."

Galileo's descriptions of the discoveries that had been made possible by the telescope were printed in his *Siderius Nuncius*, "The Messenger of the Stars," in 1610, for the purpose, as he expressed it, of "acquainting all the philosophers and mathematicians with some observations which I have made on the celestial bodies by means of my spy-glass and which infinitely amaze me." Publication of this work, justifying and supporting Copernicus, led to Galileo's first clash with the theologians. The Inquisition still ruled with unlimited power, and church officials had begun to realize the danger to the status quo inherent in the Copernican theory of the sun-centered universe.

In 1616, Galileo was denounced to the Holy Office of the Inquisition and ordered to present himself before the Grand Inquisitor, Cardinal Bellarmine. He was there commanded to "abandon his heretical opinions about the earth and the sun and the stars." Furthermore, the *Siderius Nuncius* and "all books which affirm the motion of the earth" were placed upon the *Index of Prohibited Books*. After this first brush with the Inquisition, Galileo wrote in a letter to a friend: "I believe that there is no greater hatred in the whole world, than that of ignorance for knowledge."

For fifteen years Galileo remained relatively silent. During this time, however, the election of a more liberal pope, Urban VIII, aroused hope for an enlightened and sympathetic attitude toward new scientific discoveries. In 1632, believing that circumstances were once again favorable, Galileo issued the epoch-making work upon which he had been engaged for a number of years: the *Dialogue on the Two Chief Systems of the World*. To meet the objections of the papal censor, Galileo warily included a pious preface condemning the Copernican theory on the grounds that it was contrary to the Holy Scriptures. That this was mere camouflage is obvious, for the contents of the book clearly state and support the case for the Copernican system against every variety of objection and question.

Adopting a literary usage then in vogue, Galileo's work is in the form of four dialogues between three speakers: Salviati, a convinced Copernican, obviously representing Galileo; Sagredo, an intelligent layman, who raises common-sense criticism and injects occasional humor into the proceedings; and Simplicio, a simple-minded Ptolemaist and defender of tradition who presents the usual Aristotelian objections to acceptance of the Copernican system. Invariably, Simplicio is on the losing side of the discussion.

The *Dialogue* is spread over a four-day period. In the beginning of the discussion, the old concept of a perfect and unchangeable heaven is challenged on the basis of evidence furnished by new stars and sunspots, and similarities are pointed out between the earth, moon, and planets. There follow propositions relating to the earth's rotation and to the revolution of the earth about the sun. In each argument the Copernican doctrine emerges triumphant as constituting the simplest and most logical explanation of astronomical phenomena.

Subsequent to publication of the *Dialogue*, Galileo's enemies had persuaded the pope that Simplicio was meant to be a caricature of him, since some of the arguments raised by this protagonist resembled those suggested by Pope Urban himself. A few months later, Galileo was again denounced to the Inquisition and summoned to Rome to stand trial. Then approaching his seventieth year and in poor health, Galileo was nevertheless compelled to appear before the ten cardinals of the Inquisition. Threatened with torture unless he recanted his scientific beliefs, Galileo yielded, confessed his error, and stated, "I now declare and swear that the earth does not move around the sun." There is an apocryphal story that as Galileo was led away from the tribunal he remarked under his breath, "And yet it moves."

The *Dialogue* was placed on the *Index of Prohibited Books*, where it remained until 1835. Galileo was sentenced to prison, but the sentence was never executed and he presently was allowed to return to his home in Florence. There he lived in technical confinement and continued his scientific research during the remaining eight years of his life. Shortly before his death, one of his greatest books, *Discourses on Two New Sciences* (1638), was smuggled out of the country for publication in Holland. The book presents a summary of the basic principles of dynamics and ballistics, and it is considered by some to be his most important work.

Galileo's experiments in dynamics and his astronomic observations laid the foundation of modern mathematical physics. Concerning his over-all importance and influence in the history of science, a distinguished Swiss physicist, Friedrich Dessauer, commented:

> Of all Galileo's achievements this was his greatest gift to posterity: the inductive method, the core of all exact science; extended in the years that followed, it proved to be the key to the mysteries of being, opening up ever new strata, ever new depths. And it is through the inductive method that our knowledge of the world has grown to be a million times greater than that of the ancients.[4]

The founders of modern science, such as Galileo, were faced with a dual task. They needed, first, to examine, criticize, and discredit faulty theories carried over from the ancient and medieval eras, and to replace them by theories based on scientifically demonstrated evidence — in brief, to destroy one world and to build a better one. Galileo played an instrumental role in evolving a new concept of knowledge, a new concept of science. By establishing the laws of motion and the law of falling bodies, he was a prime factor in the new scientific revolution.

25

Lawmaker for the Universe
Johannes Kepler (1571-1630)

Astronomia Nova and *Harmonices Mundi*
(The New Astronomy and Harmony of the World)

Johannes Kepler was born a little more than a generation after the death of Copernicus. One of the great creative scientists, Kepler represents both the mysticism of the Middle Ages and the positive, reasoning spirit of the Renaissance. As H. Dingle, secretary of the British Royal Astronomical Society, remarked, "There run through all Kepler's works, as inseparable threads of their texture, the search, familiar to the scientist of today, for rational co-ordination of observations, and the almost infinite remoteness of a mysticism with which we have lost touch."

The contributions of five great astronomers of the sixteenth and seventeenth centuries, from as many different nations, together solved a cosmic enigma: the motions of the heavenly bodies. Nicolaus Copernicus, a Pole, first established the theory of a heliocentric (sun-centered) universe, supplanting the accepted notion of a geocentric (earth-centered) system. With improved instruments and painstaking methods of observation, Tycho Brahe, a Dane, assembled remarkably accurate data on planetary positions. Johannes Kepler, a German, discovered the laws of planetary motion, and Galileo, an Italian, was the first to use the newly invented telescope in astronomy; his laws of dynamics were of incalculable aid in establishing the correct principles of motion. The fifth and last was an Englishman, Isaac Newton, whose law of gravitation based on Kepler's scientific discoveries provided a rational explanation for the motions of the celestial bodies and thenceforth enabled scientists to view the universe as one great system.

Though German born, Kepler's investigations in astronomy were carried on principally in Prague, where he had gone as a young man to serve as Tycho Brahe's assistant. When Brahe died, in 1601, Kepler became successor to his patron's post, with the imposing title of Imperial Mathematician to the Emperor of Bohemia. In fact, the position was that of court astrologer, with Kepler's professional duties limited to casting horoscopes and issuing prognostications, tasks he considered to be pure charlatanry but which he performed for the sake of expediency. Of immeasurable value to his scientific investigations was the fact that he inherited Tycho Brahe's voluminous unpublished collection of astronomical data. Brahe had, with utter exactness, made accurate observations of the positions of the stars and had also recorded the time of their appearance. His records, covering a period of thirty-five years, were indispensable to Kepler in carrying forward his own studies. Writing of Brahe's accumulation of data, Kepler commented, "Tycho is loaded with riches which, like most of the rich, he makes no use of."

Throughout his researches in astronomy, Kepler was determined to discover the general plan of the solar system. Since the time of the ancient Greeks, it had been universally believed that the planets move in circular paths — a theory accepted unquestioningly even by Copernicus. Kepler soon came to realize, however, that there were striking discrepancies between the circular orbit theory of planetary motion and the observed facts. Six planets — Mercury, Venus, Earth, Mars, Jupiter, and Saturn — were then known. Observations had revealed that these planets move in their courses at variable speeds, their rate decreasing as their distance from the sun increases.

Convinced that the theory of circular orbits was in error, Kepler began testing a variety of other hypotheses. After arduous labor, much trial and error, and six years spent in making innumerable calculations, he finally developed his two epoch-making "laws." His discoveries, correcting and supplementing those of Copernicus, inaugurated modern astronomy, eliminating such survivals of the Ptolemaic system as epicycles, deferents, and equants.

The two laws were first published in Kepler's *Astronomia Nova*, "The New Astronomy." According to the first law, the planetary orbits are not circular but elliptical, the sun occupying one focus of the ellipses. With this law, Kepler upset the old Aristotelian notion that the circle is a perfect figure and that therefore the planetary orbits must be circular. This departure from tradition resulted in the prompt suppression of his book by the College of Cardinals.

Kepler's second law is concerned with the fact that the speed of a planet varies as it approaches or recedes from the sun. As described by J. R. Mayer, in his *Seven Seals of Science*:

> Kepler finally discovered the curious fact that the observed variations in speed are such that planets sweep over equal areas in equal times — which is to say that, if an imaginary line is drawn from the sun to a planet moving in its elliptical path, and one end of the line is considered as fixed at the sun while the other end moves with the planet, the quasi-triangular areas swept over by the line in like periods of time are always the same.[5]

A decade went by before Kepler was ready to publish the third and last of the famous laws bearing his name. This law, appearing in his *Harmonices Mundi*, "Harmony of the World," deals with the periods of the planets, i.e., the lengths of time they take to complete their orbital paths. It had been known for centuries that the period of time varies for each planet and that the farther removed a planet is from the sun the longer the time required to complete its orbit. Kepler's goal was to determine the relationship between distance and time. As finally formulated after extensive observation and calculation, the third law reads, in mathematical terms: The squares of any two planets' periods of revolution about the sun are proportional to the cubes of their mean distances from the sun.

Having a deeply religious and even mystical nature, Kepler considered his findings to be incontrovertible evidence of the harmony of a perfect universe.

Any scientific explanation of the planets' movements escaped him, although he suspected that the sun exercises some physical control over the planets. Kepler, his spiritual beliefs not to be confounded by his scientific observations, finally came to express the belief that each planet was being held in its course by the governing power of a guiding angel. It remained for Newton's law of universal gravitation to demonstrate the physical relationship between the sun and the planets and to give the reason for the elliptical orbits.

Kepler's belief in a divine ordering of the universe is illustrated by an anecdote he relates. A new star has appeared in 1604 and the group of philosophers known as Epicureans offered a theory that the star was a fortuitous concourse of atoms. Kepler replied:

> I will tell these disputants, my opponents, not my own opinion, but my wife's. Yesterday, when weary with writing, and my mind quite dusty with considering these atoms, I was called to supper, and a salad I had asked for was set before me. "It seems then," said I aloud, "that if pewter dishes, leaves of lettuce, grains of salt, drops of water, vinegar, and oil, and slices of egg, had been flying about in the air from all eternity, it might at last happen by chance that there would come a salad." "Yes," says my wife, "but not so nice and well dressed as this of mine."

Dating from his first knowledge of it, Kepler was a thorough convert to the Copernican system. "I have attested it as true in my deepest soul," he wrote, "and I contemplate its beauty with incredible and ravishing delight." He went well beyond Copernicus, however, in his worship of the sun as the center of the universe. Kepler regarded the sun as God the Father, the sphere of the fixed stars as God the Son, and the intervening ether, through which he thought the power of the sun impels the planets around in their orbits, as God the Holy Ghost. It was a cardinal belief of Kepler's that God created the world in accordance with the principle of perfect numbers, so that the underlying mathematical harmony, the music of the spheres, is the real course of the planetary motions. This belief appears to have been the inspiring force in Kepler's life, that is, he was searching for ultimate causes, the mathematical harmonies in the mind of the creator.

Kepler's three famous laws were not by any means his only contributions to astronomy. Starting with the laws as a basis, he recalculated the motions of all the bodies in the sky and drafted the rules and facts by which their positions could be computed far in advance. This work was published near the end of Kepler's life as the *Rudolphine Tables*, named in honor of his and Brahe's imperial patron in Prague. Kepler was the first to show that the sun was more distant than had been previously estimated, though his own figure fell far short of the actual fact. He was among the first to notice the corona, the light that surrounds a sun in total eclipse. Further, he wrote an important work on comets, and noted that the tails of comets always point away from the sun.

In his writings, Kepler's mental processes are clearly revealed. He frankly describes his failures as well as his successes. Quite often he followed false trails before reaching his destination. He had tremendous patience and perseverance to go through a mass of routine computing without staff to assist him or any of the mechanical helps available in modern times.

The Copernican theory advanced rapidly after Kepler's laws became commonly known. The old astronomy was completely discredited, and to true men of science, Ptolemy and all that he stood for were gone. The astronomical structure that the medieval scholars and theologians had erected, after enduring for fifteen hundred years, had been destroyed by Kepler and such successors as Galileo and Newton.

26

Birth of Experimental Medicine
William Harvey (1578-1657)

Exercitatio Anatomica de Motu Cordis et
Sanguinis in Animalibus
(Anatomical Exercise on the Motion of the Heart
and Blood in Animals)

At the beginning of the seventeenth century, biological science and research were little more advanced than had been the study of astronomy prior to Copernicus. Physicians and medical schools still practiced and taught the anatomical and physiological theories concerning the heart, arteries, veins, and blood handed down from the great Asiatic-Greek physician, Galen, in the second century. For more than a thousand years, no substantial discoveries had been made to add to man's knowledge of blood circulation and the functions of the heart.

Aristotle thought that blood was made from food by the liver, that it flowed from the liver to the heart and went from there to all parts of the body by way of the veins. The arteries were regarded as the means by which a "spirit" or "very subtle essence" was distributed through the body. A third-century B.C. Greek physician, Erasistratus, taught that the arteries contained only air and the veins contained only blood—a theory probably based on the fact that the arteries in a dead body were found to be empty. Galen disproved the idea that the arteries contained air. Galen's other conclusions concerning the physiology of blood, however, were full of fallacies and continued to mislead the medical world for centuries afterwards. Thus the whole question was in a confused state when William Harvey appeared on the scene.

By 1600, the Renaissance in Europe had brought about an intellectual awakening immediately affecting the natural sciences. In Italy, fifty years earlier, the founder of modern anatomy, Andreas Vesalius, had disproved Galen's theory that there were pores in the septum of the heart which directly transmitted blood from the right to the left chamber. About the same time, Servetus, who was later burned at the stake for holding views considered heretical by the Calvinists, stated his belief that blood circulates through the lungs; he did not, however, recognize the heart as the pumping organ. Another important link was supplied by Fabricius of Padua in 1603, who discovered that veins have valves, though he misunderstood their purpose.

To the brilliant and incisive mind of the English physician William Harvey fell the task of discovering and formulating an orderly, systematic, and scientific set of principles which would finally unveil the mystery of blood circulation and of the various functions of the heart. As a young man, Harvey had gone to Italy to study medicine at the renowned University of Padua, for generations the medical center of Europe. There Harvey experimented on various kinds of animals and learned the art of dissection. Under the guidance and influence of the distinguished teacher Fabricius, his lifetime interest in the process of blood circulation was evidently aroused. Harvey graduated from Padua in 1602, returned to England the same year, received his medical degree at Cambridge, and in 1604 was licensed to practice medicine by the College of Physicians.

Harvey was fully acquainted with traditional views on the heart and arteries, and was ready to expose their errors. Theories of all kinds abounded, but there were three main causes of confusion: 1) the function of the arteries is to distribute air (Erasistratus), or "vital spirits" (Galen); 2) the arterial pulse was caused by expansion and contraction of the heart, motivated by a spirit; and 3) the only function of the ventricle is to "nourish" the lungs. It was generally believed that blood moved backward and forward in the body, by way of both the veins and the arteries, like the slow ebb and flow of the tides. Arterial blood from one side of the heart mixed with venous blood from the other side through minute pores. To natural facts there had become attached over the centuries much superstitious lore about the blood. More than any other part of the body, blood possessed a sacred quality, as is shown by its use in religious sacrifices and the pouring of blood upon the altars of the gods. Such ancient dogma had severely handicapped medical progress throughout the medieval era. Only a few brave souls had had the temerity to challenge and cast doubt on the precedents and sayings of the ancients.

The renascence of learning came to England later than to the continent, particularly Italy, but by the time of Harvey's birth in 1578 the nation was entering one of its greatest periods. Britain's naval might was established by the defeat of the Spanish Armada, English explorers were opening up new lands, and major names were flourishing in the literary world. The repression of thought, characteristic of preceding centuries, was beginning to lift, and men's minds were free, within certain limits, to create new ideas and to open new fields.

William Harvey's career as physician, lecturer, and writer spanned a fifty-year period. He married the daughter of Queen Elizabeth's personal physician, and subsequently served as a fellow of the Royal College of Physicians, physician to St. Bartholomew's Hospital, and physician to James I and Charles I. Throughout his life, however, Harvey was more fascinated by medical research and experimentation than by the practice of medicine. In 1616 he began lecturing before the College of Physicians on the circulation of the blood. His manuscript lecture notes still survive, written in an almost illegible mixture of Latin and English. The notes describe some of his experiments and reveal that by this date he had already become convinced of the validity of his now celebrated theories on blood circulation. "The movement of the blood," he wrote, "is constantly in a circle, and is brought about by the beat of the heart."

Twelve years passed before Harvey was ready to publish his conclusions. Why the long delay in reporting such a notable discovery to the world? There are various conjectures. Sir William Osler suggested that "perhaps it was the motive of Copernicus, who so dreaded the prejudices of mankind that for thirty years he is said to have detained in his closet the *Treatise of Revolutions*." In Harvey's own words, his theory of general circulation of the blood "is of so novel and unheard-of character, that I not only fear injury to myself from the envy of a few, but I tremble lest I have mankind at large for my enemies, so much does wont and custom, that has become as another nature, and doctrine once sown and that has struck deep root and rested from antiquity, influence all men." Neither was Harvey a man to rush into print lightly, for, in his opinion, "The crowd of foolish scribblers is scarcely less than the swarms of flies in the height of summer, and threatens with their crude and flimsy productions to stifle us as with smoke."

But eventually, after years of further experimentation and observation, Harvey decided the time was ripe. In 1628, in Frankfurt, Germany, there appeared a small volume of seventy-two pages, considered by many authorities not given to overstatement to be the most important medical book ever written. Naturally it was in Latin, the universal scholarly language. The full title was *Exercitatio Anatomica de Motu Cordis et Sanguinis in Animalibus*, "Anatomical Exercise on the Motion of the Heart and Blood in Animals." Exactly why it was issued in Germany is not known — perhaps because the annual book fair held in Frankfurt would insure its more rapid circulation amongst scientists on the continent. Harvey's atrocious handwriting was doubtless to blame for numerous typographical errors.

Two dedications graced *De Motu Cordis*. The first is to Charles I, in which the king in his kingdom is compared to the heart in the body, and this is followed by an address to Doctor Argent, president of the Royal College, "and the rest of the doctors and physicians, his most esteemed colleagues." In the latter statement, Harvey expresses the view that truth should be accepted regardless of its source and that truth is of more value than antiquity. "I profess," he said, "both to learn and to teach anatomy, not from books but from dissections; not from the positions of philosophers but from the fabric of nature." In this sentence, Harvey caught the design and spirit of modern scientific methodology.

An introduction and seventeen brief chapters, which make up the main body of the book, give a clear, connected account of the action of the heart and of the circular movement of the blood around the body. The introduction reviews the theories of Galen, Fabricius, Realdo Colombo, and other earlier writers, effectively demonstrating their errors.

In his first chapter, Harvey related some of the problems that had confronted him in his research:

> When I first gave my mind to vivisections, as a means of discovering the motions and uses of the heart, and sought to discover these from actual inspection, and not from the writings of others, I found the task so truly arduous, so full of difficulties, that I was almost tempted to think, with Fracastorius, that the motion of the heart was only to be comprehended by God. For I could neither rightly perceive at first when the systole (contraction) and when the diastole (dilation) took place, nor when and where dilation and contraction occurred, by reason of the rapidity of the movement, which in many animals is accomplished in the twinkling of an eye, coming and going like a flash of lightning.

Harvey at length became convinced that the heart's movements could be studied with less difficulty in the colder animals, such as toads, frogs, serpents, small fishes, crabs, shrimps, snails, and shellfish, than in the warm-blooded animals. In the former, he saw that the movements were "slower and rarer." The same phenomena were easily observable in dying warm-blooded animals, as the heart's action slowed down.

On the basis of his experiments, Harvey noted that the heart's contraction forces the blood out; as the heart contracts, the arteries dilate to receive the blood. The heart, a muscle serving as a kind of pump, forces continuous circulation of the blood. The blood impelled into the arteries gives rise to the pulse, "as when one blows into a glove." Contrary to the ancient ebb and flow belief, the movement is all in one direction. Harvey demonstrated that the blood passes from the left side of the heart through the arteries to the extremities, and then back by way of the veins to the right side of the heart. The direction of the circulation he determined by tying ligatures around arteries and veins at various points. The momentous discovery, in short, was that the same blood carried out by the arteries is returned by the veins, performing a complete circulation.

Harvey's description of this process is picturesque:

> These two motions, one of the ventricles, another of the auricles, take place consecutively, but in such a manner that there is a kind of harmony and rhythm preserved between them, the two concurring in such wise that but one motion is apparent, especially in the warmer blooded animals, in which the movements in question are rapid. Nor is this for any other reason than it is in a piece of machinery, in which, though one wheel gives motion to another, yet all the wheels seem to move simultaneously; or like the mechanism in firearms, where the trigger being touched, down comes the flint, strikes the steel, elicits a spark, which falling among the powder, it is ignited, upon which the flame extends, enters the barrel, causes the explosion, propels the ball, and the mark is attained—all of which incidents, by reason of the celerity with which they happen, seem to take place in the twinkling of an eye.

In thinking of the blood's movements as circular, Harvey may conceivably have been influenced by the ancient philosophers, such as Aristotle, who taught that the circular motion is perfect and the noblest of all movements. Harvey's contemporary, the astronomer Giordano Bruno, concluded that the circle is "the fundamental symbol and pattern of all life and action in the cosmos." It is significant that Harvey in his treatise uses such phrases as "motion as it were in a circle" and "motion of the blood we may be allowed to call circular."

Harvey's line of reasoning on the circulation was remarkably accurate on the whole, but there was one missing link. How did the blood get from the arteries to the veins? Harvey knew that the blood went to the arteries from the left heart and from the veins back to the right heart. However, he said, "I have never succeeded in tracing any connection between the arteries and veins by a direct anastomosis of their orifices." Lacking a microscope, he could not see the capillaries, the minute vessels through which the blood cells pass from the arteries to the veins, though he was convinced there must be such channels. The riddle was solved a few years after Harvey's death by an anatomy professor at Bologna, Marcello Malpighi. Examining a frog's lung under the newly invented microscope, Malpighi saw the network of capillaries connecting the arteries and veins, exactly as Harvey had predicted. Thus the final step in demonstrating the circulation of the blood was completed.

To win over the skeptics, further proofs of circulation were produced by Harvey. One was the application of what is known to scientists as the quantitative method. He demonstrated that in an hour's time the heart, in its some 4,000 beats, pumps out far more than the total amount of blood in the body. If the blood sent out by the heart in a single day is measured, the quantity is much in excess of all the food taken in and digested—thereby disproving the ancient Galen's theory. "In short," wrote Harvey, "the blood could be furnished in no other way than by making a circuit and returning."

Additional evidence of circulation comes from the effect of poisons on the body.

> We see in contagious diseases, in poisoned wounds, the bites of serpents or mad dogs, in the French pox, and the like the whole body may become diseased while the place of contact is often unharmed or healed.... Without doubt the contagion first being deposited in a certain spot is carried by the returning blood to the heart, from which later it is spread to the whole body.... This may also explain why some medical agents applied to the skin have almost as much effect as if taken by mouth.

Harvey's use of animals for experimental purposes was an innovation. He believed that "had anatomists only been as conversant with the dissection of the lower animals as they are with that of the human body, the matters that have hitherto kept them in a perplexity of doubt would, in my opinion, have left them freed from every kind of difficulty." Harvey may be rightly regarded as one of the founders of the science of comparative anatomy. He mentions, for example, experiments on sheep, dogs, deer, pigs, birds, chicks in eggs, snakes, fish, eels, toads, frogs, snails, shrimps, crabfish, oysters, mussels, sponges, worms, bees, wasps, hornets, gnats, flies, and lice.

> I have observed that there is a heart in almost all animals, not only in the larger ones with blood, as Aristotle claims, but in the smaller bloodless ones also, as snails, slugs, crabs, shrimps, and many others. Even in wasps, hornets, and flies, have I seen with a lens a beating heart at the upper part of what is called the tail, and I have shown it living to others. In these bloodless animals the heart beats slowly, contracting sluggishly as in moribund higher animals. This is easily seen in the snail, where the heart lies at the bottom of that opening on the right side which seems to open and close as saliva is expelled.... There is a small squid ... caught at sea and in the Thames, whose entire body is transparent. Placing this creature in water, I have often shown some of my friends the movements of its heart with great clearness.

Aside from his remarkable discoveries, Harvey's greatest contribution to science and medical research was his introduction of experimental or laboratory methods. He laid the foundation upon which for more than three centuries physiology and medicine have been built. The essence was as Harvey himself stated, "to search and study out the secrets of Nature by way of experiment." Medicine had a history going back several millenniums before the birth of Harvey. Physicians had learned to recognize and to describe accurately the principal diseases afflicting mankind. Observation, while important, is not in itself enough, and frequently leads to erroneous conclusions. This was the major difference between Harvey and his predecessors. Going beyond superficial observation, little handicapped by superstitions or by reverence for antiquated theories, Harvey drew up hypotheses and tested them by experiments. He was the first to adopt the scientific method of experiment for the solution of a biological problem. All his successors of significance since 1628 have followed the same path.

The reception of Harvey's discoveries at the time is of interest. His book was not a literary sensation; its profound import was probably not recognized even by Harvey himself. Some opposition rising from conservatism and prejudice was expressed. A contemporary society gossip, John Aubrey, wrote that "he had heard him (Harvey) say that after his book on the Circulation of the Blood came out, he fell mightily in his practice; 'twas believed by the vulgar that he was crack-brained, and all the physicians were against him."

The attitude of one of the intellectuals of the time was expressed by Sir William Temple, writing of the work of Copernicus and Harvey:

> Whether either of these be modern discoveries or derived from old foundations is disputed; nay, it is so too, whether they are true or no; for though reason may seem to favour them more than the contrary opinions, yet sense can hardly allow them, and to satisfy mankind both these must concur. But if they are true, yet these two great discoveries have made no change in the conclusions of Astronomy nor in the practice of Physic, and so have been but little use to the world, though, perhaps, of much honour to the authors.

For the most part, Harvey ignored his critics. The prolonged hostility of the University of Paris medical school, however, finally induced him to break his silence. John Riolan, professor of anatomy in the Paris school, had persuaded the faculty there to prohibit the teaching of Harvey's doctrine. In an attempt to overcome his objections, Harvey addressed to Riolan two *Anatomical Disquisitions* on the subject of the circulation of the blood. These were published in a small book in 1649, twenty-one years after *De Motu Cordis*. Therein, Harvey replied in detail to those who had condemned his work.

In the second of the *Disquisitions*, Harvey laments:

> But scarce a day, scarce an hour has passed since the birthday of the circulation of the blood that I have not heard something for good or for evil, said of this my discovery. Some abuse it as a feeble infant and yet unworthy to have seen the light; others again think the baby deserves to be cherished and cared for. These oppose it with much ado, those patronize it with abundant commendation. One party holds that I have completely demonstrated the circulation of the blood by experiments, observations, and ocular inspection against all force and strength of argument; another thinks it scarcely sufficiently illustrated, not yet cleared of all objections. There are some, too, who say that I have shown a vainglorious love of dissection of living creatures, and who scoff at and deride the introduction of frogs and serpents, flies and other of the lower animals upon the scene.... To

return evil speaking with evil speaking, however, I hold to be unworthy in a philosopher and searcher after truth. I believe that I shall do better and more advisedly if I meet so many indications of ill breeding with the light of faithful and conclusive observation.

Fortunately, Harvey lived to see general acceptance of his theories among those competent to judge them. His election to the presidency of the College of Physicians in 1654, three years before his death, is evidence of his high standing among his professional colleagues.

Also indicative of contemporary opinion is the Latin inscription on Harvey's tomb:

> William Harvey, to whose honorable name all academies rise up out of respect, who was the first after many thousand years to discover the daily movement of the blood, and so brought health to the world and immortality to himself, who was the only one to free from false philosophy the origin and generation of animals, to whom the human race owes its acquirements of knowledge, to whom Medicine owes its very existence, chief Physician and friend of their Serene Highnesses James and Charles, Monarchs of the British Isles, a diligent and highly successful Professor of Anatomy and Surgery at the College of Medicine at London; for them he built a famous Library and endowed it and enriched it with his own patrimony. Finally after triumphal exertions in observation, healing and discovery, after various statues had been erected to him at home and abroad, when he had traversed the full circle of his life, a teacher of Medicine and of medical men, he died childless on June 3 in the year of grace 1657, in the eightieth year of his age, full of years and fame.

There has been little of a basic nature added to Harvey's discovery of the circulation, though, of course a vast body of knowledge has accumulated dealing with the physiology of the heart, blood vessels, and lungs. Much is known now concerning the heart's structure, its behavior in health and disease, its complex movements, and the functions of the blood that were not even imagined in Harvey's day.

Nevertheless, as Kilgour commented:

> The direct contributions of Harvey's discovery to medicine and surgery are obviously beyond measuring. It is the basis for all work in the repair of damaged or diseased blood vessels, the surgical treatment of high blood pressure and coronary disease, the well-known "blue baby" operation, and so on. It is general physiology, however, that is most in his debt. For the notion of the circulating blood is what underlies our present understanding of the self-stabilizing internal environment of the body. In the dynamics of the human system the most important role is played by the fluid whose circulation Harvey discovered by a feat of great insight.

Perhaps no one has better summed up the meaning of Harvey's career to the progress of medicine than a great medical leader of our own time. In the annual

Harveian Oration delivered at the Royal College of Physicians in London, in 1906, Sir William Osler said of *De Motu Cordis*:

> ... it marks the break of the modern spirit with the old traditions. No longer were men to rest content with careful observation and with accurate description; no longer were men to be content with finely spun theories and dreams, which "serve as a common subterfuge of ignorance"; but here for the first time a great physiological problem was approached from the experimental side by a man with modern scientific mind, who could weigh evidence and not go beyond it, and who had the sense to let the conclusions emerge naturally but firmly from the observations. To the age of the hearer, in which men had heard, and heard only, had succeeded the age of the eye, in which men had seen and had been content only to see. But at last came the age of the hand—the thinking, devising, planning hand; the hand as an instrument of the mind, now reintroduced into the world in a modest little monograph of seventy-two pages, from which we may date the beginning of experimental medicine.

27

Beginning of Modern Scientific Method
René Descartes (1596-1650)

---

*Discours de la Méthode pour Bien Conduire sa Raison
et Chercher la Vérité dans les Sciences*
(A Discourse on the Method of Rightly Conducting the
Reason and Seeking Truth in the Sciences)

Mathematics is at the heart of modern science and has molded much of the human mind. Descartes, the greatest mathematician of his time, in his *Discourse on Method* paved the way for the application of the mathematical method to the investigation of scientific problems. In his *Origins of Modern Science*, Butterfield evaluates René Descartes' *Discourse of Method* as being "one of the really important books in our intellectual history," a ranking to which more than three centuries of pervasive influence bear testimony.

Descartes was reared and educated in a Jesuit college, and there, he tells us, "in one of the most celebrated schools in Europe," studied languages, mathematics, history, philosophy, theology, rhetoric, jurisprudence, and the sciences. "I had, in addition, read all the books that had fallen into my hands." Descartes felt, however, that instead of giving him "a clear and certain knowledge of all that is useful in life," his educational experience had been responsible for "many doubts and errors." Accordingly, "I entirely abandoned the study of letters, and resolved no longer to seek any other science than the knowledge of myself, or of the great books of the world."

Descartes was not alone in his skeptical attitude towards the sterile scholastic method handed down from the Middle Ages, a method whose remaining adherents absorbed themselves in endless hairsplitting in philosophy and theology, and who slavishly clung to the letter rather than the spririt of Aristotle's texts. Outside the schools, medieval scholasticism, with its sacred texts, its authorities, and its subtle definitions, was becoming increasingly discredited. The scientific revolution, beginning in the sixteenth century with Copernicus, hastened the process of disillusionment, and it was to this new world of science that Descartes naturally gravitated. The time had come, he was convinced, to attempt the construction of an entirely new philosophical system.

In the *Discourse on Method*, Descartes' basic assumption is that "Good sense is, of all things among men, the most equally distributed." He himself did not claim to have a superior mental capacity. But "to be possessed of a vigorous mind is not enough," Descartes declares. "The prime requisite is rightly to apply it." By describing his own thinking processes, he attempted to demonstrate how the ordinary individual can, alone and unaided, discover the truth.

Descartes' first step was to reject all ancient opinions, all the teaching that had been transmitted from the ancient and medieval world, and, with his mental slate wiped clean, to begin his thinking anew. The unreliable, the vague, and the imaginary could be eliminated only by what Descartes called "methodical doubt," a systematic skepticism which took nothing for granted except the existence of the doubter himself. "I think, therefore I am." As a historian of science, E. W. F. Tomlin points out in his *Great Philosophers*, "according to Descartes's New Method, the test of a truth was not whether it had been enunciated by Holy Writ, or St. Augustine or St. Thomas, or stated *ex cathedra* by the Supreme Pontiff, but whether it was coherent with itself and above all whether it was 'clear and distinct.' " Descartes did not advocate skepticism for its own sake; he doubted in order to find a firm basis for belief. One should, he held, trust only what can be observed with one's own senses; tradition does not make a thing true; its validity can be established only by rigid examination.

For objective testing of any opinion or theory, Descartes proposed four rules:

> The *first* was never to accept anything for true which I did not clearly know to be such; that is to say, carefully to avoid precipitancy and prejudice, and to comprise nothing more in my judgment than what was presented to my mind so clearly and distinctly as to exclude all ground of doubt. The *second*, to divide each of the difficulties under examination into as many parts as possible, and as might be necessary for its adequate solution. The *third*, to conduct my thoughts in such order that, by commencing with objects the simplest and easiest to know, I might ascend by little and little, and, as it were, step by step, to the knowledge of the more complex; assigning in thought a certain order even to those objects which in their own nature do not stand in a relation of antecedence and sequence. And the *last*, in every case to make enumerations so complete, and reviews so general, that I might be assured that nothing was omitted.

Commenting upon these four principles, the noted mathematician and philosopher Bertrand Russell says, "the second and third especially—divide difficulties into as many parts as possible and proceed from simple to complex—I personally have found it always necessary to insist upon with advanced students who were beginning research. Unless they were very able they tended to take vast problems far beyond their powers, and I find Descartes' rules exactly what one has to tell them."

Descartes was first and foremost a mathematician. One of the world's most original thinkers in this field, he created coordinate geometry, thereby uniting geometry with algebra. In his day, mathematics was the chief instrument used for discovering facts about nature. Characteristically, therefore, Descartes concluded that the mathematical method was the ideal tool to apply in every sphere of knowledge and that it would yield results of equal definitiveness and dependability in metaphysics, logic, and ethics. Like Galileo and Newton, he saw the universe as a gigantic machine in which everything is measurable; that which cannot be translated into mathematical terms is therefore unreal. According to this premise, the entire universe can be explained by mechanical and mathematical laws. Descartes' "vision of a single universal science so unified, so ordered, so interlocked," states Herbert Butterfield in his *Origins of Modern Science*, "was perhaps one of his most remarkable contributions to the scientific revolution."

Ironically, experimentation played a subordinate part in Descartes' own methodology. His insufficiency in this area was probably the result of his early educational preparation. Despite his avowed skepticism and his completion of numerous experiments, many of his accepted "facts" were actually uncritically accepted opinions of earlier scholastic writers. One of his odd theories, which had considerable vogue for a time, was that the moon and planets are carried around their orbits by "vortexes" in an unseen and unfelt substance called "ether." Even in scientific fields, Rufus Suter, writing in *The Scientific Monthly*, remarks, "the technique of pure mathematics is not enough when the thinker seeks to decode the laws of physics, chemistry, physiology, or of any other science treating of things in the physical world and presumably independent of our personal reasoning habits.... The thinker must quit his armchair and go into the laboratory." On the other hand, mathematical physicists, such as Albert Einstein, exemplify Descartes' method, depending upon little else besides pencil and paper to carry on their research. In general, however, a combination of mathematical and experimental methods adopted by later scientists, particularly in England, has largely superseded the strictly mathematical approach.

Descartes' true scientific spirit is exemplified by his statement that "the little I have hitherto learned is almost nothing in comparison with that of which I am ignorant," and he concludes the *Discourse on Method* by declaring: "I have resolved to devote what time I may still have to live to no other occupation than that of endeavoring to acquire some knowledge of Nature."

Descartes' significance in the history of science stems from his recognition that every great advance in scientific thought and discovery begins with doubt. Thus, Copernicus doubted that the sun goes around the earth; Galileo doubted that heavy bodies fall faster than light ones; and Harvey doubted that the blood flows into the tissues through the veins. Because he had a morbid fear of persecution by the Church for holding heretical views, Descartes was less outspoken, and some of his most important writings remained unpublished until after his death. His work in optics was of permanent value, but his greatest claim to fame and influence is based upon his purely philosophical contributions.

28

First Modern Chemist
Robert Boyle (1627-1691)

---

*The Sceptical Chymist: or Chymico-Physical Doubts
& Paradoxes, Touching the Experiments whereby Vulgar
Spagirists are wont to Endeavour to Evince Their Salt,
Sulphur and Mercury to be the True Principle of Things*

With the scientific achievements of Robert Boyle, the ancient grip of philosophy on science was further and irrevocably loosened. By the time of his birth, in 1627, Copernicus had published his heliocentric theory of the solar system, Brahe had recorded the motions of the planets, Kepler had proved that the planets revolve about the sun in elliptical orbits, Magellan had sailed around the earth, and Francis Bacon had published his influential discussion of inductive scientific methodology. In the following year, the publication of William Harvey's researches on blood circulation and his insistence upon actual laboratory experimentation went far toward emancipating biological studies. Everywhere the rapidly expanding field of science was affecting all branches of thought, and a revolt against scientific dogmatism was in progress.

But one area was scarcely touched by this ferment against dogmatism. Chemistry, riddled with fears, superstitions, and taboos, was kept in its infant state. The medieval cult of alchemy, with its attachment to mysticism and the occult, still swayed even the most sophisticated minds of the age, and, though emphasis had become increasingly directed toward the study of substances and their medicinal effect on the human body, the alchemists refused to give up the possibility of the transmutation of baser metals into gold and silver. Even Boyle was, to some extent, a child of his time, and not above recommending ineffectual nostrums and inept remedies for the ailments of his patients. But his keen mind and inexhaustible zeal for scientific experimentation helped raise chemistry to a science instead of a mere appendage to alchemy. Because of these qualities, Boyle played an instrumental role in establishing science as an inseparable part of man's daily existence, rather than as something apart and remote.

Boyle's scientific interests were all-encompassing. During his lifetime he conducted experiments in nearly every branch of science then known. His thirty published scientific treatises are principally concerned with physics, chemistry, physiology, and medicine, and his investigations led to discoveries concerning the effect of air in the propagation of sound, the thermometer, the barometer, freezing mixtures, the gas laws, phosphorus, phosphorescence, and electricity. Particularly significant is Boyle's law on gas, stating that the volume of gas varies inversely as the pressure.

Despite the range of his scientific talents, Boyle's first love was chemistry. His *Sceptical Chymist* is the best-known chemical work of the seventeenth century and the most influential of his extensive writings. The book is characterized by the scientific historian, William Wightman, as occupying "the same place in the history of chemistry as does Copernicus' *De Revolutionibus* in the history of astronomy."

In *The Sceptical Chymist*, Boyle undertook a critical examination of the two most popularly accepted chemical theories of his day: the Aristotelian and the Paracelsan or Spagyric. The book is written in the form of a dialogue between an Aristotelian, who believes that all matter is composed of four "elements" (earth, water, air, and fire), a Spagyrist, who supports Paracelsus' three "principles" (sulphur, mercury, salt) favored by the alchemists, and the sceptical "chymist." Boyle presides as chairman of the imaginary gathering, and addresses the others with these words:

> I am not a little pleased to find that you are resolved on this occasion to insist rather on experiments than on syllogisms. For I, and no doubt you, have long observed that those dialectical subtleties, that the schoolmen too often employ about physiological mysteries are wont much more to declare the wit of him that uses them, than increase the knowledge or remove the doubts of sober lovers of truth.

Among the alchemists and early chemists there was great confusion about the constitution of matter. The ancient Aristotelian theory held that all substances are compounded, in varying proportions of the four fundamental elements of earth, air, fire, and water. The physician and alchemist Paracelsus (1493-1541) increased difficulties by adding the three "principles," sulphur, salt, and mercury, to distinguish the separate qualities of the elements. As Boyle expressed the situation:

> Methinks the chymists, in their searches after truth, are not unlike the navigators of *Solomon's Tarshish* fleet, who brought home from their long and perilous voyages, not only gold, and silver, and ivory, but apes and peacocks too: for so the writings of several (for I say not all) of your hermetick alchemical philosophers present us, together with diverse substantial and noble experiments, theories, which either like a peacock's feathers make a great show, but are neither solid nor useful, or else like apes, if they have some appearance of being rational, are blemished with some absurdity or other, that, when they are attentively considered, make them appear ridiculous.

In *The Sceptical Chymist*, Boyle demonstrated the fallibility of the alchemistic theory that all mixed bodies could be analyzed into their elementary ingredients by reduction through fire. He further argued that no one had ever been able to divide gold into any four component parts, whereas blood could be reduced to more than four constituents. He concluded that many substances exist which are scientifically impervious to decomposition and that, until experimentation proved otherwise, these substances must be regarded as elements. In an effort to identify the elements, Boyle undertook extensive experiments (which he called "analysis") with every available substance: those that could be readily separated into simpler forms were designated compounds or mixtures; others, such as metals, remained unalterable, and they were classified as elements. Although in Boyle's day the embryo science of chemistry knew less than two dozen elements, his definition of a chemical element, as one which cannot be decomposed, still remains the accepted definition. One hundred six elements are recognized by modern chemistry. Today, however, the element is no longer considered to be the ultimate constituent, and it is believed that Boyle felt similarly.

Boyle was the first to use the term "analysis" in the modern chemical sense. Anything dissected, he held, would be found to consist of one or more elements, and the elements, such as sodium and chlorine (the elements composing salt), never change into anything else. The red mineral cinnabar is a compound, not an element, because it consists of two elements, mercury and sulphur. Boyle's *Sceptical Chymist* presents the first modern concept of an element; his hypothesis of matter was that "it consisted of atoms and clusters of atoms in motion and that every phenomenon was the result of collisions of particles in motion.

Other of Boyle's experiments provided further substantial advances in chemistry, among them being new data about the interaction of various substances. Demonstrations of the reciprocal effect of substances included, for example, the detection of hydrochloric acid by precipitation with silver solution, the isolation of iron by use of tincture of galls, and the exposure of various acids by means of paper dyed with vegetable coloring matter.

The value of Boyle's work to the science of chemistry is summarized by Wightman:

> His contributions to the progress of actual chemical discovery amounted to very little; but the progress of science depends not so much on the accumulation of facts as on the framing of clear and distinct general ideas which may serve as the framework for new facts.... In laying down guiding principles for the recognition by texts of distinct chemical individuals, Boyle made chemistry possible.[6]

Boyle viewed chemistry as an independent and vital science, thus freeing it from the limitations of alchemy and medicine. He demonstrated vividly the fruitfulness of the experimental method and cleared away a jungle of inhibiting theories. Henceforth, scientists would realize that "occult qualities" are nothing but "the sanctuary of ignorance." Boyle was the first to devote himself to chemistry for the sake of knowledge, and not with the object of making gold, the philosopher's stone, or an elixir of life.

Boyle's discoveries, aiming to elevate chemistry to a true science, were gradually accepted. The progress of chemistry was handicapped for a century, however, by a false theory, the so-called phlogiston theory. The essential point in this concept is that there is an inflammable principle, phlogiston, which escapes when a substance is burned. To regenerate a burned metal, for example, heating by some substance such as carbon, rich in phlogiston, is necessary. Antoine Lavoisier, late in the eighteenth century, conclusively disproved the phlogiston theory by showing that metallic substances actually are heavier after they are burned than before, by combining with oxygen in the air.

29

Taxonomic Pioneer
John Ray (1627-1705)

Historia Plantarum

Natural history classification is a monumental task. It is estimated, conservatively, that there are a million species of animals and plants, exclusive of a multitude of forms represented only by fossil remains. Aristotle emphasized the grouping of organisms on the basis of structural similarities. The Theophrastus classification of plants as trees, shrubs, and herbs persisted until the end of the seventeenth century. Until John Ray's time, in the second half of the seventeenth century, little progress of practical value had been achieved in classification, except by herbalists. Ray's labors, covering the classification of both animals and plants, paved the way for the great Swedish taxonomist, Linnaeus, a century later.

John Ray was born in Essex, the son of a blacksmith. His talents were recognized early, for he was sent on to Cambridge, later to become a Fellow in Trinity College and lecturer in Greek, Latin, and mathematics. From the beginning, he was also recognized as a naturalist of great promise.

At Trinity, Ray gathered around him a group of undergraduates, among them Francis Willoughby, later a close associate, all keenly interested in natural history. Together, the group drew up a scheme for the systematic investigation of the plants and animals of all accessible parts of the world. During a vacation period in 1658, Ray made the first of his mainly botanical tours, traveling on horseback through the Midland counties, North Wales, and the lowlands of Scotland, in search of rare plants and other natural curiosities.

Accompanied by Willoughby, Ray spent several years touring through the Low Countries, Germany, Switzerland, France, Bavaria, Italy, Sicily, and Malta. An expedition to the New World was planned to gather additional material, but was never realized, probably because of Willoughby's untimely death.

Though handicapped by limited means, Ray determined to complete the extensive enterprise which he and Willoughby had begun. The latter had left behind him incomplete works on birds, fishes, and insects. The first work, *Ornithologia*, completed and published by Ray in 1676, was designed to describe each species accurately. The *Ornithologia* was the first serious attempt at the classification of birds since the time of Aristotle, and has been called "the foundation of scientific ornithology." Willoughby had made a collection of pictures of birds and had others drawn for him by artists; a selection of these illustrations was included in the published work. Birds of all countries from which specimens were procurable were listed, along with such facts as measurements and weights, colors, external features, internal anatomy, descriptions of eggs, uses (medicine, cookery, falconry, etc.), and localities where found.

The ornithology takes occasion to explode a number of fables about birds, treated seriously by earlier writers on the subject. Gryphons, harpies, phoenixes, and rocs are omitted, and Ray expresses incredulity about the transformation of barnacles into geese, the renewal of their youth by eagles, the incessant flight of birds of paradise, the wool-bearing fowl, the antipathy between the lion and the cock, the six-months' sleep of the hummingbird, and the milking of goats by the nightjar or goatsucker. A fable, apparently going back to Aristotle, that some birds hibernate in the winter months did not die out until the end of the eighteenth century.

The second book left unfinished by Willoughby and completed by Ray, *Historia Piscium* (1686), treats of fishes in general and the cetaceans (whales, dolphins, porpoises, etc.), though Ray did not differentiate cetaceans from fishes. The authors had visited all the best known fishing areas in England, Holland, Germany, France, and Italy. There is little of an original nature, however, for much of the text is drawn from earlier writers. Reflecting a religious bias, the biblical story of Jonah is not dismissed, but it is concluded that the fish which swallowed Jonah must have been a shark, not a whale, because the whale has a very contracted throat and whales are seldom seen in the Mediterranean.

Willoughby had left only scattered observations about insects. Ray undertook to organize and supplement these fragmentary materials. Authorities agree that the *Historia Insectorum* (1710) added few important new observations.

Ray had acquired some experience in dissection, apparently without the use of a microscope, but by nature he was not an experimenter. His interests extended to the ecology, history, and physiology of his subjects, and thus he was more than a mere cataloger. Primarily, however, he was an enthusiastic collector and classifier, and here he showed his genius. Ray laid the foundation of modern descriptive and systematic biology, especially in botany. He was the first biologist to write treatises on the principles of taxonomy, that is the classification of animals and plants according to their natural relationships.

Ray's taxonomic concepts are exemplified in the three works discussed above, on birds, fishes, and insects, done to some extent, as noted, in collaboration with Francis Willoughby. These were carried further in his great three-volume work, *Historia Generalis Plantarum* (1686-1704). All the works combined represented by far the most complete and best-arranged survey of living nature ever attempted up to Ray's time. He was highly qualified for this monumental undertaking, possessing a talent for observation, extensive knowledge of the natural history of England and western Europe, and familiarity with the writings of ancient and modern naturalists. Important, too, was his willingness to accept new ideas, such as Nehemiah Grew's theory on the sexuality of plants, Marcello Malpighi's rejection of the ancient belief in spontaneous generation, and his own conviction that fossils were the remains of extinct species, not simply "sports" of nature.

In his series of works on systematic botany, Ray was the first to recognize the distinction between monocotyledons (plants having a single cotyledon or leaf) and dicotyledons (having two cotyledons or leaves) in the embryos of plants. By using also the root, fruit, flower, leaf, and other characteristics, he devised a natural system of classification and produced many of the plant orders still used by botanists. For the classification of animals, Ray made great use of comparative anatomy to develop a natural classification of quadrupeds, birds, and insects. He was the first taxonomist, in the case of mammals, to use such features as feet and teeth in distinguishing among ungulates, rodents, ruminants, etc., a method later adopted by Linnaeus.

The first volume of Ray's great history of plants, his *Historia Plantarum*, published in 1686, contained nearly a thousand pages. The second volume, of equal size, appeared in 1688, and the third in 1704. The three volumes contain descriptions of more than 18,000 species, far in excess of any previous work. Also of interest and importance is a fifty-eight page introduction, presenting virtually everything known during Ray's time of vegetable histology (the minute structure of plants), anatomy, and physiology.

L. C. Miall, in his *Great Naturalists*, comments: "Whatever his deficiencies, Ray did a useful service to systematic botany by gathering up all that he found valuable in his predecessors, producing thereby the best arrangement of plants hitherto published."

Natural history owes much to Ray, especially for fuller descriptions, better definitions, better associations, and better sequences. Miall finds him "the worthiest representative, with respect to knowledge at least, of systematic natural history in the seventeenth century."

30

Founder of Microscopic Anatomy
Marcello Malpighi (1628-1694)

Anatome Plantarum

The increasing perfection of the microscope during the second half of the seventeenth century opened up new worlds to conquer for a number of dedicated scientists. Among the most imaginative and creative was an Italian physician, Marcello Malpighi. Like his contemporary Anton van Leeuwenhoek, he was a pioneer in the use of lenses for examinng plant and animal tissues. The two men were alike also in both using a single lens and combinations of lenses and in the fascination which the study of the structure of living things held for them. Malpighi's researches, however, were more scientifically based.

Malpighi received his degree in medicine from the University of Bologna, and afterward was a successful practitioner and lecturer on medicine at several universities: Bologna, Pisa, and Messina. Toward the end of his career, he served as private physician to Pope Innocent XII.

The recently founded Royal Society in London was anxious to secure the cooperation of anyone who might aid in its prime object, the "advancement of natural knowledge." In 1667 the society invited communications from Malpighi. He accepted the honor with pleasure, and thereafter the results of most of his research were published by the Royal Society, by which he was elected a fellow in 1668. By that date, he had already demonstrated the existence and function of the capillaries connecting the arteries with the veins, the structure of the lungs, the layer of the skin in which is found the color of the Negro, and the surface protuberances, papillae, or taste buds of the tongue.

In his student days, Malpighi was greatly attracted to human anatomy. Because of the exceedingly complex nature of the subject, he decided to turn to the study of lower animals and then to insects. Not finding simple answers even in insects, he undertook research on plants, out of which came perhaps his most famous book, *Anatome Plantarum* in 1675-79.

When Malpighi was a student of anatomy it was believed that the lungs were a special kind of flesh, into which the ends of the small arteries, veins, and air tubes opened. The blood was supposed to mix with air before returning to the heart in the pulmonary veins. To resolve the mystery of how this theoretical process took place, Malpighi began to examine tissues from the lungs under his lenses. He soon discovered that they contained quantities of small air sacs. It was noted further than even the small arteries were divided into smaller and smaller tubes. Selecting one of the tubes, Malpighi followed its course; other tubes joined it until they were recognized as a small vein. Disproving the previous belief, the arteries and veins did not open into the tissue of the lung. They were connected by an intricate network of almost invisible vessels. In this way, Malpighi found the capillaries, the discovery for which he is most celebrated. William Harvey was convinced that the capillaries existed, but lacked the instruments to actually see them. Malpighi described the capillaries in letters written in 1660. Several years later, Leeuwenhoek, using a test tube and lenses, saw the capillary circulation in the tails of living tadpoles and fish. Blood circulation was no longer a mystery.

The demonstration of the capillary circulation in the lungs was the first discovery of prime importance ever made with a microscope since it completed Harvey's work on the circulation of the blood. Malpighi's own description of his find is dramatic:

> I see with my own eyes a certain great thing.... It is clear to the senses
> that the blood flowed away along tortuous vessels and was not poured
> into spaces, but was always contained in tubules, and that its
> dispersion is due to the multiple winding of the vessels.

The capillaries play a major role, it was eventually discovered, in the body's well being. Through the walls of these minute vessels there is a constant exchange of substances. Food and oxygen are brought to the cells and waste materials removed. Thus the nutrition of individual cells is dependent on the capillaries.

The first contribution sent to the Royal Society by Malpighi was a remarkable anatomical memoir on the silkworm. Similar studies were done on the embryology of the chick, the anatomy of the larval stages of insects, and the structure of glands. His versatility and genius are illustrated further by his studies on the anatomy of plants, the function of leaves, and the development of the plant embryo. According to one perhaps apocryphal account, while walking in a friend's garden Malpighi's attention was directed to a broken stalk of a chestnut tree, from which thread-like strands, now known as "vascular bundles," projected. When these were examined with a lens, Malpighi discovered the vessels with a spiral thickening-layer, leading him to do research on vegetable histology, a branch of anatomy dealing with the minute structure of plant and animal tissue. The same discovery was made almost simultaneously and independently by Nehemiah Grew, an English plant physiologist.

The microscope enabled Malpighi and other scientists of his time to obtain a much clearer conception of the structure of plants than had previously existed. It was assumed that there were close anatomical and physiological analogies between animals and plants. Sometimes, however, supposed analogies were misleading, such as the popular notion, eventually disproved by experiments, that the sap in plants circulates like the blood in animals. One critic, A. R. Hall, in his *Scientific Revolution*, remarks, "Malpighi, despite the excellence of his descriptions of the differing structures found in wood, pith, leaf and flower under the microscope, and of the germination of seedlings, thought too exclusively in terms of the animal form. Thus he wrongly identified the function of the spiral vessels that he observed in plant tissue with that of the tracheae in insects, and erected upon this identification a broad theory of the increasing specialization of the respiratory organs, reaching its climax in animals. He also tried to find in plants the reproductive organs familiar from vertebrate anatomy."

The microscopists in general and Malpighi in particular opened up many new paths to advance the development of biological studies. As evidence of his long-term impact, nearly a dozen structures in plants and animals are named for Malpighi, e.g., the Malpighian tubes, part of the execretory system in the bee; the Malpighian corpuscules of the spleen; the Malpighian pyramid of the kidneys; and the Malpighian layer of the human skin.

31

Pendulum and Light
Christian Huygens (1629-1695)

Horologium Oscillatorium
and
Traité de la Lumière
(Pendulum Clocks and Treatise on Light)

A contemporary rival of Isaac Newton's, though never achieving Newton's fame, was Christian Huygens, Dutch mathematician, astronomer, and physicist. In at least one field, the study of light, he proved the greater scientist.

Until the time of Huygens and Newton, only the most elementary facts were known about the principles, laws, and behavior of light. It was realized that light streams to the earth principally from the sun, it travels in straight lines, and is reflected from certain surfaces. Such phenomena as the rainbow, the aurora borealis, the shooting star, and the mirage remained mysteries. Typically, too, superstitions surrounded such spectacular events as comets, meteors, and eclipses. Comets, for example, were believed to be fire balls flung from God's angry hand, while eclipses were regarded as omens of some coming catastrophe.

Huygens was the son of a prominent Dutch family. At an early age he demonstrated enough genius in mathematics and astronomy to attract the attention of René Descartes and Spinoza, who predicted a great future for him. Throughout his career, Huygens' prodigious mental ability remained undiminished.

From his youth, Huygens was ambitious to advance astronomical knowledge. He was handicapped, however, by poor equipment. In 1655 he began working on the improvement of the telescope and found a new method of grinding and polishing lenses. Out of these improvements came his famous discovery of the rings of Saturn and the resolution into their true form of the abnormal appendages to that planet. The following year, 1656, Huygens was also the first effective observer of the orion nebula, and detected the bright region still known by his name.

For years, Huygens continued his researches on lenses and telescopes, becoming Europe's foremost authority on the subject. He produced lenses of enormous focal distances, mounted on poles and connected with the eyepiece by means of a cord, forming what were called "aerial telescopes." Three of his object-glasses, ranging in focal length up to 210 feet, are in the possession of the Royal Society, London.

Because he needed an exact measure of time in observing the heavens, Huygens began experiments with pendulums, continuing research started by Leonardo da Vinci and Galileo. Mechanical clocks, in common use, were crude. The problem of measuring time had not been satisfactorily solved, either practically or theoretically, during the Renaissance. As George Sarton comments, "many of the clocks, watches, clepsydras, and sundials made in this period were beautiful instruments, which have found a place in our museums, but they were not accurate timepieces."

The invention of the pendulum by Leonardo da Vinci and its development in Italy during the sixteenth century marked an advance, though any practical value had to await the theory and practice of pendulums in part by Galileo, but chiefly by Huygens. The latter's landmark work on pendulum clocks, *Horologium Oscillatorium*, was published in Paris in 1673.

As a result of Huygens' investigations into the mathematical properties of the curve known as the cycloid, he was able to invent the cycloidal pendulum, a time-keeping device that swung over wide distances. The invention dates from 1656, and the first "pendulum-clock" was unveiled in 1657. Other original discoveries were reported in the *Horologium*, including the first successful attempt to deal with the dynamics of a system. The concluding section, dealing with theorems on centrifugal force in circular motion, aided Newton in formulating his law of gravitation.

At the invitation of Louis XIV, in 1665, Huygens settled in Paris, where he became a member of the newly organized French Academy of Sciences. The next fifteen years were spent studying, experimenting, inventing, writing, and theorizing, combining remarkable mathematical power and practical ingenuity. In addition to perfecting the pendulum clock, Huygens invented the micrometer (an instrument for the precise measurement of minute distances) and the spiral watch spring, improved the air pump, continued to construct unusually powerful telescopes and lenses, and devised an almost perfect achromatic eyepiece, which still bears his name.

Of Huygens' various scientific theories, the most notable relate to light. In 1678, he presented to the Academie des Sciences his famous "undulatory theory," in which he attempted to answer the question "What is light?" Subsequently, his wave theory of light came into conflict with a contrary theory promulgated by Newton, leading to a historic and prolonged controversy.

An astronomer would naturally concern himself with light phenomena. What was the nature of the light from stars from immense distances away? Equally puzzling were the light of the moon and, most important of all, the light of day coming from the sun. Newton thought that light is due to infinitely minute particles constantly streaming off from luminous bodies, and that as these particles hit the eye we experience the sensation called light. This is known as the "corpuscular theory." Huygens' "undulatory theory" suggested that light comes to our eyes in waves, just as Newton had shown that sound comes to our ears in waves. According to Huygens, "light is a phenomenon of vibrations like sound, but simply on a different scale of size, the vibrations being ever so much smaller and more rapid."

Critics pointed out that there is a fundamental difference between sound and light. Sound is carried by air, which ends a short distance above the earth's surface. What would carry waves of light, say from the sun, millions of miles remote, or from the most distant star to the earth? Since there is no air between the sun and the earth, what medium exists to pass on the vibrations of the sun's light to the earth? In reply, Huygens hypothesized, "There is a medium and it pervades all space. It is highly elastic and extremely attenuated, passing between the particles of solid objects just as freely as it occupies outer space." This universal medium was called "ether" by Huygens, and the sun or any other source of light sets up vibrations in the ether. The vibrations are passed on with tremendous speed, which we now know to be about 190,000 miles per second. Huygens recognized that ether is not perceptible to the senses, that it cannot be felt or weighed or isolated. It pervades all space throughout the universe and permeates all material things.

A storm of controversy developed around the Huygens and Newtonian theories of light. The weight of Newton's superior reputation at first caused a balance of scientific opinion to favor the corpuscular over the wave theory. Long afterward, in 1850, Jean Léon Foucault of France finally settled the whole controversy, vindicating and validating Huygens' theory. The "principle of Huygen," as it came to be known, enabled its discoverer to prove the fundamental laws of optics. The theory assumed that every point on a wave front of light is a new source of wavelets and propagates an indefinite number of wave fronts.

Toward the end of his career, Huygens wrote in Latin a little book, published posthumously, entitled *Cosmotheros*, or fully translated into English, *The Celestial Worlds Discovered or, Conjectures Concerning the Inhabitants, Plants and Productions of the Worlds in the Planets*. The flights of fancy in that amusing work set a pattern long afterwards for the novels of Jules Verne and H. G. Wells.

Huygens was often in the shadow of Isaac Newton. They worked in closely related fields, but in a number of respects Huygens' contributions to science were of a different character and equally significant in their particular spheres.

32

First Microbe Hunter
Anton van Leeuwenhoek (1632-1723)

Epistolae ad Societatem Regiam Anglicam
(Letters to the Royal Society of England)

There are few lines in Enlgish literature more frequently quoted than Jonathan Swift's jingle:

> So, naturalists observe, a flea
> Has smaller fleas that on him prey;
> And these have smaller still to bite 'em,
> And so proceed *ad infinitum.*

The inspiration for this bit of doggerel was the microscopic studies of a Dutch amateur scientist and lens grinder, Anton van Leeuwenhoek, to whom historians have accorded such laudatory titles as "father of bacteriology and protozoology," "founder of microscopy," and "first of the microbe hunters." Leeuwenhoek's duties as a minor municipal official in Delft do not appear to have interfered with his avocation, a passion for constructing microscopes and for using them to observe natural phenomena, in which he indulged for most of his ninety-one years.

Though he was not the actual inventor of the microscope, Leeuwenhoek ground his own lenses, of quartz glass and diamonds, and perfected magnifying glasses of then unheard-of power: as high as two hundred and seventy to one. As a result, he was the first human being to see protozoa, bacteria, and many features of the minute structure of living organisms.

Leeuwenhoek's first step toward fame came through the intercession of Reiner de Graff, a fellow townsman already known in scientific circles. In a communication to Henry Oldenburg, secretary of the Royal Society of London, De Graff stated: "I am writing to tell you that a certain most ingenious person here, named *Leewenhoeck*, has devised microscopes which far surpass those which we have hitherto seen.... The enclosed letter from him, where he describes certain things which he has observed more accurately than previous authors, will afford you a sample of his work." The Leeuwenhoek letter describes the microscopic structure of a bee and of a louse. It was the first of several hundred communications, all in Dutch, the only language he knew, written to the Royal

Society by Leeuwenhoek over a period of fifty years. The letters, dealing with diverse chemical, physical, botanical, zoological, physiological, and medical topics, were originally published in the society's *Philosophical Transactions* and subsequently collected under the title *Epistolae ad Societatem Regiam Anglicam*. In 1680, the Royal Society unanimously elected Leeuwenhoek to membership.

Modern historians of science have said that Leeuwenhoek's investigations were scattered and unsystematic. Through his remarkable lenses he peered at everything, like a boy fascinated by a new toy. Nevertheless, despite his lack of scientific discrimination, the keen-sighted amateur naturalist was an indefatigable observer who faithfully recorded his microscopic adventures. Furthermore, every observation was verified with infinite care before being announced for publication.

Of the original discoveries credited to Leeuwenhoek, the most celebrated is that of the existence of bacteria and of protozoan life in the mouth and in water—his demonstration that the world is filled with a vast teeming universe of "little animals." Looking at a drop of rain water through one of his lenses, he found revealed an invisible horde of animal life, fast-moving creatures infinitely too minute to be seen with the naked eye. Leeuwenhoek called them "wretched beasties," and writes, "They stop, they stand still as 'twere upon a point, and then turn themselves round with that swiftness as we see a top turn round, the circumference they make being no bigger than that of a fine grain of sand." From his detailed descriptions, it is certain that he saw the three great morphological types—rod, spiral, and round—now called bacilli, spirilla, and cocci.

In a letter written October 9, 1676, Leeuwenhoek clearly and unmistakably describes both protozoa and bacteria. After noting the presence of three more or less recognizable types of protozoa, the author reports:

The fourth sort of little animals [bacteria], which drifted among the three sorts aforesaid, were incredibly small; nay, so small, in my sight, that I judged that even if 100 of these very wee animals lay stretched out one against another, they could not reach to the length of a grain of coarse sand; and if this be true, then ten hundred thousand of these living creatures could scarce equal the bulk of a coarse sandgrain. I discovered yet a fifth sort, which had about the thickness of the last-said animalcules, but which were nearly twice as long.

In another paragraph of the same letter, Leeuwenhoek describes spirilla, as well as bacteria and bacilli, discovered in pepper-water. The first representation of bacteria is to be found in a drawing accompanying one of Leeuwenhoek's communications, published by the Royal Society in 1683.

A later report, written in 1683, is also of special interest to the bacteriologist; it concerns the "scum from the teeth." Leeuwenhoek explains his research method:

'Tis my wont of a morning to rub my teeth with salt, and then swill my mouth out with water; and often, after eating to clean my back teeth with a toothpick, as well as rubbing them hard with a cloth.

Despite the elaborate cleaning operation, Leeuwenhoek found tartar still present between his teeth. In this matter suspended in rain water, he observed cocci, short rods, long thread-forms (*Leptothrix*) and spirochetes, from which he concluded that "all the people living in our United Netherlands are not so many as the living animals that I carry in my own mouth this very day." The findings were confirmed by an examination of matter from the teeth of several other persons, including an old gentleman who confessed to never having been guilty of cleaning his teeth.

Next to the observations on microbes, Leeuwenhoek's most significant claim to scientific renown is the first accurate description of the red blood corpuscles and observation of the capillary circulation. Harvey's *De Motu Cordis* in 1628 had speculated on the nature of the connection between arteries and veins that made blood circulation possible, and in 1661 Malpighi described the circulation of the bood in the capillaries of a frog's lungs. Twenty-five years later, Leeuwenhoek actually witnessed, with the aid of his microscope, the circulation of the blood in the capillaries of the tail of the tadpole and eel, the web of the frog's foot, the fins of fishes, the bat's wing, and the ears of young rabbits—all of which was duly recorded and passed on to the Royal Society. Thus he completed the proof of Harvey's theory of circulation developed a half-century earlier.

Almost everything that Leeuwenhoek saw under his microscopes was new to the world. In 1677 he described and illustrated the spermatozoa in dogs and other animals, although in this discovery Stephen Hamm had anticipated him by a few months. Disproving prevailing superstitions about spontaneous generation of low forms of animal life, Leeuwenhoek showed, for example, that the flea, "this minute and despised creature," did not consist of mere dust or sand but reproduced itself in the same manner as other winged insects and was "endowed with as great perfection in its kind as any large animal." He also recognized that the aphid was developed by parthogenesis, that is from unfertilized eggs; made accurate observations on the development of the ant and on the spinning and poison apparatus of spiders; investigated the generation of eels (at that time supposed to be produced from dew); discovered minute globular particles in fermenting liquids (he was the first to describe the yeast plant); and noted that reproduction of hydra, an aquatic animal, occurs by budding, without male intervention, and also that the hydra is the unwilling host of parasites one thousandth of its size. These were among the hundreds of marvels observed by Leeuwenhoek, all previously invisible to man's eyes.

Publication of his scientific discoveries spread Leeuwenhoek's reputation throughout Europe. As his biographer, Clifford Dobell, writes, "Kings and princes, philosophers and physicians and men of science, statesmen and clergymen and even common men went to see him and to look through his wonderful glasses."

Although he did not have the method and system of a modern scientist, Leeuwenhoek possessed a truly scientific spirit. In one of his letters he remarked:

> As I aim at nothing but Truth, and so far as in me lieth, to point out mistakes that may have crept into certain matters; I hope that in so doing those I chance to censure will not take it ill; and if they would expose any errors in my own discoveries, I'd esteem it a service; all the more, because 'twould thereby give me encouragement towards attaining of a nicer accuracy.

Though Leeuwenhoek was the first man to discover and observe the teeming new world of minute creatures, "some ferocious and deadly, others friendly and useful," as Paul de Kruif noted, there is no evidence that he theorized about their nature. He had found them in drinking water, in the mouth, in the intestines of frogs and horses, and in his own discharges. Nowhere, however, in the hundreds of letters sent to the Royal Society was there any hint of the harm that these mysterious little animals might do to men. Leeuwenhoek was cautious about calling anything the cause of something else. Modern research has demonstrated, of course, that thousands of microbes are responsible for hundreds of diseases.

Leeuwenhoek was grateful to the Royal Society for publishing his communicatons. He steadily refused to reveal the techniques by which he was able to construct such marvelous lenses, but in 1721, two years before his death, he directed his daughter to transmit a small cabinet to the society. The cabinet contained twenty-six microscopes. In a letter, he states that he ground each lens himself and that he extracted the silver in the mountings from minerals. Twenty years after the collection of microscopes was received by the Royal Society, they disappeared, leaving no record.

33

Observer of the Invisible
Robert Hooke (1635-1703)

---

*Micrographia: or Some Physiological Description
of Minute Bodies Made by Magnifying Glasses with
Observations and Inquiries Thereupon*

The Renaissance symbol of the universal man found a worthy exemplar of its ideal in Robert Hooke. His was one of the most inventive and farseeing minds in the history of physical science, and his contributions spanned the fields of physics, chemistry, meteorology, geology, biology, and astronomy. In addition, he was also a notable disciple of the arts, exhibiting skill as an architect, city planner, artist, and musician.

Hooke's astonishing versatility, however, was undoubtedly a source of weakness as well as of strength, for the fertility of his ideas was not always matched by the necessary determination and perseverance to carry them through to solid accomplishment in all the fields to which he devoted attention. Nevertheless, the range of his discoveries is amazing, and more credit belongs to him than to any other individual for the development of the modern scientific instrument.

One such instrument invented by Hooke was the first practical compound microscope, an apparatus responsible for his *Micrographia*, the first published work dealing almost exclusively with microscopical observations. The investigations described in this renowned work have earned Hooke a place beside such great founders of microscopic biological study as Anton van Leeuwenhoek in Holland, Marcello Malpighi in Italy, and Nehemiah Grew in England. Samuel Pepy's diary records how he sat up until two o'clock in the morning reading the *Micrographia*, "the most ingenious book that ever I read in my life."

Whereas Galileo, for the first time in history, was able to investigate the celestial world through the ground lenses of a telescope, Hooke and his contemporaries used the newly invented microscope to examine the hitherto unseen world of minute organisms. Their discoveries provided future scientists with an organized method of biological research.

In the *Micrographia*, Hooke predicted that, with the aid of lately perfected instruments, "the subtilty of the composition of Bodies, the structure of their parts, the various texture of their matter, the instruments and manner of their inward motions, and all the other possible appearances of things, may come to be more fully discovered." He required that the true scientist have "a *sincere* Hand, and a *faithful* Eye to examine, and to record, the things themselves as they appear."

The most celebrated and striking feature of the *Micrographia* is some sixty plates of microscopic objects, accurately and beautifully drawn by Hooke himself, with assistance perhaps from the famous English architect Sir Christopher Wren. The drawings depict a number of fundamental discoveries, many related to insect life. Among them are the compound eye of a fly, the foot of a fly, the sting of a bee, enlarged views of the structures of a flea (drawn nearly sixteen inches long), silverfish, and louse, the matamorphosis of gnat larva, and the progressive development of a mosquito. In the botanical kingdom, there are faithful representations of fungi, mould, moss, the sting of the nettle, pollen, seeds, leaves, the awn of the wild oat, and the construction of wood and cork. The facts illustrated won lasting acceptance; thus, Hooke's description of the structure of feathers remained standard for two centuries.

Hooke also examined inanimate matter such as rocks, snow crystals, raindrops, and textiles. He was the first scientist to study metals under a microscope: the point of a needle, the edge of a razor, and the minute spheres of steel struck off by a flint.

The discovery that permanently established Hooke's scientific reputation was his theory of the cell. The *Micrographia* records the first observation of the cellular structure of living tissue. Inspecting an exceedingly thin slice of cork under the microscope, Hooke was amazed to find it was composed of tiny "little boxes or cells" much like the compartments of a honeycomb. His use of the word "cell" is responsible for its application to the protoplasmic units of modern biology. Hooke's method of thin-sectioning or slicing to obtain a specimen for microscopic study has become a standard laboratory technique.

A certain amount of controversy has centered around the origin of the cell theory. Some biology textbooks still attribute the discovery to the German scientists Theodor Schwann and Mattias Schleiden. The record was cleared by Edwin Grant Conklin, a noted American biologist, who stated that Schleiden and Schwann's "theory was a special and in important respects an erroneous one. There is no present biological interest in their theory.... Cells were first seen, named, described by Robert Hooke 170 years before the work of Schleiden and Schwann. Hooke described among many other things the little chambers or cells which he had seen with his simple microscope in sections of cork."

Another widely prevailing misconception was that the early microscopists, such as Hooke and Nehemiah Grew, saw only the cell's outer membrane, and not the inner mass. Edwin B. Matzke, writing in *Science*, refuted this error by citing evidence from the *Micrographia* itself:

> From these quotations it is evident that Hooke and Grew fully realized that cells in living plants had contents. Of course they had no knowledge of the internal structure and organization of the cell, of its nucleus and other constituent parts, of the protoplast as we know it to-day. They apparently did not appreciate the importance of the cell as a unit in the organism. However, they thought of liquids or juices moving within the plant through the cells, foreshadowing, unconsciously, much more recent work on hormones, vitamins, viruses and the translocation of substances in plants.[7]

The fact that Hooke was at all times a humble servant of science is reflected in the closing words of the *Micrographia*: "Wherever the Reader finds that I have ventured at any small conjectures, at the causes of things that I have observed, I beseech him to look upon them only as uncertain guesses and not as unquestionable conclusions, or matters of unconfutable science."

The *Micrographia* is full of discoveries and inventions in various branches of science. It has particular interest for the biologist because of Hooke's application of his improved compound microscope to the study of plants and animals. One interesting example is Hooke's description of the development of mosquitoes.

The actions of the mosquitoe larvae first attracted Hooke's attention. He noted that the larvae hung suspended from the surface of the water with their heads downward. They reminded him of an American animal he had seen in London which suspended itself by the tail, evidently an opossum. Hooke also described the pupal and adult stages of the mosquitoe and raised doubts about the popular belief that mosquitoes were formed from decaying matter in the water, rather than developing from eggs.

Hooke's actual contributions to scientific thought were many. Except for development of the microscope for biologic studies and naming of the cell, however, he was a much greater physicist than a biologist.

34

Plant Anatomist

Nehemiah Grew (1641-1712)

The Anatomy of Plants Begun

By the second half of the seventeenth century, the world of the naturalists was expanding rapidly. The study of man remained the prime focus of biologists' attention, but increasingly the discoveries of the human anatomists and physiologists, the chemists, and the physicists were being complemented by researches on plants and lower animals. While the description and cataloging of flora and fauna remained the principal tasks, there was evidence of attempts at interpretation and deeper understanding.

A pioneer in this endeavor was an English plant anatomist and physiologist, Nehemiah Grew. Grew was trained as a physician and practiced medicine in Coventry and London. He appears to have spent most of his time, however, in the study of plants. Much of his research activity paralleled that of his contemporary, Marcello Malpighi in Italy.

Grew's writings show a strong religious orientation, perhaps reflecting the fact that he was the son of a Puritan minister. Henemiah relates that in 1664, while studying animal anatomy, it occurred to him that as both plants and animals "came at first out of the same Hand, and were, therefore, the contrivances of the same Wisdom ... it could not be a vain design to seek it in both"—a philosophical notion that sometimes led him astray in seeing exact analogies between the plant and animal kingdoms.

Grew began his plant observations by watching the germination of seeds in his graden, noticing differences between that of wheat and of the bean, recognizing the foliar nature of the cotyledons (the first leaf or one of the first pair of leaves developed in seed plants), and the existence in the seed-coat of the micropyle (the minute orifice in the integuments of an ovule through which the pollen tube penetrates to the embryo sac), naming the descending axis and the cellular tissues "extending much alike both in the length and breadth."

Grew describes seed, root, trunk, leaves, flower, and fruit in order. In the flower he distinguishes the calyx, the corolla, and the stamens, the last containing pollen. As to the uses of the pollen, Grew had no conception except to suggest it as an "ornament or distinction to us, or food for other animals," such as insects.

Grew was well aware that the work of naturalists up to his time fell far short of a true "knowledge of nature." In his *Philosophical History of Plants* (1672), he outlined some of the tasks, as he saw them, confronting workers in this field:

> First, by what means it is that a *plant*, or any *part* of it, comes to *grow*, a *seed* to put forth a *root* and *trunk*. How the aliment by which a *plant* is fed, is duly prepared in its several *parts*.... How not only their *sizes*, but also their *shapes* are so exceeding various.... Then to inquire, what should be the reason of their various *motions*; that the *root* should *descend*; that its descent should continue to be *perpindicular*, sometimes more *level*: That the *trunk* doth *ascend*, and that the ascent thereof, as to the space of *time* wherein it is made, is of different *measures*.... Further, what may be the causes as of the *seasons* of their *growth*; so of the *periods* of their *lives*; some being *annual*, others *biennial*, others *perennial* ... and lastly in what manner the seed is prepared, formed and fitted for propagation.

In his *Scientific Revolution*, A. R. Hall comments that many of the problems stated by Grew remain unsolved. Attempts at answers were made by Grew himself. One of his brilliant deductions was that plants reproduce sexually, the flower being hermaphrodite (containing both male and female reproductive organs), with the stamens acting as the male organs. Grew also examined plant substance by combustion, calcination, distillation, and other experimental methods of chemistry, but the techniques were too primitive at the time to be particularly useful. It was shown, however, that the matter of the pithy or starchy part of the plant was quite different from that of the woody or fibrous part.

Grew's religious convictions came through in his account of plant nutrition. As he saw it, there was no reason to think:

> that there is any contradiction, when *philosophy* teaches that to be done by *nature*, which *religion*, and the *Sacred Scriptures*, teach us to be done by *God*; no more, than to say, that the ballance of a *watch* is moved by the next *wheel*, is to deny that *wheel*, and the rest, to be moved by the *spring*; and that both the *spring*, and all the other *parts*, are caused to move together by the *Maker* of them. So *God* may be truly the *Cause of This Effect*, although a thousand other *causes* should be supposed to intervene. For all nature is as one *great engine*, made by, and held in *His Hand*.

Like Malpighi, Grew failed to recognize the cambium, the soft tissue which gives rise to new tissues (wood, bark, etc.) in the stems and roots of certain plants. Consequently, they both mistakenly supposed analogies with animal anatomy. On the other hand, Grew made a number of valuable observations; among them, he noted the alteration of the floral whorls; described a bulb as "a great bud underground"; and gave an account of winged and plumed fruits and seeds, and of the explosive dispersal of seeds. At one point, he drew a quaint analogy between a book and a plant, suggesting "that a plant is as it were, an animal in quires, as an animal is a plant, or rather several plants, bound up into one volume," a strange metaphor, though with some scientific validity.

Grew's earliest botanical researches were published in 1671 by the Royal Society, under the title of *The Anatomy of Vegetables Begun*, a work done for the most part without a microscope and containing three plates. The first chapter describes the germinating seed of the garden bean, followed by discussion of the stem, the bud, the leaf, the flower, the fruit, and the seed before germination. On the basis of this work, Grew was appointed by the Royal Society as curator of the Anatomy of Plants, at a salary of fifty pounds. Encouraged by favorable notice, he continued his researches and in 1673 published *Idea of a Phytological History Propounded, with an Account of the Vegetation of Roots.* The aim therein was to establish a basis for a natural system of classification which was to include ecology, properties, chemical characters, and both external and internal anatomy.

Subsequent writings by Grew were *The Anatomy of Leaves, Prosecuted with the Bare Eye and with the Microscope* (1676), *The Anatomy of Flowers* (1676), and *The Anatomy of Fruits* and *The Anatomy of Seeds* (1677). All these works and earlier writings in revised form were brought together and published in 1682 in Grew's best-known work, *The Anatomy of Plants Begun,* with 83 plates. "The beautiful and accurate draughtsmanship of the plates," remarks one commentator, "is a constant source of surprise to those seeing them for the first time."

Both Grew and Malpighi attempted to explain the functions of the structures they described, sometimes accurately and in other cases entirely mistakenly. For example, both believed that the sap was pumped through the vessels of the wood by a sort of rhythmical pulsation, corresponding to the circulation of the blood in animals. Since the plant has no heart, they invented the rhythmical squeezing of the wood vessels to take its place. Not long afterward, another biologist, Stephen Hales, showed that no such squeezing takes place and that there is no circulation in the plant comparable to blood circulation in animals.

35

System of the World
Isaac Newton (1642-1727)

Principia Mathematica

Of all the books which have profoundly influenced human affairs, few have been more celebrated and none read by fewer people than Sir Isaac Newton's *Philosophiae Naturalis Principia Mathematica* (*Mathematical Principals of Natural Philosophy*). Deliberately written in the most abstruse and technical Latin, profusely illustrated by complex geometrical diagrams, the work's direct audience has been limited to highly erudite astronomers, mathematicians, and physicists.

One of Newton's chief biographers has stated that when the *Principia* was published in the last quarter of the seventeenth century there were not more than three or four men living who could comprehend it; another generously stretched the number to ten or a dozen. The author himself admitted that it was "a hard book," but he had no apologies for he had planned it that way, making no concessions to the mathematically illiterate.

Notable men of science hold Newton to be one of the great intellectual figures of all time. Laplace, a brilliant French astronomer, termed the *Principia* "pre-eminent above any other production of human genius." Lagrange, famous mathematician, asserted that Newton was the greatest genius who ever lived. Boltzmann, a pioneer of modern mathematical physics, called the *Principia* the first and greatest work ever written on theoretical physics. An eminent American astronomer, W. W. Campbell, remarked, "To me it is clear that Sir Isaac Newton, easily the greatest man of physical science in historic time, was uniquely the great pioneer of astrophysics." Comments from other leading scientists over the past two-and-a-half centuries have been phrased in like superlatives. The layman must necessarily accept these judgments on faith, and on the basis of results.

Newton was born on Christmas day, 1642, almost exactly a century after the death of Copernicus, and in the same year as Galileo's death. These giants in the world of astronomy, together with Johannes Kepler, furnished the foundations upon which Newton continued to build.

Newton was a mathematical wizard in an age of gifted mathematicians. As Marvin pointed out, "the seventeenth century was the flowering age of mathematics, as the eighteenth was of chemistry and the nineteenth of biology, and the last four decades of the seventeenth saw more forward steps taken than any other period in history." Newton combined in himself the major physical sciences—mathematics, chemistry, physics, and astronomy—for in the seventeenth century, before the era of extreme specialization, a scientist could encompass all fields.

In his early years Newton saw the rise and fall of Oliver Cromwell's Commonwealth government, the Great Fire, which practically destroyed London, and the Great Plague, which wiped out a third of the city's population. After eighteen years spent in the little hamlet of Woolsthorpe, Newton was sent to Cambridge University. There he was fortunate to come under the guidance of an able and inspiring teacher, Isaac Barrow, professor of mathematics, who has been called Newton's "intellectual father." Barrow recognized, encouraged, and stimulated the growing genius of young Newton. While still in college, Newton discovered the binomial theorem.

Because of the plague, Cambridge was closed in 1665, and Newton returned to the country. For the next two years, largely cut off from the world, he devoted himself to scientific experimentation and meditation. The consequences were astounding. Before he had reached the age of twenty-five, Newton had made three discoveries that entitle him to be ranked among the supreme scientific minds of all time. First was the invention of differential calculus, termed "fluxions" by Newton because it deals with variable or "flowing" quantities. The calculus is involved in all problems of flow, movement of bodies, and waves, and is essential to the solution of physical problems concerned with any kind of movement. "It seemed to unlock the gates guarding the storehouse of mathematical treasures; to lay the mathematical world at the feet of Newton and his followers," according to one commentator.

Newton's second major discovery was the law of composition of light, from which he proceeded to analyze the nature of color and of white light. It was shown that the white light of the sun is compounded of rays of light of all the colors of the rainbow. Color is therefore a characteristic of light, and the appearance of white light—as Newton's experiments with a prism demonstrated—comes from mixing the colors of the spectrum. Through knowledge gained from this discovery, Newton was able to construct the first satisfactory reflecting telescope.

Even more noteworthy was Newton's third revelation—the law of universal gravitation, which is said to have stirred the imaginations of scientists more than any theoretical discovery of modern times. According to a well-known anecdote, the flash of intuition which came to Newton when he observed the fall of an apple led to formulation of the law. There was nothing particularly new in the idea of the earth's attraction for bodies near its surface. Newton's great contribution was in conceiving the gravitation law to be universal in application—a force no less powerful in relation to celestial bodies than to the earth—and then producing mathematical proof of his theory.

Curiously enough, Newton published nothing at the time on these three highly significant discoveries on the calculus, color, and gravitation. Possessed of an extremely reticent, even secretive nature, he had an almost morbid dislike of public attention and controversy. Consequently, he was inclined to suppress the results of his experiments. Whatever he published later was done under pressure from friends, and afterward he nearly always regretted surrendering to their entreaties. Publication led to criticism and discussion of his work by fellow scientists, something which Newton, with his sensitive nature, completely detested and resented.

Following the enforced isolation and leisure of the plague years, Newton returned to Cambridge, received a master's degree, and was appointed a fellow of Trinity College. Shortly thereafter, his old teacher, Barrow, withdrew, and Newton, at the age of twenty-seven, became professor of mathematics, a position which he held for the next twenty-seven years. For the next decade or two, little was heard of Newton. It is known that he continued his investigations of light, and published a paper on his discovery of the composite nature of white light. Immediately he became involved in controversy, first because his conclusions on the subject of light were in opposition to those then prevailing; and second, because he had included in the paper a statement on his philosophy of science. In the latter, he had expressed the point of view that the chief function of science is to carry out carefully planned experiments, to record observations of the experiments, and lastly to prepare mathematical laws based on the results. As Newton stated it, the "proper method for enquiring after the properties of things is to deduce them from experiments." While these principles are in complete accord with modern scientific research, they were by no means fully accepted in Newton's day. Beliefs founded on imagination, reason, and the appearance of things, usually inherited from ancient philosophers, were preferred to experimental evidence.

Attacks on his paper by such established scientists as Huygens and Hooke so angered Newton that he resolved to escape future irritations by doing no more publishing. "I was so persecuted," he said, "with discussions arising from the publication of my theory of light, that I blamed my own imprudence for parting with so substantial a blessing as my quiet to run after a shadow." He even expressed an acute distaste for science itself, insisting that he had lost his former "affection" for it. Later, he had to be "spurred, cajoled and importuned" into writing his greatest work, the *Principia*. In fact, creation of the *Principia* appears to have come about more or less by chance.

In 1684, through computations by Picard, the earth's exact circumference was determined for the first time. Using the French astronomer's data, Newton applied the principle of gravitation to prove that the power which guides the moon around the sun is the force of gravity. The force varies directly with the mass of the attracted bodies and inversely as the square of their distances. Newton went on to show that this accounts for the elliptical orbits of the planets. The pull of gravity kept the moon and the planets in their paths, balancing the centrifugal forces of their motions.

Again, Newton failed to reveal his phenomenal discovery of nature's greatest secret. As it happened, however, other scientists were engaged in a search for a solution of the same problem. Several astronomers had suggested that the planets were bound to the sun by the force of gravity. Among these was Robert Hooke, Newton's severest and most persistent critic. But none of the theorists had been able to offer mathematical proof. By now Newton had won considerable reputation as a mathematician, and he was visited at Cambridge by the astronomer Edmund Halley, who requested his help. When Halley stated the problem, he learned that it had been solved two years before by Newton. Further, Newton had worked out the principal laws of motion of bodies moving under the force of gravity. Characteristically, though, Newton had no intention of publishing his findings.

Halley at once recognized the significance of Newton's accomplishment, and used all his powers of persuasion to convince the stubborn Newton that his discovery should be developed and exploited. Moved by Halley's enthusiasm and with his own interest rekindled, Newton began the writing of his masterpiece, the *Principia*, termed by Lange "a veritable reservoir of mechanistic philosophy, one of the most original works ever produced."

Not the least remarkable feature of the *Principia* was that its composition was completed in eighteen months, during which, it is said, Newton was so engrossed that he often went without food and took little time to sleep. Only the most intense and prolonged concentration could have brought forth such a monumental intellectual achievement in so brief a period. It left Newton mentally and physically exhausted.

Furthermore, during the time of writing, Newton's peace of mind was intensely disturbed by the usual controversies, particularly with Hooke, who maintained he should receive credit for originating the theory that the motion of the planet could be explained by an inverse square law of attraction. Newton, who had finished two-thirds of the *Principia*, was so incensed by what he considered an unjustified claim, that he threatened to omit the third and most important section of his treatise. Again, Halley used his influence and prevailed on Newton to complete the work as first planned.

The role played by Edmund Halley in the whole history of the *Principia* deserves the highest commendation. Not only was he responsible for inducing Newton to undertake the work in the first place, but he obtained an agreement with the Royal Society to publish it, and unselfishly dropped everything he was doing to supervise the final printing. Finally, when the Royal Society reneged on its promise to finance the publication, Halley stepped in and paid the entire expense out of his own pocket, though he was a man of moderate means with a family to support.

Surmounting all obstacles, the *Principia* came from the press in 1687, in a small edition selling for ten or twelve shillings a copy. The title page bore the imprimatur of Samuel Pepys, then president of the Royal Society, "although it is to be doubted," remarked one commentator, "whether the learned diarist could have understood so much as a single sentence of it."

Any brief summary of the *Principia* in nontechnical language is a difficult, if not impossible, undertaking, but some highlights may be indicated. The work as a whole deals with the motions of bodies treated mathematically, in particular, the application of dynamics and universal gravitation to the solar system. It begins with an explanation of the differential calculus or "fluxions," invented by Newton and used as a tool for calculations throughout the *Principia*. There follow definitions of the meaning of space and time, and a statement of the laws of motion, as formulated by Newton, with illustrations of their application. The fundamental principle is stated that every particle of matter is attracted by every other particle of matter with a force inversely proportional to the square of their distances apart. Also given are the laws governing the problem of bodies colliding with each other. Everything is expressed in classical geometrical forms.

The first book of the *Principia* is concerned with the motion of bodies in free space, while the second treats of "motion in a resisting medium" such as water. In the latter section, the complex problems of the motion of fluids are considered and solved, methods discussed for determining the velocity of sound, and wave motions described mathematically. Herein is laid the groundwork for the modern science of mathematical physics, hydrostatics, and hydrodynamics.

In the second book, Newton effectively demolished the world system of Descartes, then in popular vogue. According to Descartes' theory, the motions of the heavenly bodies were due to vortexes. All space is filled with a thin fluid, and at certain points the fluid matter forms vortexes. For example, the solar system has fourteen vortexes, the largest of them containing the sun. The planets are carried around like chips in an eddy. These whirlpools were Descartes' explanation for the phenomena of gravitation. Newton proceeded to demonstrate experimentally and mathematically that "the Vortex Theory is in complete conflict with astronomical facts, and so far from explaining celestial motions would tend to upset them."

In the third book, entitled "The System of the World," Newton was at his greatest as he dealt with the astronomical consequences of the law of gravitation.

> In the preceding books I have laid down the principles of philosophy [science]; principles not philosophical but mathematical.... These principles are the laws and conditions of certain motions, and powers or forces.... I have illustrated them here and there ... with ... an account of such things as are of more general nature ... such as the density and the resistance of bodies, spaces void of all bodies, and the motion of light and sound. It remains that, from the same principles, I now demonstrate the frame of the System of the World.

Explaining why he had not popularized his work, Newton revealed that:

> Upon this subject I had, indeed, composed the third Book in a popular method, that it might be read by many, but afterwards, considering that such as had not sufficiently entered into the principles could not easily discern the strength of the consequences, nor lay aside the prejudices to which they had been many years accustomed, therefore, to prevent the disputes which might be raised on such accounts, I chose to reduce the substance of this Book in the form of Propositions (in the mathematical way), which should be read by those only who had first made themselves masters of the principles established in the preceding Books; not that I would advise anyone to the previous study of every Proposition of those Books; for they abound with such as might cost too much time, even to readers of good mathematical learning.

For this reason, the style of the *Principia* has been described as "glacial remoteness, written in the aloof manner of a high priest."

At the outset, Newton makes a fundamental break with the past by insisting that there is no difference between earthly and celestial phenomena. "Like effects in nature are produced by like causes," he asserted, "as breathing in man and in beast, the fall of stones in Europe and in America, the light of the kitchen fire and of the sun, the reflection of light on the earth and on the planets." Thus was discarded the ancient belief that other worlds are perfect and only the earth is imperfect. Now all were governed by the same rational laws, "bringing order and system," as John MacMurray said, "where chaos and mystery had reigned before."

A mere listing of the principal topics covered in the third book is impressive. The motions of the planets and of the satellites around the planets are established; methods for measuring the masses of the sun and planets are shown; and the density of the earth, the precession of the equinoxes, theory of tides, orbits of the comets, the moon's motion, and related matters discussed and resolved.

By his theory of "perturbations" Newton proved that the moon is attracted by both the earth and the sun, and therefore the moon's orbit is disturbed by the sun's pull, though the earth provides the stronger attraction. Likewise, the planets are subject to perturbations. The sun is not the stationary center of the universe, contrary to previous beliefs, but is attracted by the planets, just as they are attracted to it, and moves in the same way. In later centuries, application of the perturbations theory led to the discovery of the planets Neptune and Pluto.

The masses of different planets and the masses of the sun Newton determined by relating them to the earth's mass. He estimated that the earth's density is between five and six times that of water (the figure used by scientists today is 5.5), and on this basis Newton calculated the masses of the sun and of the planets with satellites, an achievement which Adam Smith called "above the reach of human reason and experience."

Next, the fact that the earth is not an exact sphere, but is flattened at the poles because of rotation, was explained, and the amount of flattening was calculated. Because of the flattening at the poles and the slight bulge at the equator, Newton deduced that the force of gravity must be less at the poles than at the equator—a phenomenon that accounts for the precession of the equinoxes, the conical motion of the earth's axis, resembling a gyroscope. By studying the shape of the planet, furthermore, the possibility of estimating the length of day and night on the planet was shown.

Another application of the law of universal gravitation was Newton's exploration of the tides. When the moon is fullest, the earth's waters experience their maximum attraction, and high tide results. The sun also affects the tides, and when the sun and moon are in line, the tide is highest.

Still another subject of popular interest on which Newton shed light was comets. His theory was that comets, moving under the sun's attraction, travel elliptical paths of incredible magnitude, requiring many years to complete. Henceforth, comets, which were once regarded by the superstitious as evil omens, took their proper place as beautiful and harmless celestial phenomena. By using Newton's theory of comets, Edmund Halley was able to identify and to predict accurately the reappearance about every seventy-five years of the famous Halley's Comet. Once a comet has been observed, its future path can be accurately determined.

One of the most amazing discoveries made by Newton was his method for estimating the distance of a fixed star, based on the amount of light received by reflection of the sun's light from a planet.

The *Principia* made no attempt to explain the *why* but only the *how* of the universe. Later, in response to charges that his was a completely mechanistic scheme, making no provision for ultimate causes or for a supreme creator, Newton added a confession of faith to the second edition of his work.

> This most beautiful system of the sun, planets, and comets could only proceed from the counsel and dominion of an intelligent and powerful Being.... As a blind man has no idea of colours, so have we no idea of the manner by which the all-wise God perceives and understands all things.

The function of science, he believed, was to go on building knowledge, and the more complete our knowledge is, the nearer we are brought to an understanding of the cause, though man might never discover the true and exact scientific laws of nature.

Brilliant achievement that the *Principia* was, it was not written in a vacuum, as Newton's most ardent admirers concede. I. Bernard Cohen stated:

> The great Newtonian synthesis was based on the work of predecessors. The immediate past had produced the analytical geometry of Descartes and Fermat, the algebra of Oughtred, Harriot and Wallis, Kepler's law of motion, Galileo's law of falling bodies. It had also produced Galileo's law of the composition of velocities — a law stating that a motion may be divided into component parts, each independent of the other (for example the motion of a projectile is composed of a uniform forward velocity and a downward accelerated velocity like that of a freely falling body). The afore-mentioned are but a few of the ingredients present and waiting for the grand Newtonian synthesis. But it remained for the genius of Newton to add the master touch; to show finally, and once and for all, in just what manner the ordered universe is regulated by mathematical law.

It was evident that the world needed, as Sir James Jeans described Newton, "a man who could systematize, synthesize and extend the whole, and it found him in superlative excellence in Newton."

Newton himself recognized that his "System of the World," his mechanics of the universe, was built upon the work begun by Copernicus and so notably carried on by Tycho Brahe, Kepler, and Galileo. "If I have seen farther than other men," Newton said, "it is by standing on the shoulders of giants."

In fact, the probable cause of the controversies that dogged Newton's life was the intellectual ferment prevailing in his time. The air was full of new theories, and many able scientists were exploring them. It is not surprising that two men would make the same discovery almost simultaneously and quite independently. Precisely this appears to have happened in Newton's two principal controversies, those with Leibnitz and Hooke. Leibnitz invented the differential calculus, and Hooke advanced a theory of universal gravitation, both somewhat later than Newton's, but announced to the world first, because Newton had neglected to publish his work.

The contemporary reception of the *Principia* was more cordial in England and Scotland than on the Continent, but everywhere slow. As Newton had foreseen, an understanding of it required great mathematical ability. The extraordinary nature of the performance was acknowledged, however, even by those who had only a dim conception of Newton's contribution. Gradually, scientists everywhere accepted the Newtonian system, and by the eighteenth century it was firmly established in the world of science.

After the *Principia*, Newton appears to have lost all active interest in scientific research, though he lived for forty years after its publication. During this period he was the recipient of many honors: he was appointed master of the Mint, knighted by Queen Anne, elected president of the Royal Society from 1703 until his death in 1727, saw publication of the second and third editions of the *Principia*, and, in general, was held in the highest respect and esteem.

Scientific discoveries in the twentieth century have modified or shown inadequacies in Newton's work, especially in relation to astronomy. Einstein's theory of relativity, for example, maintains that space and time are not absolute, as Newton had taught. Nevertheless, as various authorities in science and technology have pointed out, the structure of a skyscraper, the safety of a railroad bridge, the motion of a motor car, the flight of an airplane, the navigation of a ship across the ocean, the measure of time, and other evidences of our contemporary civilization still depend fundamentally on Newton's laws. As Sir James Jeans wrote, the Newtonian principles are "inadequate only with reference to the ultra-refinements of modern science. When the astronomer wishes to prepare his 'Nautical Almanac,' or to discuss the motions of the planets, he uses the Newtonian scheme almost exclusively. The engineer who is building a bridge or a ship or a locomotive does precisely what he would have done had Newton's scheme never been proved inadequate. The same is true of the electrical engineer, whether he is mending a telephone or designing a power station. The science of everyday life is still wholly Newtonian; and it is impossible to estimate how much this science owes to Newton's clear and penetrating mind having set it on the right road, and this so firmly and convincingly that none who understood his methods could doubt their rightness."

The tribute paid Newton by Einstein should remove any question of rival philosophies: "Nature to him was an open book, whose letters he could read without effort. In one person he combined the experimenter, the theorist, the mechanic and, not least, the artist in expression."

Newton's own estimate of his career, made near the end of a long life, was characteristic of his modesty: "I do not know what I may appear to the world, but to myself I seem to have been only like a boy on the seashore, and diverting myself in now and then finding a smoother pebble or a prettier shell than ordinary, while the great ocean of truth lay all undiscovered before me."

36

Plant Physiologist
Stephen Hales (1677-1761)

Vegetable Staticks: or, An Account of Some
Statical Experiments on the Sap in Vegetables

Stephen Hales belongs to a small group of late seventeenth- and early eighteenth-century naturalists—Nehemiah Grew, Marcello Malpighi, John Ray, and a few others—who were blazing new trails in plant and animal discoveries. All were stimulated and supported by the Royal Society of London for Improving Natural Knowledge by Experiment, founded in 1645. Hales has been termed the Harvey of plant physiology. His *Vegetable Staticks*, published in 1727, laid the foundations of the physiology of plants by making "plants speak for themselves" through his experiments.

Hales was a student of divinity at Cambridge when Newton was teaching there. Whether he came under the latter's direct influence is uncertain, but in any case he became thoroughly imbued with the scientific spirit, and learned as much about physics and chemistry as he did about theology. In 1708, Hales was appointed to the curacy at Teddington on the Thames, where he remained for the rest of his life, and where all his scientific work was carried on. He appears to have been an exemplary parish priest, fully discharging his duties to the poor. Nevertheless, he found time to proceed with a series of investigations in his garden at Teddington.

Hales' best-known experiments related to sap pressure. Nehemiah Grew had believed in the circulation of sap in plants, similar to that of blood in animals, and imagined that he saw the sap being pumped up the vessels of the wood by rhythmical squeezing. Skeptical of this conclusion, Hales undertook a series of ingenious experiments, and soon convinced himself that the sap did not circulate. Instead, it ascended and there was no pulsation in the wood vessels. There was, however, pressure that varied according to changes in temperature, light and darkness, seasons of the year, and other conditions. The continuous but varying stream ascended from the roots to the leaves where the surplus water was exhaled as vapor through the stomata.

The pressure exerted by the ascending sap and the rate at which it flowed were measured by Hales by means of a simple instrument called a manometer, consisting of a twice-bent tube, one leg of which was attached to the stem of the plant while the other hand contained mercury. At the start, the mercury was at the same level in both legs, but as the sap exuded from the stem it pressed the mercury down in the nearer leg and caused it to rise in the other. Thus, any variations in the heights of the mercury indicated variations in the pressure of the sap. Hales attached the manometers to several branches of the same tree and in that way was able to observe the variations of pressure in different parts under different conditions.

Hales had no knowledge of stomata (small openings in the epidermis of a plant) or chlorophyll (the green photosynthetic coloring matter of plants), and considered the leaves to be mainly organs of transpiration to raise the sap from the root through the stem by suction; still, he recognized that the air contributed to the building up of the plant, as well as the liquid absorbed by the roots. In that connection, he raised the question: "May not light, which makes its way into the outer surface of leaves and flowers, contribute much to the refining of the substances in the plant?"

Hales was mildly critical of the observations previously made by Grew and Malpighi, as he states in his *Vegetable Staticks*:

> Had they fortuned to have fallen into this statical way of enquiry, persons of their great application and sagacity had doubtless made considerable advances in the knowledge of the nature of plants. This is the only sure way to measure the several quantities of nourishment which plants imbibe and perspire, and thereby to see what influence the different states of air have on them. This is the likeliest method to find out the sap's velocity and the force with which it is imbibed. As also to estimate the great power that nature exerts in extending and pushing forth her productions by the expansion of the sap.

Fresh pure air was almost a fetish with Hales, for plants, animals, and human beings. When the Princess Augusta began laying out her botanical garden at Kew in 1761, Hales designed the flues for heating the "Great Stove." On another occasion, when the Royal Society was asked to investigate the high death rate in prisons, Hales, as a member of the committee to study the problem, invented a ventilator which was installed in Newgate Prison. Prior to its installation, seven or eight people had died there each week from "jail fever." The death rate dropped to about two a month after better ventilation was established. An improved version of the ventilator was installed in the holds of ships by Captain James Cook, the famous explorer.

Some years after his pioneer investigations in the plant world, Hales applied his "statical way of enquiry" to animals, in order to find the pressure of the blood in horses, dogs, and deer. The second volume of his *Vegetable Staticks* (1733) contains reports of experiments on the "force of the blood" in various animals, its rate of flow, and the capacity of the different vessels. On the basis of such research, it has been suggested that Hales should be regarded as one of the originators of experimental physiology. Beyond theoretical findings, too, Hales undertook practical applications, such as a search for a solvent for stones in the bladder or kidneys. According to the testimony of the sergeant surgeon to George II, a form of forceps devised by Hales extracted stones with "great ease and readiness."

Other Hales inventions included a "sea gauge" for sounding, and processes for distilling fresh from sea water, for preserving corn from weevils by fumigation with brimstone, and for salting animals whole by passing brine into their arteries.

Gilbert White, author of *Natural History of Selborne*, a younger contemporary, noted that Hales' "whole mind seemed replete with experiment," and continued:

> His attention to the inside of ladies' tea-kettles, to observe how far they were incrusted with stone, that from thence he might judge of the salubrity of the water of their wells—his advising water to be showered down suspicious wells from the nozzle of a garden watering-pot in order to discharge damps, before men ventured to descend; his directing air-holes to be left in the out-walls of ground-rooms, to prevent the rotting of floors and joints ... his teaching the housewife to place an inverted teacup at the bottom of her pies and tarts to prevent the syrup from broiling over, and to preserve the juice ... are a few, among many, of those benevolent and useful pursuits on which his mind was constantly bent.

In his researches on plant life, Hales owes little to his predecessors. His methods were original and precise. In summary, he marked and measured growing roots; used a graduated column of mercury to determine the amount of root pressure; and constantly weighed and re-weighed. With Hales, it became clear, for the first time, that green plants derive an important element of their food from the atmosphere, and also that the leaves play an active part in the movements of fluids up the stems and in eliminating superfluous water through evaporation. His many experiments with gases demonstrated the dependence of plants on air, and that plants inspire and give off "air."

37

Electrical Wizard
Benjamin Franklin (1706-1790)

Experiments and Observations on Electricity

The Grolier Club's list of *One Hundred Books Famous in Science* includes only five books of American origin, and a single title precedes the 1830s: Benjamin Franklin's *Experiments and Observations on Electricity, Made at Philadelphia in America* (1751), one of the most widely read and discussed books ever written on a scientific subject.

The highly versatile Franklin was both a scientist and an inventor; he created more useful devices than any American prior to Thomas A. Edison. The range of his scientific experimentation and study drew him into many fields—physics, chemistry, oceanography, geology, meteorology, astronomy, aeronautics, geography, and medicine—and to such practical applications as heating stoves, ventilation, treatment of lead poisoning, fertilizers, bifocal glasses, and lightning rods.

But it was in the field of electricity that Franklin conducted his most sensational and original scientific investigations. Though he devoted only a few years to science before his energies were almost completely absorbed by public affairs, Franklin's contributions to the understanding and possible uses of the new branch of knowledge won for him international fame. His imagination and mechanical ingenuity were brought into play at a critical moment in the history of electrical theory. As a side effect, Franklin's prestige in science was an important factor in his rise in politics and subsequently in his notable achievements as a republican diplomat in Paris.

Benjamin Franklin was nearly thirty-seven years of age when he first became aware of the "wonders of electricity." This occurred in a visit to Boston, probably in 1743, when he witnessed demonstrations by Archibald Spencer, a popular lecturer, who, as Franklin wrote, "was lately arrived from Scotland, and showed me some electrical experiments. These were imperfectly perform'd, as he was not very expert; but being on a subject quite new to me, they equally surpris'd and pleased me."

From *Famous American Books* by Robert B. Downs. Copyright © 1971, McGraw-Hill, Inc. Used with the permission of McGraw-Hill Book Company.

By this time, Franklin was an established businessman, a successful publisher and journalist, and a prominent citizen of Philadelphia. Earlier in his career, during a sojourn in England, he had become acquainted with a number of English scientists. After returning home he took the lead in forming a discussion club called the "Junto," which later became the American Philosophical Society, the first scientific society in America.

Shortly after Franklin's interest in electricity had been aroused by Spencer's demonstrations, he tried out some experiments on his own account with apparatus sent by Peter Collinson of London to the Library Company of Philadelphia, another organization founded by Franklin. All of Spencer's equipment was purchased by Franklin and added to the items acquired from London. For the next several years he and his friends carried on experiments with electricity, manufacturing for themselves any other equipment needed. Franklin writes, "I eagerly seized the opportunity of repeating what I had seen in Boston: and, by much practice, acquir'd great readiness in performing those also which we had an account of from England, adding a number of new ones."

In a letter to Collinson in March 1747, Franklin reports, "I never was before engaged in any study that so totally engrossed my attention and my time as this has lately done." Franklin promised to report to Collinson, a fellow of the Royal Society of London, "some particular phenomena that we look upon to be new," though he modestly admitted that it was possible "some one or other has hit on the same observations" in Europe. Collinson turned out to be a valuable friend. He not only provided the first equipment for Franklin's researches but communicated news of the latter's discoveries and theories to English scientists and to the Royal Society. Collinson was also responsible for collecting the reports from Franklin and having them published in book form.

Centuries before Franklin's time, men of scientific bent had been tantalized by the question, What is electricity? In the sixth century B.C., Thales of Miletus had found that amber, when rubbed, would attract such objects as pieces of dry leaves and straw. (The Greek word for amber was *elektron*.) Later experimenters learned that light objects could also be attracted by sealing wax rubbed with fur and glass rubbed with silk. These two discoveries led to further investigations. A rod of sealing wax rubbed with fur was held near a small pith ball suspended by a silk thread; strangely, the pith ball was repelled. The same test was made with a glass rod rubbed with silk; in this instance, the pith ball was attracted. The conclusion was drawn, therefore, that there are two kinds of electricity, one called vitreous (glass) and the other resinous (amber). This was the two-fluid theory of electricity—a theory later rejected by Franklin.

Immediately prior to Franklin's work in the electrical field, important advances had been made in the construction of large glass frictional machines, which could produce strong sparks and electrify various objects. A new device, invented by Pieter van Musschenbroek of Leyden in 1745, proved to be a major contribution for laboratory purposes. This was the Leyden jar, an instrument made of a glass bottle, coated on the outside with metal foil, and filled with metal shot or water into which a wire hook was inserted. The Leyden jar was a primitive condenser, capable of storing a large electric charge from frictional electric glass tubes. Long sparks could be produced by applying a conductor to the two sides of the bottle. Popular entertainers used the marvelous invention to electrocute chickens, roast steaks, set alcohol aflame, blow out flames, transmit shocks across streams, and produce mysterious lights in the dark. People suffering from paralysis were given electric shocks as a possible cure.

Franklin's scientific fame was first solidly established by his analysis of the Leyden jar. He proceeded on the assumption that electricity is a single fluid, not two. Step by step, Franklin discovered that the charge in a Leyden jar is negative on the inside and positive on the outside and that the two charges balance each other; that is, they are always equal. By testing the bottle one element at a time, it was found that the charge was not in the wire, the cork, the water, or the foil, but always in the glass itself. Franklin substituted glass plates for the bottle — thereby inventing the parallel-plate condenser — and showed that the charge resides in the glass because it is a nonconductor. This was a step toward the development of the battery.

The Leyden jar experiments were the origin of the series of electrical terms coined by Franklin, some of which became standard terminology. He was the first to designate the two states of electricity as *positive* and *negative*, and he introduced other, now everyday, words in the field of electricity: *armature, charge, discharge, condenser, conductor, nonconductor, electrical shock,* and *electrician.* As a graphic expression to describe the shock produced by a number of Leyden jars combined, Franklin took over a military term, *battery.* In a report to Collinson on April 29, 1749, he told of making, for the first time in history,

> what we called an electrical battery, consisting of eleven panes of large sash-glass, armed with thin leaden plates pasted on each side, placed vertically and supported at two inches' distance on silk cords, with thick hooks of leaden wire, one from each side, standing upright, distant from each other, and convenient communications of wire and chain from the giving side of one pane to the receiving side of the other; that so the whole might be charged together and with the same labour as one single pane.

Earlier, Franklin had written Collinson that he had "observed some particular phenomena, which we looked upon to be new." "The first," he continued, "is the wonderful effect of pointed bodies, both in drawing off and throwing off the electrical fire." Franklin demonstrated that sharply pointed conductors were more effective than blunt ones in the transmission of electrical charges across gaps. From his experiments with pointed conductors evolved both Franklin's greatest experiment and his most famous invention.

Scientists before Franklin had noted the obvious resemblance between the electric spark and lightning. Franklin, believing that they are identical, observed in one of his notebooks: "Electrical fluid agrees with lightning in these particulars: giving light, color of the light, crooked direction, swift motion, being conducted by metals, crack or noise in exploding, subsisting in water or ice, rending bodies it passes through, destroying animals, melting metals, firing inflammable flames, sulfurous smell." To demonstrate the truth of his theory that the thunderstorm and the artificial spark differ only in intensity, Franklin proposed an experiment. According to his hypothesis or "doctrine of points," lightning or electricity could be attracted from the air during a storm by means of an iron rod shaped like a needle placed at the top of a tall building. There was no spire in Philadelphia at the time high enough to attract the electrical charge, and Franklin was awaiting the construction of a steeple on Christ Church. The Franklin proposal for an experiment was published abroad, and a French scientist, Jean François D'Alibard, put it to a successful test. The identity of lightning and electricity was confirmed.

Meanwhile, back in Philadelphia, Franklin thought of a simpler method of drawing fire from the heavens—by a kite armed with a long point. The plan was to fly a kite as high as possible and by this means to reach an electrified cloud, in order to bring the lightning flash down to earth. The kite was made by stretching a piece of silk over two sticks placed crosswise. A pointed wire was fastened to the top of the kite, and to the lower end of the hempen kite string were tied a metal key and a piece of silk ribbon. As a thunderstorm approached, Franklin and his son William raised the kite, and when the string had become wet enough to conduct electricity, they were able to draw sparks from the key and to charge a Leyden jar from it. No doubt remained that lightning is attracted by metallic points, as are electric sparks.

The perils of the Franklin experiment have often been the subject of comment. If the hemp cord of his kite had been thoroughly wet, he could have been electrocuted. A Swedish physicist, G. W. Richman, visiting the Imperial Academy of Saint Petersburg, was instantly killed trying to repeat the experiment, when a flash of lightning reached him through a wire he was holding in his hand. Franklin used the precaution, however, of holding the kite by the piece of silk ribbon, a nonconductor, and standing inside a shed to keep himself dry while flying the kite.

As one of Franklin's biographers, Ralph L. Ketcham, pointed out:

> When Franklin proved that lightning was a great discharge of static electricity produced by natural movements of air, he placed electricity beside heat, light, and gravity as one of the primordial forces of the universe.... Lightning's dramatic effects, and the superstitions which had long surrounded it, heightened the awe with which its captor was sure to be held.

The practical-minded Franklin, after establishing the nature of lightning, at once began thinking of useful applications of his discovery. Since the experiment had proved successful, he wrote:

> If the fire of electricity and that of lightning be the same ... may not the knowledge of the power of points be of use to mankind, in preserving houses, churches, ships, etc. from the stroke of lightning, by directing us to fix on the highest parts of those edifices, upright rods of iron made sharp as a needle, and gilt to prevent rusting, and from the foot of those rods a wire down the outside of the building into the ground, or down around one of the shrouds of a ship, and down her side until it reaches the water? Would not these pointed rods probably draw the electricity silently out of a cloud before it came nigh enough to strike, and thereby secure us from that most sudden and terrible mischief?

Here was the concept of the lightning rod invented by Franklin, a device called an "electrical conductor" in the eighteenth century. A well-grounded, pointed metal rod alongside a house, Franklin concluded, can rob the clouds of their dangerous electrical charge before it can do any damage, exactly as under laboratory conditions one can draw off the charge from a metal sphere by a needle held in the hand. Actually, lightning rods do not "steal thunder" from the cloud but attract the actual lightning discharge themselves and conduct it safely into the ground.

The lightning rod was the first economically important application of electrical principles. It immediately became the popular symbol of Franklin's fame as an electrical wizard. Many people in Philadelphia were persuaded to use his newest invention, and in the summer of 1752 lightning rods were raised on the academy and statehouse spires. Over his own house, Franklin attached bells to the rod; when electricity from the skies was drawn off into the experimental bottles, the bells would ring. Nevertheless, acceptance of the protective rod was slow because of popular ignorance, superstition, and religious prejudice. Franklin felt vindicated to some degree when the British government contracted with him to plan a system of lightning rods for arsenals.

As news of the Philadelphia experiments traveled abroad, much interest began to be aroused among Europeans, especially in England and France. Peter Collinson shared the reports received from Franklin with other members of the Royal Society. Franklin's letters were cited in the Society's *Philosophical Transactions*, and they reached a wider public in the *Gentleman's Magazine*. In April 1751, a compilation was printed by Edward Cave in London under the title *Experiments and Observations on Electricity Made at Philadelphia in America, by Mr. Benjamin Franklin, and Communicated in Several Letters to Mr. P. Collinson, of London, F.R.S.* This eighty-six-page pamphlet was the first edition of probably the most famous and influential book to come out of America in the eighteenth century. The wide popularity of the book led to the publication of ten editions before the American Revolution — five in English, three in French, and one each in German and Italian.

Paul K. Conkin in his *Puritans and Pragmatists* concludes that Franklin's reputation in the field of electricity rests on two main achievements. First, during a period of "experimental ferment and theoretical confusion," he "contributed simple theoretical principles that successfully explained or predicted all but one of the existing electrical phenomena." Second, by proving the electrification of clouds, he made electricity a respected branch of natural science.

Franklin's modest approach to the study of electrical matters is revealed in an early statement: "In going on with these Experiments, how many pretty Systems do we build, which we soon find ourselves oblig'd to destroy! If there is no other use discover'd of Electricity, this, however, is something considerable, that it may *help to make a vain man humble.*"

A Nobel Prize-winning United States physicist, Robert A. Millikan, sums up Franklin's career as a scientist:

> Franklin lives as a physicist because, dilettante though he is sometimes called, mere qualitative interpreter though he actually was, yet it was he who with altogether amazing insight laid the real foundations on which the whole superstructure of electrical theory and interpretation has been erected.

38

Father of Systematic Biology
Carolus Linnaeus (1707-1778)

Systema Naturae
(System of Nature)

"Nomenclature," wrote Carolus Linnaeus, eighteenth-century Swedish naturalist, "is one of the foundations of botany." He went on to lament, "How great a burden has been laid on the shoulders of botanists by disagreements in names, which is the first step toward barbarism." It was imperative, Linnaeus held, that "botanists come to an agreement among themselves about the fixed laws in accordance with which judgment can be pronounced on names, that is to say, good names can be absolutely distinguished from bad ones, the good ones maintained and the bad ones banished without any exception, so that botany firmly built on immovable principles may remain a fortress inviolable and unshaken." To this cause, Linnaeus devoted most of an active career, striving to make order out of chaos by bringing systematic organization to an increasingly complex field badly handicapped by lack of logic and method.

Though Linnaeus is commonly accepted as one of the great figures in the history of science, his position is a peculiar one. It has been observed that his name is not associated with any epoch-making hypothesis, not with a single important discovery, and not with one fundamental law or generalization in any branch of science. Linnaeus' role was a different one. He is the only scientist of first rank whose work was almost entirely of a descriptive or classificatory nature. As Arthur O. Lovejoy pointed out on the occasion of the bicentenary of Linnaeus' birth, "He was an unsurpassed organizer, both of scientific material and of scientific research; he introduced form and order, clearness and precision, simple definitions and plain delimitations of boundaries, into sciences previously more or less chaotic or confused or impeded with cumbrous and inappropriate categories and terminology."

The lack of systematic terminology and nomenclature in the biological sciences early in the eighteenth century, when Linnaeus began his activities, paralleled the condition that Lavoisier later found in the field of chemistry. Plants and animals were called by long Latin names, containing as many as fifteen or twenty words, with no attempt made to show relationships among species. Rousseau characterized the prevailing scheme as "a tirade of Latin names which sounded like a conjuration of hobgoblins." The muddled situation was further confused by world travelers bringing back specimens of plants and animals that had never been seen before on the Continent. Schwartz and Bishop estimated that 6,000 plants had been recognized by the year 1600, and that in the century that followed some 12,000 more were discovered.

Attempts at classification were frequent but inadequate. In botany, schemes were developed to group plants by the colors of their flowers, by the shapes of their leaves, or by the presence or absence of thorns. More scientific was the work of several of Linnaeus' predecessors, on whose discoveries he drew, notably that of John Ray (1627-1705), the "father of English natural history," Joseph Tournefort (1658-1708), professor at the Jardin des Plantes in Paris, scene of many botanical researches in the eighteenth century, and August Quirinus Rivinus (1652-1723), noted German botanist. These three had made definite progress toward classifying the subjects of natural history.

It remained for Linnaeus, however, to conceive of the system of nomenclature which, with later corrections and modifications, has remained in use to the present day. This is the two-name or binomial method of naming organisms. Every plant or animal is given two scientific names in Latin, one for the species and the other for the group or genus within the species. To illustrate: man, standing at the top of the biological ladder, was termed *Homo sapiens* (reasoning man) by Linnaeus, and the orangutan was called *Homo troglodytes* (anthropoid man — reportedly to the disgust of many of Linnaeus' contemporaries). Primroses, *Primula*, were subdivided as *Primula vulgaris* (common primrose), *Primula farinosa, Primula veris*, etc. All roses are *Rosa*, with such sub-groups as *Rosa gallica* (French rose), *Rosa odorata* (fragrant tea rose), and so on.

Linnaeus first applied his system of binomial nomenclature to zoology in the tenth edition of his *Systema Naturae* (1758), having applied it to plants in his *Species Plantarum* (1753). The first edition of the *Systema Naturae* (1735) was only a dozen pages in length; the twelfth edition in 1766, the last issued during Linnaeus' lifetime, had grown to three volumes, totaling 2,400 pages.

More complicated was the matter of classification. Linnaeus' plan was to assign a plant's or animal's position in nature by class, order, genus, and species. Plants were identified by the number and position of their male stamens and female pistils, the class being based on the number of stamens and the order depending on the number of pistils. The arrangement by genera and species was determined by natural distinctions, providing a basis for the two-name scheme of identification.

Linnaeus recognized that his system of classification was an artificial one, and he regarded it simply as a temporary convenience to be supplanted by a natural system whenever the fundamental relationships of plants and animals should become better known. Darwin's theory of evolution in the nineteenth century provided some of the principles needed for a natural system, but the broad outlines of the Linnaean scheme were retained.

Despite the generally acknowledged value of his contributions, historians of science have been inclined to criticize certain aspects of Linnaeus' work. Typical is the American educator Andrew D. White's comment: "In the second half of the eighteenth century a great barrier was thrown across this current scientific progress — the authority of Linnaeus.... The atmosphere in which he lived and moved and had his being was saturated with biblical theology, and this permeated all his thinking." Reference here is to Linnaeus' contention that each species of animal originated from a single pair and to his citing as incontrovertible proof the

Mosaic account of the creation. The possibility of evolution did not occur to him; species could not change, new species could not be created, and none could disappear. In holding this view, a century before Darwin, Linnaeus was merely reflecting the persuasions of his own age.

Linnaeus has also been censured for limiting his work to naming and classifying, for his lack of interest in the physiology of plants and animals, for neglecting to make use of the microscope, and for failing to carry on laboratory experiments. But perhaps the critics expect too much. Linnaeus was preeminently a classifier, and believed that the groundwork of science required first of all the arrangement and naming of species. The study of natural history is indebted to him for three significant advances in science: the development of the principle of binomial nomenclature; the introduction of clear, terse descriptions; and the focusing of attention upon species, this last leading to increased interest in the question of their origin and paving the way for the theories of Darwin, Wallace, and others.

Linnaeus' influence on his own time and long afterwards was immense. He appears to have been an inspiring teacher, highly successful in publicizing his ideas, a prolific author, and a leader in organizing scientific expeditions to every corner of the world. He was also a supreme egotist; his arrogance has been compared to that of Dr. Samuel Johnson's. His contributions to biological science represented a great step forward, a foundation on which to build, but as William Wightman comments in his *Growth of Scientific Ideas*, "Forces were gathering — to which in some measure he yielded later in life — which were to break through his iron-clad system, whose very completeness carried the implication of its own destruction."

39

Spirit of Enlightenment

Denis Diderot (1713-1784)

Encyclopédie ou Dictionnaire Raisonné des
Sciences, des Arts et des Métiers
(Encyclopedia, or Systematic Dictionary of the
Sciences, Arts, and Crafts)

Denis Diderot has been called "the most typical, yet the least known, of the leading thinkers of the French Enlightenment." Of the four major prophets who prepared the way for the French Revolution—Voltaire, Rousseau, Montesquieu, and Diderot—the last, though the least brilliant writer, was the ablest organizer and the most effective journalist. His "role was greater than his work."

Though a prolific author on a variety of subjects, Diderot never created what may be termed a masterpiece. Of all his literary endeavors, his greatest contribution, unquestionably, was the editorship of the French *Encyclopedia*, the great rationalist compendium of the period of Enlightenment. To Diderot alone belongs the honor of conceiving, carrying on in the face of almost insurmountable difficulties, and finally completing this huge undertaking. "In accomplishing this extraordinary feat," remarked the American historian J. Salwyn Schapiro, "Diderot raised editorship from a critical function to a creative art of the first order." There had, of course, been encyclopedias prior to Diderot's work, but his striking innovations—making the *Encyclopédie* the collective work of famous specialists, and including articles dealing with science, agriculture, commerce, and industry—provided a model on which later encyclopedias of merit were patterned.

Diderot first became associated with the enterprise in about 1745. The original plan had been for him merely to translate into French the two-volume English Chambers' *Cyclopaedia, or Universal Dictionary of the Arts and Sciences*, but he persuaded the publisher, Le Breton, to produce a work more original and ambitious in scope and more distinctly French in outlook. Under his expert guidance, the *Encyclopédie* became the first large-scale synthesis of all knowledge.

In an article appearing in the *Encyclopédie*, Diderot described the aim of his work: "to assemble the knowledge scattered over the face of the earth; to explain its general plan to the men with whom we live, and to transmit it to those who will come after us, so that the labors of past centuries may not be useless to future times; so that our descendants, by becoming better informed, may in consequence be happier and more virtuous; and so that we may not die without having deserved well of the human race." In these lines was epitomized the spirit of the "Age of Enlightenment."

In his brilliant list of contributors, Diderot had to vie with sensitive and often conflicting temperaments. His colleagues included D'Alembert on mathematics, Turgot on economics, Quesnay on agriculture, Buffon on nature, Rousseau on music, Montesquieu on taste, and Voltaire on a variety of topics. Diderot himself dealt with philosophy, the arts, and industry. For diverse reasons, usually controversial, Rousseau, D'Alembert, and several others dropped out before the project was finished.

No other encyclopedia ever had such a stormy career. Embodying, as it did, the essential spirit of the democratic and scientific movement in France immediately before the revolution, bitter reaction from the entrenched forces of conservatism was inevitable. The powerful ecclesiastics and the despotic French court recognized instinctively that the work challenged blanket acceptance of the traditional explanations of natural phenomena and severely threatened autocratic authority. Directly or indirectly, numerous articles condemned religious intolerance, despotic government, arbitrary restrictions on the growth of commerce and industry, unfair taxation, and infringements on personal liberty. "Around the Encyclopedia," commented Lester Crocker, a Diderot biographer, "the greatest and most crucial fight of the century was waged," and Diderot was its hero.

The first volume of the *Encyclopédie* appeared in 1751, and the second followed early the next year. Then the Jesuits and absolutist critics bore down heavily. The King's Council forbade printing, reprinting, or sale of the *Encyclopédie* on the grounds that it tended "to destroy royal authority, establish the spirit of independence and revolt, and, under obscure and equivocal terms, lay a foundation for error, corruption, irreligion, and incredulity." The ruling applied, however, only to the first two volumes, and further publication was not specifically banned. Thereafter, a volume was issued each year until a second major crisis developed in 1759, caused by a new wave of repression. Publication was ordered suspended, and several of Diderot's collaborators, tired of suffering continual indignities, withdrew; the enterprise appeared doomed.

To circumvent the ban, Diderot and his publisher decided to print the remaining volumes in secret; the names of the editors and authors were omitted, and a false imprint of Neuchatel, Switzerland was inscribed. Not until 1772 was the complete series, consisting of seventeen volumes of text and eleven volumes of plates, off the press. It had occupied Diderot for more than a generation.

At the moment of apparent triumph, however, Diderot suffered the crowning blow when he discovered that Le Breton, apprehending government disapproval, had been systematically censoring copy for the encyclopedia after Diderot had returned corrected page proofs to him; though retaining its essential spirit, the work was irreparably damaged.

The *Encyclopédie* devotes much space to technical articles on different trades and manufactures of the period, to medicine, mathematics, physics, chemistry, biology, grammar, cookery, gardening, and numerous other subjects. Of primary interest today are the articles dealing with religion, philosophy, and political and social ideas. A small sampling of quotations follows:

On *Political Authority*: "No man has received from nature the right of commanding others. Liberty is a present from Heaven, and every individual of the human species has the right to enjoy it as soon as he enjoys reason." In condemning the cruelty of treatment of criminals in eighteenth-century France, the article on *Torture* states that this method is "a sure means of convicting an innocent man who is physically weak and of acquitting a guilty person born with great endurance." On *Sovereigns*: "Men have entered into society in order to be free, but experience always teaches us that the greater the power of men is, the more their passions lead them to its abuse." On *Consecrated Bread*: "Religion does not consist in adorning temples, in delighting the eyes or the ears, but in paying sincere reverence to the Creator, in following Jesus Christ." On *Almshouses*: "It would be far more important to work at the prevention of misery than to multiply places of refuge for the miserable." On *Man*: "The net profit of a society, if equally distributed, may be preferable to a larger profit, if it be distributed unequally, and have the effect of dividing the people into two classes, one gorged with riches, the other perishing in misery."

The influence of the *Encyclopédie* was by no means limited to France, but extended over the whole of Europe and to America. The English biographer Francis Gribble aptly said of Diderot that he was "the first great editor; and it is unlikely in view of the extraordinarily difficult circumstances surrounding his work—that there has ever been a greater one."

From the point of view of scientific thought, publication of the encyclopedia was a landmark. It collected and focused attention on many branches of knowledge. Most of the great French scientists of the period contributed articles. Science and technology as a whole are amply treated. A major result was greatly to encourage expansion of the crafts, sciences, and technology in the second half of the eighteenth century. It also left an unmatched record of the industry of the period. More than three thousand engraved plates graphically illustrate the current state of the arts and sciences.

40

Pioneer of Modern Geology
James Hutton (1726-1797)

Theory of the Earth; or an Investigation of the
Laws Observable in the Composition, Dissolution, and
Restoration of Land upon the Globe

An odd aspect of the history of science is that man's study of the earth and its physical characteristics did not, until relatively recent times, keep pace with astronomy, the study of distant stars. The fascination of the remote and unattainable far exceeded interest in the commonplace world. Theories were not lacking, however, on the origin of the earth. Among the bizarre hypotheses current in the eighteenth century, for example, was that in the beginning the earth was a solid mass of ice, becoming animated after being struck by a comet. Another held that the original globe was a mass of water, with vapors containing solid elements floating over it, and that eventually these elements precipitated to form a crust upon the water.

Great pains were taken, not only by theologians but even by most geologists, to reconcile any theory of physical geology with the Mosaic revelation, literally interpreted. If, as the theologians contended, the earth was created in 4004 B.C., its present state could be explained only by a series of cataclysmic events, perhaps an ocean which covered the highest mountains, devastating floods, earthquakes, and volcanic eruptions. Conceptions of natural phenomena were strongly influenced by the religious belief dating back to remote times that destructive geological occurrences had been inflicted on an erring humanity.

The first important effort to establish a scientific view of the operations of natural forces in the earth's geological history was made by a Scotsman, James Hutton, late in the eighteenth century. Hutton, trained as a physician, occupied his early years as a gentleman farmer. He settled on a farm in Norfolk where he examined chemically not only the nature of the soils on which he grew his crops, but also the peculiarities of the underlying rocks. Later he took over a small estate near Edinburgh, inherited from his father. For the next fourteen years, Hutton read all available treatises on geological subjects, especially the writings of French geologists, and attempted to verify their statements by his own first-hand observations.

As an increasing amount of time was being taken up by his studies, Hutton, at the age of forty-two, gave up his farm, moved to Edinburgh, and devoted the remainder of his life entirely to scientific research. He was a notably keen observer of natural phenomena, accustomed to going directly to nature to find the facts. His data were collected on extensive travels through Scotland, England, and the Continent.

Based on his observations of familiar ditches, pits, and river beds, Hutton recognized that the stratification of rocks and creation of fossils were processes still going on in sea, river, and lake. As he stated, "No powers are to be employed that are not natural to the globe, no action to be admitted except those of which we know the principle."

Hutton's general outline on earth structure was presented in preliminary form to the Royal Society of Edinburgh, an organization of which he was one of the founders. The paper was published in the society's *Transactions*, and immediately drew a scathing attack by a celebrated Irish chemist and mineralogist, Richard Kirwan. Hutton responded to the criticism by rewriting the whole paper in his great two-volume work, *Theory of the Earth*, issued in 1795. Literary critics have characterized the book as "appallingly repetitive and leisurely in style," "abstruse," and "almost unreadable," but as a trailblazer, exploring new frontiers in science, it has vital historical significance.

Hutton's announced purpose in the *Theory of the Earth* was "to examine the construction of the present earth, in order to understand the natural operations of time past; to acquire principles by which we may conclude with regard to the future course of things, or judge of those operations by which a world so wisely ordered, goes into decay; and to learn by what means such a decayed world may be renovated, or the waste of habitable land be repaired."

The scheme of the earth as outlined by Hutton is simple and convincing. His essential thesis was that the past should be interpreted, as far as possible, in the light of the present. The earth's features are constantly changing, he states in discussing erosion: "From the top of the decaying pyramids to the sea, throughout the whole of this long course, we may see some part of the mountain moving some part of the way." Rocks disintegrate, soil is carried away by rivers, coasts are worn down, and all loose material moves toward the sea. Through the action of wind, rain, and frost, and by chemical decomposition, mountains, rock, and soil are steadily wearing away, and the debris ends up on the ocean floor, where it forms strata or layers of rock. In the process, mountains are carved out and valleys formed.

If the changes described by Hutton continued indefinitely, with the earth disintegrating and filling up the oceans, eventually the earth would be covered with water. But, Hutton theorized, over eons of time, the process is reversed. The sediment in the sea is continually building new continents. Subterranean heat solidifies the ocean beds, and at times that heat becomes so intense that it produces volcanic upheavals, lifting the overlying rock masses. Evidences of the gigantic convulsions are rugged mountains, broken and tilted rock strata, and folds. Hutton dismissed as nonsense the "convulsions of Nature," "sudden and great catastrophes," and "universal debacles" previously used to explain these phenomena.

The general thesis propounded by Hutton is "that there is nothing new under the sun." What is occurring today is the same as what happened in past ages. Below the soil lie beds of limestone, sandstone, shale, or gravel, all derived from disintegrating mountains and lower lands. The rocks observed today are the consolidated sediments from rivers of the past, solidified by the weight of succeeding layers laid down on them over the ages. Hutton recognized primary and secondary rocks, all baked by subterranean heat and squeezed or crushed into cakes or strata.

Transformation of the earth's surface, continuing slowly but incessantly, in Hutton's view exhibited "no vestige of a beginning, no prospect of an end." None before Hutton had fully realized the immensity of geological time. In terms of geology, recorded history is only yesterday. "Time, which measures everything in our idea, and is often deficient to our schemes, is to Nature endless and as nothing," declared Hutton, for countless ages are required to form mountains, rocks, and soil.

Near the beginning of his *Theory of the Earth*, Hutton observes:

> A solid body of land could not have answered the purpose of a habitable world; for a soil is necessary for the growth of plants; and a soil is nothing but the materials collected from the destruction of the solid land. Therefore the surface of this land ... is made by nature to decay, in dissolving from that hard and compact state in which it is found below the soil; and this soil is necessarily washed away, by the continual circulation of the water, running from the summits of the mountains towards the general receptacle of that fluid. The heights of our land are thus level with our shores; our fertile plains are formed from the ruins of the mountains; and those travelling materials are still pursued by the moving water, and propelled along the inclined surface of the earth.

Such radical doctrine was too strong for most of the author's contemporaries to stomach. Hutton was soon charged with heresy for expounding ideas contrary to the Scriptures and was condemned as an enemy of religion. One critic pronounced Hutton's theories "not only hostile to sacred history, but equally hostile to the principles of probability, to the results of the ablest observations on the mineral kingdom, and to the dictates of rational philosophy."

A useful service was performed for Hutton, a few years after his death, by his friend John Playfair, who brought out a work entitled *Illustrations of the Huttonian Theory of the Earth*, discussing, explaining, and illustrating Hutton's beliefs. Written in a clear, readable, and understandable style, Playfair's book aided substantially in popularizing the Hutton thesis. Even so, the theories did not win wide acceptance for another fifty years.

With the progress of science, some of Hutton's views have been modified and a few rejected, but the essential features, for the most part, have been confirmed by later investigators. Though ignored or attacked by his contemporaries, Hutton's theory marks the beginning of modern geological science.

Hutton's "uniformitarian theory" became generally accepted after later scientists validated his views—notably, William Smith, who assigned ages to rocks according to their fossilized contents; George Cuvier, who reconstructed extinct mammalian forms from fossils and bones found near Paris; Jean Baptiste de Lamarck, who classified and compared recent and fossil shells; and Charles Lyell, who collected in his *Principles of Geology* all available evidence relating to the manner and extent to which the earth continues to be molded into new forms by water, volcanoes and earthquakes, as well as all known facts about fossils.

41

Analyzer of Water
Henry Cavendish (1731-1810)

Experiments on Air

One of the most eccentric characters in the history of science was a wealthy English recluse, Henry Cavendish, a striking contrast to one of his ancestors, the noted freebooter Thomas Cavendish, the second Englishman to circumnavigate the globe. Henry Cavendish belonged to one of the oldest families in England. He inherited a large fortune, to become the richest man in England, which gave him complete freedom to live as he wished—in solitude and retirement, completely absorbed in scientific research. Four years were spent at Cambridge, but Henry left without taking a degree because he was averse to the strict religious tests applied to candidates for degrees at the universities. Thereafter he lived almost continually in London.

Cavendish's scientific experiments are distinguished for their wide range and for their exceptional exactness and accuracy. The papers published during his lifetime form an incomplete record of his numerous contributions and discoveries. Many of the results he obtained did not become known until long after his death.

The subject of Cavendish's first recorded investigation was arsenic, about 1764. Two years later he began sending communications to the Royal Society on the chemistry of gases, one of his chief claims to fame. Three papers published in 1766 deal mainly with "inflammable air" (hydrogen), which he was the first to recognize as a distinct substance, and "fixed air" (carbon dioxide).

It was not until 1784 that Cavendish made his great discovery on the composition of water, which he announced in his work called *Experiments on Air*. For that purpose he made use of the knowledge gained from his previous experiments on the properties of hydrogen. He obtained hydrogen by pouring dilute sulphuric acid over zinc, and collecting the gas given off by means of a pneumatic trough. When he mixed a measured volume of this gas with about two and a half times its volume of ordinary air and set fire to the mixture, an explosion took place and the wall of the container became dim with dew, which was identified as water.

The next step was to determine the exact proportions of the two gases, hydrogen and oxygen. For that experiment, Cavendish invented an instrument which he called a eudiometer. A mixture of 195 volumes of oxygen and 370 volumes of hydrogen in a bell-jar was prepared, and from this reserve a pear-shaped bulb of the eudiometer was filled. All the ordinary air had been extracted with an airpump. A tap was then closed and an electric spark sent through the terminals. According to Cavendish's own words, the gas "lost its elasticity and became liquid water." The experiment was repeated a number of times with the same results. There was no question that the water was produced by the chemical union of two volumes of hydrogen and one volume of oxygen. The water formed, however, was distinctly acid, an impurity Cavendish identified as nitric acid. He also showed that the weight of the water formed is equal to the weight of the two gases that have disappeared.

This surprising and unexpected result, of the production of water from the newly discovered gases, soon became widely known and made Cavendish famous among his contemporaries. It was the key, finally, to the composition of water, which since ancient times had been considered a simple element. The discovery stimulated other scientists. Thenceforth, rapid progress was made in learning the composition of other bodies made up of gases.

Another Cavendish discovery was that a certain proportion of the mixture of air and oxygen remained unchanged even after long passage of the electric sparks. This substance called argon, was recognized as a separate element more than a century later. It is now known that argon is a regular constituent of atmospheric air very similar to nitrogen.

An entirely different kind of investigation, and Cavendish's last great achievement, was his series of experiments to determine the density of the earth, published in 1798. The work, which occupied his last years, required great skill in the art of quantitative observation. The ingenious apparatus used measured the force of gravity between two terrestrial masses small enough to be contained in an ordinary room. Newton had shown earlier in his study of celestial bodies that two masses exert an attraction upon one another dependent upon their magnitude and distance apart. The proof of the force, however, had not been demonstrated experimentally.

Cavendish's research concluded that the mean density of the earth is about 5.5, a figure confirmed by much later measurements, often by means of very different methods. It is theorized that since the mean density of all substances on the surface of the earth is much smaller, heavy substances, doubtless metals, must be predominant in the center of the earth. This is a logical conclusion, if the earth was originally a molten mass and the heavy substances collected near its center. We know from the findings of Cavendish and his successors that these substances must be present in disproportionate amounts in the earth's interior.

Cavendish was a superb experimenter. Science to him was primarily a matter of measurement. For example, he gathered hundreds of samples of air from as many different places as he could reach, and then subjected the samples to numerous experiments, weightings, and calculations. He was led to the conclusion that the atmosphere has an almost uniform composition, despite its complex nature. Cavendish was the first accurate analyst of the air. He discovered that air contains twenty percent oxygen by firing it with pure oxygen in a glass tube. The nitrogen of the air was changed into nitrous acid by repeated sparking of the air in an enclosed vessel. The experiments were made possible by the use of the Leyden jar, invented by a Dutch physicist, which produced sparks of electricity at the operator's will.

Cavendish's work on electricity remained unpublished until 1879. His papers in that field reveal that he anticipated the discoveries of Michael Faraday and others. He investigated the capacity of condensers and constructed a series of condensers with which to measure the capacity of various pieces of apparatus. The idea of potential was introduced by him in 1771 in a paper entitled "Attempt to Explain Some of the Principal Phenomena of Electricity by Means of an Elastic Fluid." Also investigated was the power of different substances to conduct electrical discharges. Cavendish also had considerable interest in geology and made several tours in England to explore various geological phenomena, though he does not appear to have published in this field.

In summary, Henry Cavendish was a scientist of amazing genius and versatility. He determined the specific gravity of hydrogen (the true nature of which he was the first to recognize) and carbon dioxide; discovered that water is produced by the union of hydrogen and oxygen; discovered the composition of nitric acid; isolated the element argon; anticipated certain researches in electricity; and devised experiments to measure the density of the earth. His scientific curiosity knew no bounds.

42

Architect of Modern Chemistry
Antoine Laurent Lavoisier (1743-1794)

Traité Élémentaire de Chimie
(Elementary Treatise of Chemistry)

On May 8, 1794, in the midst of the revolutionary Reign of Terror in France, Antoine Laurent Lavoisier was guillotined because of his prior association with the deposed government. Hearing of his friend's death, the mathematical genius Lagrange exclaimed: "It took a moment to cut off that head, but it will take France a century to produce another like it." Lagrange underestimated, for it is nearly two hundred years later, and no figure comparable to Lavoisier has yet appeared.

When Lavoisier was born, in 1743, chemical thought was, in many respects, still medieval. Chemistry was regarded as no more than an adjunct to medicine. The state of the art may be judged from an episode in England, where in 1739 a woman chemist, Joanna Stephens, was awarded a £5,000 prize for a "scientific remedy" that had "cured Mr. Walpole, the Prime Minister, who had been suffering from the stone." The ingredients included "Eggshells and Snails, a Ball of Soap, Swines' Cresses burnt to a Blackness, Burdock Seeds and Honey." Other chemists of the period claimed to be able to transform one element into another; to transform water into wood; and to transmute water into earth.

Scientific chemistry did not, however, originate with Lavoisier. Since the beginning of the seventeenth century, such men as Van Helmont, Boyle, Glauber, Lemery, and Stahl had been developing an important body of chemical knowledge. Lavoisier's own investigations were substantially aided by the discoveries of some of his contemporaries, notably Black, Priestley, and Cavendish. It has been remarked, in fact, that Lavoisier "discovered no new substances, devised no really novel apparatus, and worked out no improved methods of preparation." His major contribution consisted in establishing order among the experiments that had preceded him and in drawing from them meanings which were to place chemistry on a new foundation.

When Lavoisier began his work, the doctrine of phlogiston was the dominant theory in chemistry. The idea was an ancient one: that all things that burned contained an essence of fire called "phlogiston," which flowed out of inflammable substances as they burned. The more inflammable the substance, the more phlogiston was supposed to be present. Georg Ernst Stahl (1660-1734), the originator of the notion, argued that differing substances—wood, metal, coal, paper, cloth—can be burned and therefore must have phlogiston in common. In his view, the ash which remains when wood is burned, for example, is the original substance minus phlogiston.

It was Lavoisier who completely demolished the phlogiston theory and who first presented the true explanation of combustion. "Chemists have made phlogiston a vague principle," he objected, "which is not strictly defined and which consequently fits all the explanations required of it; sometimes the principle has weight, sometimes it has not.... It is a veritable Proteus that changes its form every instant. It is time to lead chemistry back to a stricter way of thinking." Burning, stated Lavoisier, is the union of the burning substance with oxygen, the name he gave to the "dephlogisticated air" discovered by Joseph Priestley. Using extremely delicate balances, he observed that the ashes of burned-out metals weighed more than the original metal because of the weight of the air which combined with the burning body. Combustion, whether it takes place inside the body, a furnace, or an engine, was thus seen as a chemical combination of other elements with oxygen. The process, known as oxidation, occurs at different rates of speed—slowly, as when iron rusts, or rapidly, as when gasoline explodes. Lavoisier also concluded that respiration in animals is a kind of slow combustion.

The explanation for the combustion of "inflammable air" (hydrogen) came to Lavoisier when he heard of Cavendish's discovery that the burning of inflammable air produced pure water. Lavoisier experimented and concluded that water is a compound of the two gases, oxygen and hydrogen.

From his various experiments, Lavoisier evolved the law of the conservation of matter, a cornerstone of modern chemistry—not a new concept, but one which had never before been so accurately demonstrated. The principle makes possible the expression of chemical changes in the form of equations in which the combined weight of materials used must be equal to the total weight of the products. Again, by resorting to his balance, Lavoisier showed that every chemical operation ends in an equation, and though matter may be altered by the chemical process, it does not change in amount. Briefly stated, matter can neither be created nor destroyed. Even life moves in a circle—dust to dust.

Lavoisier's success in establishing the composition of water and other compounds and formulating the law of the conservation of matter was immensely facilitated by his three delicate balances, the most sensitive of which could weigh the five-hundredth part of a grain. He insisted upon absolute exactness in measurements, the magic key to the new chemistry. With his balances, he weighed chemical elements and compounds, before and after reactions, and he designed equipment for weighing gases. Trattner, noted scientific historian, comments: "By introducing the balance into chemistry as an instrument of precision, Lavoisier placed the new science upon the definite quantitative basis of an exact discipline. It provided the *coup de grace* to the whole system of outworn methods.... By the keen temper of his logic Lavoisier realized from the outset that there could be no progress without the ability to weigh and measure all things chemical."

Another essential reform was a revised nomenclature for chemistry. For the most part, chemical terms had come down from the ancient days of alchemy, a pseudo-science filled with barbarous and meaningless expressions. Lavoisier and a small group led by him set out to introduce a comprehensive revision of the language. "Butter of arsenic" became arsenic chloride, "flowers of zinz" was changed to zinc oxide, "dephlogisticated air" to oxygen, and "phlogisticated" or "inflammable air" to hydrogen. Terminations were invented to describe classes of substances, such as oxide, sulphide, and phosphide, corresponding to their chemical composition. Many of the terms invented by Lavoisier have become the international vocabulary of chemists.

A table of elements was devised by Lavoisier, containing thirty-three names, of which twenty-three are still regarded as elements: carbon, hydrogen, oxygen, nitrogen, phosphorous, sulphur, antimony, arsenic, bismuth, cobalt, copper, gold, iron, lead, manganese, mercury, molybdenum, nickel, platinum, silver, tin, tungsten, and zinc. Several others listed by Lavoisier—lime, magnesia, baryta, alumina, and silica—are oxides which could not be decomposed with the chemical means available to him.

Among Lavoisier's experiments was one to show that plants are not merely "quantities of water transformed into quantities of wood," but compounds of various substances derived from the water and the earth and the air in which they live and upon which they feed. His next step was to investigate the nature of some of the substances, especially the composition of air. In this connection, Lavoisier applied the term oxygen for the first time.

After numerous experiments of a similar nature, Lavoisier stated four general principles or laws as the basis for a new chemistry. First, substances burn only when "vital air" (oxygen) is present. Second, non-metals, such as phosphorous, sulphur, or carbon, when burnt in vital air give rise to phosphoric, sulphuric, or carbonic acids. (Actually, hydrochloric acid contains no oxygen). Third, a metal when burnt in air forms a calx by combining with oxygen, becoming heavier in the process. Finally, there is no such thing as phlogiston, and combustion results, under proper conditions, from the union of the combustible body with the oxygen of the atmosphere.

Here, then, Lavoisier laid the foundation for the modern science of chemistry. Within his relatively brief life span, he had succeeded in revolutionizing the world in which he felt most at home, the field of chemistry.

The publication of his *Elementary Treatise of Chemistry* marked the culmination of Lavoisier's years of experimentation and investigation. This first modern textbook of chemistry is divided into three parts. The first deals with the formation and properties of gases, oxidation, fermentation, and putrefaction, and with the composition of air, water, acids, gases, and salts; the second relates to chemical elements, listing thirty-three substances then regarded as elements, and contains detailed tables of nomenclature of chemical compounds; the third part is concerned with apparatus and methods of chemical experimentation, and includes many engraved plates drawn by Lavoisier's talented wife. The *Elementary Treatise* was immensely successful from the outset, and Lavoisier's ideas and terminology set down therein were almost universally adopted.

Lavoisier's philosophy of science is summed up in these words: "Thoroughly convinced of these truths, I have imposed upon myself as a law, never to advance but from what is known to what is unknown; never to form any conclusion which is not an immediate consequence necessarily flowing from observation and experiment."

43

Invertebrate Zoologist
Jean Lamarck (1744-1829)

Natural History of Invertebrate Animals

The theory that species do not remain fixed, that gradual changes take place in them over long periods of time, aroused bitter controversy in the intellectual world, reaching its most violent stage in the second half of the nineteenth century. Inseparably linked with the concept of a progressive development of species are the names of Jean de Lamarck and Charles Darwin. Each developed his own theory of the origin of species. The idea that species change goes back to the ancient Greeks. A variety of factors (man's ego, religious prejudice, lack of objective evidence, etc.) caused its rejection. Many scientists at the beginning of the nineteenth century doubted the records of fossils, not believing that they were stone images of animals that had once lived. There was general acceptance (even by Lamarck) of spontaneous generation, the birth of animals without parents. The theory of special creation was universally held, and when Lamarck denied it, he was called an atheist. The ice ages in the history of the earth had not yet been demonstrated by geologists. Indeed, the notion was widely accepted that the world was less than six thousand years old and had been fashioned by God's own hands.

Lamarck was the youngest member of a family of eleven. While still in his teens, he enlisted in the French army and became a hero in the Seven Years War. When the war ended, he went to Paris and spent four years in the study of medicine, supporting himself by working in a banker's office. He became interested in meteorology and chemistry, but his main attention turned to botany.

For ten years Lamarck concentrated on research and writing for his *Flore Française*, long a standard reference work, published in 1778. Recognition for the author came through election to the Academy of Sciences and appointment in 1779 as keeper of the herbarium in the royal garden. For two years, 1781-82, Lamarck traveled across Europe, under the title of botanist to the king, sending back to Paris plants and seeds, animals, and minerals. On his return, he wrote two voluminous works, *Dictionaire de Botanique* and *Illustrations de Genres*.

By reason of a reorganization of the Jardin du Roi, where he had held a botanical appointment since 1788, Lamarck was chosen as professor of invertebrate zoology. The appointment marked a turning point in Lamarck's life. His work in botany had earned for him the name of the "French Linnaeus." Now he began to apply himself as rigorously to invertebrate zoology as he had previously to botany.

From the beginning, Lamarck started to develop a system for the classification of invertebrates, previously grouped roughly into insects and vermes. The two were divided by Lamarck into four groups: *Infusoria, Annelida, Archmida*, and *Crustacea*. His research on living forms was extended to a study of fossilized invertebrates. A work on fossil shells, published in 1806, was the first scientific book on paleontology, a fact that perhaps entitles Lamarck to be regarded as the founder of paleontology, a claim also made for Georges Cuvier.

Lamarck's earlier work in botany aided him in recognizing relationships between animals and plants. He coined the word "biology" in 1802 to cover the field of both plants and animals.

Belief in the immutability of species was almost universal among scientists of Lamarck's time, a natural derivative of the special creation theory. Lamarck was not convinced, however, and he suddenly emerged as an evolutionist. In 1800 he delivered a lecture in which he first stated his theory of evolution. The following year his views were published as a preface to his *Système des Animaux sans Vertebrès*. A later work, *Philosophie Zoologique*, published in 1809 (the year Darwin was born), contains a fuller explanation of his theory of descent.

"Neither man nor anything else in the world," wrote Lamarck, "is the result of special creation. That belief is childish, fit only for a primitive people. Theologians count time as 4,004 years from Adam to Christ, fixing thus neatly the age of the world. Reading these fossils and the stones in which they are found, I count the age of the world in thousands and thousands of years. What is time to Nature, that gigantic force which has no clocks? Read, you, the stones and the messages in the running waters that have worn and changed this earth." Lamarck added, "and throw away that silly notion of cataclysms, as of a violently wrenched earth or destructive floods. These changes of which I write came slowly, imperceptibly, a tiny bit at a time."

According to Lamarck's theory of the origin of species, animals became changed in order to make them better adapted to living in a particular environment. As an example, he explained the webbed feet of birds by concluding that they had moved from dry land to swamps, and the long neck of the giraffe developed from long periods of stretching for food. Such modifications were not sudden, Lamarck believed, but came about through ages of time.

One of the most frequently expressed objections to Lamarck's theory concerned his conclusion that characteristics acquired by an individual during its lifetime can be passed on to its offspring. On the basis of innumerable later experiments on plants and animals, the notion that acquired characteristics are inheritable was discredited. A well-known English scientist, J. B. S. Haldane, calls Lamarckism "a socially harmful doctrine," and notes that "human behavior depends much more on environment than ancestry."

Lamarck and Charles Lyell, geologist, were influential in convincing scientists and others that the earth was tremendously old. Both shared the belief, also, that natural forces operating in the present had operated in the past.

In the introduction to his *Histoire Naturelle*, Lamarck states four laws to explain the organization of animals and formation of different organs:

1. Life by its proper forces tends continually to increase the volume of every body possessing it, and to enlarge its parts, up to a limit which it brings about.

2. The production of a new organ in an animal body results from the supervention of a new want continuing to make itself felt, and a new movement which this want gives birth to and encourages.

3. The development of organs and their force of action are constantly in ratio to the employment of these organs.

4. All which has been acquired, laid down, or changed in the organization of individuals in the course of their life is conserved by generation and transmitted to the new individuals which proceed from those which have undergone these changes.

The second law, Lamarck's hypothesis of the evolution of organs in animals, holds that altered wants in animals lead to altered habits, resulting in the formation of new organs and modifications in existing organs. The fourth law deals with the inheritance of acquired characteristics.

As a naturalist, Lamarck possessed outstanding ability in precise descriptions. He excelled also in the wide scope of his interests and in fertility of ideas. His greatest claim to fame as a zoologist was his detailed investigation of living and fossil invertebrates. He was the first to distinguish vertebrate from invertebrate animals by the presence of a vertebral column. In a further step, he divided invertebrates into three major groups. Lamarck's permanent place in the history of science will doubtless be based on his influential theory of the origin of the diversities of animal forms.

Lamarck's last years were devoted to completion of his monumental work, *Natural History of Invertebrate Animals*, in seven volumes. Before finishing the sixth volume, he had become totally blind, and the remainder of the work had to be dictated to his daughter Cornelie.

44

Discoverer of Vaccination
Edward Jenner (1749-1823)

---

*An Inquiry into the Causes and Effects of the Variolae
Vaccinae, a Disease Discovered in Some of the Western
Counties of England, particularly Gloucestershire,
and Known by the Name of the Cow Pox*

Of all the ancient scourges of mankind, the most deadly and devastating was smallpox, a disease which can be traced back at least to Egyptian mummies more than three thousand years ago. Only leprosy, influenza, cholera, typhus fever, and bubonic plague were as dreaded, and over the centuries none of these had rivaled smallpox in its dire consequences. In Europe alone, sixty million people died of smallpox in the eighteenth century. One out of every fourteen persons born in England during these years succumbed to the disease. Many occupants of the French throne, among them Louis XV, died of the affliction, as did Mary II, Queen of England and consort of William II (at age thirty-two). A favorite theme of novelists was the pathetic disfigurement of beautiful women by smallpox. Victims of the disease who survived were usually marred for life and frequently blinded.

Credit for relieving the human race of this awful pestilence belongs to an English country physician, Edward Jenner. The idea of preventive inoculation for smallpox was not original with Jenner. Long before his time, the practice of injecting small doses of matter, from a smallpox sore on a patient with a mild case, under the skin of a well person to cause the latter to build up an immunity had been known in the East. An English traveler, Lady Mary Wortley Montague, had brought the idea from Turkey as early as 1721. The method, however, had serious faults; the resulting disease was often not mild, and sometimes it proved fatal. Furthermore, each inoculated person was a source of infection to other people.

A tradition among the dairy folk of the Gloucestershire countryside led to Jenner's epochal discovery. Dairy maids who had contracted cowpox when milking were believed by the farmers to be ever afterward immune from smallpox. Jenner noted also that persons who had had smallpox in a mild form acquired immunity against a second attack. He determined to undertake a series of experiments to test the prevailing folklore. His first operation was performed in 1796 upon an eight-year-old country boy, James Phipps, using matter from the hand of a milkmaid, Sarah Nelmes, who was suffering from a typical case of cowpox. About eight weeks later, the boy was inoculated with smallpox virus. In a letter to a friend, Jenner described the results:

> A boy named Phipps was inoculated in the arm from a pustule on the hand of a young woman who was infected by her master's cows. Having never seen the disease but in its casual way before, that is, when communicated from the cow to the hand of the milker, I was astonished at the close resemblance of the pustules in some of their stages to the variolous [smallpox] pustules. But now listen to the most delightful part of my story. The boy has since been inoculated for the small-pox which, as I ventured to predict, produced no effect. I shall now pursue my experiments with redoubled ardor.

Thus was marked the first successful vaccination for smallpox in history. Over the next two years Jenner continued his experiments, by the end of which period he had demonstrated in twenty-two cases that vaccination with cowpox matter gave complete protection against smallpox. Sixteen of the cases had occurred accidentally among people working with cows and horses; the others were contrived under Jenner's direction.

The evidence was beyond question. To announce the great medical triumph, Jenner published in 1798 one of the masterpieces of scientific literature, *An Inquiry into the Causes and Effects of the Variolae Vaccinae*, a thin quarto of seventy-five pages with four colored plates. Full descriptions were included of the cases personally directed or observed by Jenner. In somewhat florid opening paragraphs, the author began:

> The deviation of Man from the state in which he was originally placed by Nature seems to have proved to him a prolific source of diseases. From the love of splendour, from the indulgencies of luxury, and from his great fondness for amusement, he has familiarized himself with a great number of animals, which may not originally have been intended for his associates.
>
> The Wolf, disarmed of ferocity, is now pillowed in the lady's lap. The Cat, the little Tyger of our island, whose natural home is the forest, is equally domesticated and caressed. The Cow, the Hog, the Sheep, and the Horse, are all, for a variety of purposes, brought under his care and dominion.

The *Inquiry* went through several editions and within a few years had been translated into a number of other languages, spreading knowledge of Jenner's discovery around the world. Soon the results of vaccination began to be felt in the declining death rate from smallpox. Napoleon Bonaparte, for example, had all of his soldiers vaccinated, and his armies were thereafter free of the disease.

Nevertheless, conservative opposition in medical and lay circles was vociferous. Ministers denounced vaccination from their pulpits as man's interference with the ways of God. Antivaccinationist societies, some of which are still in existence, were formed. The fantastic idea was circulated that vaccination would cause the human subject to sprout horns, grow a tail, low like a cow, bellow like a bull, and acquire other bovine characteristics. Overzealous advocates of vaccination harmed its reputation by using contaminated vaccine matter, producing serious illnesses. Such obstacles, however, were gradually surmounted. A grateful Parliament recognized Jenner's work by two grants, totaling 30,000 pounds, to cover his expenses, and in his later years he was accorded numerous honors.

In succeeding generations, Jenner's original discovery has been vastly expanded by other research workers in the development of a formidable battery of toxins and antitoxins and various forms of inoculation to protect the individual against many contagious diseases. Jenner's successful solution to the smallpox problem has probably saved more lives and suffering than any other single accomplishment in the history of medicine. As Thomas Jefferson stated in a letter to Jenner, May 14, 1806: "You have erased from the calendar of human afflictions one of the greatest. Yours is the comfortable reflection that mankind can never forget that you have lived; future nations will know by history only that the loathsome small-pox has existed, and by you has been extirpated."

In December, 1977, the World Health Organization announced the end of the last known case of virulent smallpox anywhere in the world, 181 years after Jenner's discovery.

45

Mathematical Astronomer
Pierre Laplace (1749-1827)

Traité de Mécanique Céleste
(Celestial Mechanics)

Sir Isaac Newton's investigations of astronomic phenomena led him seriously to question the stability of the universe. Believing that the movements of the planets were affected not only by the sun but also by other planets, he feared that eventually the whole system would become deranged. When or if this occurred, only divine intervention could restore equilibrium and order.

Pierre Simon Laplace, often referred to as "the Newton of France," one of the greatest intellects in the history of science, devoted his masterpiece, *Mécanique Céleste*, to proving the essential stability of the solar system. Laplace's life work was a detailed application of the Newtonian hypothesis of universal gravitation to the universe. The *Mécanique Céleste* may be rightly regarded as the mathematical masterpiece of the nineteenth century, comparable in many respects to Newton's *Principia*.

Living in a deeply troubled era and being a political opportunist of the first water, Laplace had a most complex personality. As Eric T. Bell remarked, "On the human side he is perhaps the most conspicuous refutation of the pedagogical superstition that noble pursuits necessarily ennoble a man's character." Coming from poor parents in Normandy, Laplace transferred his allegiance in succession from Louis XVI to the revolution, to Napoleon Bonaparte, and, finally, to the restored monarchy, ending as a marquis of the Restoration—a decided contrast to, for example, his contemporary and one-time collaborator, Lavoisier, who died on the guillotine during the revolution, at the height of his career.

Laplace's *magnum opus*, the *Mécanique Céleste*, appeared in five volumes over a period of twenty-six years. The work is a highly technical treatise on mathematical astronomy; Laplace declared its purpose to be the treatment of astronomy "as a great problem of mechanics, from which it is important to banish as much as possible all empiricism," that is, largely to omit observation and experiment, while reducing all known phenomena of the universe to strict mathematical principles. By carrying forward and completing Newton's investigations of the motions of the planets, satellites, and comets, Laplace proposed "to present a connected view of these theories."

Beginning with the discoveries previously made by Galileo, Huygens, and Newton, the *Mécanique Céleste* gives an exposition of all existing knowledge of physical astronomy. The solar system is exhibited as a vast and complex machine, every movement of which is a mere working out of the laws of mechanics and gravitation. Valuable mathematical methods are developed for studying the motion of the planets, the moon, and ocean tides, including formulas for calculating the disturbances of planets and moons by their mutual gravitational forces. Applying mathematical theories of probability to celestial bodies, Laplace concluded that the apparent changes in the motion of the planets and their satellites are changes over tremendously long periods, and that, consequently, the solar system is in all probability very stable.

Laplace's conception of the universe was purely mechanistic, for he was unwilling to concede any divine hand in its creation or control. According to a favorite story, the author presented a copy of his work to Napoleon, who remarked, "You have written this huge book on the system of the world without once mentioning the author of the universe." Laplace replied, "Sir, I had no need of that hypothesis."

Closely associated with Laplace's name is the nebular hypothesis, though the famous German philosopher Immanuel Kant had suggested the same idea about a half-century earlier. The theory was first advanced by Laplace in his *Exposition of the System of the World* (1796), an earlier and simpler version of *Mécanique Céleste*, with most of the mathematics omitted. The nebular hypothesis attempts to explain the origin of the planets by assuming that the sun began as a vast heated nebula, composed of gas. As the gas gradually cooled, it shrank and, traveling in rotary fashion, whirled faster and faster. The sun threw off the hot, rotating gases, and these contracted and solidified to form planets, meanwhile continuing their rotation around the sun. According to Laplace, the speed of rotation caused the sun to break up and produce planets. In common with the other planets, the earth began in a hot, gaseous state, finally cooling and contracting until it could support life.

The nebular hypothesis captured the imagination of the scientific world and held sway for more than a century. Various technical objections to it, as new facts accumulated, however, caused this Laplacian conception to be superseded in recent decades by the planetesimal theory developed by T. C. Chamberlin.

Laplace's rank as a mathematician is on a par with his fame as an astronomer. His *Analytic Theory of Probabilities* (1812), for example, is a classic in its field. But Laplace is reported to have had no interest in mathematics except as a tool for solving technical problems. His work in the theory of probabilities was inspired by the need for it in mathematical astronomy.

"Laplace's Equation" has been of great value in the theoretical developments of a number of branches of physics, such as gravitation and electricity, and has also been used to solve specific problems in these fields.

One connection between Laplace's work and the American scene is worthy of note. Nathaniel Bowditch translated *Méchanique Céleste* into English. Issued in Boston, 1829-1839, in four volumes, this was the first work of such major scientific significance to be published in America.

46

Comparative Anatomist
Georges Cuvier (1760-1832)

The Animal Kingdom

Georges Cuvier was an outstanding figure among paleontologists of the first half of the nineteenth century. As a biologist, he played an instrumental part in establishing comparative anatomy as a distinct branch of science, formulating the principles and methods still followed for the study of fossil vertebrates.

Cuvier's interest in natural history began early. As a child he was exposed to Buffon's *Histoire Naturelle*, and proceeded to color the pictures with paints and pieces of silk according to descriptions in the text. At age eighteen, Cuvier became tutor to a family living on the Normandy coast. There the sea washed up a variety of specimens (starfish, mollusks, marine worms, and other animals) for the budding young scientist to examine and dissect. A group of people interested in science in nearby villages met occasionally and developed into a small scientific society, with Cuvier as secretary. Cuvier's expert draftsmanship attracted the attention of an agriculturist, Alexandre-Henri Tessler, who recommended him to the newly appointed professor of comparative anatomy in Paris. This led to an appointment as assistant at the Museum of Natural History—and Cuvier's scientific career was on its way.

In a short time Cuvier was appointed professor of comparative anatomy, and in 1799 became professor of natural history in the Collège de France. Thenceforth he lived a busy life, dissecting, drawing, teaching, and writing. His influence with Napoleon and other leaders promoted him to a dominant position in the French scientific and educational world during the first quarter of the nineteenth century.

In 1803 Cuvier was appointed perpetual secretary of the Institut National in the department of the physical and natural sciences. In that capacity, he devoted himself to three fields of investigation: one dealing with the structure and classification of mollusca; the second with the comparative anatomy and systematic arrangement of fishes; and the third mainly with fossil animals and reptiles, with some attention to living forms. Cuvier's published *Histoire Naturelle de Poissons* contained descriptions of 5,000 species of fishes.

Cuvier was a pioneer among early anatomists. He dissected many animals which had not been previously examined, he insisted on the anatomical basis of classification, and he recognized three great branches of the animal kingdom: the vertebrates, the molluscan, and the articulate. One of Cuvier's earliest papers dealt with a comparison of living and extinct elephants, in accordance with his belief that living and fossil forms must be studied together.

An important aspect of Cuvier's first writings was his so-called correlation theory. He saw a close relationship between the internal and external structure of an animal and its habits of life. For example, a carnivorous animal is likely to have claws adapted for catching and holding its prey. Its teeth are sharp and so placed in the jaws that they can tear flesh. A plant-eating animal, on the contrary, may lack claws and has a different teeth formation. Carrying these points further, Cuvier went on to demonstrate that the digestive systems and other parts of the internal structure of flesh-eating and plant-eating animals are different.

The reconstruction of fossils remains one of Cuvier's remarkable achievements. His thorough knowledge of comparative anatomy made it possible for him to sort out the bones of different kinds of animals when they were found together in a fossil bed. Thus, Cuvier astonished the world by reconstructing prehistoric forms of animal life whose existence had not even been imagined. His work on skeletal remains was the beginning of the modern science of comparative paleontology. Following his methodology, many models of prehistoric animals have been constructed for natural history museums, even when some of the bones of the fossilized skeletons are missing.

Despite such noteworthy contributions to scientific knowledge, especially in the fields of comparative anatomy and paleontology, historians of science conclude the Cuvier retarded scientific thought and progress. He had no sympathy for the views of Hutton or Lamarck, who had so clearly disproved biblical chronology and given infallible evidence of the earth's immense age.

In one of his most famous books, the *Discourse on the Revolutions of the Surface of the Globe*, Cuvier attempted to prove the reality of the Deluge and the brief history of man on the earth. He reviewed the traditions of a deluge among ancient nations, some preceding biblical chronology, in support of his belief in such happenings. In fact, Cuvier was convinced that the world had gone through numerous catastrophic earthquakes, floods, and volcanic eruptions. These cataclysmic events produced a series of faunas year after year. All living things, except a small remnant, were destroyed during each world-shaking catastrophe and new organisms were created by natural or supernatural forces. New forms also came in from areas which had not undergone calamities. This was Cuvier's explanation for differences in fossil species found in upper and lower strata of rocks.

In 1802 a discovery was made in Siberia which Cuvier believed gave support to his theory. A mammoth was found frozen in the ice. The flesh of the animal was so well preserved that it was devoured by dogs after removal from the ice. In Cuvier's mind, the finding of the mammoth in such a perfect state of preservation was proof that a catastrophe had occurred. The bones of animals found in caves, he believed, had been deposited there by tremendous floods.

Since Cuvier was adamant in his theory that new species were created after each catastrophe, it was natural for him to defend his stand on the fixity of species. Each species, he held, was distinct from any other, and had remained unchanged since its creation.

The formations of the Paris Basin studied by Cuvier had alternate strata of marine fossils, fresh-water fossils, and material without fossils. The alterations, he concluded, were the result of sudden revolutions in the state of the sea. Supernatural causes alone explained the revolutions. The deposits made between revolutions were considered to come from natural forces and time. In this fashion did Cuvier build up an elaborate defense against the theory of evolution. If each species had a limited ability to vary, the divine origin of species was irrefutable. Meanwhile, Hutton, Lamarck, Erasmus, Darwin, Lyell, and others were busy tearing down this beautiful structure.

In another area, Cuvier remained wedded to discredited theories of earlier naturalists. In spite of the work of Anton van Leeuwenhoek and similar evidence, he was a firm believer in spontaneous generation of life from inorganic or dead material. He thought, also, that the fertilized egg contained within it the whole adult organism in miniature, and that development was merely an unfolding or expansion of its parts.

But aside from such weaknesses and mistaken opinions, Cuvier was primarily responsible for opening up a major new field, that of comparative anatomy. In his important textbook on the subject, he dealt with the minute structure of both higher and lower animals. Cuvier's greatest work was *The Animal Kingdom Arranged According to Its Organization*, published in 1817. In this four-volume treatise, he divided animals into four types: the Vertebrata, including those with a bony skeleton and a backbone; Mollusca, such as snails, limpets, mussels, etc., soft-bodied animals, often with shells; Articulata, jointed animals like lobsters, worms and insects; and Radials, like starfish, sea anemones, and polyps. Needless to say, later biologists made drastic revisions in this crude classification. At the head of the animal kingdom Cuvier proudly placed the "only two-legged, two-handed animal, man."

47

Birth of the Atomic Theory
John Dalton (1766-1844)

A New System of Chemical Philosophy

A century and a half ago it was possible for relatively uneducated and untrained experimenters, such as John Dalton and Michael Faraday, to make scientific discoveries of immense significance. Today, when scientists are customarily required to go through long periods of formal preparation, when a tremendous body of complex knowledge has accumulated for the major branches of science, and research is carried on in expensive and elaborately equipped laboratories, important scientific advances are likely to result from team rather than individual effort.

John Dalton, son of a poor Quaker hand-loom weaver, born in Cumberland, and largely self-taught, earned a living throughout his life as a private tutor of children. His acquaintance with John Gough, the blind philosopher, was of material assistance to him. With Gough as teacher, he learned some Latin, French, and Greek, mastered differential calculus, and studied the works of English mathematicians. From Gough, too, he learned to keep a meteorological journal.

In his Cumberland days, Dalton began to study the weather systematically. Over a period of fifty-seven years, he recorded two hundred thousand weather observations and laid the foundations of meteorology as a science. His *Meteorological Observations and Essays* (1793) offered the now accepted hypothesis that the aurora borealis is purely electrical in origin. The investigation of weather phenomena led Dalton to "speculate upon the nature and the constitution of the atmosphere," a study that set in motion his subsequent ideas on the atomic theory.

Dalton was not, and never claimed to be, the first to propose an atomic theory of matter. As early at 1200 B.C., Hindu literature shows the existence of a theory that regarded matter as a union of tiny particles, separated by empty space but naturally attracted to one another. Later, the Greeks held similar views, adding, however, the notion that the particles are indestructible and always in motion. One of the first exponents of these ideas was Democritus (460-360 B.C.). During the medieval era, atomic speculations lingered among the Arabs, though they were generally rejected by Christian theologians. A revival of interest among seventeenth-century and eighteenth-century scientists caused Newton, for example, to conceive of atoms as "solid, massy, hard, impenetrable, movable particles."

But despite such pioneer attempts at explanation, atomic theories prior to Dalton were chiefly in the realm of philosophy, for lack of quantitative evidence. Dalton's distinctive contribution was in specific measurement. "Are all atoms," he asked himself, "alike in size and weight?" He suggested the hypothesis that the atoms of the same element are uniform and always fixed and never vary, but that the atoms of different elements are unlike in both form and weight. Every element, according to this postulate, is composed of atoms, and an atom of carbon or sulphur is identical with every other carbon or sulphur atom, but is distinct from the atoms of other elements.

From his investigations and deductions, Dalton came to the conclusion that chemical combination takes place in the simplest possible way: an atom of one element combines with an atom of another element. Combining atoms of oxygen and hydrogen, to illustrate, produces water, erroneously assumed by Dalton at first to contain an equal number of atoms of each element. Later he discovered that water contains twice as many atoms of hydrogen as of oxygen.

On the basis of experiments with a variety of compounds, Dalton formulated the principle for which he is most famous, the "law of multiple proportions." As stated by him: "If two elements combine in more than one proportion, then the volumes of one of these elements combined with a fixed volume of the other are in simple numerical proportion." More simply put, many pairs of elements combine to form more than one compound. The same elements combined in different proportions by weight produce different results.

Concerning the mechanism of chemical combination, Dalton writes:

> Chemical analysis and synthesis go no further than the separation of particles one from another, and to their reunion. No new creation or destruction of matter is within the reach of chemical agency. We might as well attempt to introduce a new planet into the solar system, or to annihilate one already in existence, as to create or destroy a particle of hydrogen.

Observing the proportions by weight by which elements combine, Dalton reasoned that it was possible to determine the *relative* weights of the atoms of which an element is composed. Atoms are much too small to see or weigh singly, he conceded, but the weights could be obtained through measures of chemical composition. Accordingly, through his own experiments and those of fellow scientists, Dalton prepared the first table of atomic weights. Starting with the lightest element known, hydrogen gas, as a standard, all other elements were assigned weights in ratio to hydrogen. Dalton's original table of relative atomic weights contained twenty-one elements. The table was necessarily crude and inaccurate, since the available laboratory equipment was too primitive for exact experimentation.

In 1808 Dalton presented a brief account of his atomic theory in the first volume of his *New System of Chemical Philosophy*, with the table of atomic weights and plates of chemical symbols.

Though an awkward, cumbersome scheme, Dalton originated the first system of atomic notation or chemical shorthand. In his formulas for the various elements, he introduced a complicated series of circles with markings within the circles to denote the atoms of each element. The oxygen atom was represented, for example, by a simple circle, the hydrogen atom by a circle with a dot in the center, and the nitrogen atom by a vertical line bisecting a circle. Compounds were indicated by joining one circle to another. Ultimately the elaborate scheme was discarded, and notations designed by Berzelius, a Swedish chemist, in use to the present day, were adopted, indicating elements by letters and compounds by letters and Arabic numerals.

Dalton's atomic theory differs in important respects from modern theory, but it laid a solid foundation for future progress. Since his day, an overwhelming mass of experimental verification has accumulated to support the atomic concept. As early as 1811, Avogadro made a distinction between the atoms of a chemical element and its molecules, and an army of scientific investigators is currently concerned with such aspects of atomic research as analysis of the electron, proton, neutron, and positron.

Every scientific advance must have a beginning, and contemporary advanced research in atomic theory can be traced back directly to its foundations in Dalton's work. In the words of the science historian J. Newton Friend, "Just as a crystal dropped into a solution may yield a vast crop of crystals entirely unrelated in quantity to the size of the original crystal, so Dalton's theory has been a nucleus around which have collected, and are still collecting, new laws, hypotheses and theories."

48

Father of English Geology
William Smith (1769-1839)

Geological Atlas of England and Wales

James Hutton, Charles Lyell, and, later, Charles Darwin were deeply indebted to an obscure practicing surveyor, William Smith, for solid evidence to support their evolutionary theories. Smith, the son of a mechanic, was a native of Oxfordshire. At the age of eighteen, he became assistant to a surveyor for the areas of Oxfordshire, Gloucestershire, and other districts, giving him an exceptional opportunity to study their varieties of strata and soils. As he worked in different parts of England, Smith noted the position, extent, and composition of sedimentary rocks, collected fossils from each stratum, and recorded his observations on colored geological maps and sections. He noted that certain fossils appeared in the same beds at different localities, and each fossil species was embedded in a definite formation. Here was established the principle of identification of strata by the residue or organic remains. Vertically, successive layers were the keys to the order of organic periods.

Smith was not a writer, and he recorded nothing in writing. He had a phenomenal memory, however, and in 1799 dictated a list of fossils in the order in which they could be gathered from a succession of rocks, ranging from what are now known as the Carboniferous to the Cretaceous systems.

At the urging of fellow geologists, Smith prepared a series of colored maps, culminating in 1815 in his *Geological Atlas of England and Wales*, the first of its kind in the world. Geologists for all time were provided with a method of correlating rocks from all areas of the earth.

Smith had no thought, apparently, that his discoveries would shed any light on the problem of evolution. He was never an evolutionist in the Darwinian sense. Though his work was not published in completed form until 1815, a general outline of his ideas had been communicated to a few associates earlier. His general conclusions were presented to the public by one friend, the Reverend Joseph Townsend, in a work entitled *The Character of Moses Established for Veracity as an Historian, Recording Events from the Creation to the Deluge* (Bath, 1813), giving full credit to Smith. Neither Townsend nor Smith recognized the time element in laying down the successive strata or in examining fossil remains. In fact, both thought that they were supporting Mosaic views on the creation of the world. Townsend denounced Hutton for the sacrilegious notion that the earth's age should be measured in millions of years, and for questioning that supernatural agents had caused various types of unheavals on the earth's surface.

Nevertheless, William Smith's methods and discoveries were of inestimable importance in spreading the concept of geological and biological evolution. No one was more profoundly influenced than was Charles Darwin.

In his matter-of-fact way, Smith laid a secure foundation of modern stratigraphy. It became gradually accepted that fossils provided the surest means for the comparative study of sedimentary rocks. Fossils are now seen as an infallible tool for answering questions of time and order of succession, and the correlation of widely separated beds. William Smith, chiefly by being an acute and intelligent observer, found the way to read the history of the earth — a truly extraordinary contribution to science.

Smith's geological map-making continued after publication of his 1815 atlas, in a series of county maps. His collection of fossils was purchased by the British Museum, and in 1817 a descrptive catalog was published under the title *Strategraphical System of Organizing Fossils*. Smith also began publication of another work, *Strata Identified by Organized Fossils*, of which only four parts were issued.

Recognition of Smith's achievements came from several sources during his last years: the Geological Society of London's Wollaston medal (the citation which described him as Father of English Geology), an honorary degree from Dublin, and a life pension from the British government.

The practical utility of fossils has been realized since Smith's time. The dating of fossils plays an important role in the search for oil. Consequently, many paleontologists are employed by oil companies to assist them in finding potential oil-producing areas.

49

Universal Man
Alexander von Humboldt (1769-1859)

Cosmos

Simón Bolívar once declared that "Baron Humboldt did more for the Americas than all the conquistadores." Without doubt, the Great Liberator's judgment was correct, for Humboldt's early-nineteenth-century expeditions revealed a new America. His voluminous publications, his varied influence on American growth and development, his encouragement to the Latin American liberators, and his aid to innumerable later explorers entitle Humboldt to a unique position in the annals of American history.

Alexander von Humboldt's extraordinary career ended in 1859 in his ninetieth year. Since the early years of the nineteenth century, he had been a world-famous figure, second in renown only to Napoleon. Evidence of the esteem in which he was held is furnished by the numerous geographical features named for him in the New World: Humboldt Current (off the Pacific coast of South America), Humboldt Glacier (Greenland), Humboldt Peak (Venezuela and Colorado), Humboldt Bay (California), Humboldt Range (Nevada), and perhaps a score of American cities and counties.

In the universality of his interests, Humboldt has been compared to Pericles and also to Leonardo da Vinci. Son of an aristocratic family in Prussia, he received the best education then available in Europe, studying under famous savants at the universities of Frankfurt and Göttingen. Subsequently, he was to shine brilliantly as an explorer, cosmographer, biologist, diplomat, engineer, and citizen of the world. Among his friends and associates were Agassiz, Ampère, Bolívar, Chopin, Cuvier, Faraday, Franklin, Frederick the Great, Gauss, Goethe, Irving, Jefferson, Lavoisier, Liszt, Lyell, Morse, Pitt, Gilbert Stuart, and other public leaders of his time. His admirers included Charles Darwin, who called him "the greatest scientific traveler who ever lived." Yet, despite his contemporary fame and the near adulation in which he was held, Humboldt today is largely a forgotten personality, and his most celebrated book, *Cosmos*, little read.

Probably more than any other single factor, Humboldt's career was shaped by his travels in Latin America, during the five years from 1799 to 1804. Starting in Venezuela, he explored the Orinoco and upper Amazon valleys, climbed Chimborazo (then believed to be the world's highest mountain), studied the Inca civilization in Peru, corrected the figures for the latitudes of South America, calculated a route for the Panama Canal (approximately the present site), investigated changing vegetation from the steaming tropical jungles to the top of the Andes, collected, with the aid of his botanist companion, Aimé Bonpland, sixty thousand plant specimens, provided the first accurate data on cinchona (source of quinine) and rubber trees, and assembled a vast collection of animals, insects, and geological fragments. Before returning to Europe, Humboldt visited Mexico and Cuba and stopped over for a stay with Thomas Jefferson at Monticello.

Twenty-five years later, at the age of sixty, Humboldt undertook an extended tour, subsidized by the czar of Russia, into the interior of Asia. His scientific labors during the ensuing three decades of his career, however, were chiefly influenced by the impressions and observations gained from his American travels. No less than thirty published volumes were drawn from the extensive notes he made while on that odyssey to South and Middle America—scientific studies relating to botany, geology, zoology, and geography, as well as narratives of popular travel and discussions of economic, social, and political conditions.

At the age of seventy-six, Humboldt resolved to undertake his most ambitious work: to coordinate and synthesize all the knowledge of his era into a harmonious whole. Everything that he had previously written or done he regarded as prologue, mere preparation for the gigantic project now begun. As the author outlines his plan in a letter:

> I have been seized with the mad idea of representing in a single work the whole material world, everything that we know today concerning the phenomena of the heavens and of the earth, from the nebulae to the geography of mosses on granite rocks.... Every great and important idea, which anywhere shines forth, must here be given together with the relevant facts. It must represent an epoch of the mental development of humanity as regards its knowledge of Nature.

The result of this audacious enterprise was *Cosmos*, subtitled *Sketch of a Physical Description of the Universe*, issued in five volumes over the period 1845 to 1862. Humboldt was preeminently qualified for the task to which he now set himself because of his extensive knowledge of many fields of learning, varied experiences as a traveler, and the resources of the scientific and literary world at his disposal. Collaborators pledged to his assistance included the greatest scientists of his generation, leaders in chemistry, astronomy, anatomy, mathematics, mineralogy, botany, and other areas. Not since Aristotle had any writer attempted to deal with the universe in such comprehensive fashion.

In *Cosmos*, Humboldt combines the broad philosophical ideas of the eighteenth century with the more exact scientific knowledge of the nineteenth century. His basic purpose is stated in the introduction to the first volume:

> The most important aim of all physical science is this: to recognize unity in diversity, to comprehend all the single aspects as revealed by the discoveries of the last epochs, to judge single phenomena separately without surrendering to their bulk, and to grasp Nature's essence under the cover of outer appearances.

Beginning with a general "portrait of Nature," Humboldt examines outer space—the Milky Way, cosmic nebulae, and planets—and then proceeds to the earth and its physical geography; climate; volcanoes; relationships among plants, animals, and mankind; evolution; and the beauty of nature. The second part, on the history of science, is concerned with "the difference of feeling excited by the contemplation of Nature at different epochs," that is, the attitudes toward natural phenomena among poets, painters, and students of nature through the ages. The three final volumes are devoted to a more detailed account of scientific studies in astronomy, the earth's physical properties, and geological formations.

Cosmos was both a literary and a scientific achievement, immensely popular among nineteenth-century readers. Humboldt's object, "to represent Nature as one great whole, moved and animated by internal forces," was successfully accomplished. Since his day, the natural sciences have, of course, made tremendous progress, and *Cosmos*, though still highly readable, has become outdated in important particulars.

In retrospect, Humboldt's work gave a strong impetus to scientific exploration throughout the nineteenth century, inspiring, for example, the voyage of the *Beagle*, with Darwin aboard as the ship's naturalist. It may rightfully be claimed also that he laid the foundations of physical geography and meteorology. But, without question, Humboldt's most enduring contribution to scientific progress is his conception of the unity of science, of nature, and of mankind.

50

Seaman's Bible

Nathaniel Bowditch (1773-1838)

The New American Practical Navigator

The natural perils of the sea were vastly increased for early sailors by faulty systems of navigation. Ancient seamen lacked compasses, sextants, chronometers, and of course the electronic devices in common use today. The timid stayed close to shore and sailed only during daylight in fair weather; the more intrepid dared to sail out of sight of land and, using the sun, stars, and winds, managed to reach their destinations without the aid of mechanical devices.

By the sixteenth century, substantial advances had been made. Ferdinand Magellan's expedition to circumnavigate the globe was equipped with sea charts, a terrestrial globe, theodolites, quadrants, compasses, magnetic needles, and hour glasses. Still missing was a vital element: an accurate method of determining longitude. That huge obstacle was overcome two centuries later with the invention of the chronometer. Another basic step was the publication of the first official nautical almanac.

Beginning with the original edition in 1772, John Hamilton Moore's *Practical Navigator* was the leading navigational text until superseded thirty years later by an American work, Nathaniel Bowditch's *New American Practical Navigator* (1802), subtitled *Being an Epitome of Navigation; Containing All the Tables Necessary to Be Used with the Nautical Almanac in Determining the Latitude; and the Longitude by Lunar Observations; and Keeping a Complete Reckoning at Sea: Illustrated by Proper Rules and Examples: The Whole Exemplified in a Journal, Kept from Boston to Madeira: In Which All the Rules of Navigation Are Introduced: Also the Demonstration of the Most Useful Rules of Trigonometry: With Many Useful Problems in Mensuration, Surveying, and Gauging: And a Dictionary of Sea-Terms, with the Manner of Performing the Most Common Evolutions at Sea. To Which Are Added. Some General Instructions and Information to Merchants, Masters of Vessels, and Others Concerned in Navigation, Relative to Maritime Laws and Mercantile Customs.*

Born in 1773, Nathaniel Bowditch was a native of Salem, Massachusetts. From early youth he was recognized as a brilliant mathematician and linguist, though denied an opportunity for any formal education after age ten because of family poverty. In the seafaring town of Salem, Bowditch was naturally drawn to the study of navigation. At age thirteen he learned the rudiments of the subject from an old British sailor. A year later he began to study surveying and assisted in a survey of the town of Salem. While still in his early teens, he devised an accurate calendar and constructed a barometer and sundial.

Bowditch's seagoing career began at age twenty-one, when he went on a year-long voyage to the Indian Ocean. Four other trips to sea were made over a period of about nine years, the last as captain and part owner of the three-masted *Putnam* on a thirteen-month voyage to Sumatra and Mauritius.

Accurate time was no more available to the average naval or merchant vessel during this period than it was in earlier centuries. The chronometer had been invented about sixty years earlier, but was too expensive for most shipowners to afford. Ships navigated by a combination of dead reckoning and parallel sailing (a system of sailing north or south to the latitude of the destination and then west to the destination).

During his first voyage and afterwards, Bowditch found innumerable errors in Moore's *Practical Navigator*. He began recording the mistakes and undertook, through a Newburyport publisher, Edmund M. Blunt, to issue a revised edition of the work. A total of some ten thousand errors in Moore were corrected in two editions edited by Bowditch. Then he and his publisher decided to bring out their own work, rather than to continue to correct Moore's blunders. They were encouraged in the undertaking by a report of a committee of the East India Marine Society of Salem, which stated:

> After a full examination of the system of Navigation presented to the society by one of its members, (Mr. Nathaniel Bowditch) they find, that he has corrected many thousand errors, existing in the best European works of the kind; especially those in the Tables for determining the latitude by two altitudes, in those of difference of latitude and departure, of the sun's right ascension, of amplitudes, and many others necessary to the Navigator. Mr. Bowditch has likewise, in many instances, greatly improved the old methods of calculation, and added new ones of his own. That of clearing the apparent distance of the moon, and sun or stars, from the effect of parallax and refraction, is peculiarly adapted to the use of seamen in general.... He has much improved the table of latitudes and longitudes of places, and has added those of a number on the American coast hitherto very inaccurately ascertained.

In an advertisement inserted at the beginning of the book, publisher Blunt comments ironically: "While he is tendering his thanks to such as have assisted in the establishment of the work, it would be highly criminal to omit those due to *John Hamilton Moore*; and with the greatest frankness it is acknowledged that he contributed largely to its establishment, as his late editions have been so erroneous that no person would hazard his interest, much less life, in navigating his vessel by the rules there laid down." Bowditch's biographer, Robert E. Berry, notes that some of the errors made by Moore had been fatal to ships — the faulty tables of declination, for example. The year 1800 had been shown as a leap year in the tables, resulting, several masters claimed, in the loss of their ships.

Except in form, *The New American Practical Navigator* incorporated nothing from Moore which Bowditch had not verified at first hand. For instance, in presenting the model of a journal of a sea voyage, Bowditch substituted the record of his own voyage from Boston to Madeira for Moore's log of a voyage between England and the island of Tenerife.

Bowditch's aim was to compile a work which would be intelligible to the average seaman—in effect serving as a text for every member of a crew. In addition to improving methods of determining longitude, *The New American Practical Navigator* gave the ship's officer information on winds, currents, and tides; directions for surveying; statistics on marine insurance; a glossary of sea terms; instructions in mathematics; and numerous tables of navigational data. Berry observes that a diligent student of Bowditch "learned how to observe an amplitude or azimuth by the compass, to find the moon's declination, to find the time at sea and regulate a watch, to calculate the sun's altitude at any time, and to calculate the altitude of the moon and stars." He could also learn to survey a coast from a ship's deck, survey a harbor from shore, and find the time of high tide.

The first edition of *The New American Practical Navigator* was a large, well-produced book, running to nearly 600 pages in length. The reception of the work was gratifying, making the author known around the world. Copies were soon in the sea chests of every American captain and sailor, and "Bowditch" became standard equipment for seagoing men.

Bowditch's knowledge of navigation was not limited to theory; he was equally skilled in practice. According to one anecdote, on Christmas Day in 1803, returning to Salem from a long voyage on the *Putnam*, he ran into a blizzard. While other ships were standing off shore waiting for the snow to stop, Bowditch headed his ship straight into the rocky harbor and landed safely at night in one of the worst storms on record.

Ten editions of *The New American Practical Navigator* appeared prior to Bowditch's death in 1838, and twenty-five other editions came out through 1867, when the copyright was purchased by the U.S. Navy Hydrographic Office. The title has been changed to the *American Practical Navigator*, but Bowditch's name still appears on the title page. A total of more than 700,000 copies in about seventy editions have been published since 1802.

Bowditch was a prolific writer throughout a long and active career. He prepared and published charts of the Salem, Beverly, and Manchester harbors, and wrote twenty-three papers for the *Memoirs of the American Academy of Arts and Sciences* on the orbits of comets, meteors, applications of Napier's rules, magnetic variation, eclipses, calculations of tides, and other astronomical and nautical matters. His most monumental achievement, however, was the translation into English of the first four volumes of LaPlace's *Mécanique Céleste* (Paris, 1799-1805), accompanied by a voluminous commentary that considerably more than doubled the size of the original.

Many honors came to Bowditch in recognition of his accomplishments. Offers of professorships, which he refused, were received from Harvard University, the University of Virginia, and West Point. Honorary M.A. and LL.D. degrees were conferred on him by Harvard, and he was elected a member of numerous American and European scientific societies.

Major credit belongs to Bowditch for the reputation which Yankee shipmasters achieved for their skill, dexterity, and know-how as navigators. Even before publication of *The New American Practical Navigator*, American ships were engaged in worldwide trade and naval cruises, and their captains were known as able seamen. Bowditch supplied them with the basic scientific and technical knowledge which they had hitherto lacked.

The high esteem in which Bowditch was held by his contemporaries is demonstrated in a eulogy from the Salem Marine Society:

> Not this community, nor our country only, but the whole world, has reason to do honor to his memory.... No monument will be needed to keep alive his memory among men; but as long as ships shall sail, the needle point to the north, and the stars go through their wonted course in the heavens, the name of Dr. Bowditch will be revered as of one who helped his fellowmen in a time of need, who was and is a guide to them over the pathless ocean.

51

Ornithologist Supreme

John James Audubon (1785-1851)

The Birds of America

If Americans were asked to name their favorite naturalist, past or present, the name of John James Audubon would doubtless head the list. Framed reproductions of his paintings hang in innumerable American homes, and his fame is perpetuated through the National Audubon Society, the Canadian Audubon Society, and similar groups dedicated to wildlife conservation and preservation. After examining Audubon's double-elephant-folio edition of *The Birds of America*, his most celebrated achievement, the famous French biologist Georges Cuvier pronounced it "the greatest monument ever erected by art to Nature"—and so it has remained.

Audubon's artistic temperament shines through in every phase of a long and frequently tempestuous career. His one consuming passion was painting birds and animals as he found them in nature; all else was subordinated to this driving ambition.

Considerable mystery surrounds Audubon's early years. The most authentic evidence supports the belief that he was born in 1785 in Les Cayes, Santo Domingo (now Haiti), the illegitimate son of a French sea captain, Jean Audubon, and a native Creole girl, Mlle. Rabin. After his mother's early death, the four-year-old child was taken to France to be educated. His youth was carefree, spent in rambling through woods and fields, collecting snakes and turtles and birds' eggs, and studying music and drawing, the latter under a well-known teacher, Jacques Louis David. Young Audubon first saw the United States at the age of eighteen, when he was sent to manage his father's estate in Pennsylvania.

Audubon showed no interest in or talent for business, but in a year spent at the "Mill Grove" farm, near Philadelphia, he began his study of American birds, devoting much of his time to observing and drawing the avifauna around him. During that period he met, became engaged to, and several years later married a neighbor's daughter, Lucy Green Bakewell, whose loyal support contributed immensely to her husband's subsequent success. The young couple began their life together in Louisville, Kentucky. After several attempts to operate stores, mills, and commission businesses, all of which were failures, Audubon spent an increasing amount of time in the Kentucky wilderness with his gun and sketchbook, making and selling crayon portraits and teaching drawing, music, and dancing. While at Louisville, in 1810, he was visited by Alexander Wilson, then America's foremost ornithologist; a certain degree of rivalry later developed between them, spurred on by friends of both.

Audubon abandoned business altogether after 1819, and henceforth was solely preoccupied with his artistic efforts and attendant publication problems. At this time, apparently, he had fully determined to publish his ornithological studies and paintings. The first of a series of long expeditions took him down the Ohio and Mississippi rivers to New Orleans, during which he explored the country for birds. Another tour gave him an opportunity to study the bird life of the Lake Ontario and Lake Champlain region. Meanwhile, for the next several years the family's principal support came from his wife's salary as a governess. Near the end of 1822, Audubon received his first instruction in the use of oils from John Stein, an itinerant portrait painter. Later, Thomas Sully, a famous early-American portrait painter, gave Audubon free lessons in oil painting.

The concept of his monumental work, *The Birds of America*, seems to have been in the back of Audubon's mind for a considerable time before it reached maturity. He came to visualize the undertaking as a great portfolio of all the known birds of the North American continent, life-size, perched upon cliffs or tree branches, painted in true colors. Life-size pictures for the largest birds would require pages 3 feet by 2½ feet in size. The artistic side of the project was far simpler than the problem of financing publication and seeing the work through the press.

Visits to Philadelphia and New York in 1824 convinced Audubon that there was no hope of having his paintings published in America. The technical skill was lacking. After a two-year delay to accumulate travel funds, he sailed for England to find a publisher and to raise subscriptions for the huge folio set. Audubon landed at Liverpool on July 21, 1826, and remained abroad nearly three years. Through influential references his drawings were exhibited at the Royal Institution a week after his arrival and were an immediate success.

The original plans for publication of *The Birds of America* provided for the issuance of the drawings in parts of five plates each, at two guineas a part, all to be engraved on copper, life-sized, and colored after Audubon's paintings. The number of parts was estimated at eighty, to be completed in fourteen years. Actually, the finished work consisted of eighty-seven parts of 435 plates, in four volumes, representing more than a thousand individual birds, plus thousands of American trees, shrubs, flowers, insects, and animals of the entire continent. The end was reached in twelve years, from 1827 to 1838.

The specifications for the prodigious enterprise are contained in a prospectus issued in London, after ten numbers had been completed. The details were as follows:

> The Engravings in every instance to be of the exact dimensions of the Drawings, which, without any exception, represent the Birds of their natural size.
> The Plates will be coloured, in the most careful manner, from the original Drawings.

The Size of the work will be Double Elephant, and printed on the finest Drawing Paper.

Five plates will constitute a Number; one Plate from one of the largest Drawings, one from one of the second size, and three from the smaller Drawings.

There are 400 Drawings; and it is proposed that they shall comprise Three Volumes, each containing about 133 Plates, to which an Index will be given at the end of each, to be bound up with the Volume.

Five Numbers will come out annually.

The Price of Each Number will be Two Guineas; payable on delivery.

The price to each, subscriber — £182 14s. in England and $1,000 in America — was enough to give pause to persons of moderate means, and the roll of patrons never reached the level anticipated by Audubon. Actually, the number fluctuated during the twelve years that the work was in process of production. Some of the early subscribers tired of waiting, became dissatisfied, and dropped out, while new customers were picked up along the way. There were 279 names on the original list of patrons who had subscribed to 284 sets. By the time the project was completed, the number of names had declined to 161 for 166 copies (84 in Europe and 82 for America). Thus many original subscribers were left with incomplete sets on their hands.

After Audubon had been in England for three months, he journeyed to Edinburgh and there met William Home Lizars, a painter and engraver, who agreed to produce a specimen number of *The Birds of America*; the five plates for the first number were ready early in 1827. By the time he had finished ten plates, however, Lizars had become discouraged and withdrew from the project. At this stage Audubon had the great good fortune to meet and to form a partnership with another engraver, Robert Havell, Jr., then thirty-two years old. It was Havell who carried *The Birds of America* through to completion eleven years later and whose superb technique never faltered. His friendship with Audubon induced him to emigrate to the United States following completion of the long, drawn-out undertaking.

Concerning Havell's contribution to *The Birds of America*, Constance Rourke writes, "He remains one of the greatest artists in the difficult medium of aquatint. He lavished immense skill, conscience, even affection upon this work." The magnitude of the job undertaken by Havell may be better understood if one realizes that every illustration in Audubon's *Birds* was first engraved by hand on a copper plate; that is, each original picture was copied in every detail by etching or cutting lines on a piece of sheet copper. From the engravings, black-and-white reproductions were printed, following which each impression (numbering about 100,000) had to be colored in watercolor paints by hand, as nearly identical to the original painting as possible. The day of modern photoengraving and color printing lay far in the future.

In the course of publication, Audubon returned to America on several occasions to search for additional specimens of bird life. His journeys took him up and down the north and south Atlantic coasts, as far north as Labrador and as far south as Florida, including explorations in New Brunswick, Maine, New Jersey, and South Carolina, supplemented by further expeditions down the Ohio and Mississippi rivers, and in Louisiana and Texas. These far-flung travels account for the expansion of *The Birds of America* beyond the original estimate of size.

The four enormous volumes of *The Birds of America*, when they finally came from the press, were approximately 3 feet 3 inches high and 2 feet 5 inches wide; each volume was three inches thick and weighed between forty and forty-five pounds.

The exact number of complete sets of Audubon's masterpiece presently surviving is unknown. Some volumes have been broken up by dealers and the plates sold separately for framing. Waldemar H. Fries, in his *Double Elephant Folio* (Chicago, ALA, 1974), attempted to record every known copy. He found 134 complete and six incomplete sets. Audubon's own set, with added plates, sold at auction for $216,000 in 1970. *American Book Prices Current* recorded two sets sold at auction in London: in 1977 for $320,000, and in 1978 for $360,000.

Concurrently with *The Birds of America*, Audubon was engaged upon another large and ambitious enterprise, his *Ornithological Biography*, intended to be a complementary work. Preparation began in 1830 with the assistance of William MacGillivray of Edinburgh, and the first volume appeared the following year. The five-volume set, consisting of the life stories of the birds pictured in *The Birds of America*, was completed in 1839, followed immediately by *The Synopsis of the Birds of North America*, a systematic index listing all the birds that Audubon knew, a total of 491.

With the completion of these several major publications, Audubon and his family returned to the United States in the late summer of 1839. Fermenting in his mind were two additional projects. The first was an octavo, or miniature, edition of *The Birds of America*, which began to be issued in parts in 1839 and was in press for four years. The set, published in Philadelphia, grew to seven volumes, illustrated with 500 lithographic, colored plates, picturing seventeen new birds and many new trees and flowers. To Audubon's gratification, the work was an immediate success, attracting a total of 1,198 subscribers.

The second and last of Audubon's American publishing ventures, one which he did not live to complete, was *The Viviparous Quadrupeds of North America*. A large folio edition was issued in two volumes in 1845-1846, and an octavo edition in three volumes appeared during the period from 1846 to 1854. Only the first volume of the latter work was seen by Audubon before his death in 1851.

A century and a half ago, when Audubon was collecting specimens for *The Birds of America* and other writings, the balance of nature in America was relatively undisturbed. The coming of "civilization" in the interim has caused dramatic changes in the environment. Many species and subspecies once numerous are extinct or in imminent peril of becoming extinct. Some species, such as the carrier pigeon, man has slaughtered wholesale. The native habitats of others have been altered so drastically that the birds can no longer exist. To a certain extent, therefore, Audubon has left a record of bird life no longer visible in nature. As Constance Rourke comments in her biography of Audubon:

> The parroquets are no longer a cloud of green among leafless sycamores. The bold ivory-billed woodpecker can be found only in the deep swamps of the far South. The traveler in winter along the Mississippi will not see, as Audubon saw, a flock of trumpeter swans rising with a beating of white wings and a great clangor.[8]

There are evidences, on the other hand, that the American people are awakening to the importance of wildlife preservation, and through the efforts of such conservation organizations as the Audubon societies and the creation of refuges and sanctuaries the destructive trend is being reversed.

52

Case of the Wounded Stomach
William Beaumont (1785-1853)

Experiments and Observations on the Gastric
Juice and the Physiology of Digestion

An unfathomed mystery of medical science at the beginning of the nineteenth century was the physiology of digestion. The knowledge gap was not from lack of curiosity or of widespread experimentation. There were theories by the hundreds, but rarely were they based on facts. The existing understanding of the subject was summed up by William Hunter, a leading anatomist of the time, in these words: "Some physiologists will have it that the stomach is a mill, others, that it is a fermenting vat, others, again, that it is a stew pan; but in my view of the matter, it is neither a mill, a fermenting vat, nor a stew pan, but a stomach, gentlemen, a stomach."

Erroneous theories of digestion are traceable to such ancients as Hippocrates and Galen. Not until the eighteenth century were there significant advances in the knowledge of digestive physiology. The names of several pioneer experimenters of that era stand out. Réaumur, French scientist and inventor, performed the first systematic experiments on digestion in birds and mammals; for example, he persuaded a pet buzzard to swallow small perforated tubes containing fragments of sponge, to obtain samples of gastric juice. A contemporary, Lazzaro Spallanzani, Italian biologist, carried out numerous experiments on fish, frogs, snakes, cattle, horses, cats, dogs, and other animals, as well as on himself, finally proving that digestion is a chemical process, though he erroneously questioned the acid nature of the gastric juice. A third notable name is that of William Prout (1785-1850), the first English physiological chemist, who demonstrated that the gastric juice contained hydrochloric acid—a major discovery.

It remained, however, for an American, "a backwoods physiologist," William Beaumont, to learn what actually happens in the stomach during the digestion of food and to present a detailed and comprehensive picture of the whole cycle of gastric digestion in a book which Harvey Cushing, a century later, called "the most notable and original classic of American medicine."

Beaumont's opportunity to achieve medical immortality came about by a freak accident. Beaumont, a native of Lebanon, Connecticut, born in 1785, was not a medical school graduate—few doctors of the period were—but had served an apprenticeship with a practicing physician in St. Albans, Vermont. After two years of study he enlisted in the army as an assistant surgeon. Following the War of 1812, he was stationed at Fort Mackinac, where Lake Michigan and Lake Huron join.

Mackinac, a primitive frontier community in the Michigan territory, had become a center for John Jacob Astor's American Fur Company. Early each summer, there was an influx of Indians, half-breeds, trappers, and Canadian voyageurs, bringing in their winter's collection of pelts to sell or barter at the company's retail trading post. It was in this crowded store, on the morning of June 6, 1822, that a gun went off accidentally and a young French Canadian, Alexis St. Martin, fell with a huge wound in his side. His shirt caught fire and burned until it was quenched by the flow of blood. Dr. Beaumont was sent for and arrived within minutes.

As described by Beaumont, the charge, consisting of powder and buck shot, was received in the left side of the nineteen-year-old youth, who had been standing not more than a yard from the muzzle of the gun. A portion of the lungs as large as a turkey's egg protruded through the external wound, lacerated and burned; below this was another protrusion resembling a portion of the stomach, "which at first sight I could not believe possible to be that organ in that situation with the subject surviving," wrote Beaumont, "but on closer examination I found it to be actually the stomach with a puncture in the protruding portion large enough to receive my forefinger." The frightful wound had torn open the chest wall, leaving a hole as large as the palm of a hand, and ribs were fractured. A mixture of food, blood, and splinters of bone escaped from the wounded stomach. Further, "The whole mass of materials forced from the musket, together with fragments of clothing and pieces of fractured ribs, were driven into the muscles and cavity of the chest."

Beaumont proceeded to render first aid, cleansing the wound and applying a superficial dressing, though he was convinced that it was impossible for the patient to survive twenty minutes. The surgeon underestimated the tenacity and toughness of the dark, wiry little half-breed. About an hour later, the wound was dressed more thoroughly—Beaumont still "not supposing it possible or probable for him to survive the operation of extracting the fractured fragments of bones and other extraneous substances." But "to the utter amazement of everyone he bore it without a struggle or without sinking." Before the protruding lung could be returned into the cavity of the thorax, Beaumont was forced to cut off with a penknife the point of a fractured rib on which it was caught, and thereafter the lung had to be held in place by pressure to avoid its being forced out by coughing.

The patient was removed to the primitive base hospital, and there under Beaumont's expert care he rallied slowly, though his body was still full of shot, wadding, and splintered bone. After four months, St. Martin's miraculous tissues began to expel all foreign matter. For the better part of a year, day after day, and month after month, Beaumont continued to treat the youth, dressing the terrible wound at frequent intervals, opening successive abscesses, removing fragments of indriven cartilage or bone, as the damaged region began gradually to form healthy scar tissue.

A new kind of crisis developed some ten months following the accident. The town officials refused further assistance to the destitute patient, now a pauper without funds, relatives, or friends. Beaumont was confronted with a dilemma: He had the alternative of packing the youth off in an open bateau to his native place fifteen hundred miles away, a voyage which he could scarcely have survived, or of taking him into his own home. Impelled by motives of charity and kindness, Beaumont chose the latter course—a decision he could ill afford, since he was supporting a family on an army surgeon's salary of forty dollars per month. Nonetheless, Beaumont moved the patient into his household, where he nursed, fed, clothed, and lodged him, while continuing with the daily dressing of the slowly healing wound. By the end of another year, Alexis had recovered his health and strength sufficiently to do household chores for the Beaumonts, but was still incapable of earning his own living. Thus began a long relationship between the military surgeon and the young French Canadian who was destined to go through life with a hole in his stomach.

After the first year, the skin tissue around the opening had healed. St. Martin, however, stubbornly refused to submit to an operation to suture the lips together. A most fortunate circumstance was that instead of dropping back into the abdominal cavity the rim of the stomach puncture adhered to the rim of the external wound. As a result of the union of the lacerated edges of the stomach and the intercostal muscles, a phenomenon known to medical men as a gastric fistula developed. Eventually an inner coat of St. Martin's stomach folded across the opening, forming a leakproof valve. A round hole, large enough to admit the doctor's forefinger directly into the stomach, remained permanently. The valve held the food in "but was easily depressed with the finger," Beaumont reported.

Quite early in his treatment of young Alexis, Beaumont came to realize that he was being presented with a unique opportunity to explore the great mystery of human digestion. In May 1825, about three years after the gunshot episode, Beaumont began his first series of gastric experiments on the patient, who by now was fully recovered. In the daily routine of dressing the wound, Beaumont made a momentous discovery. When Alexis lay on his right side, causing the stomach to fall away from its attachment to the margins of the healing wound, "I can look directly into the cavity of the stomach," Beaumont wrote, "observe its motion, and almost see the process of digestion. I can pour in water with a funnel and put in food with a spoon, and draw them out again with a siphon.... The case affords an excellent opportunity for experiment upon the gastric juices and the process of digestion. It would give no pain or cause the least uneasiness to extract a gill of fluid every two or three days, for it frequently flows out spontaneously in considerable quantities; and I might introduce various digestible substances into the stomach and easily examine them during the whole process of digestion."

The walls of the fistula could be pushed apart with a thermometer, giving Beaumont a chance to peer five or six inches into the interior of the cavity. He found that the stomach walls were pale pink in color, soft and velvety-looking, and lined with a mucous coat. When a few bread crumbs were inserted, the stomach brightened in color, hundreds of tiny droplets began to rise through the mucous film and trickle down the walls—the "gastric juice," as Spallanzani had called it, tasting of hydrochloric acid. Here was the first step in the digestive process.

There followed over a period of years a variety of experiments, using all of the foods found in a frontier community. The surgeon passed into the stomach through the fistula pieces of raw beef, cooked beef, fat pork, stale bread, raw sliced cabbage, and other vegetables. In all, hundreds of foodstuffs were tested with regard to the length of time required for their digestion in the stomach. The items were tied to a long piece of silk string at spaced intervals and pushed individually through the opening, which was about two and one half inches in circumference. An hour later, Beaumont withdrew the food particles and found the cabbage and bread about half-digested. At the end of a second hour, they had vanished completely, along with the pork and boiled beef. Hourly examinations throughout the day showed the other foods being digested at a slower rate. The raw meat turned out to be almost wholly indigestible.

Another ingenious experiment was concerned with artificial digestion. Through a tube, as Beaumont describes the operation, he "drew off one ounce of pure gastric liquor, unmixed with any other matter, except a small proportion of mucus, into a three ounce vial. I then took a solid piece of *boiled, recently salted beef*, weighing three drachms, and put it into the liquor in the vial; corked the vial tight, and placed it in a saucepan, filled with water, raised to the temperature of 100° (found by Beaumont to be the stomach's normal temperature) and kept at that point, on a nicely regulated sand bath. In *forty minutes* digestion had distinctly commenced over the surface of the meat. In fifty minutes the fluid had become quite opaque and cloudy; the external texture had begun to separate and become loose. In *sixty minutes* chyme began to form." Not until ten hours after the test began, however, was the meat completely digested. A similar piece of meat suspended in the stomach was fully digested in two hours.

Beaumont was the first person in history to isolate pure human gastric juice, but lacking chemical training he was unable to analyze it. He observed, however, that the liquid is "a clear, transparent fluid; inodorous, a little saltish; and very perceptibly acid." It was concluded, too, that the gastric juice is "powerfully antiseptic," and is "the most general solvent in nature, of alimentary matter — even the hardest bone cannot withstand its action." From its behavior, Beaumont had no doubt that the fluid was a chemical agent. The gastric juice, he found, does not accumulate in the stomach during a period of fasting — thus a starving person would produce no gastric fluid — but only appears in response to the partaking of food or artificial stimulus. Beaumont suggested the possible presence of another agent in digestion, though he could not identify it. Researches by Theodor Schwann, German botanist and physiologist, a few years later isolated the substance; he gave it the name of pepsin.

In an effort to learn more about the nature of gastric juice, Beaumont sent samples for analysis to two of the leading chemists in America, Robley Dunglison of the University of Virginia and Benjamin Silliman of Yale University. The former reported that the major active ingredient was hydrochloric acid; Silliman also found hydrochloric acid present, but was otherwise vague, evading the issue with the statement that "the laws of the Creator were often incomprehensible equally in His nature and His works." A specimen sent to the famous Swedish chemist Berzelius elicited a reply too late and too indecisive to be of value.

Beaumont's investigations did not proceed smoothly and without incident in other respects. Feeling the need for a laboratory and medical library, he asked for a transfer eastward, and received an assignment to Niagara Falls, taking his patient with him. Two such different personalities, however, were incompatible, and there was constant friction between them. Alexis St. Martin resented being treated as a human guinea pig and hated the discomfort of having interminable tubes, strings, and bags moving in and out of his stomach, and being required to go on diets and fasts. His meals were frequently eaten lying down, while Beaumont watched the food pass through the gullet; he was ordered to carry small bottles under his armpits — Beaumont's method of demonstrating that animal heat is not different from ordinary heat – and many of the experiments made him ill. He was illiterate, addicted to drunken binges, homesick for his old life in the forest, and longed for the girl he had left behind him in Canada.

It is scarcely surprising, therefore, that in the new post, so temptingly near his native land, St. Martin tied his belongings in a bundle one night and vanished. Beaumont was deeply distressed to have his promising experiments interrupted so suddenly and apparently permanently. While he searched without avail for his missing patient, Alexis had gone off to marry Marie Jolly, father two children, and to resume his career as a voyageur in the Indian country for the Hudson Bay Company. Four years passed before the truant was found, living in a village near Montreal. Reluctantly he agreed to return and to submit to a new series of experiments, but only on condition that his family accompany him and he be generously compensated. To ensure Alexis' loyalty, a detailed legal contract was drawn up, to which the young Canadian affixed his mark. The financial burden on Beaumont was removed by enrolling St. Martin in the army and assigning him to the medical service.

The surgeon was happy to find that despite the four-year break, the patient's "stomach and side were in a similar condition as when he left me in 1825. The aperture was open, and his health good." As reported by Beaumont:

> I commenced another series of experiments on the stomach and gastric fluids and continued them uninterruptedly until March 1831. During this time, in the intervals of experimenting, he performed all the duties of a common servant, chopping wood, carrying burdens, etc., with little or no suffering or inconvenience from the wound. He labored constantly, became the father of more children, and enjoyed as good health and as much vigor as men in general. He subsisted on crude food in abundant quantities, except when on a prescribed diet for particular experimental purposes and under special observation.

With the resumption of his experiments, Beaumont kept a meticulous record of his observations – to appear later in printed form – noting the movements of the stomach during digestion, studying the effects of temperature, sleep, and anger on the flow of gastric juice, describing the results of starvation and of overeating. His charts represented the fluctuations of gastric secretion under a variety of conditions, and he timed the exact hours and minutes required for the digestion of numerous foods from both the animal and vegetable kingdoms. After Alexis' frequent alcoholic sprees, his stomach's condition was checked by Beaumont. Fundamental facts on human diet, nutrition, and digestion emerged from the long drawn-out experiments.

A preliminary report on his findings was published by Beaumont in 1825 in the *Medical Recorder* under the title "A Case of Wounded Stomach." At the conclusion of his 238 experiments, there was printed in 1833, at Plattsburgh, New York, Beaumont's definitive work, *Experiments and Observations on the Gastric Juice and the Physiology of Digestion*, an octavo volume of 280 pages in an edition of one thousand copies. The book was cheaply printed at the author's expense and sold by subscription for two dollars per copy. The current value on the rare book market ranges between five hundred and a thousand dollars.

Beaumont writes in an unpretentious, direct style. His "Preliminary Observations," discussing the physiology of digestion in general, fill approximately one hundred pages, divided into seven sections: Of Aliment, Of

Hunger and Thirst, Of Satisfaction and Satiety, Of Mastication, Insalivation, and Deglutition, Of Digestion by the Gastric Juice, Of the Appearance of the Villous Coat and the Motions of the Stomach, and Of Chylification and Uses of the Bile and Pancreatic Juice. The second major division of the book is a detailed description in chronological order of the experiments, followed by a brief summary of fifty-one "inferences" or conclusions.

Many of Beaumont's diverse findings have entered into general knowledge. Concerning the matter of overloading the stomach, for example, he points out, "There is always disturbance of the stomach when more food has been received than there is gastric juice to act upon it." Overeating is an all too common human failing, in the view of the author, who asserts that "the quantity of food generally taken is more than the wants of the system require; and such excess, if persevered in, generally produces not only functional aberration, but disease of the coats of the stomach." It is recognized that individual needs vary; for example, "Persons who do not exercise much, require less nutritious diet than those who are in the habit of constant labor.... Young people who are growing, require more nutriment in proportion to their size than those who have arrived at adult age."

Beaumont's researches support the objections of religious and temperance groups to use of alcohol and stimulating beverages. "The whole class of alcoholic liquors, whether simply fermented or distilled," he states, "may be considered as *narcotics* ... and the use of *ardent spirits* always produces disease of the stomach, if persevered in." Water is the only fluid called for by the human system; "Even coffee and tea, the common beverages of all classes of people, have a tendency to debilitate the digestive organs." Also having religious sanction, ancient in this instance, is the statement, "The digestibility of most meats is improved by incipient putrifaction, sufficient to render the muscular fibre slightly tender."

Among numerous other conclusions reached by Beaumont were these: Meats and "farinaceous substances" are easier to digest than vegetables; oily substances are digested with great difficulty; fish (not including shellfish) are easily digestible; condiments are non-nutritious and, except for salt and vinegar, should be avoided. Actually, in Beaumont's opinion, "the stomach is a creature of habit. It can become accustomed to any kind of diet; and sudden changes are likely to derange its healthy actions. To those accustomed to what is called high living, such as strong meats, strong drinks, and high seasoned food, of all kinds, the transition to a meat diet, which contains a considerably lowered stimulation, would probably be an imprudent change."

Moderate exercise, Beaumont found, contributes to healthy and rapid digestion. "Severe and fatiguing exercise, on the contrary, retards digestion." There is a close relation, too, between emotional states and the digestive process. Fear and anger check the flow of the gastric juices, and "the latter causes an influx of bile into the stomach, which impairs its solvent properties." Bile is not present in a healthy stomach if the subject is in "an equable frame of mind."

Beaumont attempted to verify the results of his experiments during a six-month stay in Washington, DC, where he had access to most of the available medical literature on digestion. Some authorities supported his conclusions; others, lacking Beaumont's unique opportunities for first-hand observation, were full of beautiful but erroneous theories, mainly based on observations of animals. Beaumont pays his respects to the latter group of writers in these words:

> It is unfortunate for the interests of physiological science, that it generally falls to the lot of men of vivid imaginations, and great

powers of mind, to become restive under the restraints of a tedious and *routine* mode of thinking, and to strike out into bold and original hypotheses to elucidate the operations of nature, or to account for the phenomena that are constantly submitted to their attention. The process of developing truth, by patient and persevering investigation, experiment and research, is incompatible with their notions of unrestrained genius. The drudgery of science, they leave to humbler, and more unpretending contributors. The flight of genius is, however, frequently erratic.

The reception of Beaumont's book at home and abroad was gratifying. As George Rosen brings out in detail in his *The Reception of William Beaumont's Discovery in Europe*, the Beaumont revelations were even more fully appreciated abroad during the early years after publication than they were in his native country — partially, no doubt, because of the European physicians' greater sophistication and familiarity with scientific method. German, French, and Scottish editions soon appeared, and both the medical and lay press carried numerous articles describing and evaluating the findings. Because of Beaumont's precise observations and careful recording of the experiments, there was little inclination anywhere to question his conclusions. In John F. Fulton's judgment, "William Beaumont may be ranked with Benjamin Franklin and Weir Mitchell as one of three Americans whose writings exerted a profound influence upon medical thought of Europe prior to 1900." In America, reprint editions and a second, revised edition were issued within a few years.

Perhaps the most important of Beaumont's contributions were his investigations on the influence of the psyche on gastric secretion, leading a half century later to Pavlov's famous experiments on dogs; his research on the problem of nervous dyspepsia and gastritis; and studies on the effects of intemperance and unwholesome diet on digestion. The subsequent development of studies in gastric physiology, pathology, and therapy owe a great debt to Beaumont's pioneer discoveries. A foremost historian of medicine, Sir William Osler, felt justified in calling Beaumont "the first great American physiologist."

In 1834, presumably for a visit, Alexis St. Martin was given leave to return to Canada. At approximately the same time, Beaumont was transferred by the military authorities to St. Louis, where he resided for the remainder of his career. Efforts over a period of twenty years to persuade St. Martin to return, for a continuation of the experiments, were fruitless. Thus ended the strange alliance so inadvertently begun. Alexis St. Martin outlived his partner in medical research by twenty-seven years and sired seventeen children in all; at the time of his death in 1880, he was chopping cordwood for a living, having lived for fifty-eight years with a hole in his vitals. After his death, his family adamantly refused to permit an autopsy, and to ensure that he would not be dug up, buried him secretly in an unmarked grave eight feet deep.

53

Birth of Photography
Louis Daguerre (1789-1851)

History and Description of the Process of Daguerreotype

So omnipresent are photographic processes in modern life, it is difficult to realize that they were invented and came into practical use less than a century and a half ago. Present-day books, periodicals, and newspapers would seem barren without the products of highly sophisticated cameras, and large corporations and industries have been built to meet the demands for pictorial material.

The first practical photographic process was invented by a Frenchman, Louis Daguerre, in the 1830s. Daguerre was a painter and a physicist. Early in his career he helped to execute a series of panoramic views of Rome, Naples, London, Jerusalem, and Athens. Subsequently, he opened in Paris an exhibition called a Diorama ("double view"), pictorial views, with effects heightened by changes in the light thrown upon them. A similar show was later arranged by Daguerre in London.

Daguerre and another French experimenter, Joseph Nicéphore Niépce, appear to have begun attempts to develop a photographic process near the same time. Since 1814, Niépce had been seeking a means of obtaining permanent pictures by the action of sunlight. When he learned that Daguerre was similarly occupied, he suggested that they join forces. In 1829, he forwarded to Daguerre details of his method of fixing the image produced in the "camera lucida" by making use of metallic plates coated with a composition of asphalt and oil of lavender.

Daguerre and Niépce continued their joint investigations to produce "heliographic pictures" from 1829 to 1833, when the latter died. Daguerre continued his experiments, eventually discovering the process associated with his name, the daguerreotype. As announced by Daguerre, the procedure consisted of six steps: 1) a sheet of copper, plated with silver, was polished to mirror-like brilliance; 2) the plate was placed in a box over particles of iodine, the vapor of which, reacting with the silver, formed light-sensitive silver iodide; 3) the sensitized plate was exposed in a camera from twenty to forty minutes; 4) the exposed plate was suspended over heated mercury, which formed an amalgam in proportion to the amount of light received by the plate; 5) the unexposed silver iodide was washed away with sodium thiosulphate; and, finally, 6) the daguerreotype was rinsed with distilled water and dried.

The first full account of both process and technique was embodied in Daguerre's famous brochure, *Historique et Description des Procédés de Daguerreotype et du Diorama* (Paris, 1839). A number of issues of the work appeared within a short time.

A well-known French scientist, François Arago, learned of Daguerre's invention and reported the discovery to a meeting of the Academy of Sciences early in 1839, pointing out the importance of the new device. On the basis of recommendations made by Arago to the French government, Daguerre was appointed an officer in the Legion of Honor. At the same time, a bill was introduced in the French Parliament to acquire the invention. An appropriation was approved to pay annuities to Daguerre and to his deceased partner's son, Isodore Niépce. By agreement, Daguerre's process, together with his system of transparent and opaque painting, was published by the government, and soon became widely known.

A phenomenal growth of photography occurred during the months following announcement of the invention. In response to popular demand, Daguerre offered instruction in the new art of photography.

As time passed, the elaborate process of 1839 became simplified, and steady improvements were made. In 1839, William Henry Fox Talbot introduced the negative-positive process, the basis for today's photography. In the same year, Sir John Herschel discovered hyposulfite of soda, "hypo," as the fixing agent in photographic processing. The collodion, or wet-plate process was invented by Frederick Scott Archer in 1851, using a glass negative. The wet plate was used by Matthew B. Brady for his celebrated Civil War pictures, and by William H. Jackson in early Western explorations. The development of the dry plate greatly simplified the taking of pictures, and in the 1880s George Eastman applied its principle to roll film used in hand cameras.

54

Electrical Pioneer
Michael Faraday (1791-1867)

Experimental Researches in Electricity

Michael Faraday's career fulfills all the specifications for a Horatio Alger hero: son of a poor blacksmith, industrious, persevering, honest, and unselfish, having almost no formal education, winning the good will and support of highly placed persons, and rising at last to become one of the most eminent scientists of all time, offered a knighthood and the presidency of the Royal Society, and loaded with other honors.

Modern civilization, based so largely upon electricity, owes more to Michael Faraday and his discoveries than to any other individual. Out of his extraordinary researches grew the principles of the generator and the electric motor, which provided a method of producing electrical energy by mechanical rather than chemical action. Faraday's experiments also revealed the principle of the transformer, making it possible to transmit electric current over long distances.

At the beginning of the nineteenth century, in Faraday's youth, electricity was nothing more than a laboratory toy. To fascinated scientists, it represented one of nature's most elusive secrets, but it could not be said to have any practical significance. The first great breakthrough was achieved by Alessandro Volta, an Italian physicist, when, in 1800, he invented a chemical source of electricity, the voltaic cell or pile, generating a steady flow of electric current. Volta's process was to place copper and zinc plates alternately, insert cloths soaked in a dilute acid between them, and then connect the end plates. Voltaic piles containing as many as two thousand plates were put together. The method was costly and produced only low-power current. It led, however, to the construction of the electromagnet, important for further research efforts.

Faraday's scientific career started with his appointment as assistant to Sir Humphry Davy, director of the Royal Institution's laboratory and a notable teacher. From the outset, Faraday demonstrated genius in chemical experimentation, discovering the fundamental laws of electrolysis (chemical decomposition by the action of electric current), liquefying various gases, and isolating benzene for the first time. But, increasingly, electrical researches claimed Faraday's interest and attention, and it is in this area that he was destined to gain his greatest fame.

The finding of a relation between magnetism and electricity had been announced in 1820 by a Danish physicist, Hans Christian Oersted. By running a current through a wire, he found that he could induce a movement in a nearby magnet. Oersted suggested that a magnetic field surrounded the wire conductor. Davy and Faraday promptly became interested in the new electromagnetic discovery, and repeated experiments made by Oersted, Ampère, and other scientists of the time.

After repeated failures, Faraday, in September 1821, working alone, demonstrated electromagnetic rotation. He found that the flow of electric current caused a magnet to revolve around a wire-carrying current or a wire-carrying current to revolve around a fixed magnet. Such motions continued as long as the current continued to flow. Here was the principle of the electric motor.

For the next ten years, Faraday was preoccupied with the problem of converting magnetic force into some form of electrical force. In his mind, the central question was: If an electric current could yield magnetism, could not a magnet produce electricity? Among other experiments, he tried to induce current in a wire by placing a magnet near it, but the attempt failed. Later he realized that it was the motion of the electric current in the wire that produced magnetism.

In the summer of 1831, Faraday began another experiment to solve the problem, an effort that culminated in his most epoch-making discovery. The experiment that succeeded now appears extremely simple: a coil of insulated wire, connected to a galvanometer (an instrument for measuring a small electric current by movement of a magnetic needle), was wound on a hollow paper cylinder. As a magnet was thrust in and pulled out of the cylinder or the cylinder was moved over the magnet, the galvanometer registered the passage of an electric current in the coil of wire.

A short while later, in October 1831, Faraday built the world's first generator, consisting of a copper disk rotating between the poles of a large magnet, mounted on an axle and operated by turning a crank. Thus was electricity finally generated from magnetism—the principle of the dynamo. It is upon this basic principle that all commercial electricity is produced today, for a modern electric generator is essentially a coil of wire (an armature) rotated between the poles of a set of magnets.

Faraday reported his results to the Royal Society within a month and formulated the discovery into a paper for publication, the first of a series of twenty-nine papers, eventually brought together in three volumes under the title *Experimental Researches in Electricity.*

The solution to the mystery of electromagnetic induction was not enough to satisfy Faraday's insatiable curiosity about natural phenomena. He wanted to know *why* a moving magnet induced an electric current in a conductor. The answer he proposed was that the space surrounding the magnet was filled with lines of force. In fact, Faraday concluded that all space is filled with various kinds of force: magnetic, electric, radiant, heat, and gravitational.

In direct contrast to Newton, who had conceived of space as rigid, absolute emptiness, Faraday imagined space as being alive with moving, flexible, ever-changing electromagnetic forces. Here is the historic origin of the theory of the electromagnetic field, considered by many scientists to be Faraday's greatest contribution.

A younger contemporary of Faraday's, James Clerk Maxwell, was profoundly impressed by the field theory. By mathematical analysis, he proved that electromagnetic disturbances and waves of light are transmitted by the same medium and at the same speed. Consequently, Maxwell was able, in 1873, to announce the electromagnetic theory of light. In the hands of later scientists—Hertz, Marconi, and others—there developed out of these highly theoretical investigations such practical applications as wireless telegraphy, radio, and television.

Faraday himself had no interest in inventing devices to use electricity. Commercially feasible generators, electric lights, electric motors, and all the remaining paraphernalia of the age of electricity awaited the inventive genius of later generations of engineers and scientists.

Faraday's philosophy of scientific research is revealed in these comments:

> Let the imagination go, guarding it by judgement and principle, but holding it in and directing it by experiment.... In the most successful instances (of scientific investigation) not a tenth of the suggestions, the hopes, the wishes, the preliminary conclusions have been realized.... Nature is our best friend and best critic in experimental science if we only allow her intimations to fall unbiased on our minds. Nothing is so good as an experiment which, while it sets an error right, gives as a reward for our humility an absolute advance in knowledge.

55

Interpreter and Synthesizer

Charles Lyell (1797-1875)

*Principles of Geology, Being an Attempt to Explain
the Former Changes of the Earth's Surface, by
Reference to Causes Now in Operation*

It has been remarked that James Hutton, on whose theories a large share of the superstructure of modern geology now rests, was born fifty years too soon. Neither scientists nor the lay public found his radical beliefs acceptable, and he died virtually unhonored and unsung.

By coincidence, in the year of Hutton's death, 1797, there was born another Scotsman, Charles Lyell, who was to champion and expand the Huttonian teachings and play an instrumental part in obtaining their adoption by the world of science. This was accomplished by Lyell through his *Principles of Geology*, a work which for more than a century and a half has exercised an immeasurable influence on the development of geological science.

While other sciences were moving ahead in the eighteenth and early nineteenth centuries, the progress of geology was seriously retarded. During these years, the biblical story of the Creation and the Flood remained the fundamental textbook of geology. Fossils were believed to be the remains of animals lost in Noah's Flood. Geologists in general held the view that the whole history of the earth consisted of a series of sudden and violent catastrophes, by which the bed of the ocean was suddenly raised and its waters precipitated onto the land, carrying with it universal ruin and extermination of all life. Following such catastrophes, there would be periods of quiet, during which the new earth was repopulated, by direct act of creation, with new forms of life adapted to the new conditions. Species of life were unchanged until another universal cataclysm exterminated them.

Still raging in Lyell's youth was the controversy between the Neptunists, who argued that the earth's crust was formed by layers deposited or precipitated by an ocean that once covered the entire surface of the globe, and the Vulcanists, who maintained that the earth's present contours are accounted for by volcanic action. Into this murky atmosphere came Charles Lyell, with extraordinary talent for synthesizing the findings of other scientists and for interpreting the most varied natural phenomena. Coupled with this ability were powers for keen observation and a clear, logical writing style. It was said of Lyell by Sir Andrew Ramsay, "We collect the data and Lyell teaches us to comprehend the meaning of them." While still in his early thirties, Lyell produced the first edition of the *Principles of Geology*, a work that was to go through a dozen editions during his lifetime.

The dominant idea in Lyell's writings is that geological causes and processes, i.e., past events, can be discovered only by studying the forces at work on the earth today. Fully convinced that the present is the key to the past, he amassed overwhelming data to support his theory. His observations were that mountains and continents are being built, strata are being folded and broken, igneous and sedimentary rocks are being formed, and fossils are being buried in the same manner now as in past ages. There have been no vast cataclysms or devastating floods. All processes have been orderly and uniform.

Thus arose the uniformitarian doctrine to oppose the theories of the apostles of catastrophism. According to Lyell, given eons of time, all the phenomena in geological history can be accounted for by natural forces in daily operation. Catastrophic changes in either the organic or inorganic world were ruled out.

Strong support for the uniformitarian approach came from the researches on fossil remains of plants and animals, especially in relation to strata formation, carried on by such scientists as William Smith in England and Cuvier in France. This branch of geology, paleontology, was almost unknown in James Hutton's time. Year by year it became evident that the earth's crust contained materials for a history of organic nature from early geological periods to the present. Fossils also provided evidence on the nature and order of physical changes, such as alternations of sea and land and revolutions in climate. The scattered observations of numerous individuals concerned with paleontology were assembled by Lyell and generalized upon in his *Principles of Geology*. Lyell's work served as a trailblazer for the later acceptance of Darwin's theory of evolution.

Lyell's *Principles* was, in effect, a rewriting of the whole of the existing science of physical and historical geology, a systematic synthesis and interpretation of all prevailing knowledge of the subject. Lyell was not content, however, to depend entirely upon investigations by others. To verify facts, to clarify doubtful points, and to reinforce his own conclusions, he traveled widely through Great Britain, the Continent, and North America, examining peaks, precipices, snow fields, glaciers, and lakes in the Alps and Pyrenees; the cones, craters, and lava streams of the Vesuvius and Etna volcanoes; and similar natural phenomena of geological interest. Traveling he considered "as the first, second and third requisite for a modern geologist in the present adolescent state of the science."

Lyell and Charles Darwin were close personal friends, and Darwin was encouraged by Lyell to publish the *Origin of Species*. In his journals, Darwin has recorded the deep impression made on his mind by the first reading of the *Principles of Geology*. The book had been taken with him on the celebrated *Beagle* expedition around the world. On the occasion of Lyell's death, Darwin wrote, "How completely he revolutionized geology; for I can remember something of Pre-Lyellian days—I never forget that almost everything which I have done in science I owe to the study of his great works."

56

Paths of the Sea
Matthew Fontaine Maury (1806-1873)

The Physical Geography of the Sea

The founder of the modern science of oceanography spent his youth some 450 miles inland from the Atlantic, but from early boyhood the sea held an irresistible fascination for Matthew Fontaine Maury. His inspiration doubtless came from an older brother who had been marooned in the South Seas, sailed on the *Essex* under Porter against British men-of-war, fought on Lake Champlain, and was flag captain of the squadron that destroyed the pirates of the West Indies.

Maury was born on a farm near Fredericksburg, Virginia in 1806, and as a five-year-old moved with his family to Franklin, Tennessee, near Nashville. In 1825, as a protégé of Sam Houston, then a congressman from Tennessee, Maury received a midshipman's warrant and reported to the Secretary of the Navy for training. His tour of naval duty included a voyage to France on a ship that carried Lafayette home after his last visit to the United States; circumnavigation of the globe on the *Vincennes*, the first American warship to sail around the world; and sailing master aboard the sloop-of-war *Falmouth* on a cruise around the Horn into the Pacific, to join the American squadron there in patrolling the west coast of South America.

After nine years of almost continuous sea duty, Maury returned home. In the course of his long voyages he had been impressed with the meagerness of the information then available to mariners concerning the ocean's prevailing winds and currents which favor or retard the progress of ships under sail. Maury had learned during his seagoing experience that adverse winds or the drift of currents could force a vessel far off its projected route. He also found that a ship could double its speed by taking advantage of favorable currents. The problem was how to develop a science out of these facts.

During the period when Maury was a young naval officer, a voyage to South America was a leisurely, zigzagging affair. Because of legends that the northeastern extremity of Brazil was swept by dangerous currents, early navigators first sailed to Europe in order to follow an old and tried route. If their destination was Australia or China, they would cross the Atlantic again to round the Cape of Good Hope.

It cannot be claimed that Maury was the first to recognize the need for reliable information for navigation purposes. The Greek sailors of antiquity had learned how to utilize the etesians—the northerly summer winds of the Aegean Sea—and the monsoons, which, changing their direction twice a year, make the round-trip voyage to India easy sailing. After the fifteenth century, the trade winds of the Atlantic and Pacific began to be understood and used by sailors. The astronomer Halley charted the ocean winds over the intertropical region of the globe in 1688, despite the scanty data then available. Benjamin Franklin produced a usable map of the Gulf Stream in 1770, and from 1809 to 1811 Captain James Horsburgh published full accounts of the winds of the Eastern sea routes. None of these earlier efforts, however, rivaled in completeness, accuracy, and comprehensiveness the sea charts to be prepared by Matthew Fontaine Maury. He was indeed the first great "pathfinder of the seas."

Maury's first scientific article, "On the Navigation of Cape Horn," based on his own experience, described graphically the dangers of the passage of Cape Horn, and gave specific information concerning the winds and the peculiar rising and falling of the barometer in those latitudes. Encouraged by the response to his initial writings, Maury embarked on a larger enterprise, a book on navigation, printed in 1836 under the title *A New Theoretical and Practical Treatise on Navigation*, the first nautical work of science to come from the pen of an American naval officer. Among those who commended the book was Nathaniel Bowditch, of whose *New American Practical Navigator* Maury was an avid student. The Maury work went through several editions, was adopted as a textbook by junior officers in the navy, and became the basis for the author's later, more famous book, *The Physical Geography of the Sea*.

In a series of anonymous articles appearing in the Richmond *Whig and Public Advertiser* and the *Southern Literary Messenger*, Maury criticized the low quality of education of U.S. Navy midshipmen and called for reorganization and drastic change in other navel matters. The articles urged the establishment of a naval academy similar to the army's West Point; broader education for naval officers, including foreign languages and international law; higher ranks and better pay for naval officers; and a large navy, better harbor defenses, vigorous enforcement of the law against the African slave trade, and greater protection for merchant shipping against the Chinese pirates.

Because of a crippling accident which precluded further sea duty, Maury was placed in charge, in 1842, of the Depot of Charts and Instruments, from which later developed the Hydrographic Office and the Naval Observatory. Still later, the Weather Bureau took over the task of collecting marine weather statistics. Here began Maury's in-depth studies of the meteorology of the ocean.

In the building of the Depot of Charts and Instruments, stored away in cellar, closets, and attic, were bundles of old logbooks covered with dust. The books had been deposited by hundreds of captains after thousands of voyages. They told the stories of the windjammers which had sailed all over the world. Therein were recorded the observations of sea captains who had watched the winds, weather, and currents. The new superintendent at once recognized the mine of information that could be extracted from the primary records. Maury's method of work is described as follows by Harold A. Calahan, naval authority:

If he found that a ship encountered northwest winds in latitude 40°
north, longitude 60° west in the month of July, he went through the
log of every ship that had sailed near that spot in that month in the
60-odd years of his records to see what winds she had encountered.
Presently there began to emerge a picture of the ocean — winds,
currents, temperatures, storms, waves, ice, whales, everything. Maury
reasoned that if ships found the same conditions in the same seasons
in the same parts of the ocean for 60 years, there would be a strong
probability that ships in the future would find the same conditions at
the same time in the same places.

Altogether, Maury and his assistants cataloged more than 10,000 ships' logs.
Slowly they pieced together an imperfect picture of the sea. There were blank
spots for which no data were available, but after five years Maury felt sufficiently
confident of his facts to publish the first *Wind and Current Chart of the North
Atlantic* (1847). Some 5,000 copies were distributed to skippers along the Atlantic
seaborad.

To fill gaps in the record, Maury knew that additional, more complete data
were required. A year after the original chart was issued, therefore, he devised
and printed thousands of blank charts on which sea captains were asked to mark
the tracks of their ships from day to day. As described by Maury's biographer,
Charles L. Lewis:

They were to enter in this log the latitude and longitude every day at
noon; the hourly rate of the currents expressed in knots; the variation
of the compass; the reading of the thermometer, in both air and water,
at nine o'clock each morning; the state of the barometer just before,
during, and just after a gale of wind with the changes and time of
changes in the direction of the wind during the gale; careful entries as
to the direction and force of the winds every eight hours; and other
marine phenomena such as whales, flocks of birds, rains and fogs,
etc., etc.

By 1851, fully a thousand skippers were cooperating with Maury, sending in
logs of winds and weather from far and near on all the oceans. As fast as the
information came in, Maury revised his charts and brought out new editions. A
long series of charts appeared, accompanied by texts, relating to winds, currents,
and other matters of practical interest to sailors, including the average frequency
of rain, fog, and thunderstorms in different areas, the temperature of the sea,
and the locations of profitable whaling grounds. About 200,000 copies of the
charts and 20,000 copies of sailing directions in book form were distributed free
to the mariners who cooperated in gathering the information.

The results were spectacular, and quickly converted skeptics among the sea
captains who had doubted the value of the charts. The average voyage by a sailing
vessel from New York to Rio had been 55 days; by following Maury's directions
the time was reduced to 35 to 40 days. Two weeks were cut off the trip to Lisbon,
a week saved to Dublin. The average time from New York to San Francisco had
been 180 days, and Maury's wind and current charts reduced it to 133 days. Use
of the charts by American shipping alone saved owners more than $2 million
annually, while Britain gained by $10 million.

On one occasion Maury actually rescued a ship by long-distance methods. The vessel had foundered off Cape Hatteras in a hurricane and was stranded for several weeks. An appeal was made to Maury, who ascertained the position of the ship when struck, then traced on his charts the probable drift of a derelict at sea and marked its course on a map. "If afloat you will find her here," Maury is reported to have said. The ship was recovered in the exact longitude and latitude predicted by Maury.

Another contribution made by Maury was the laying down of lanes for steamers in the North Atlantic, where collisions between ships had been frequent. In 1855 he published a chart defining proposed "ocean lanes." Two tracks of lanes, twenty miles wide, were laid down. Steamers westward bound were to follow the northern lane, and east-bound ships would stay in the southern lane. The Secretary of the Navy immediately ordered navy ships to observe the lanes, and gradually they were adopted also for commercial shipping. The lanes were designed to keep ships away from icebergs and fog, as far as possible, as well as to avoid collisions. Thereafter, a drastic drop occurred in the accidents which had previously befallen vessels sailing the stormy North Atlantic.

Maury's researches for the laying of the first Atlantic cable were likewise of a pioneering nature. As early as 1848 he had come to the conclusion, in the course of his investigations of winds and currents, that there existed between Newfoundland and Ireland a broad and level plateau at a comparatively moderate depth. In a report to the Secretary of the Navy, February 1854, the results of a series of deep sea soundings were summarized:

> From Newfoundland to Ireland the distance between the nearest points is about 1,600 miles, and the bottom of the sea between the two places is a plateau which seems to have been placed there especially for the purpose of holding the wires of the submarine telegraph, and of keeping them out of harm's way. It is neither too deep nor too shallow; yet it is so deep that the wires but once landed will remain forever beyond the reach of the anchors of vessels, icebergs, and drifts of any kind, and so shallow that they may be readily lodged upon the bottom.

A topographic map of the North Atlantic ocean floor was constructed by Maury, and he served as adviser to Cyrus W. Field in the actual laying of the first cable. After several failures, the undertaking was finally successfully concluded. At a dinner given in New York in 1858 to celebrate the arrival of the first message across the Atlantic, Field is reported to have said, "I am a man of few words; Maury furnished the brains, England gave the money, and I did the work."

In time, Maury became an international figure. In August 1853 he was the leading spirit at the first International Meteorological Conference, held at Brussels. For seventeen days scientists from nine principal maritime nations discussed the many problems associated with ocean traffic. Steam was gradually replacing sail, but sea charts were as urgently needed as in the past. The conferees agreed on plans to enlist sailors of all nationalities in a vast campaign of nautical and meteorological observations according to Maury's methods. Even in time of war, the records were to be preserved and regarded as inviolate.

A bibliography of forty pages is required to list the titles of Maury's published works. His most famous and popular book was *The Physical Geography of the Sea*, which appeared in 1855—the first classic work of modern oceanography. Nine American and nineteen English editions and at least a half-dozen translations into European languages were issued. The book was designed for the general reader and written in nontechnical language. In the introduction, the author outlines the work's contents and general scope: "I shall treat of the economy of the sea and its adaptations—of its salts, its waters, its climates, and its inhabitants, and of whatever there may be of general interest in its commercial uses or industrial pursuits, for all such things pertain to its Physical Geography."

The second chapter of *The Physical Geography of the Sea* is devoted to a subject which Maury had studied intensively for years—the Gulf Stream. His opening statement is classical:

> There is a river in the ocean; in the severest droughts it never fails, and in the mightiest floods it never overflows; its banks and its bottom are of cold water, while its current is of warm; the Gulf of Mexico is its fountain, and its mouth is in the Arctic Seas. It is the Gulf Stream. There is in the world no other such majestic flow of waters. Its current is more rapid than the Mississippi or the Amazon, and its volume more than a thousand times greater. Its waters, as far out from the Gulf as the Carolina coasts, are of an indigo blue. They are so distinctly marked that their line of junction with the common sea-water may be traced by the eye.

Maury was the world's pioneer investigator on subjects covered by two other chapters—"The Depths of the Ocean" and "The Basin of the Atlantic"—both popular with readers. Practically no aspect of the broad field was neglected, as other divisions dealt with such topics as the atmosphere, rains and rivers, sea currents, salts of the sea, the cloud region and sea fogs, the geological effects of winds, sea routes, monsoons, climates of the sea, tide-rips and sea drift, storms, hurricanes and typhoons, and the Antarctic regions.

Because Maury was an original thinker and investigator and too ready to rush in with theories when factual support was lacking, some of his concepts in later years were found to be erroneous. A number of errors were corrected in subsequent editions. As one Maury biographer, Patricia Jahns, points out, "The book has passages that show that if Maury had had infinite capacity for taking pains that characterizes genius, he would have produced a great work." A detailed analysis of the *Physical Geography* reveals that it is accurate in statements of observed facts concerning ocean phenomena, but is often wrong in assumption and analysis—in part, at least, because of the limitations of knowledge at the time that Maury was writing. Maury was a bold workman who believed that beginnings should be made, even if in time they had to be revised or corrected.

A leading meteorologist, John Leighly, in an introduction to a 1963 reprint of the *Physical Geography*, sums up the case: "There is in fact a great deal of sound information in the book, but the reader now, as a hundred years ago, must weigh each paragraph and sort out its content of objective fact, of material selected to support Maury's interpretations, and of fantasy. The most valuable parts are those in which he describes investigations done under his supervision, such as his account of deep-sea soundings." Leighly concludes that the *Physical Geography* is read today "as the highly personal testament of an energetic and self-assertive man unacquainted with the rigorous methods practiced in the academies, but possessing first-hand knowledge of ships and the sea, boundless self-confidence, and a pen well exercised in persuasive writing."

Maury's later career was an anticlimax. At the outbreak of the Civil War, he resigned from the U.S. Navy to serve as chief of sea coast, river and harbor defenses of the Confederacy. For several years following the war he considered himself a refugee, living first in England and then in Mexico. Maury returned to the United States in 1868 and served as professor of meteorology at the Virginia Military Institute until his death in 1873.

The permanent significance of Maury's contributions to maritime science is indicated by the inscription placed on the pilot charts issued by the Hydrographic Office (since 1962 the Naval Oceanographic Office) of the Navy Department.

Founded upon the researches made in the early part of the nineteenth century by Matthew Fontaine Maury, while serving as a lieutenant in the United States Navy.

57

Case of the Wandering Boulders
Jean Louis Agassiz (1807-1873)

Études sur les Glaciers
(Studies on Glaciers)

A lone boulder seventy feet high stands on the shore of Lake Geneva in Switzerland, and in the western part of the country, in Neuchâtel, is a huge rock sixty-two feet high and forty feet across. Other massive boulders are scattered for many miles around but are most numerous in the mountain region.

Peasant folktales variously account for the wandering boulders by reference to supernatural forces or credit them to prehistoric giants. Among early nineteenth-century scientists, several theories were in vogue. A famous geologist, Leopold von Buch, held that the rocks had reached their present sites as the result of great upheavals which had hurled huge stones from mountain to mountain and into the lowlands. Others regarded them as a residue of Noah's Flood. The most generally accepted hypothesis was Charles Lyell's: land surfaces had often been submerged beneath the sea, and, while so covered, icebergs had deposited the boulders over the land.

The true explanation had occurred to James Hutton, in Scotland, toward the end of the eighteenth century. Though Hutton never saw the boulders himself, he speculated that they were ice-carried, and his disciple, John Playfair, concluded that "a glacier is the only agent we now see capable of transporting them to such a distance, without destroying that sharpness of the angles so distinctive of these masses." Hutton and Playfair were not alone. During the first quarter of the nineteenth century, Jean de Charpentier, director of the mines at Bex, and M. Venetz, a civil engineer, had become converted to the glacial theory. The Alps, they were convinced, had once been embedded in a mass of ice.

In 1836, Charpentier brought these ideas to his friend, Louis Agassiz, a brilliant young Swiss biologist. Skeptical at first, Agassiz began an investigation on his own and soon became an enthusiastic advocate of the theory of glacial action. Furthermore, the imaginative Agassiz immediately perceived far greater implications in the theory than had Charpentier. Not only the Alps but also many other regions of the northern hemisphere, he decided, had once been covered with an ice sheet. Everywhere he saw evidence of the work of glaciers: transported boulders, scratched and polished outcropping rocks, moraine-like deposits, and glacial drift, as soil left by glaciers is called. In travels through Scotland and Wales, Agassiz observed similar signs of the work of long-vanished glaciers.

Agassiz's theory was introduced to the world in 1837 in a paper read to the Helvetic Association of Neuchâtel. Three years later, his famous *Études sur les Glaciers*, "Studies on Glaciers," was published. In his address, he announced his belief that a great ice age, due to a temporary fluctuation of the globe's temperature, had covered the surface of the earth with an ice sheet extending at least from the North Pole to Central Europe and Asia. In Agassiz's words:

> Siberian winter established itself for a time over a world previously covered with a rich vegetation and peopled with large mammalia, similar to those now inhabiting the warm regions of India and Africa. Death enveloped all nature in a shroud, and the cold, having reached its highest degree, gave to this mass of ice, at the maximum of tension, the greatest possible hardness.

Agassiz's *Études sur les Glaciers*, consisting of one large volume of text and an atlas, presented a historical résumé of all previous work on glaciers, followed by an account of observations made by Agassiz and his companions during several years' study of the Alpine glaciers. New facts were reported on the appearance and structure of these streams of slowly moving ice, their method of formation, their internal temperature, and their rock loads. From the local phenomena of the Alpine valleys, Agassiz restated in almost poetic terms the vast conclusions that he had reached earlier:

> The surface of Europe adorned before by a tropical vegetation and inhabited by troops of large elephants, enormous hippopotami, and gigantic carnivora, was suddenly buried under a vast mantle of ice, covering alike plains, lakes, seas, and plateaus. Upon the life and movement of a powerful creation fell the silence of death. Springs paused, rivers ceased to flow, the rays of the sun, rising upon this frozen shore (if, indeed, it was reached by them), were met only by the breath of the winter from the north and the thunders of the crevasses as they opened across the surface of this icy sea.

For the next half-dozen years, Agassiz's researches on glaciers continued. He climbed the Jungfrau and other "unscalable" mountains, spent several summers camping upon the Aar glacier, measured the depth and forward movement of glaciers, braved their treacherous crevasses, and studied the flora and fauna of the ice fields. The results of the later investigations were described in Agassiz's *Système Glaciaire*, "Glacial System," published in 1846.

After his appointment to the Harvard University faculty in the 1840s, Agassiz tested his glacial theories further by examining North and South American geology. He explored for evidences of ice action the area extending from the Atlantic Coast to the Rocky Mountains and from the Great Lakes to the Gulf of Mexico, everywhere north of the thirty-fifth parallel finding abundant proof of the Ice Age. The whole northern part of the North American continent, he asserted, was modeled by a moving ice sheet, a statement verified by all subsequent investigators.

Like all other revolutionary scientific conceptions, Agassiz's theories met with opposition and violent criticisms when first announced. His own countrymen scoffed at the Ice Age theory, and the leading English geologists considered him insane. Before his death in 1873, however, Agassiz had the satisfaction of seeing the views which he had first advanced in 1837 gain worldwide acceptance.

Since Agassiz's time, research in glacial geology has immensely expanded in variety and complexity. Among fields of interest to present-day geologists are: the petrography of the drift; mountain summit and mountain valley sculpture by the snow field and the valley glacier; the involved history of the Great Lakes region during the retreat of the last ice sheet; the changes of land level associated with glaciers; the history of the Ice Age (possibly a million years in duration), including effects on plant and animal life and on man; the study of vastly older glacial ice ages; and theories concerning their causes. Scientists are now generally agreed that the last glacial stage, ending approximately 20,000 years ago, was one of a series reaching back into the remote geological past. Furthermore, it has been suggested that the present is merely an interglacial stage and that another glacial stage, with its almost incalculable consequences for the human race, is beginning to take shape.

58

Survival through Natural Selection

Charles Darwin (1809-1882)

*On the Origin of Species by Means of Natural Selection,
or the Preservation of Favoured Races in the
Struggle for Life*

The basic principles of Charles Darwin's theory of evolution, as set forth in *The Origin of Species*, are today almost universally accepted in the scientific world, though controversies have raged around them for more than a century.

The most important event in Darwin's life, determining his whole career, was his five-year voyage as naturalist on HMS *Beagle*, 1831-1836. During this period, the *Beagle* touched on nearly every continent and major island as she circled the world. Darwin was called upon to serve as geologist, botanist, zoologist, and general man of science — superb preparation for his subsequent life of research and writing.

Everywhere Darwin went, he made extensive collections of plants and animals, fossil and living, earth-dwelling and marine forms. He investigated, with the eye of a naturalist, the pampas of Argentina, the dry slopes of the Andes, the salt lakes and deserts of Chile and Argentina, the dense forests of Brazil, Tierra del Fuego, and Tahiti, the deforested Cape de Verde Islands, geological formations of the South American coast and mountains, active and dead volcanoes on islands and mainland, coral reefs, fossil mammals of Patagonia, extinct races of man in Peru, and the aborigines of Tierra del Fuego and Patagonia.

Of all the regions visited, none impressed Darwin so forcibly as the Galapagos Islands, five hundred miles off the west coast of South America. There he saw giant tortoises, elsewhere found only as fossils, huge lizards long since extinct in other parts of the world, enormous crabs, and sea lions. The birds on the islands were similar to those on the neighboring continent, but not identical. The strange phenomena of the Gallapagos Islands, added to certain facts previously noted in South America, reinforced the ideas on evolution beginning to take shape in Darwin's mind.

Immediately upon his return to England, Darwin began keeping a notebook on evolution and collecting facts on the variation of species, thus taking the first steps toward his *Origin of Species*. In the beginning, the great riddle was how to explain the appearance and disappearance of species. Why did species originate, become modified with the passage of time, diverge into numerous branches, and often vanish from the scene completely?

The key to the mystery for Darwin came through a chance reading of Malthus' *Essay on Population*. Malthus had shown that mankind's rate of increase was retarded by such checks as disease, accidents, war, and famine. It occurred to Darwin that similar factors might keep down the populations of animals and plants. Thus was born the famous Darwinian doctrine of natural selection, struggle for existence, or survival of the fittest—the foundation stone for *The Origin of Species*. For twenty years, Darwin's notebooks expanded to substantiate his theories. He read a vast range of literature, talked with expert breeders of animals and plants, studied skeletons of wild and domesticated birds, made crossing experiments with pigeons, and investigated seed transport.

Strong support for the principle of natural selection, Darwin thought, came from a study of "artificial selection." In the case of domestic animals and plants, man has selected and bred the varieties most advantageous to his own need, causing radical modifications from their wild ancestors. If evolution could be brought about by artificial selection, Darwin reasoned, nature might function in the same manner, except that natural selection would result from the struggle for existence. Among all forms of life, he observed, an enormous number of individuals must perish; only a fraction of those born can survive. Some species furnish food for other species. The battle goes on ceaselessly, and the fierce competition eliminates animals and plants unfit to survive. Variations in species take place to meet the conditions necessary for survival.

The first announcement of the theory of evolution by natural selection came in 1858, shortly after Darwin learned that a fellow scientist, Alfred Russel Wallace, carrying on natural history observations in the Malay Archipelago, had reached the same conclusions. *The Origin of Species* was published the following year.

At the outset, Darwin describes the changes that have occurred in domesticated animals and plants as a result of human control, and these are compared with variations resulting from natural selection. Wherever there is life, it is concluded, change is constant. To variation there is added the struggle for existence, and Darwin offers dramatic illustrations of how far the ability of living organisms to reproduce outstrips their capacity to survive.

The Origin of Species demonstrates the operation of the principle of natural selection in checking population increases. Some individuals in a species are stronger, can run faster, are more intelligent, more immune to disease, sexually more aggressive, or better able to endure the rigors of climate than their fellows. These will survive and reproduce as the weaker members perish. In the course of many millenniums, variations lead to the creation of essentially new species.

As expressed by Darwin: "Natural selection is daily and hourly scrutinizing, throughout the world, the slightest variations; rejecting those that are bad, preserving and adding up all that are good." In this fashion is the theory of unending evolution presented in *The Origin of Species*.

The contemporary reception of Darwin's celebrated book has been compared to "a conflagration like lightning in a full barn." If the revolutionary new theory were valid, the biblical story of creation could no longer be accepted. Church authorities immediately viewed the Darwinian thesis as dangerous to religion, and roused a storm of opposition. In *The Origin of Species*, Darwin intentionally softpedaled any discussion of man's beginning, because he thought that any emphasis on this phase of evolution would cause his entire theory to be rejected. In a later work, *The Descent of Man*, however, a massive amount of evidence is advanced to demonstrate that the human race is also a product of evolution from lower forms.

Viewed in retrospect, Darwin's impression on nearly all major fields of learning was, and continues to be, profound. The doctrine of organic evolution has been accepted by biologists, geologists, chemists, and physicists, by anthropologists, psychologists, educators, philosophers, and sociologists, and even by historians, political scientists, and philologists.

Because he was an extraordinarily acute observer and experimenter, Darwin's findings for the most part have stood up well against the test of time. Even though his theories have been modified by the discoveries of modern science, Darwin succeeded in foreshadowing in a remarkable fashion the ideas prevailing today in genetics, paleontology, and a variety of other fields.

Nevertheless, violent controversy continues to rage around the evolutionary theory, especially in the United States. Even a U.S. president has expressed doubts as to its validity, and fundamentalist religious groups, known as creationists, continue to bring pressure on state legislatures to require the biblical account of creation to be taught on an equal basis, or as an alternative, to the theory of evolution. Many years after the famous 1925 "Monkey Trial" of John Scopes for teaching evolution in Dayton, Tennessee, stormy debates go on in educational, religious, and legislative circles.

59

Professional Homicide
Oliver Wendell Holmes (1809-1894)

The Contagiousness of Puerperal Fever Read before
the Boston Society for Medical Improvement and
Published at the Request of the Society

The conditions prevailing in early nineteenth-century hospitals in Europe and America can only be compared to a chamber of horrors. A pervading stench emanated from the saturation of wounds with pus. Four diseases took a heavy death toll: septicemia, a form of blood poisoning caused by pathogenic bacteria in the bloodstream; pyemia, with abscesses spread throughout the body; hospital gangrene, characterized by mortification of the tissues; and erysipelas, a contagious skin disease. The death rate from operations ranged from twenty-five to forty percent, and ran considerably higher for amputations.

The notable researches of Louis Pasteur on fermentation and applied bacteriology, of Joseph Lister on aseptic surgery, and Robert Koch's demonstrations that specific bacteria cause specific diseases all came after the middle of the century. Until then, few medical men suspected that lack of sanitation might be responsible for widespread infection and innumerable deaths. Surgical instruments were cleaned only casually; silk threads used for stitches were carried in the surgeon's lapel or pocket; when his hands were otherwise busy, the surgeon held the operating knife in his teeth; his coat, covered with stains and blood, was seldom if ever washed; and the surgeon did not trouble to wash his hands when going from one type of disease to another or from an autopsy to a living patient. Microorganisms naturally flourished and multiplied.

Particularly perilous was childbirth in the hospitals—so hazardous indeed that it came near ruining the new science of obstetrics. When men doctors began to replace midwives, using forceps and making frequent examinations during labor, there was an immediate and rapid increase in "child-bed fever." The cases ordinarily began with a chill on the fourth day after the birth, fever rose, the abdomen became distended, and death nearly always followed. Autopsies revealed peritonitis and the formation of pus throughout the body.

Child-bed fever had long been known in the medical profession, but its causes remained a dark mystery. An English surgeon, Charles White, devoted the first chapter of his *Treatise on the Management of Pregnant and Lying-in Women* (1773) to "The Causes and Symptoms of the Puerperal or Child-bed Fever." The devastating plague was common throughout Europe. Dr. Logan Clendening cites a report of Paris' largest hospital, which lost more than half of the women in maternity cases, and in Vienna in 1846 the First Clinic of the University lost from child-bed fever over eleven percent of the 4,010 patients it delivered.

A number of years earlier, alert observers among the doctors had begun to speculate on the reasons for the deadly infections. Alexander Gordon of Aberdeen published in 1795 *A Treatise on the Epidemic of Puerperal Fever*, in which he states, "By observation, I plainly perceived the channel by which it was propagated, and I arrived at that certainty in the matter, *that I could venture to foretell that women would be affected with the disease upon hearing by what midwife they were to be delivered, or by what nurse they were to be attended, during their lying-in; and almost in every instance, my prediction was verified.*" Dr. Gordon confessed, "It is a disagreeable declaration for me to mention, that I, myself, was the means of carrying the infection to a great number of women." Many of the leading doctors, medical school teachers, and nurses of the period, on the other hand, ridiculed the notion that they might be guilty of transmitting the deadly disorder.

Child-bed fever was no less a curse in America than abroad. In the Boston area, puerperal fever became prevalent in the spring of 1842. At meetings of the Boston Society for Medical Improvement, of which Dr. Oliver Wendell Holmes, professor of anatomy at Harvard University, was a member, various physicians reported and discussed cases coming to their attention. Some fourteen or fifteen cases had occurred in Salem, and the disease was frequently seen on Cape Cod. There had been fifteen fatal cases of puerperal fever in Boston and the vicinity within a period of about a month. New York was also suffering from an epidemic.

A shocking new turn of events came later in the year when several men contracted child-bed fever. A Dr. Whitney of Newton and two students, all of whom had lesions on their hands, did a postmortem examination of a women dying of puerperal fever. The three became desperately ill, showing the usual symptoms of the disease, and a few days later died. A similar case was reported from Lynn, where a Dr. Barker made an examination of a patient who had died of puerperal fever. It was reported that "he had at the time several open sores on each hand, and pricked himself while sewing up the body." The following day he was ill and six days later dead—doubtless not helped by the excessive bleeding which had been prescribed by the attending physician.

The cases thus reported to the Boston Society for Medical Improvement led to "animated discussion," and a question rose as to the contagion of puerperal fever and the possibility of physicians communicating it from one patient to another. The suggestion that the disease was probably communicable struck a spark with Dr. Holmes, and three weeks later, on February 13, 1843, he had a paper, revolutionary in its impact, ready to read to his fellow members. The title was "The Contagiousness of Puerperal Fever." By vote of the membership, the essay was published the following April in *The New England Quarterly Journal of Medicine and Surgery*.

Holmes was more celebrated in his own time, as he is today, as a literary light than as a man of medicine. Though presently little read except in textbook anthologies, devoted admirers of his light verse and essays among his contemporaries were numerous, especially in New England. In writing his utterly convincing argument against needless deaths in childbirth, Holmes' superb literary powers and his knowledge of medicine were combined in the most telling fashion.

Essentially, "The Contagiousness of Puerperal Fever" presents a long array of facts in support of the contention that the disease was contagious, was usually transmitted by the doctor or the nurse, and was due to a specific infection. Holmes opens with a declaration that every well-informed member of the medical profession realizes puerperal fever is sometimes passed on from one person to another. Anyone who thinks otherwise has not examined the evidence. "No negative facts, no opposing opinions," he writes, "be they what they may, or whose they may, can form any answer to the series of cases now within the reach of all who choose to explore the records of medical science."

To those who asserted that the case for contagion was not proven because not all exposed patients contracted child-bed fever, Holmes retorted, "Children that walk in calico before open fires are not always burned to death; the instances to the contrary may be worth recording; but by no means if they are to be used as arguments against woolen frocks and high fenders."

Illustrating the misinformation being disseminated by medical authorities, Holmes cites Dewees' standard *Treatise on the Diseases of Females*, which states unequivocally, "In this country, under no circumstances that puerperal fever has appeared hitherto, does it afford the slightest ground for the belief that it is contagious." On the contrary, Dr. Holmes was fully persuaded that "the disease known as Puerperal Fever is so far contagious as to be frequently carried from patient to patient by physicians and nurses."

Holmes concedes that little of a positive nature was known about how infection occurs, why some patients were susceptible and others escaped, how the disease is propagated, or why epidemics wax and wane. The clinching argument, in his view, was "that if it can be shown that great numbers of lives have been and are sacrificed to ignorance or blindness on this point, no other error of which physicians or nurses may be occasionally suspected will be alleged in palliation of this; but that whenever and wherever they can be shown to carry the disease and death instead of health and safety, the common instincts of humanity will silence every attempt to explain away their responsibility."

Further reference was made to the 1795 treatise by Dr. Gordon of Aberdeen, who had observed that the only women who contracted puerperal fever were those who had been attended by a physician or nurse who had previously been in contact with patients suffering from the disease. According to Dr. Gordon, "the infection was as readily communicated as that of the small-pox or measles, and operated more speedily than any other infection with which I am acquainted."

Other citations to the professional literature on the subject, British and American, were offered by Dr. Holmes, all arriving at the same conclusion—that a direct relationship existed between the incidence of the disease and the doctor's or nurse's previous contacts with afflicted patients or postmortems. A Dr. Blundell, quoted by Holmes, was so discouraged "that in my own family I had rather that those I esteemed the most should be delivered, unaided, in a stable, by the manger-side, than that they should receive the best help, in the fairest apartment, but exposed to the vapors of this pitiless disease."

Based on numerous first-hand accounts, it is, said Holmes, "the plain conclusions that the physician and the disease entered, hand in hand, into the chamber of the unsuspecting patient."

After reviewing a "long catalogue of melancholy histories" of individual doctors and nurses responsible for multiple cases of puerperal fever, Holmes philosophizes on how much kinder nature unaided "deals with the parturient female, when she is not immersed in the virulent atmosphere of an impure lying-in hospital, or poisoned in her chamber by the unsuspected breath of contagion." Under other circumstances, the percentage of deaths from childbirth was extremely low.

Given the general atmosphere prevailing in the maternity hospitals of Holmes' time, there were long odds against a patient when she entered the doors. "Within the walls of lying-in hospitals," Holmes wrote, "there is often generated a miasma, palpable as the chlorine used to destroy it, tenacious so as in some cases almost to defy extirpation, deadly in some institutions as the plague ... the loss of life occasioned by these institutions completely defeats the objects of their founders."

Near the conclusion of his paper, Holmes rises to a high point of eloquence in pleading his case:

> It is as a lesson rather than as a reproach that I call up the memory of these irreparable errors and wrongs. No tongue can tell the heartbreaking calamities they have caused; they have closed the eyes just opened upon a new world of life and happiness; they have bowed the strength of manhood into the dust; they have cast the helplessness of infancy into the stranger's arms, or bequeathed it with less cruelty the death of its dying parent. There is no tone deep enough for record, and no voice loud enough for warning. The woman about to become a mother, or with her new-born infant upon her bosom, should be the object of trembling care and sympathy wherever she bears her tender burden, or stretches her aching limbs. The very outcast of the street has pity upon her sister in degradation when the seal of promised maternity is impressed upon her. The remorseless vengeance of the law brought down upon its victims by a machinery as sure as destiny, is arrested in its fall at a word which reveals her transient claims for mercy. The solemn prayer of the liturgy singles out her sorrows from the multiplied trials of life, to plead for her in the hour of peril. God forbid that any member of the profession to which she trusts her life, doubly precious at that eventful period, should regard it negligently, unadvisedly, or selfishly.

Eight conclusions were drawn by Holmes from his research and studies, all based upon practical experience and common sense. Among them were these: A physician engaged in the practice of obstetrics should not participate actively in the postmortem examination of cases of puerperal fever; if a physician is present at such autopsies, he should bathe thoroughly, change all his clothing, and allow twenty-four hours to pass before treating a patient; similar precautions should be taken in dealing with cases of erysipelas; a physician in whose practice a single case of puerperal fever has occurred "is bound to consider the next female he attends in labor" to prevent carrying the infection to her; if a physician has two cases of puerperal fever occurring within a short space of time, "he would do wisely to relinquish his obstetrical practice for at least one month," and try to rid himself of any contamination he may be carrying; if three closely connected cases occur in the practice of one individual, it "is *prima facie* evidence that he is the vehicle of contagion"; the physician should also take every precaution against nurses or other assistants transmitting the disease.

Holmes' eighth and last recommendation is so cogently expressed that it deserves to be quoted in full: "Whatever indulgence may be granted to those who have heretofore been the ignorant causes of so much misery, the time has come when the existence of a *private pestilence* in the sphere of a single physician should be looked upon, not as a misfortune, but as a crime; and in the knowledge of such occurrences the duties of the practitioner to his profession should give way to his paramount obligations to society."

Predictably, the conservatives and traditionalists reacted violently and adversely to the Holmes thesis. Such a forthright, forceful statement challenging fixed ideas was certain to arouse the antagonism of those whose teachings had been for years diametrically opposed to the concept of the contagiousness of puerperal fever. At the time, Philadelphia was the American center for the teaching of obstetrics, and two of the biggest guns in that city were wheeled out to demolish the upstart Holmes. Charles D. Meigs, professor of obstetrics at the Jefferson Medical College, and Hugh Lenox Hodge, professor of obstetrics and of the diseases of women and children at the University of Pennsylvania, attacked Holmes vituperatively. Meigs pointed to the many cases of women during an epidemic of child-bed fever who did not contract the disease. "I prefer to attribute them (puerperal fever attacks) to accident, or Providence," he disclaimed, "of which I can form a conception, rather than to a contagion of which I cannot form any clear idea, at least as to this particular malady." In 1852 Hodge published an essay on the non-contagious character of puerperal fever, in which he asserted: "The result of the whole discussion will, I trust, serve, not to exalt your views of the value and dignity of our profession, but to divest your minds of the overpowering dread that you can ever become, especially to woman, under the extremely interesting circumstances of gestation and parturition, the minister of evil; that you can ever convey, in any possible manner, a horrible virus, so destructive in its effects, and so mysterious in its operations as that attributed to puerperal fever."

Undaunted, Holmes returned to the fray. In 1855 he reprinted his original essay, unchanged, in pamphlet form, in order to give it wider circulation, but retitled *Puerperal Fever as a Private Pestilence*, preceding it with a lengthy introduction and bringing his facts up to date. The introduction is prefaced with a quotation from the 1852 edition of Copland's *Medical Dictionary*, designed to put Drs. Hodge, Meigs, and their kind to shame:

> Boards of health, if such exist, or, without them, the medical institutions of a country, should have the power of coercing, or of inflicting some kind of punishment on those who recklessly go from cases of puerperal fevers to parturient or puerperal females, without using due precaution; and who, having been shown the risk, criminally encounter it, and convey pestilence and death to the persons they are employed to aid in the most interesting and suffering period of female existence.

Point by point, Holmes replied to his critics, exposing the fallacies of their arguments. Referring to the strong and personal language used by Meigs, he says: "I take no offense and attempt no retort; no man makes a quarrel with me over the counterpane that covers a mother with her new-born infant at her breast." Holmes was especially concerned that medical students might be led astray by the statements of the two distinguished professors, which seemed to him to condone, if not actually encourage, professional homicide. One famous paragraph of the introduction, directed at students, suggests, "They naturally have faith in their instructors, turning to them for truth, and taking what they may choose to give them; babes in knowledge, not yet able to tell the breast from the bottle, pumping away for the truth at all that offers, were it nothing better than a professor's shrivelled forefinger."

Holmes concludes with a strong appeal to reasonable men: "The teachings of the two professors in the great schools of Philadelphia are sure to be listened to, not only by their immediate pupils, but by the profession at large. I am too much in earnest for either humility or vanity, but I do entreat those who hold the keys of life and death to listen to me also for this once. I ask no personal favor; but I beg to be heard in behalf of the women whose lives are at stake, until some stronger voice shall plead for them."

Dr. Holmes was being heard. The circulation of the *New England Quarterly Journal of Medicine and Surgery* was necessarily limited, but twelve years later, by the time the second edition of Holmes' work appeared, he could report, "I have abundant evidence that it has made many practitioners more cautious in their relations with puerperal females." His arguments had been prepared with such care that before long they became accepted facts among enlightened members of the medical profession. His essay undoubtedly saved many a mother from an untimely death. As a commentator for the Grolier Club's catalog of *One Hundred Influential American Books* phrased it, "No American publication in the nineteenth century saved more lives than this unassuming pamphlet, founded solely on the evidence of observed cases."

In his *The Professor at the Breakfast Table*, published some years later, Holmes indulged in reminiscences: "When, by the permission of Providence, I held up to the professional public the damnable facts connected with the conveyance of poison from one young mother's chamber to another's—for doing which humble office I desire to be thankful that I have lived, though nothing else good should ever come of my life—I had to bear the sneers of those whose position I had assailed, and, as I believe, have at last demolished, so that nothing but the ghosts of dead women stir among the ruins."

"At the time it was delivered," states the medical historian Dr. Henry R. Viets, "this paper was the most important contribution made in America to the advancement of medicine." The assertion may be questioned, if originality is the criterion, for William Beaumont's researches on the physiology of digestion were far more pioneering in character. As a matter of fact, Holmes laid no claim to great originality. Toward the end of a long life, he wrote that "others had cried out with all their might against the terrible evil, before I did, and I gave them full credit for it. But I think I shrieked my warning louder and longer than any of them, and I am pleased to remember that I took my ground on the existing evidence before the little army of microbes was marched up to support my position."

The story would not be complete without reference to a young Hungarian physician, Ignaz Philipp Semmelweis, a graduate of the University of Vienna's medical department. When Semmelweis became an assistant in the obstetrical clinic at Vienna in 1848, he required students to wash their hands in chlorine water before entering the clinic. Later, a solution of chloride of lime was used. Immediately there occurred a dramatic decrease in the previously high mortality rate from puerperal fever. Thereafter, Semmelweis continuously preached the doctrine that the obstetrician must come to his patients aseptically clean. Like Holmes, he was attacked viciously by the diehards, driven from one hospital to another, and eventually died insane. To Semmelweis, nevertheless, belongs the major credit for our first knowledge of the means to eliminate the horrible pestilence of puerperal fever.

60

First Great American Botanist
Asa Gray (1810-1888)

Elements of Botany

What John James Audubon accomplished in identifying and describing the avifauna of America, his contemporary Asa Gray did for the botanical kingdom. When Gray began his labors in the early 1830s, North America, botanically speaking, was virgin territory, and its rich flora was awaiting discovery and scientific study. Because virtually everything was new, the classification of plants — mainly flowering plants — was practically the whole of botany through most of Gray's career. The botanist was preoccupied with forest and field, with outdoor rather than laboratory investigations, as he sought to find hitherto unknown plants and to accumulate material for research. Aside from amateurish manuals for New England and the middle and southern Atlantic states, botanical literature was extremely limited and largely unreliable. The unsatisfactory state of botanical knowledge was accentuated by the opening of the western territories, which were constantly bringing new discoveries to light.

Asa Gray was born in 1810 in upstate New York, the son of a farmer and tanner. His sketchy education in a local grammar school and academy was roughly equivalent to two years in a modern high school. Even with such restricted preparation, he was admitted to a small provincial medical college in Fairfield and graduated with the M.D. degree in 1831.

Several years earlier, however, Gray's lifetime passion for botany had been aroused by reading an article in the *Edinburgh Encyclopedia*, which surveyed the subject comprehensively in 343 double-columned pages, beginning with the ancient Greeks. Gray was also stimulated by a study of Eaton's *Manual of Botany for the Northern States*. As John M. Coulter commented, "This seems to have been like putting a brand to a mass of dry fuel, for his interest became a consuming one and the fire was never extinguished." The problem was how to earn a living. Botany was a part-time avocation for the clergymen, doctors, lawyers, and teachers concerned with the field. But Gray wanted to spend all his time on plant study. The first seven years after he reached the decision to be a professional botanist were a race with starvation.

Gray's first opportunity came in 1833, through his acquaintance with John Torrey, professor in the New York College of Physicians and Surgeons, at the time the best-known American botanist. In the 1820s, Torrey had published some parts of his *Flora of the Northern United States*. Mutual interest in plants attracted Torrey to the young physician, and he proceeded to offer Gray an appointment as his assistant, to gather new material. Unfortunately, a shortage of funds soon terminated the arrangement. Not long afterward, Gray became curator and librarian of the New York Lyceum of Natural History, an institution which Torrey had helped to establish. Despite a small salary, Gray wrote that "it will be a fine situation for scientific pursuits." His collaboration with Torrey on the *Flora* continued.

The first of Gray's several influential textbooks, *Elements of Botany*, was published in 1836. Succeeding editions of this work, of the *Manual of the Botany of the Northern United States,* and other texts dominated botanical instruction in the United States for the next several generations. Though only twenty-six when the *Elements* appeared, Gray had already developed a smooth, graceful writing style, and his material was logically and systematically arranged. At the beginning, he urged the student to "in the first place direct his attention to the study of plants as organized and living beings, and become familiar with all the ordinary forms of structure." Four chapters were devoted to morphological and physiological subjects, the fifth dealt with flowerless plants, previously generally neglected, and the last with systems of classification.

In *Elements of Botany*, Gray argued vigorously for the natural system of classification, then coming into vogue among European scientists. Previously, Linnaeus' theory of classification of plants based on their system had prevailed. The Linnaean system was founded on the number of stamens and styles as a convenient method of grouping plants. Gray pointed out, on the other hand, that the botanist who simply counted stamens was lost when those parts were missing or when the number varied from species to species. The natural system is based on the form and structure of plants (morphology), establishing their relationships according to various kinds of parts in addition to sexual characteristics.

Following the publication of *Elements of Botany* and joint authorship with Torrey of several parts of the *Flora of North America*, Asa Gray sailed for Europe in 1838, where he remained for a year, purchasing books for the newly established University of Michigan and traveling and studying widely in Britain and on the Continent. This was the first of six highly rewarding and stimulating European tours taken by Gray over a period of nearly fifty years. His chief purpose was to study original plants in the European herbaria. English travelers in North America had collected plant specimens extensively. In fact, nearly all the earlier collections of North American plants were sent to Europe for description, and Gray had an opportunity to examine in detail the actual plants upon which published descriptions had been based. A knowledge of the plants in European collections, Gray was convinced, was essential to establishing a firm foundation for American botany. His labors abroad involved an immense amount of detailed and exact observations, as well as good judgment and a retentive memory.

A collateral benefit growing out of Gray's European travels was the close personal relations which he established with the leading European botanists. The friendships thus formed continued until his death in 1888. In addition to the herbaria of England and Scotland, Gray visited those of Paris, Lyons, Geneva, Munich, Berlin, Halle, Hamburg, and Vienna.

Shortly after returning from his first European expedition, the president of Harvard University offered Gray the position of professor of natural history and curator of the Botanic Garden. The offer was accepted. As described by William G. Farlow, "On Dr. Gray's accession there was no herbarium, no library, only one insignificant greenhouse, and a garden all in confusion, with few plants of value." When Gray retired, some thirty-one years later, the Harvard herbarium had become the largest and most valuable in America, comparable to the best in Europe, and an excellent library had been formed. The herbarium was a center for the active working botanists of the country and attracted many young men who were subsequently to become leaders in botanical studies throughout the United States.

Gray's travels were not restricted to Europe. He particularly enjoyed field studies and first-hand collecting. Early journeys took him into the southern Appalachians, where he was particularly fascinated with the high-mountain flora of North Carolina. Another collecting mission was to the White Mountains of New Hampshire. The completion of the transcontinental railroad enabled Gray to fulfill a long-held ambition to visit the West Coast, in the summer of 1872. High points of the expedition, from Gray's viewpoint, were the Great Plains, the Utah-Nevada desert, the redwoods and Yosemite valley of California, and the Rockies.

Throughout his long and fruitful career, a stream of publications flowed from Gray's pen. For several years following his first voyage to Europe, he continued to collaborate with John Torrey on completion of the *Flora of North America*, subtitled "Containing Abridged Descriptions of All the Known Indigenous and Naturalized Plants Growing North of Mexico, Arranged According to the Natural System." After publication of the second volume in 1843, however, further work was suspended indefinitely because the authors were unable to keep abreast of new material pouring in. A series of great transcontinental surveys had begun, each returning with extensive collections of the plants of various regions of the country. Years later, when the amount of new material being reported had declined, Gray began the preparation of a revised work, the *Synoptical Flora of North America*, two parts of which were published shortly before his death.

Doubtless the most widely used of Gray's many writings was his *Manual of Botany*, a descriptive work including all plant species of the northern United States east of the Mississippi and north of North Carolina and Tennessee. The first edition appeared in 1848, and the second to the fifth during the author's lifetime. Complementing the *Manual* was a series of textbooks, beginning with *Elements of Botany* and continuing with the *Botanical Text-book for Colleges, Schools, and Private Students* (1842), *First Lessons in Botany and Vegetable Physiology* (1857), *How Plants Grow: A Simple Introduction to Structural Botany* (1858), *Forest, Field and Garden Botany* (1868), *How Plants Behave* (1872), and *Structural Botany* (1879). The *Manual* has been republished frequently, with minor modifications, for more than a century, and despite the availability of more modern floras, it has remained a standard work. The eighth edition is currently in print.

Of historical significance and human interest is Gray's long association with Charles Darwin. The two men first met in 1838 in London, when Gray was twenty-eight and Darwin a year older. The acquaintance grew into close friendship on subsequent visits. Darwin's theory of the origin of species was foreshadowed in a letter from Gray to another English scientist, Joseph D. Hooker, in 1854, stating: "Scientific systematic botany rests upon species created with almost infinitely various degrees of resemblance among each other." The communication fell into Darwin's hands, and confidential correspondence with Gray followed over the next several years. In 1856 Darwin wrote to Gray as follows:

> Nineteen year ago it occurred to me that whilst otherwise employed on Natural History I might perhaps do good if I noted any sort of facts bearing on the question of the origin of species, and this I have since been doing. Either species have been independently created, or they have descended from other species, like varieties from one species. As an honest man I must tell you that I have come to the heterodox conclusion that there are no such things as independently created species — that species are only strongly defined varieties.

In another letter, September 5, 1857, Darwin sent a detailed account of his theory of evolution to Gray. An advance copy of *The Origin of Species* reached Gray before the publication date. The book became an immediate best-seller and was violently denounced by theological conservatives, as well as by certain scientists, such as Louis Agassiz. Gray, though devoutly religious, became the foremost defender of Darwin's theory of natural selection, in part because he believed that scientific investigation should be free from theological domination and further because he felt that the theory had much merit and did not conflict with religious beliefs. Gray's scattered writings in defense of Darwin were brought together in his *Darwiniana* (1876) and *Natural Science and Religion* (1880). His advocacy of Darwin's unorthodox theories was instrumental in gaining wide acceptance for them in the United States.

Sir Joseph D. Hooker, who in his time was called "the greatest living systematic botanist," summed up Gray's career and attainments in the following comments:

> When the history of the progress of botany during the nineteenth century shall be written, two names will hold high positions: those of Prof. Augustin Pyrame De Candolle and of Prof. Asa Gray.... Each devoted half a century of unremitting labor to the investigation and description of the plants of continental areas, and they founded herbaria and libraries, each in his own country, which have become permanent and quasi-national institutions.... There is much in their lives and works that recalls the career of Linnaeus, of whom they were worthy disciples, in the comprehensiveness of their labors, the excellence of the methods, their judicious conception of the limits of genera and species, the terseness and accuracy of their descriptions, and the clearness of their scientific language.

61

Indestructible Energy
Hermann von Helmholtz (1821-1894)

On the Conservation of Force

A recurring phenomenon in the history of scientific thought has been the almost simultaneous discovery by a number of scientists, working independently, frequently in different countries, of some great principle projecting forward the frontiers of knowledge. The essential thought appears to be in the air, and investigators converge upon it from various directions. The point is well illustrated by the case of surgical anesthesia, whose priority of discovery was disputed by several claimants. Even better known is the theory of evolution, with its long pre-Darwinian history.

A similar instance of coincidental development is that of the concept of energy conservation. Quite independently of one another, two German physicians, Julius Robert Mayer and Hermann von Helmholtz, and an English physicist, James Prescott Joule, began to meditate on a possible relationship between heat and force. Each, following a different line of reasoning, arrived at the idea of the mechanical equivalent of heat and the principle of the conservation of energy. The first paper containing a clear statement of the law of conservation of energy and attempting to determine the mechanical equivalent of heat was published by Mayer in 1842. Being neither a mathematician nor a physicist, Mayer offered no experimental proof to support his theory. The following year, Joule's paper, advancing the same theory but citing experimental justification, appeared in the *Philosophical Magazine.*

The broadest and most definitive formulation of the law of the conservation of energy, and the one that was to have the greatest influence on scientific circles, however, was the work of the German physicist, physiologist, and philosopher Hermann von Helmholtz. His statement was supported by a wealth of illustrations from mechanics, electricity, heat, and biology, and it also presented mathematically the law's profound general implications. At the time Helmholtz published his account of energy conservation in 1847, he was not a practicing scientist but a young doctor, only twenty-six years of age, in the Prussian army. Helmholtz has been ranked with Willard Gibbs of Yale as one of the greatest thinkers of all time. His scientific accomplishments were extraordinarily wide in range, including major contributions to medicine, physiology, psychology, physics, and mathematics. In the course of his experimental work, he invented many instruments, among them the ophthalmoscope, ophthalmometer, and telestereoscope.

Helmholtz had long been preoccupied with thoughts on the conservation of energy, his interest first being aroused by research in biology. A lively issue among scientists of the period was the theory of vitalism. What was the source of the energy to be observed in living forms? Helmholtz was skeptical of the prevailing notion that living organisms are governed by an "indwelling vital force." He set out to answer the question propounded by the great German chemist Justus von Liebig: "Are the mechanical energy and heat produced by an organism entirely the product of its own metabolism?" Helmholtz's first investigations into the metabolism of muscle, that is, the chemical changes in living cells, showed that the heat of the body comes entirely from the foodstuff and oxygen supplied to it. For example, he found that the heat given off by an animal was equivalent to that produced by burning the animal's food in a calorimeter. No residue remained to indicate the operation of a vital force.

Late in the eighteenth century, the French chemist Lavoisier had established the principle of the indestructibility of matter. Now, a half-century later, Helmholtz stated a corollary law: the indestructibility of energy. "Nature as a whole," he concluded, "possesses a store of energy which cannot in any wise be added to or subtracted from." The quantity of energy is as eternal as the quantity of matter. Like matter, energy cannot be created or destroyed but only transformed.

This idea proved to be one of the most revolutionary in the history of physical science. As A. C. Crombie, a noted science historian, pointed out, "Its implications and the problems it posed dominated physics in the period between the electromagnetic researches of Faraday and Maxwell and the introduction of the quantum theory by Planck in 1900." On the foundation which Helmholtz had provided, Clausius, Boltzmann, Kelvin, and other physicists constructed the modern science of thermodynamics. With the acceptance by physiologists of the principle of energy conservation, the fantastic theory of vitalism disappeared, and the body came to be regarded as a machine which converts food and oxygen into heat and work. As research continued, it became evident that the doctrine of the conservation of energy was applicable everywhere—in inanimate objects as well as in living things.

In his epoch-making paper of 1847, Helmholtz assumed that perpetual motion is impossible. What, then, are the relations among the various known forces of nature? Since these forces cannot arise out of nothing, mechanical energy can be generated naturally only through the expenditure of energy. Illustrating the principle that energy cannot be lost, Helmholtz noted that in a weight-powered clock a quantity of energy may disappear when the weight reaches the bottom, but the kinetic (motion) energy of the clock's mechanisms has been transformed into an equivalent quantity of heat. In other applications, Helmholtz showed how to compare the kinetic energy of a moving body, the electrical energy produced by a thermo-couple (a thermoelectric couple used to measure temperature differences), the energy of a magnet moved by electricity, and simple heat energy. Kinetic energy or energy in motion was the yardstick used to measure all other forces.

Helmholtz concluded with the statement: "I think in the foregoing that I have proved that the above-mentioned law (conservation of energy) does not go against any hitherto known facts of natural science, but is supported by a large number of them in a striking manner. I have tried to enumerate as completely as possible what consequences result from the combination of other known laws of nature, and how they require to be confirmed by other experiments."

In a tribute to Helmholtz, James Clerk Maxwell, noted nineteenth-century physicist, commented: "To appreciate the scientific value of Helmholtz' little essay on the Conservation of Force, we should have to ask those to whom we owe the greatest discoveries in thermodynamics and other branches of modern physics, how many times they have read it over, and how often during their researches they felt the weighty statements of Helmholtz acting on their minds like an irresistible driving power."

Through the work of Albert Einstein and other twentieth-century physicists, concepts of energy and matter or mass now tend to merge. The law of the conservation of energy has therefore been interpreted in a new light. Energy cannot be created or destroyed, but it may be increased or decreased in proportion to mass. Thus a single embracing principle covers the two fundamental laws relating to the conservation of energy and the conservation of matter.

62

Explorer of Unseen Worlds
Louis Pasteur (1822-1895)

Mémoire sur la Fermentation Appelée Lactique
(Treatise on the Fermentation Known as Lactic)

Two centuries before Louis Pasteur's researches in bacteriology, Robert Boyle, "the father of chemistry," made the prophetic statement, "He that thoroughly understands the nature of ferments and fermentations shall probably be much better able than he that ignores them to give a fair account of divers phenomena of certain diseases (as well fevers as others) which will perhaps be never properly understood without an insight into the doctrine of fermentation." Boyle's prediction came true with the first man to understand the nature of fermentation, Louis Pasteur.

Ever since the phenomenon had first been observed by man, fermentation had been surrounded by mystery and superstition. Most widely accepted by scientists was the theory of spontaneous generation of living creatures—a theory that goes back at least to Aristotle and was treated as an unquestionable fact by Ovid, Pliny, Lucretius, and Vergil. Living matter, it was believed, came from dead substances. Vergil tells of bees swarming to life from the body of a dead bull. As late as the seventeenth century, it was the popular belief that eels, salamanders, lizards, flies, bees, and other lower forms originated by spontaneous generation. An Italian scientist, Buonanni, taught that "a certain timberwood after rotting in the sea produced worms which engendered butterflies, and these butterflies became birds," and a noted chemist handed down an infallible recipe for making mice: "Place a piece of soiled linen in a vessel; add a few grains of corn; and in twenty-one days the mice will be there, fully adult, and of both sexes."

The greatest chemist of Pasteur's time, Justus Liebig, had a somewhat different explanation for ferments. "The changes designated by the terms fermentation, decay, and putrefaction," he maintained, "are chemical transformations," a process caused by the decomposing of dead yeast cells whose bursting molecules sped up the decomposition of the fermentable matter. Liebig and many other chemists continued to hold this view for years after Pasteur's famous experiments had destroyed the idea of spontaneous generation. So overwhelming, however, was Pasteur's evidence that scientists generally promptly subscribed to the thesis. In defending his position before the Sorbonne, Pasteur stated that "there is no circumstance known in which it can be affirmed that microscopic beings come into the world without germs — without parents similar to themselves."

Pasteur's epoch-making investigations into fermentation began in 1854, with his appointment, at the age of thirty-two, as dean of the science faculty at the University of Lille. There, in a center for the manufacture of alcohol, Pasteur, a trained chemist, was called upon to study the problems of the beet-root alcohol industry. Spoilage and variation in quality of the product, Pasteur found, were caused by the lactic acid formed in a living ferment. Subsequent experiments with wine, vinegar, and milk demonstrated that fermentation and souring invariably resulted from the presence of microorganisms. Further, it was shown that such organisms are neither spontaneously nor chemically created. They are always introduced from the outside, that is, from the air or by infection. Consequently, fermentation could be prevented by protection from the atmosphere and from contamination. Through the simple procedure of heating wine, milk, and other liquids at a relatively low temperature, the method now known as *pasteurization*, harmful bacteria could be killed.

His early researches on fermentation were published by Pasteur in 1857 in his *Mémoire sur la Fermentation Appelée Lactique*, "Treatise on the Fermentation Known as Lactic." Thus began the experimentation and research in a field which was to occupy Pasteur for the remainder of his life and produce one revolutionary discovery after another. The fascination which this branch of science held for him and the importance he attached to it are revealed in a letter to a friend: "I am pursuing as best I can these studies on fermentation which are of great interest, connected as they are with the impenetrable mystery of life and death."

If bacteria caused wine and milk to sour, butter to become rancid, and meat to putrefy, might they not also be responsible for disease in men and animals? This was the startling question that occurred to Joseph Lister in Scotland, after reading Pasteur's paper, and that led him on to the discovery of the cause of wound infection.

Pasteur first applied his findings on microorganisms to silk worms. Disease among the caterpillars threatened to wreck the silk industry in the south of France and elsewhere. After three years of research, Pasteur discovered two different diseases caused by bacteria, showed the silk growers how to breed healthy stock, and restored the prosperity of the industry. Next, at the urging of the distressed farmers of France, Pasteur undertook a study of anthrax, a disease which had reached epidemic proportions and appeared likely to wipe out the nation's sheep and cattle stocks. Following the principles established by Jenner some seventy years earlier for smallpox vaccination, Pasteur prepared a weak form of virus; when injected into an animal, the attenuated virus caused a mild attack and thereafter gave immunity. Another contagious disease, chicken cholera, was prevented by similar means.

Pasteur's most spectacular triumph came in the perfection of a vaccine for rabies or hydrophobia, a dreadful disease caused by the bite of a rabid animal, previously 100% fatal to its victims. Rabies is an acute infectious disease caused by a virus, first identified by Pasteur in 1881. The treatment developed by Pasteur in 1885 has some modern modifications, but is still basically the same as the original Pasteur treatment.

Like all other great innovators and trailblazers, Pasteur soon found that his career inevitably engendered controversy. Jealous colleagues called him a "circus performer, a charlatan, and a clown." On one occasion, when being attacked in a meeting of the Académie des Sciences, Pasteur turned to one of his critics and said, "You are incapable of observing!," and to another, "You are incapable of reasoning!" When members of the academy protested, Pasteur replied, "My vivacity has carried me away. I present my apologies to my colleagues." Then he hesitated—"May I, now that I have admitted my faults and made amends, make a statement in extenuation? What I said was true, absolutely true!" Pasteur is also quoted as remarking, "A man of science should think of what will be said of him in the following century, not of the insults or the praise of one day."

In view of much current discussion on the merits of applied versus pure science, it is of interest to note that Pasteur's researches were directed nearly always toward the solution of practical problems, especially those of economic importance, such as were posed to him by brewers, dairymen, vintners, and silk growers. Pasteur's pragmatic approach is revealed in his comment that "nothing is more agreeable to a man who has made science his career than to increase the number of his discoveries, but his cup of joy is full when the result of his observations is put to immediate practical use."

The genius of Pasteur lay in his understanding of scientific method, acute powers of observation, imaginativeness, and limitless patience in producing experimental proof. These extraordinary qualities enabled him to establish bacteriology on a sound basis and to transform that science into an invaluable ally of the medical world.

63

Riddle of Heredity
Gregor Mendel (1822-1884)

Experiments in Plant Hybridization

Approximately three centuries after the passing of Nicolaus Copernicus, who had won preeminence as the father of modern astronomy, another Catholic churchman, Gregor Johann Mendel, entered the hall of fame by founding the modern science of genetics. Further, Mendel, an Austrian, was born and spent his active career only a short distance from Copernicus' native Poland.

Heredity has long been viewed as one of the fundamental biological problems. Investigators had been accumulating a mass of facts prior to Mendel's mid-nineteenth-century experiments, but interpretations of the data were hopelessly muddled. There was no agreement except on the observation that offspring resemble one or the other parent or are intermediate between them. It is now recognized that Mendel's predecessors failed in their heredity studies because they concerned themselves with species or races as a whole, instead of concentrating attention on a few clearly defined characteristics — an error avoided by Mendel. His solution of the strange riddle of heredity came through the investigation of individual, sharply contrasted characteristics.

Questions of heredity began to interest Mendel as early as 1855. While serving as an Augustinian monk in Brünn (now Brno in Czechoslovakia), he was assigned a garden plot for his experiments in plant hybridization. During the eight years from 1856 to 1864 he observed over 10,000 specimens. After careful consideration, Mendel chose the ordinary edible pea as a subject for his experiments. The pea met several essential requirements: there are many distinct varieties, differing in inherited characteristics; it is an annual, growing a new generation year after year; and the sex physiology of the pea flower is ideal, since it is self-fertilizing, containing both male and female sex elements, and well protected from pollen contamination by other plants.

Following the selection of peas for his experiments, Mendel obtained seeds of thirty-four varieties and spent two years testing them to make certain that they were pure-breeding types. From the total, twenty-two were chosen for experimentation. There were then singled out for study seven different pairs of contrasting characteristics: differences in the shape of ripe seeds, round or irregular; the color of the leaves, yellow or green; the color of the seed coat, gray-brown or white; the form of the ripe pods, inflated or constricted between the seeds; the color of the unripe pods, green or yellow; the position of the flower, along the main stem or bunched at the top of the stem; and the length of the stem, tall or dwarf.

Among the pea varieties were a giant growing seven feet tall and dwarfs of less than two feet. Using his careful cross-fertilization or hybridization techniques, Mendel crossed the two. The seeds were saved and planted the following season, with the astonishing result that all produced giants. In the next generation, however, there were three giants to one dwarf. Even more surprising was the fourth generation; the seed from the dwarfs produced only dwarfs, but the seed from the tall plants produced both giants and dwarfs. Records showed that out of six tall plants, two would grow only tall plants, and never anything else, while the other four would produce tall and dwarf in the proportion of three giants to one dwarf. These ratios held true through all succeeding generations.

Similar crosses were made by Mendel with each of his other six pairs, producing identical results. Always the parents transmitted characteristics to their offspring in definite numerical proportions. Mendel concluded that somewhere in the plants' hereditary constitution there were "units," now called genes, which determine character. The stronger units he described as "dominant" and the weaker as "recessive." For example, in the first generation raised from his crossbreds or hybrids, Mendel discovered that there were seventy-five percent dominants and twenty-five percent recessives—indicating that tallness was not the dominant quality. He concluded that the recessive genes are not destroyed or lost, but simply latent or suppressed, ready to produce their effects upon a definite proportion of the succeeding generations. The genes remain pure indefinitely, never fusing.

The first report of his pioneer work was presented by Mendel before the Brünn Society for the Study of Natural Science in 1865. The following year the paper, *Versuche über Pflanzen-Hybriden* (Experiments in Plant Hybridization), was published in the society's proceedings. Copies went to institutions at home and abroad—with a complete lack of response. Not until 1900, sixteen years after Mendel's death, did the world of science become aware of the extraordinary importance of Mendel's discoveries. Then, by an odd coincidence, Hugo De Vries in Holland, Karl Correns in Germany, and Erich Tschermak in Austria almost simultaneously rediscovered Mendel's long-neglected report. The Mendelian experiments were repeated, the findings confirmed, and the study of genetics thereby given a tremendous impetus toward becoming, as it is today, one of the most dynamic of the biological sciences.

Various scientists and social scientists have pointed out that the basic laws of heredity discovered in the plant and animal world are also applicable to man. Certain human abnormalities represent dominant traits and are transmitted from generation to generation. A famous example is hemophilia, a tendency to bleed, long a curse of European royalty. Experiments following Mendelian principles have thrown light on other hereditary diseases and on certain forms of nervous disorders and feeble-mindedness.

In the introduction to his 1865 report, Mendel commented: "It requires indeed some courage to undertake a labor of such far-reaching extent; this appears, however, to be the only right way by which we can finally reach the solution of a question the importance of which cannot be overestimated in connection with the history of the evolution of organic forms."

After more than a century, the essential accuracy of Mendel's laws has been confirmed by a host of research workers on sex, cytology, embryology, albinism, genetics, eugenics, and heredity. Mendel's demonstration that by careful selection and observation pure types can be produced has proven of immense significance to plant and animal breeders as well as to those who, whether for the betterment or destruction of their fellow men, attempted to apply his precepts to the human being. Thus, a half century after Mendel's death, his principles of genetics, combined with the Nietzschean ideal of the superman, were mutilated and misused to provide a pseudo-scientific basis for Hitler's attempt to exterminate an entire race.

64

Founder of Antiseptic Surgery
Joseph Lister (1827-1912)

On the Antiseptic Principle in the Practice of Surgery

Medical historians are virtually unanimous in holding that Joseph Lister represents the beginning of a new era in medicine, and that he was directly responsible for extraordinary progress in the control of human suffering. As noted in the chapter on Oliver Wendell Holmes, and his great concern with puerperal fever, conditions prevailing in nineteenth century hospitals were incredibly bad. A terrible stench pervaded rooms and corridors, caused by the suppuration of wounds. A heavy death toll resulted from septicema, a form of blood poisoning; pyemia with abscesses spread throughout the body; hospital gangrene, characterized by mortification of the tissues; and erysipelas, a contagious skin disease. The death rate from operations ranged from twenty-five to forty percent and was even higher for amputations. In military hospitals, fatalities were as much as ninety percent. Napoleon's surgeon, Larrey, reported only two survivals in several thousand amputations at the hip. Excessive overcrowding led to complications in diseases. A Paris hospital had only 1,200 beds for 3,000 patients.

Joseph Lister, then a young surgeon in a Glasgow hospital, was appalled at the prevailing situation. Why, he asked, did every wound in the surgical wards become infected and suppurate? Why did so many of the surgeon's patients die, and what could be done to save them? One distinguished surgeon declared that "a man laid on the operating table in one of our surgical hospitals is exposed to more chances of death than the English soldier on the field of Waterloo."

Lack of sanitation, Lister suspected, might be one source of infections. Surgical instruments were cleaned only casually; silk threads used for stitches were carried in the surgeon's lapel or pocket; when his hands were otherwise busy, the surgeon held the operating knife in his teeth; his coat, covered with stains and blood, was seldom if ever washed; and the surgeon did not trouble to wash his hands when going from one type of disease to another or from an autopsy to a living patient. Naturally, microorganisms flourished and multiplied to claim their victims. Acting upon the theory of better sanitation, Lister's wards became models of cleanliness. Still the death rate did not decrease.

Among Lister's colleagues at Glasgow was Dr. Thomas Anderson, professor of chemistry. One day in conversation, Anderson drew Lister's attention to an article written by a Frenchman, Louis Pasteur, on the processes of fermentation and putrefaction. Immediately after reading the article, Lister was convinced that he had found a solution to the questions that had continually perplexed him. The germs Pasteur had discovered causing fermentation in wine could perhaps contaminate wounds, causing fermentation or pus formation in infections. "It occurred to me that decomposition in the injured part might be avoided, without excluding the air," Lister wrote, "by applying as a dressing some material capable of destroying the life of the floating particles."

How could the deadly little organisms be killed off and excluded from wounds? Lister learned that municipal authorities at Carlisle had successfully used a new German invention, carbolic acid, to disinfect and deodorize the sewage system. From his chemist friend Anderson, Lister was able to obtain a supply of the acid for experimentation.

On August 12, 1865, Lister's great opportunity arrived. An eleven-year old boy had been run over by a cart and was brought to the Glasgow hospital with a compound fracture. Lister had the wound dressed with a piece of lint saturated in carbolic acid, set the bones, and applied another carbolic acid dressing. The boy made a rapid recovery, with none of the customary inflammation, pus formation, or other complication. "This, no doubt, was a favourable case," Lister wrote in his famous 1867 paper, "and might have done well under ordinary treatment. But the remarkable absence of suppuration, and the immediate conversion of the compound fracture into a simple fracture (a fracture with unbroken skin) with a superficial sore, were most encouraging facts."

Delighted with his success, Lister began to use carbolic acid on everything that came into contact with the patients. Bandages, instruments, and ligatures were dipped in it; the operating table was washed with it; the surgeon and his assistants scrubbed their hands in a dilution of the acid; and even the air in the operating room was sprayed with it by means of a complex apparatus. The odor of carbolic acid replaced the smell of decay and death.

Certain that he was on the right track, Lister turned from accident wounds to abscesses, again using the carbolic acid technique. The results obtained from treating abscesses antiseptically were even more astonishing than those obtained from the antiseptic treatment of compound fractures. Patients who previously almost certainly would have succumbed from their infections made quick and satisfactory recoveries.

The results of his experiments were reported by Lister in his notable article, "On the Antiseptic Principle in the Practice of Surgery," published in *The Lancet*, 1867. He described the successful application of his methods in cases of compound fractures and other severe injuries, in the antiseptic treatment of abscesses, and for the improvement of hospital sanitation. Concerning the last, he wrote:

> Since the antiseptic treatment has been brought into full operation, and wounds and abscesses no longer poison the atmosphere with putrid exhalations, my wards, though in other respects under precisely the same circumstances as before, have completely changed their character; so that during the last nine months not a single instance of pyemia, hospital gangrene, or erysipelas has occurred in them.

In common with virtually all great discoveries, Lister's findings at first met with violent criticism and opposition from conservative members of his profession, especially from the senior surgeons who disliked change and who clung to the old methods of treatment. Acceptance came more readily from German, French, and other Continental physicians than from the English diehards. But long before his death at the ripe age of eighty-five, Lister had seen worldwide approval and adoption of his ideas. Among numerous honors conferred upon him were those of being raised to the peerage by Queen Victoria in 1897 and election to the presidency of the Royal Society from 1894 to 1900.

Lister himself was responsible for continual improvements in medical practice after his original discoveries. The advances in surgery since his day have, of course, been phenomenal. Sir St. Clair Thompson, eminent London physician, pointed out that "Listerism is the foundation of the vast edifice of hygiene and preventive medicine. The investigations leading to the discovery of the control of typhoid, cholera and plague; the investigation of tropical diseases; the establishment of blood transfusion and other remedial measures were made possible by the methods of Listerian surgery."

65

Greatest American Scientist
Josiah Willard Gibbs (1839-1903)

On the Equilibrium of Heterogeneous Substances

Josiah Willard Gibbs is ranked by historians of science as probably the greatest of American scientists, and by world standards some would place him beside Newton and Maxwell, on the ground that he did for thermodynamics and physical chemistry what they did for mechanics and electromagnetics. Gibbs' name means little or nothing, however, to the man of the street, and a majority of scientists recall only that he discovered a principle of great importance called the "phase rule" and expressed it in terms which hardly any of his contemporaries could understand.

Why, in view of his lofty rank in the world of science, has Gibbs remained a relatively obscure and little-known figure? Primarily, the difficulty lies in his method of expression: an application of mathematical principles to a solution of fundamental problems of chemistry and physics. Reading Gibbs with any understanding requires mathematical facility of a high order. One is reminded of Sir Isaac Newton's "glacial remoteness" of style. Yet, Gibbs, who spent his entire active career as professor of mathematical physics at Yale University (1871-1903), is universally credited with creating the systems on which much of the modern industrial and scientific world rests.

The epoch-making work that assured Gibbs a permanent niche in the hall of fame is entitled *On the Equilibrium of Heterogeneous Substances*, published in three installments (1876-1878) in the *Transactions* of the Connecticut Academy of Arts and Sciences.

The nineteenth century was the age of steam. It was natural, therefore, that Gibbs should have directed his attention to thermodynamics, the branch of science dealing with the laws of one of the forms of energy — heat. The field of thermodynamics, however, was simply a springboard or point of departure for Gibbs, who went on to work out a series of universal laws governing the conditions or "phases," as he called them, of heterogeneous matter — any matter, anywhere. In his paper, Gibbs was concerned essentially with the famous "second law of thermodynamics," which, highly simplified, states that heat must always pass from hot to cold. "Heat cannot of itself, without the performance of work by some external agency, pass from a cold to a warmer body." This is the scientific reason why it is impossible to invent a "perpetual motion" machine. The "second law" has been defined as meaning simply that hot bodies cool off, that water must be raised if it is to fall, that clocks must be wound up after they have run down, that the universe is doomed to chaos.

Gibbs followed the principles laid down by Rudolph Clausius, German mathematical physicist: "The energy of the world is constant. The entropy of the world tends toward a maximum." The term "entropy," invented by Clausius, stands for a measurable quantity; when no heat reaches it, this quantity remains constant, but when heat enters or leaves the body the quantity increases or diminishes. Gibbs undertook to demonstrate mathematically the relations existing among temperature, volume, pressure, energy, and entropy.

Another complex term as interpreted by Gibbs is "equilibrium." In the pre-Newtonian era, equilibrium was thought of as a state of balance in which all things are motionless. The idea was expanded by Newton to include motion: for example, a planet moving in orbit. A further extension was made by Gibbs, who included in the concept of equilibrium the way in which matter changes its state and identity. For example, ice becomes water, water becomes steam, steam becomes oxygen and hydrogen. Hydrogen combines with nitrogen and becomes ammonia. In brief, every process in nature means change, and Gibbs discovered the laws determining such change. To establish the number of physical phases or states possible to a specific chemical system in equilibrium, Gibbs evolved his celebrated "phase rule" or law. The fundamental importance of the discovery may be illustrated by noting that the mathematical formulas of the phase rule made it possible to determine in advance the exact concentration of various substances that were to be used in making a required mixture. The formulas stated the temperatures and pressures best suited to produce a final mixture whose components would remain in equilibrium with each other and not separate out and destroy the mixture. Using the phase rule, an experimenter could also calculate the conditions necessary for making physical separations of one or more of the substances found in a complex mixture of salts or metals.

Though Gibbs devoted only four pages to the development of the phase rule, it has been estimated that other scientists have subsequently printed over 11,000 pages describing applications of Gibbs' phase rule to mineralogy, petrology, physiology, metallurgy, and every other branch of science.

Gibbs' paper contains, as far as general principles are concerned, practically the whole of the science which is now called physical chemistry and which had scarcely been begun when the paper was written. The rules formulated by Gibbs have enormously facilitated and cheapened a great variety of industrial processes — for example, in metallurgy, refrigeration, fuel and power engineering, and the manufacture of synthetic chemicals, ceramics, glass, and fertilizers. Today, chemistry has become the basis of the world's greatest industries, and a substantial share of the progress in the field can be traced to Gibbs' remarkable discoveries.

Gibbs was far in advance of his time, and his paper was published in an obscure journal. Thus the significance of his work was not recognized for ten years. At first it was used almost exclusively by Germans and Hollanders, who began to apply it in the interpretation of chemical phenomena. In 1901 the Royal Society's Copley Medal was awarded Gibbs for applying his analytical methods to determining the relations between chemical, electrical and thermal energies.

66

Founder of American Psychology
William James (1842-1910)

The Principles of Psychology

Until the coming of William James in the last quarter of the nineteenth century, modern psychology was a science yet unborn. Previously, the approach to the field had been philosophical, with emphasis on its ethical and moral aspects. It was James who played a pioneer role in creating a "new psychology allied with the natural sciences and combining," as Ralph Barton Perry noted, "the methods of observation with those of speculation and reflection."

William James was born in New York City, the son of a theologian, Henry James, and the brother of the novelist Henry James. His background provided ideal preparation for a reexamination of psychology as a science. After a period of study in England, France, Switzerland, and Germany, James entered the Lawrence Scientific School at Harvard in 1861 and in the ensuing years studied chemistry, anatomy, physiology, and medicine, receiving the M.D. degree from Harvard in 1869. From 1872 to 1907, James was a member of the Harvard University faculty, beginning as an instructor in anatomy and physiology, and then serving successively as professor of psychology and professor of philosophy. In 1876, he was the leading spirit in founding at Harvard the first laboratory for psychological research in the United States. James also had the advantage of being well acquainted with accomplishments in psychology in England, France, and Germany, doing much to reshape into lively and understandable language the complicated, overly technical writings of the European psychologists.

Charles Darwin's theory of biological evolution deeply influenced James, and the system of psychology which the latter developed was a comprehensive attempt to explain mind in terms of evolution. After his work in anatomy, physiology, and medicine, James found unacceptable a psychology that stressed the soul and ignored the body. The psychological aspects of life, he held, could be explained satisfactorily only in terms harmonizing with the general theory of evolution. "A real science of man," James wrote in 1875, "is now being built up out of the theory of evolution and the facts of archaeology, the nervous system, and the senses." In a letter to the president of Harvard University the same year,

James expressed the view that "psychology cannot be taught as a living science by anyone who has not a first-hand acquaintance with the facts of nervous physiology." As a medical student and teacher of physiology, James had acquired all that was currently known about the nervous system, how it received stimuli through the sense organs and transmitted the impulses to the brain.

The climax of James' career as a psychologist was the publication in 1890 of his *Principles of Psychology*, a two-volume work 1,400 pages in length, on which he had labored for twelve years. The publication of the *Principles* was hailed at home and abroad as an event of first importance in the psychological world. It was not only a comprehensive survey of an essentially new subject, synthesizing the facts of psychology, but a major contribution to the field. The book treated psychology as a natural science, with emphasis on the biological aspects. A recent writer, John J. McDermott, calls the *Principles* "actually a running commentary on the total human experience as well as a rich expression of much of its untold psychic activity. To this day, the chapter on 'Habit' is the classic statement on that aspect of human life. No detail is too slight to be given a full and complete hearing in the mèlange of sensations which is open to James's analysis."

As a biologist, James saw the mental processes as inseparable from the activities of living creatures — processes, indeed, which are essential to survival in the world of nature. The American school of psychology known as functionalism grew out of this theory. Further, James stresses throughout the *Principles* the irrational side of human nature and demonstrates that man is a creature of emotion and action as well as of knowledge and reason. The intellect is governed by definite physiological conditions, James was convinced, and belief is determined by emotion and will. The earlier concept of man as a rational being is largely rejected.

One of the most influential doctrines presented in the *Principles* is the "stream of consciousness," a stream of thoughts from which a functioning brain makes selections. The process of selection is synonymous with the mind, and thinking or intelligence may be defined as the ability to select. As summarized by Gay Wilson Allen, James' biographer, James maintained that "the mind or consciousness is never empty, even in sleep; something is always in it, and the content is always changing, accumulating new images, points of attention, or 'thoughts' in the process, so that, like a river, it seems to flow in one direction. Even when the mind attempts to retrace its course, it is never the same course because the contents have changed in many subtle ways."

The British philosopher John Locke had divided ideas into simple and complex categories, arguing that the mind takes simple ideas and combines them into complex structures in any process of logical reasoning. James rejected such a classification and also the doctrine of "association of ideas," which had previously prevailed. So-called reasoning, he held, is usually nothing more than rationalizing, in an attempt at self-justification or to satisfy emotional needs. Thus all thought is shaped by the individual thinker's needs, likes, dislikes, and peculiarities. According to James, the primary mental fact is that thinking of some kind goes on, but he insisted that "no one ever had a simple sensation by itself. Consciousness, from our natal day, is of a teeming multiplicity of objects and relations, and what we call simple sensations are results of discriminative attention, pushed often to a very high degree."

Another concept with which James' name is closely associated is his celebrated theory of the emotions, sometimes referred to as the James-Lange theory, since the Danish physiologist Carl George Lange presented a similar idea almost simultaneously. The essence of the theory is that the causes of emotion are entirely physiological; bodily changes follow perception of the stimulus, and the subjective feeling of these changes, such as quickened heart beats, shallow breathing, and trembling, as they occur, constitutes the emotion. As James expresses the hypothesis, "We feel sorry because we cry, angry because we strike, afraid because we tremble, and not that we cry, strike, or tremble, because we are sorry, angry, or fearful, as the case may be." Interpreting the meaning of his theory of emotions in its psychological applications, James continues:

> It makes us realize more deeply than ever how much our mental life is knit up with our corporeal frame, in the strictest sense of the term. Rapture, love, ambition, indignation, and pride, considered as feelings, are fruits of the same soil with the grossest bodily sensations of pleasure and pain.

In developing the theory of emotions, James was influenced by Darwin's ideas, which inclined him to link the emotions with the instincts. A recent critic of James' psychological teaching, Margaret Knight, questions the theory. She does not deny that emotions have physical causes, adding, "but modern research has shown that they are caused primarily by processes in the thalamic region of the brain ... which give rise (via the autonomic nervous system) to the involuntary physical changes by which the emotion is accompanied."

Closely associated with James' theory of consciousness was his doctrine of the will. A basic question is whether human beings are largely automatons whose behavior is determined by their environment and heredity, or whether it is possible for them, through exertions of will, to act otherwise. No system of ethics, for example, is possible without free will. Individual differences, of course, are inevitable, as James points out:

> When a dreadful object is presented, or when life as a whole turns up its dark abysses to our view, then the worthless ones among us lose their hold on the situation altogether, and either escape from its difficulties by averting their attention, or if they cannot do that, collapse into yielding masses of plaintiveness and fear.... But the heroic mind does differently. To it, too, the objects are sinister and dreadful, unwelcome, incompatible with wished-for things. But it can face them if necessary, without for that losing its hold upon the rest of life.

The latter type of mind can maintain some control over its destiny and learn to play the game of life to its own advantage. A person with such a mind becomes a master of life, able to direct his own experience and to influence the lives of others, for, James asserted, "we draw new life from the heroic example."

Perhaps the most famous of all James' chapters is "Habit." The benign effect of routine and the cumulative significance of little acts are summed up by James in the statement: "Sow an action, and you reap a habit; sow a habit and you reap a character; sow a character and you reap a destiny." The importance of *first experience* in shaping future experiences was emphasized by James, who noted that once a neural path has been established by habit, it will be traveled again and again unless some stronger force breaks a new path. The effects of the "law of habit" are described as follows:

The great thing, then, in all education is *to make our nervous system our ally instead of our enemy.* It is to fund and capitalize our acquisitions, and live at ease upon the interest of the fund. The more of the details of our daily life we can hand over to the effortless custody of automatism, the more our higher powers of mind will be set free for their own proper work. There is no more miserable human being than one in whom nothing is habitual but indecision. Full half the time of such a man goes to the deciding, or regretting, of matters which ought to be so ingrained in him as practically not to exist for his consciousness at all.

Good habits, James maintains, are a great boon to man and should be carefully cultivated; by taking advantage of the "plasticity of the living matter in our nervous system" they make the difficult easy. Beginning as early in life as possible, useful actions should be made automatic and habitual. By adulthood, the good and bad habits which man has formed effectively suppress most natural impulses. In the adult, James says, "nine hundred and ninety-nine thousandths of our activity is purely automatic and habitual." It is thus clear that in forming habits man is shaping his own future self. As a method of forming good habits, James suggests four rules:

> We must take care to *launch ourselves with as strong and decided initiative as possible.... Never suffer an exception to occur till the new habit is securely rooted in your life.... Seize the very first possible opportunity to act on every resolution you make and on every emotional prompting you may experience in the direction of the habits you aspire to gain.... Keep the faculty of effort alive in you by a little gratuitous exercise every day.*

Reflecting his medical training, James emphasized "exceptional mental states" in his writings, thus pioneering in the study and development of abnormal psychology and psychopathology. He drew freely on the researches of three French psychologists and neurologists, Jean Martin Charcot, Pierre Janet, and Alfred Binet, who had undertaken the first important investigations of the phenomena of disassociation. Such matters as multiple consciousness, subconsciousness, hallucination, the hypnotic trance, and various aspects of hysteria were extensively treated by James. He was fascinated by unusual psychical phenomena, devoted years of thought and research to reports of occult phenomena, and served as president of the Society for Psychical Research. These activities were condemned by most contemporary psychologists on the ground that they were unscientific. But their disapproval in no way deterred James, who was a nonconformist by nature, hospitable to the examination of all doctrines, even those of the "faith healers" and "mental healers," no matter how much despised by the orthodox. His keen interest in mental illness and citation of numerous case histories drawn from clinical psychology anticipated psychoanalysis and psychiatry. James was among the first proponents of a theory of the subconscious mind.

After publication of the *Principles*, James expressed frankly his views on the state of psychology in his time. As a science, he wrote, "psychology is the condition of physics before Galileo and the laws of motion, of chemistry before Lavoisier and the notion that mass is preserved in all reactions. The Galileo and the Lavoisier of psychology will be famous men indeed when they come, as come they some day surely will, or past successes are no index to the future." James regarded his own monumental treatise as exploratory and provisional. Eventually, he hoped, laws would be discovered that would make possible the prediction and control of mental life.

In summing up the impact of James' work, Lloyd Morris, in his *William James: The Message of a Modern Mind*, concludes:

> *The Principles* appears to be one of the major watersheds of twentieth-century thought. Directly or indirectly, its influence has penetrated politics, jurisprudence, sociology, education and the arts. In the domain of psychology, it has foreshadowed nearly all subsequent developments of primary importance. Viewed retrospectively, the permanent significance of *The Principles* was incentive. It explored possibilities and indicated directions.[9]

Largely because of James, American psychology made a smooth transition from mental philosophy to a science. Henceforth, the distinction between philosophical matters, such as the problems of the soul and the psychological aspects of life, could be established with reasonable exactitude. In James' time, psychology lacked the hard facts essential to the creation of a mature science, but he showed that such facts must be obtained on the basis of experience and of experimental verification. As Knight states, the *Principles*, "though it is inevitably out of date on points of detail, is most startlingly modern in its general approach. Most of the unsolved problems with which James was preoccupied—such as the relation between brain-processes and consciousness, or the physiology of the learning process—are still unsolved, and still burning questions, to-day." Unquestionably, James was years ahead of his time in his view that psychology should be more closely allied with biology and physiology than with philosophy. James' recognition that psychology was in a state of infancy when he was writing is evidenced by a passage in his last chapter:

> Even in the clearest parts of psychology our insight is insignificant enough. And the more sincerely one seeks to trace the actual course of *psychogenesis*, the steps by which as a race we may have come by the peculiar mental attributes which we possess, the more clearly one perceives "the slowly gathering twilight close in utter night."

67

Bacillus Hunter

Robert Koch (1843-1910)

The Etiology of Tuberculosis

Both Louis Pasteur and Robert Koch are frequently referred to as the "father of bacteriology." Each unquestionably is entitled to share that high honor. The difference between their respective achievements in this field is that Koch was a great research bacteriologist and Pasteur was perhaps the greatest of applied bacteriologists.

A striking similarity may be noted in the early careers of Koch in Germany and Edward Jenner in England. They began as country doctors, with only the crudest laboratory apparatus available for experimental purposes. Both were extraordinarily keen observers with a passion for scientific research. Jenner, however, was content to spend most of his years in the rural environment where he started, while Koch was called to Berlin in his early thirties, and thereafter the world was his stage.

Koch's first significant research, commenced before he gave up his country practice at Wollstein, was on the bacteria of anthrax, a disease that had occupied much of Pasteur's time. Other bacteriologists had noted that the blood of animals dying of anthrax contained numerous minute, rod-shaped bodies. Working in his poorly equipped laboratory, Koch cultivated the anthrax germs outside the animal body, using broth as a culture medium. The artificial cultures of anthrax bacilli were then used to inoculate mice and rabbits. In a short time, the laboratory animals exhibited the typical symptoms of anthrax. Here was the first demonstration in medical annals that specific bacteria or bacilli caused a specific disease.

His investigations into anthrax and other diseases, as well as researches by later scientists, were vastly aided by two new laboratory techniques developed by Koch. The first technique was a method of obtaining pure cultures. Before Koch, bacteriologists experienced great difficulty in separating one variety of bacteria from another. Cultures were grown in test tubes, usually in beef, chicken, or mutton broth, but it was impossible to separate one kind of organism from another or to avoid contamination from the air. One day Koch observed numerous spots different in color and shape on a piece of potato left on his laboratory table. Examination by microscope revealed that each spot represented a distinctive colony of bacteria. Later, Koch substituted a sterile meat extract containing liquid gelatine for the potato. This mixture solidified when poured on a glass plate. A second highly valuable technique perfected by Koch was the use of analine dyes for staining bacteria for easier identification, a laboratory method followed to the present day.

The scientific discovery that will always be most closely associated with Koch's name is the isolation of the tubercle bacillus, *Mycobacterium tuberculosis*, the cause of the "white plague." Infinite patience had been required, for the tuberculosis germ grows slowly, developing over a period of weeks, in contrast to hours characteristic of most bacteria. In reporting the discovery to the Berlin Physiological Society on March 24, 1882, Koch stated that he had found the rod-like bacillus present in every case and type of tuberculosis examined; the bacillus had been isolated from the human body and grown in a pure culture; and with this culture he had been able to give the disease to healthy animals. The complete story of his investigations and findings is contained in Koch's *Die Aetiologie der Tuberculose*. In the future, he asserted, "the fight against this terrible plague of mankind will deal no longer with an undetermined something, but with a tangible parasite, whose living conditions are for the most part known and can be investigated further."

Prior to Koch's epochal discovery, it was believed that tuberculosis was caused by bad heredity or weakened constitutions. Over the centuries it had established itself as the most ruthless killer in human history. In the fourth century, B.C., Hippocrates wrote that of all diseases tuberculosis caused the most suffering and the greatest number of deaths. In the nineteenth century, it was estimated that 14 million people died in war, while 30 million succumbed to consumption. During the period of Koch's discovery, tuberculosis was the leading cause of death throughout the Western world.

By demonstrating that tuberculosis is an infectious disease caused by a specific bacillus and spread from man to man, Koch laid the groundwork for public health measures that have immeasurably reduced the incidence of the disease throughout the world.

Only thirty-nine when the tuberculosis discovery was announced, Koch turned his brilliant research abilities to other major diseases. During outbreaks of cholera in Egypt and India, he isolated and identified the comma-shaped bacillus causing the disease, then showed how it was transmitted by drinking water and, therefore, how it might be prevented.

For the remaining years of an extremely active life, until his death in 1910, Koch carried on teaching and research at home and engaged in scientific expeditions abroad. In the course of a dozen years, he and his assistants discovered the causes of ten important diseases. In addition to tuberculosis and cholera, these included typhoid fever, diphtheria, erysipelas, tetanus, glanders, pneumonia, epidemic meningitis, and bubonic plague.

Early in his career, Koch developed four "postulates" or rules which he and later investigators found infallible in the study of disease-producing organisms. A parasite cannot be regarded as the cause of a disease unless all these conditions are met: first, the germ must be found in large numbers in the blood and tissues of the diseased animal; second, the germ must be grown outside the body of the animal in a pure culture; third, the pure form, when injected into other animals, must produce the same disease; and, fourth, the germs must be recoverable from the blood and tissues of the second animal.

Koch covered a wide field of medical investigation and made solid contributions to many phases of his profession. Methods developed by him or his followers for the control of bacterial infections in man, animals, and plants play a major role in making modern life possible, notably through such practices as the purification of water supplies, disposal of sewage, sterilization of food supplies, measures to insure a supply of pure and clean milk, cleanliness in personal living, and techniques for the prevention of specific diseases.

68

Doyen of Experimental Physiologists
Ivan Petrovich Pavlov (1849-1936)

Conditioned Reflexes: An Investigation of the Physiological Activity of the Cerebral Cortex

---

George Bernard Shaw and Ivan Petrovich Pavlov were strikingly similar in appearance, each sporting a luxuriant beard, and their long lifetimes were almost exactly contemporaneous. Shaw, the uncompromising antivivisectionist, exhibited no fraternal feeling, however, for his twin. His *Black Girl in Search of God* is represented as encountering "a very short-sighted elderly man in spectacles [Pavlov] who was sitting on a gnarled log." The man addressed the black girl as follows:

> In running away you were acting on a conditioned reflex. It is quite simple. Having lived among lions you have from your childhood associated the sound of a roar with deadly danger. Hence your precipitate flight when that superstitious old jackass brayed at you. This remarkable discovery cost me twenty-five years of devoted research, during which I cut out the brains of innumerable dogs, and observed their spittle by making holes in their cheeks for them to salivate through instead of through their tongues. The whole scientific world is prostrate at my feet in admiration of this colossal achievement and gratitude for the light it has shed on the great problem of human conduct.[10]

The black girl ridicules the old gentleman by remarking that she could have told him as much in twenty-five seconds without hurting any dogs, and points out that he is sitting on a crocodile mistakenly taken for a log. But despite the Shavian satire, the description of Pavlovian methods is not greatly exaggerated.

Pavlov, perhaps the outstanding scientist produced by Russia in modern times, devoted his early years to investigating the functions of the alimentary tract. Most of the facts relating to digestion now known either had their origin, or were established, in Pavlov's laboratory. For these researches, he received the Nobel Prize for Physiology and Medicine in 1904.

From 1902 until his death in 1936, Pavlov went on to explore a new branch of knowledge — the physiology of higher nervous activity. In his own words:

> For many years previously I had been working on the digestive glands.
> I had studied carefully and in detail all the conditions of their activity.
> Naturally I could not leave them without considering the so-called
> psychical stimulation of the salivary glands, i.e., the flow of saliva in
> the hungry animal or person at the sight of food or during talk about
> it or even at the thought of it.

During Pavlov's work on the digestive system he had observed that a dog secretes saliva and gastric juice not only as the result of being fed, but even in response to the sight or smell of food or to signs that it is about to be fed. Here was the beginning of his experiments extending over many years.

Pavlov's primary aim was to understand the working of the human brain. For laboratory purposes he chose dogs because of the simplicity of their mental processes and because they are close enough to man in the evolutionary scale to have brains essentially comparable.

The Pavlovian experiments were centered around reflex actions. Reflexes were divided into two groups: natural and conditioned. The ordinary inherited reflexes, sometimes referred to as "instincts," were called *unconditional*, and such acquired responses as those of the burnt child or the beaten dog, *conditional* reflexes.

Pavlov's basic method was to take a hungry dog and place it in a room from which all outside distractions of sight, sound, or smell were shut out. In one experiment, a metronome, an instrument with an audible tick, was used. When the metronome had ticked a few seconds, a plate of food was swung down to the floor, the dog ate the food, and the plate was pulled out of sight. At intervals, the ticking of the metronome followed by the appearance of food was repeated until the two became closely associated in the dog's mind and its salivary glands became active at the sound of the metronome. This is a simple example of a conditioned reflex. In other experiments a flash of light, the ringing of a bell, a touch upon a certain part of the body, the twang of a tuning fork, or squares of black-and-white cloth were used as signals. Soon the dog would learn that a certain sign meant food; its tail would wag and its mouth water before the food actually appeared.

Succeeding Pavlov experiments were designed to decondition a conditioned reflex. An animal conditioned to the ringing of bells would be subjected to a series of rings but no food would follow. At first the dog's mouth watered and its tail wagged. After a number of disappointments, however, it would no longer lick its lips. The dog had unlearned its original lesson. This process was termed inhibition by Pavlov. Inhibition takes various forms. To illustrate, dogs learned to discriminate that a flash of light with a noise meant food but a flash alone did not.

On the basis of experiments with numerous dogs, Pavlov found that animals varied greatly in the speed with which conditioned reflexes were formed and in the permanence of the reflexes. Some dogs became greatly excited during the experiments and developed nervous disorders. The neurotic states were evidently caused by conflicts between the reflexes that excited and those that inhibited. The dogs showed different temperaments and individual peculiarities, not unlike human beings. Confronted by insurmountable obstacles, the animals succumbed to nervous breakdowns, but the symptoms of the emotional strains, worries, or shocks were shown in diverse fashions: intense excitement comparable to insanity, a state of deep depression characterized by sleepiness, etc.

Pavlov's findings led psychologists to conduct extensive investigations of experimental neuroses. New approaches to phenomena of mental instability were suggested by the Pavlovian discoveries. As interpreted by Pavlov, fears, phobias, hates, and other irrational behavior are caused by reflexes conditioned by some earlier happenings, such as those associated with frightening or disturbing experiences. Near the end of Pavlov's life a psychiatric and psychoneurological clinic was added to his laboratories. Here an effort was made to analyze various cases of human neuroses by applying the criteria revealed in experiments on animals.

The first full account of Pavlov's work to appear in English was his *Conditioned Reflexes: An Investigation of the Physiological Activity of the Cerebral Cortex.*

It is generally agreed that in the development of modern psychology, conditioned reflexes have played a major part. Important trends of psychological investigation now in progress are based largely on the accomplishments of the Pavlov laboratories. The behavioral school founded by two Americans, Watson and Yerkes, in great vogue during the 1920s though now somewhat passé, was inspired by the Russian. Unquestionably, the study of conditioned reflexes has made fundamental contributions to the understanding of the nature of sleep, neuroses, and temperament. To Pavlov belongs the honor of being the first scientist to investigate the functions of the whole central nervous system from a physiological point of view. Some of his theories have been rejected by physiologists and neurologists, but his basic facts remain beyond dispute.

Pavlov's extraordinary achievements and influence are widely acknowledged among psychologists, psychiatrists, medical practitioners, and other specialists whose fields were touched by his researches. Because of Pavlov, psychology is now a branch of science rather than a subdivision of philosophy. Physiologists are indebted to him for developing a method of studying the brain in healthy animals, and psychiatrists for his investigations in experimental neurosis.

Critics of Pavlov's teachings have pointed out certain sinister aftermaths of his discoveries. Since his viewpoint was completely mechanistic, Pavlov concluded that even such concepts as freedom, curiosity, and religion were conditioned relfexes of the brain. Psychologists under authoritarian regimes have endeavored to apply these principles to the conditioning or "brainwashing" of masses of the population.

69

Founder of Modern Psychiatry
Sigmund Freud (1856-1939)

Civilization and Its Discontents

Of all branches of science, it is generally conceded that psychology is most mystical and obscure, the least susceptible to scientific proof. In the nature of things, the elusiveness and unpredictability are inescapable because the psychologist is dealing with the most mysterious of natural phenomena: the mind of man. A theory in chemistry or physics can be verified or disproved by laboratory techniques, but the validity of a psychological theory may be impossible to demonstrate. Thus the storm of controversy that has raged around Sigmund Freud and psychoanalysis throughout the present century.

But whether demonstrable or not, Freudian theories have exerted a profound influence on twentieth-century thought. Scarcely any facet of contemporary life and culture has remained unaffected by Freud's explorations of the subconscious regions of the mind. Such Freudian concepts as the influence of the subconscious on consciousness, the sexual basis of neuroses, the existence and importance of infantile sexuality, the function of dreams, the Oedipus complex, repression, resistance, and transference are now accepted as commonplace. The prejudices which Freud had to overcome to spread his doctrines were even more intense than those encountered by Copernicus and Darwin.

Freud is, without question, the founder of modern psychiatry and psychoanalysis. Prior to his time, psychiatry was concerned with such symptoms of insanity as schizophrenia and manic-depressive psychosis, requiring confinement in an institution. Beginning his clinical work with the treatment of repressions and conflicts of neurotics, Freud soon came to the conclusion that such conflicts were not peculiar to neurotics, but were also characteristic of well-adjusted persons. Further, neuroses were not diseases in the accepted sense, but psychological states of mind. Upon his observations, experiments, and experience with many patients around the turn of the century, Freud built the foundation of psychoanalysis.

Freud was one of the most prolific scientific writers of all time, and the variety of new concepts and psychological contributions flowing from his pen is distributed among many books and articles. One of his own favorites was *The Interpretation of Dreams*, issued in 1900, which contains most of his fundamental observations and ideas. In an earlier work, *Studies in Hysteria*,

1895, he had indicated his belief that sexual disturbances were the *"essential factor in the etiology of both neuroses and psychoneuroses"*—one of the cornerstones of psychoanalytic theory. Within the next few years, Freud had also worked out his concepts of resistance, transference, childhood sexuality, relationship between unpleasant memories and fantasies, defense mechanisms, and repression.

In his old age, Freud became interested in the application of psychoanalytic principles to society and its problems. One of the results was the writing of *Civilization and Its Discontents*, a searching analysis of modern civilization and its besetting ills. After a lifetime of specialized scientific investigations and experiments, Freud, in this general work, presents the broad impressions which his immense knowledge of innumerable individual cases had given him. The over-all effect is highly pessimistic.

Civilization as we know it, says Freud, is made possible only by man's heroic sacrifice of instinct. The instinctive life of man is one of unrestrained aggression and egoistic self-satisfaction. But civilization is built upon prohibitions and curbs of the natural impulses. From infancy, man is trained to become a member of a community organized for mutual assistance and is inhibited against murdering the man who stands in his way or raping the woman he desires. Thus in every civilized individual there is developed a force commonly called conscience, termed by Freud "the super-ego," to censor and judge every act and every desire. Without this mechanism, there could be no civilization.

The renunciation by individuals of instinctive gratifications, however, has created intense inner antagonisms and conflicts in mankind, accounting, according to Freud, for the turmoil of present-day civilization. Freud attaches high importance to the sexual privations, but places chief emphasis on the universal instincts of aggression and destruction. Countering the instinct of self-preservation, he believes, is a "death instinct," from which the instinct of aggression is derived. The instinct of aggression is the most powerful obstacle to culture and frequently threatens its destruction.

Assuming that the purpose of human life is the pursuit of happiness, Freud considers the principal barriers to its attainment:

> Suffering comes from three quarters: from our own body, which is destined to decay and dissolution, and cannot even dispense with anxiety and pain as danger signals; from the outer world which can rage against us with the most powerful and pitiless forces of destruction; and finally from our relations with other men. The unhappiness which has this last origin we find perhaps more painful than any other.

Yet, though our goal of happiness appears unattainable, the struggle to realize it continues. Among the means enumerated by Freud as ordinarily utilized to reduce unhappiness are powerful diversions of interests, leading us to forget our miseries; substitute gratifications, such as art, "illusions in contrast to reality"; intoxicating substances, making us insensitive to hard facts; personal delusion or religions, which "must be classified as mass delusions"; or the seeking of happiness through loving and being loved.

In his endless and restless search for happiness, man has gone far toward conquering nature. "In the last generations," Freud points out, "man has made extraordinary strides in knowledge of the natural sciences and technical application of them, and has established his dominion over Nature in a way never before imagined.... But men are beginning to perceive that all this newly won power over space and time, this fulfillment of age-old longings, has not increased the amount of pleasure they can obtain in life, has not made them feel any happier." This is no reason, though, in Freud's view, for concluding that technical progress is worthless from the standpoint of happiness. It merely means that power over nature is not the only condition of human happiness, nor is it the only goal of civilization's efforts.

The hostility of men toward one another, declares Freud, is a perpetual menace threatening the disintegration of society. His review of Marxist socialism's solution for the problem is of interest:

> The Communists believe they have found a way of delivering us from this evil. Man is whole-heartedly good and friendly to his neighbor, they say, but the system of private property has corrupted his nature.... If private property were abolished, all valuables held in common and all allowed to share in the enjoyment of them, ill-will and enmity would disappear from men.... I cannot enquire into whether the abolition of private property is advantageous and expedient, but I am able to recognize that this theory is founded on an untenable illusion. By abolishing private property one deprives the human love of aggression of one of its instruments, a strong one undoubtedly, but assuredly not the strongest. To do this in no way alters the individual differences in power and influence which are turned by aggressiveness to its own use, nor does it change the nature of the instinct in any way.

The moral conscience is dwelt upon at length by Freud. Conscience in the child is a relatively simple affair, usually manifested by dread of losing the love of its parents. In the adult, the phenomenon is more complicated, marked by tension and conflict between the strict "super-ego" and the "ego," the latter defined as the sense of guilt. Freud stresses the basic significance of this factor because he wishes "to represent the sense of guilt as the most important problem in the evolution of culture, and to convey that the price of progress in civilization is paid in forfeiting happiness through the heightening of the sense of guilt." The feeling of guilt, while causing the multiple discontents of civilization, increases our sense of responsibility to the community. Out of guilt comes not only wretchedness but progress.

The meaning of the evolution of culture, as defined by Freud, is clear: "It must present to us the struggle between Eros and Death, between the instincts of life and the instincts of destruction, as it works itself out in the human species.... The evolution of civilization may be simply described as the struggle of the human species for existence." Freud concludes his treatise with these penetrating observations:

> The fateful question of the human species seems to me to be whether and to what extent the cultural processes developed in it will succeed in mastering the derangements of communal life caused by the human instinct of aggression and self-destruction. In this connection, perhaps the phase through which we are at this moment passing deserves special interest. Men have brought their powers of subduing the forces

of nature to such a pitch that by using them they could now very easily exterminate one another to the last man. They know this—hence arises a great part of their current unrest, their dejection, their mood of apprehension. And now it may be expected that the other of the two "heavenly forces," eternal Eros, will put forth his strength so as to maintain himself alongside of his equally immortal adversary.

Present-day psychiatrists are split into two or more opposing camps, pro and con Freud. Even his disciples have modified their full acceptance of the theories over the past eighty years. Nevertheless, the changes and developments during this period have not diminished Freud's stature or influence, despite the fact that many of his ideas and concepts have had to be modified by his successors in the light of further experience.

70

Most Civilized Englishman
Havelock Ellis (1859-1939)

Studies in the Psychology of Sex

When, as a young man growing up in Australia, Havelock Ellis resolved to become a physician and to devote himself to a lifetime study of sexual phenomena, the subject was surrounded by social taboos. Ellis became the first notable English writer to discuss sex openly and with detachment. Starting with Ellis and Sigmund Freud late in the nineteenth century, human physiology began to be seriously investigated and sex to be studied not as if it were a disgraceful function but as something normally common to the human race. That everything relating to sex can be freely discussed in the twentieth century is owing largely to the work of these two trailblazing scientists.

Among Western peoples, attitudes toward sex during the nineteenth century were doubtless conditioned by the Victorian reaction against the frank language and easy morality of the preceding century. The study of sex was the one field still shunned by scientists. Actually, the need for sexual enlightenment was as great among the medical profession as among laymen. Ignorance was equated with morality. When Thomas Henry Huxley wrote his *Elementary Lessons in Physiology* (1866), for example, he was compelled to omit the fact that the human body possessed sexual organs. Normal sexual interests and attributes were assumed to exist only among the "low," such as professional prostitutes and country boys and girls. Nevertheless, it was in such an atmosphere of severe legal restrictions, public prejudice, professional attacks, and social ostracism that Ellis carried on his research and writing.

In the preface to his monumental *Studies in the Psychology of Sex*, Ellis states the motives that impelled him to undertake the work:

> As a youth, I had hoped to settle problems for those who came after; now I am quietly content if I do little more than state them. For even that, I now think, is much: it is at least the half of knowledge. In this particular field the evil of ignorance is magnified by our efforts to suppress that which can never be suppressed, though in the effort of suppression it may become perverted. I have at least tried to find out what are the facts, among normal people as well as abnormal people; for, while it seems to me that the physician's training is necessary in

order to ascertain the facts, the physician for the most part only obtains the abnormal facts, which alone bring little light. I have tried to get at the facts, and, having got the facts, to look them simply and squarely in the face. If I cannot, perhaps, turn the lock myself, I bring the key which can alone in the end rightly open the door: the key of sincerity. That is my one panacea: sincerity.

After returning to England and completing his medical training, Ellis began the investigations for his *magnum opus* that were to be his chief occupation for the remainder of a long lifetime. The first volume, dealing with *Sexual Inversion*, of the seven-volume work was issued in London in 1897. Almost immediately, the publisher, George Bedborough, was arrested and charged with "having unlawfully and wickedly published and sold, and caused to be procured and to be sold, a wicked, bawdy, and scandalous, and obscene book." Found guilty, Bedborough was released on condition that he destroy the stock and publish nothing further of a similar nature. Because of the savage stand taken by the English courts, Ellis determined to issue none of the succeeding volumes in England. Instead, the entire set was brought out by F. A. Davis Company of Philadelphia, with the sale limited to members of the legal, medical, and educational professions.

While Ellis undertook a certain amount of original investigation for *Studies in the Psychology of Sex*, his writings are based chiefly upon already published work scattered through hundreds of learned journals and innumerable books, many of them exceedingly obscure. To the study of sex, Ellis proposed to apply the same objective research methods followed by other scholars in anthropology, politics, and the social sciences. His seven-volume work was directed primarily at the education of normal people—the general public—to persuade them that a rational attitude toward sex is essential to human happiness. Only incidentally was Ellis concerned with the problems of medical practitioners and with sexual abnormalities.

Studies in the Psychology of Sex has been termed "the world's first scientific encyclopedia of sexual information." Ellis' purpose, as stressed in his preface, was to discover the facts—the socially tabooed facts, knowledge of which was forbidden by church and state, the "real natural facts of sex apart from all would-be moralistic or sentimental notions."

Though he began his series with a monograph on homosexuality, Ellis emphasizes the normal expressions of sex and documents his study with a wide background of historical, psychological, and anthropological data. The physiological and psychological aspects of sex are treated as inseparable parts of a single process. Ellis was convinced that men's capacity to love sexually should be valued, developed, and educated, and is as basic to his happiness as the capacity to think, to play, to create, or to exercise any other function belonging to normal existence.

Summing up Ellis' achievements, the American psychiatrist Karl Menninger concludes:

Substantially, he did three things. In the first place, he made a careful, thorough, and honest collection of data relating to a phase of biology which the hypocrisy and prudery of medical science had, until Ellis, caused to be ignored for the most part. In the second place, he evolved and advocated a hedonistic philosophy of life tempered if not determined by the sane, scientific attitude toward sex which his studies engendered. In the third place, he presented his scientific findings and philosophical beliefs to the world with that artistic combination of directness and delicacy which made them acceptable to non-scientific readers.[11]

H. L. Mencken described Ellis as "undoubtedly the most civilized Englishman of his generation," a judgment that has won wide concurrence. Ellis has been more responsible than any other man for lifting the puritan taboo upon sex, for bringing the subject into the clear light of science, and for preparing public opinion for objective research in the field of sex and marriage. He paved the way for the reception of Freud and Jung in psychological theory, for such literary figures as Joyce and Proust, and for such further investigations in his own chosen field as those of Alfred Kinsey.

Preceding Ellis by a few years was another pioneer, the German psychiatrist Richard Krafft-Ebing, who in 1887 began publishing his monumental treatise on abnormal sexual behavior, entitled *Psychopathia Sexualis*, a work that has gone through numerous editions and many translations.

71

Discoverers of Radium

Marie (1867-1934) and Pierre Curie (1859-1906)

Researches on Radioactive Substances

Marie and Pierre Curie, discoverers of two new elements, are undoubtedly the most celebrated man and wife team in the history of science. Their complete dedication to scientific research overcame years of poverty, inadequate laboratories, and ill health.

Marie Curie (born Manya Sklodowska) was the daughter of a professor of physics at the Warsaw High School, and her mother was an accomplished pianist. The mother died when Marie was only ten. Subsequently, the family was left in desperate financial straits when the father lost his position for agitating freedom for Poland from repressive Russian rule. For the same reason, Marie was forced to leave Warsaw for taking part in revolutionary activity.

In Paris, where Marie became a student in the faculty of science at age twenty-three, her intellectual interests were omnivorous; she became immersed in physics, chemistry, mathematics, poetry, music, and astronomy. In the end, she received master's degrees and later doctorates in physics and mathematics.

Marie met Pierre Curie at the Sorbonne, and they were married in 1895. Pierre, the son of a French physician, had become a bachelor of science at sixteen and a master of physics at eighteen. Other achievements were impressive: he was head of the laboratory at the Parisian School of Chemistry and Physics, and in the course of his researches had formulated the principle of symmetry in the structure of crystals, discovered the important phenomenon of the generation of electricity by means of pressure, invented a new apparatus for precise measurement of minute quantities of electricity, and constructed a highly sensitive instrument, the "Curie Scale," for checking the results of scientific experiments.

The Curies' marriage turned out to be a partnership of genius. Both had become deeply interested in the experiments of Henri Becquerel, an eminent French physicist who, while examining the salts of uranium, had discovered that these salts emitted a ray which could penetrate opaque objects. A compound of uranium placed on a photographic plate surrounded by black paper made an impression on the plate through the paper. Here was the first known observation of the penetrating quality of certain rays, in short, the discovery of radioactivity.

Following Becquerel's observations on radioactivity in 1896, Marie chose for her doctoral dissertation at the Sorbonne to continue Becquerel's investigations, in particular to test most of the known elements for radioactivity. She found that only two, thorium and uranium, produced significant ionization. In further examinations of uranium contained in pitchblende ore, she found that the ore was much more radioactive than could have been anticipated from an analysis of its uranium content. On the basis of that discovery, Marie concluded the pitchblende must contain still another element not yet identified.

At this stage, Pierre Curie dropped all other research and began to collaborate with his wife in a laborious search for the new element, an undertaking which required minute analysis of tons of the complex ore. Several years later, in 1898, the Curies had succeeded in isolating the hitherto unknown element and named it polonium, after Marie's native land. The new element was so rare that it consisted of only a millionth part of the pitchblende ore, a major factor in attempts to isolate it. At the same time, it was far more radioactive than uranium.

A serious handicap for the Curies' experiments was the cost of pitchblende. It was an expensive ore mined in Bohemia for the extraction of the uranium salts used in the manufacture of glass. The price was far beyond the Curies' means. A practical solution was to use the residue of the pitchblende after the uranium had been extracted. Considerable quantities of the residue could be obtained for little more than the cost of transportation.

At the end of four years of arduous experiments, the Curies had found not only one but two new elements. In addition to polonium, they discovered another substance which they called radium. Radium's power of radiation was almost incomprehensible; it exceeded that of uranium by a factor of a million and a half. The processing of eight tons of pitchblende resulted in the isolation of a single gram of pure radium salts. The atomic weights of both radium and polonium were determined by the Curies.

In recognition of their extraordinary discoveries, the Curies and Henri Becquerel shared the 1903 Nobel prize in physics. Meanwhile, Marie continued her investigations of radium chloride, while Pierre studied the physical properties of the rays emitted by the new elements. He became convinced that they had therapeutic value, and spoke before meetings of physicians on the subject. Radium was found effective in the treatment of cancer and in healing certain types of skin lesions. Though the substance could cause dangerous and even fatal burns, it was highly efficient in destroying infected cells and stopping harmful growths. The Curies were urged to patent the process of extracting the element, but refused to profit financially from the discovery, holding that "radium is an instrument of mercy and it belongs to the world."

Further official recognition of the Curies' achievements came with Pierre's appointment as a professor in the Sorbonne and the promise of a well-equipped laboratory, which they had previously lacked. Their improved status was destined to be of short duration, however, for two years later Pierre was killed in a traffic accident. After Pierre's death, Marie was appointed his successor at the Sorbonne as professor of physics, the first woman to hold such a position in a French university. In 1911, she was awarded a second Nobel prize, in chemistry, for successfully isolating pure metallic radium. Nobel prizes ran in the family: Marie's older daughter, Irène, who assisted her mother after 1918, and later married the physicist Frédéric Joliot, was awarded the 1935 Nobel prize in chemistry, jointly with her husband, for the discovery of artificial radioactivity.

The Curies were prolific contributors to scientific literature. The principal writings of Marie Curie were *Le Polonium et le Radium, leir Découuverte pour les Rayons de Becquerel* (1899), *Recherches sur les Substances Radioactives* (1903), and *Tralté de Radioactivité* (1910).

Marie Curie died in 1934 of pernicious anemia, caused by excessive exposure to radioactivity. Thus she became a martyr to her work.

72

Harbinger of the Atomic Age
Albert Einstein (1879-1955)

Relativity, the Special and General Theory

The theory of relativity, universally associated with the name of Albert Einstein, has doubtless influenced the thinking and the lives of twentieth-century man more than any other scientific concept. Since the theory deals with the relationship between physical and mathematical events, it can be adequately expressed only in abstract mathematical language—placing it beyond the comprehension of the layman. Nevertheless, certain features of the Einstein cosmos can be suggested without resort to mathematical symbolism.

Einstein published his first paper on the theory of relativity while serving as a member of the staff of the Swiss Patent Office. What is now known as the special theory of relativity was presented by him, in 1905, in a paper entitled "The Electrodynamics of Bodies in Motion," in the *Annalen der Physik*. Eight years later, Einstein put forward the general relativity theory and published the whole in his *Relativity, the Special and General Theory*. By 1917, the combined theory had been extended, verified, and accepted, and, with the quantum theory, it now forms the essential basis of modern physics.

The special theory of relativity is so called because it is concerned with a special kind of motion: uniform motion in a straight line, that is, with constant velocity. In describing the motion of a body, it is necessary to refer to another body, e.g., the motion of a railroad train with reference to the ground, of a planet with reference to all visible stars. The motion of each is relative to the other. In his conception of space, Einstein added a fourth dimension, time, to the three classical dimensions of length, breadth, and height.

A major principle on which the special relativity theory rests is that of the constancy of the velocity of light in a vacuum. The speed of light is constant as measured by all observers anywhere and with all possible varieties of motion with respect to each other. According to the special theory, no material body can move with a velocity greater than that of light—186,000 miles per second. Further, any measuring rod for length, such as a yardstick, if moving with a speed approaching that of light as a limit, would become shorter and shorter, approaching zero in length as that speed was approached. Likewise, a clock moving with a speed approaching that of light would slow down and stop at the speed of light. Mass also is changeable. As velocity increases, the mass of an object becomes greater. Particles of matter speeded up to eighty-six percent of the speed of light weigh twice as much as when at rest—a fact that had tremendous implications for the development of atomic energy.

In a brief sequel to his original paper, Einstein introduced the most famous equation in history: $E = Mc^2$, energy equals mass multiplied by the square of the velocity of light. Energy and mass are thus demonstrated to be identical, differing only in state. The formula shows that the energy in a single uranium nucleus would be 220,000,000,000 electron volts if all its mass could be converted into energy. Only one-tenth of one percent of the total energy content is released by splitting the uranium nucleus, or fission.

In his general theory of relativity, Einstein advanced a new concept of gravitation. Gravity had been regarded by Isaac Newton as a "force." Einstein proved, however, that the space around a planet or other celestial body is a gravitational field similar to the magnetic field around a magnet. A massive body, he said, causes a distortion of space and time. To check Einstein's general theory, an expedition was sent out by the Royal Society in 1919 to observe an eclipse of the sun; as Einstein predicted, photographs revealed that light rays bend toward the sun. When a planet is closest to the sun in its orbit and the gravitational field greatest, the planet reaches its greatest speed. This fact was used by Einstein to explain a constant shift in the orbit of Mercury, nearest planet to the sun, again confirmed by experimental evidence.

Einstein suggested that the universe may be finite and that space itself may be curved, though no definite boundaries can be established. An alternative hypothesis is that space may be curved but still is infinite. Also a matter of speculation is the shape of the universe: a plane surface, a sphere, or a cylinder, the last theory preferred by Einstein.

Einstein's equation stating that mass can be converted into energy or energy into mass has formed the basis of today's atomic reactors and thermonuclear releases of energy. The title of "the father of the release of atomic energy" was disclaimed by Einstein. In his *Atomic War or Peace* he writes, "My part in it was quite indirect. I did not, in fact, foresee that it would be released in my time. I believed only that it was theoretically possible. It became practical through the accidental discovery of chain reaction, and this was not something I could have predicted." Despite this modest denial, it was Einstein's letter to President Roosevelt in 1939, describing the incredible power of atomic energy, that led to the construction of the Manhattan atom-bomb project.

Einstein's later years were devoted to a unified field theory, attempting to discover a completely inclusive explanation of the energy in all scientific phenomena, including electric, magnetic, and gravitational fields of force. According to his view, physical laws for the minute atom should be equally applicable to immense celestial bodies. The unified field theory, he felt, would demonstrate the existence of a well-ordered universe. Einstein's final statement of the theory in 1953, two years prior to his death, has failed to find support among leading physicists.

Concerning the present status of relativity, an international conference of theoretical physicists at Berne, Switzerland recently agreed that the foundations of the special and general theory have been universally accepted. Experiments have conclusively confirmed the special theory and are convincing for the general theory. The special theory has been incorporated into general physics and is used continually in atomic and nuclear physics.

For a number of years, the general theory was applied mainly to cosmology and cosmogony, but lately relativity is being applied to microphysical problems. The relationship to the quantum theory is still quite undetermined. It is apparent that general relativity provides a new approach to the ultimate properties of space and time. If true, the theory may have as much bearing on the physics of the very small as of the very large. The increasing worldwide interest in general relativity indicates that scientists believe the theory may add further to our understanding of the universe as an organic whole.

73

The Proper Study of Man
Alfred Kinsey (1894-1956)

Sexual Behavior in the Human Male

Prior to the investigations conducted by Alfred Kinsey and his associates at Indiana University's Institute for Sex Research, human sexual behavior was the least explored area of biology, psychology, and sociology. As Dr. Kinsey points out in a historical introduction to his pioneer work, *Sexual Behavior in the Human Male* (1948), "Scientifically more has been known about the sexual behavior of some of the farm and laboratory animals." The subject was largely taboo because of religious, legal, and social restrictions. A breakdown of Victorian conventions and interdictions in the twentieth century, however, led to an increasing demand for objective data among physicians, psychiatrists, and persons concerned with such matters as sexual adjustments in marriage, the sexual guidance of children, and sex education. The prevailing situation was described by Alan Gregg of the Rockefeller Foundation's Medical Sciences Division in a preface to the Kinsey work:

> Certainly no aspect of human biology in our current civilization stands in more need of scientific knowledge and courageous humility than that of sex. The history of medicine proves that in so far as man seeks to know himself and face his whole nature, he has become free from bewildered fear, despondent shame, or arrant hypocrisy. As long as sex is dealt with in the current confusion of ignorance and sophistication, denial and indulgence, suppression and stimulation, punishment and exploitation, secrecy and display, it will be associated with a duplicity and indecency that lead neither to intellectual honesty nor human dignity.[12]

Years of strict scientific discipline had prepared Dr. Kinsey for his task. A biologist who had spent decades of research on a minute field of specialization, Dr. Kinsey's previous publications had borne such esoteric titles as *The Gall Wasp Genus Cynips, The Gall Wasp Genus Neuroterus, The Origin of Higher*

Categories in Cynips, and *Edible Wild Plants of Eastern North America*. (A report on a single species of gall wasp was based on 150,000 individual specimens.) His concern with studies of human sexual behavior began late and appears to have been inspired originally by the inability to answer students' questions on the subject. Current research was practically nonexistent, and available publications had so little solid basis that they were almost worthless.

Ten years passed between the start of Dr. Kinsey's work in his new field of inquiry and the appearance of the first report, *Sexual Behavior in the Human Male*. During that period he was joined by Wardell B. Pomeroy, a clinical psychologist, and Clyde E. Martin, a specialist in statistical procedures, both of whom aided in perfecting the methodology for the investigation and participated in the thousands of interviews which form the foundation for the book. Various psychologists and scientists from other disciplines also took part in the project as full-time staff members or consultants. Financial support came from Indiana University and the Rockefeller Foundation's Division of Medical Sciences.

Throughout his researches, Kinsey had one objective: to study all aspects of human sexual behavior without "preconception of what is rare or what is common, what is moral or socially significant, or what is normal and what is abnormal." At the outset, Dr. Kinsey announces his intention strictly to avoid social or moral interpretations of facts discovered, though some critics question whether he is fully successful in that aim.

As the first in a projected series of reports, *Sexual Behavior in the Human Male* places specific limitations on its scope: the data are confined to information collected from 5,300 white American males (omitting Europeans and Negroes), chiefly from the northeastern quarter of the United States. Social groups represented include inmates of penal institutions and the underworld in general, laborers, clerks, farmers, business executives, lawyers, physicians, high school students, college students and professors, and clergymen. The population is subdivided by race-cultural group, marital status, age, age at adolescence, educational level, occupational class (ten categories), occupational class of parents, rural-urban background, religion, degree of religious adherence, and geographic origin.

One reviewer commented that "Kinsey has studied the sex behavior of the American male as though the American male, too, were a gall wasp." His book is described by Kinsey himself as "a taxonomic study of the frequencies of sources and sexual outlets among American males." Data were obtained in intimate personal interviews in which each individual was asked between 300 and 500 questions. The interviews lasted from one to six hours, and elaborate care was exercised to make them valid, painless, and confidential.

Courage was required to gather data for the study and later to publish the findings. The mere news that the investigation was in progress aroused violent opposition in some quarters. Kinsey notes in his introduction that he and his associates were:

> repeatedly warned of the dangers involved in the undertaking and were threatened with specific trouble ... there were attempts by the medical association in one city to bring suit on the ground that we were practicing medicine without a license, police interference in two or three cities, investigation by a sheriff in one rural area, and attempts to persuade the University's administration to stop the study or to prevent the publication of the results, or to dismiss the senior

author from his university connection, or to establish a censorship over all publications emanating from the study.

In one city the president of the school board, a physician, dismissed a teacher because he had assisted in obtaining histories outside of the school. A hotel manager refused to allow interviews under his roof. But for every individual or group that opposed the study, hundreds cooperated, ranging from Harvard and Columbia universities to the Kansas state police and the Salvation Army's Home for Unwed Mothers.

Why should a report of a scientific investigation prepared by an Indiana University zoologist arouse so much antagonism and cause so many attempts at suppression even before publication? The primary reason, of course, was the fact that it dealt with a tabooed subject. Another factor doubtless was the fear of what the inquiry might disclose. Those who had reason to be nervous about the findings were justified, for when the book came off the press its revelations upset numerous popularly held opinions, prejudices, and superstitions.

Among the most important findings of the Kinsey report, in summary, are that the sex impulse exists in every individual, of whatever age, beginning in infancy; in nearly every person it is extremely powerful; and it has numerous forms of expression. Further, there is a vast difference between the moral pretensions of the community and actual behavior, that is between what we do and what the conventions say that we should do. There is a wide range in the sexual activity of individuals, sexual activity begins much earlier and continues longer than is commonly believed, and the period of highest activity in the male comes much earlier than is generally supposed.

Sexual Behavior in the Human Male includes findings about masturbation, petting, intercourse, prostitution, and homosexuality. The book is filled with such facts as these: 88% of single men between sixteen and twenty practice masturbation; 99% of American boys begin having a sexual life at adolescence; 37% of young married males and 22% of men aged sixty have extramarital relations; 27% of the youngest unmarried group have had some form of homosexual experience, and that figure increases to 39% among unmarried males over thirty-six years old; 70% of pre-adolescent boys report sex play with other children between the ages of five and fourteen; 75% of boys who go no further than high school have premarital heterosexual experiences, in contrast to those who go to college, of whom 42% have indulged in teenage premarital sex relations.

Kinsey verifies Sigmund Freud's theories of infantile sexuality. The former's data show that sexual activity in the male is present from birth to death. The popular belief in "sex conservation" as a reason for continence is refuted by Kinsey, who finds that boys who attain early puberty and begin sex activity earlier have the highest rate of sex activity and continue such activity longer. The facts clearly make nonsense of the oft-repeated warning that early indulgence will weaken the sexual powers in later life; the exact opposite appears to be true. Prior to Kinsey, it had not been recognized that maximum sexual activity occurs in the teens. Boys between sixteen and seventeen have more frequent sexual arousals than at any other period in their lives. By fifteen years of age, 95% of males were found to be regularly active. This is a fact of challenging significance in the light of the increasing lag between biological maturity and economic security and marriage. During the years when a boy's sexual drive is at its highest, no socially approved outlet is provided. The boy seeks his outlet in various forms, all of which are banned by society and give rise to much anxiety and conflict in the individual. Concerning the physical and psychological harm caused thereby, Kinsey remarks:

> Whether there should be sex instruction, and what sort of instruction it should be, are problems that lie outside the scope of an objective scientific study; but it is obvious that the development of any curriculum that faces the fact will be a much more complex undertaking than has been realized by those who think of the adolescent boy as a beginner, relatively inactive, and quite capable of ignoring his sexual development.

With advancing age, Kinsey's data show, there is a slow and steady decline in sexual activity, but no evidence was found of sudden male climacteric. The indications are that even at seventy years of age only 30% are impotent.

Another unexpected finding of the Kinsey study is that sexual behavior is influenced in many significant and complex ways by social level, as measured by educational attainment, grade school, high school, or college graduation. Social levels are not supposed to exist in a democratic society, but realistically there are an "upper class" and a "lower class," and "most people do not in actuality move freely with those who belong to other levels." There are wide and consistent differences in the sphere of sexual behavior between educational and occupational classes. Single males with only grade school education practice only half as much masturbation as do the college group, and tend to be more ashamed of it, while their frequency of intercourse is, in the lower-age levels, almost three times as high. Lower-level groups are also inclined to frown on nudity, petting, oral eroticism, and unconventional poses in intercourse—all practices which the upper-level population indulges in frequently. Among the lower economic and sociological groups, intercourse with prostitutes is six times more frequent than in the upper.

Grade school graduates show considerable extramarital intercourse during the first years of marriage, but with time become increasingly faithful to their wives, whereas the college population begins marriage with high fidelity and in time become increasingly promiscuous. Dr. Kinsey comments, "Some persons may interpret the data to mean that the lower level starts out by trying promiscuity and as a result of that trial, finally decides that strict monogamy is a better policy; but it would be equally correct to say that the upper level starts out by trying monogamy and ultimately decides that variety is worth having." Another commentator suggests that the changing pattern may simply be a matter of opportunity. Upper-level males are surrounded by a surplus of unmarried, divorced, and widowed women and also have more money and freedom to arrange liaisons with such women, while the lower-level male has fewer women available and less means to maintain his personal attractiveness.

The incidence of homosexuality among males is considerably higher than was realized prior to the Kinsey investigation, which indicates that "at least thirty-seven percent of the male population has some homosexual experience between the beginning of adolescence and old age." Actually, the high percentage may be misleading, as the author notes, for it applies to men who have had any kind of homosexual experience in their lives; in some instances, this may have been a single experience. Nevertheless, the figures show that 10% of men between the ages of sixteen and sixty-five are homosexuals for at least three years, and 4% are entirely homosexual throughout their lives.

The legal implications of the Kinsey report are obvious. Numerous commentators have suggested that important changes in our laws and social customs are desirable to close the wide gap between what we preach and what we practice. The dimensions of the problem are startling: 85% of the total male population have premarital intercourse, 37% have had homosexual experience, 59% have experienced oral-genital contacts (a criminal offense in a number of states), 30 to 45% have extramarital intercourse, nearly 70% have had relations with prostitutes, and 17% of farm boys have intercourse with animals — altogether a total of 95% of the entire male population involved in illicit activities. As Dr. Kinsey remarks, the periodic call for a "clean-up of the sex offenders in a community is, in fine, a proposal that five percent of the population should support the other 95 percent in penal institutions," if strict legal penalties were enforced.

The psychological effects of the Kinsey findings are also significant. Millions of people, Kinsey points out, carry around with them feelings of guilt, believing that they belong to a small minority that has transgressed moral law. Some individuals are so conscience-smitten that they break down under the burden and end up in psychiatrists' offices or hospitals. Such people still regret their actions, but their feelings of remorse might be less acute knowing that they belong to 90% instead of 1% of the population.

A barrage of criticism greeted the Kinsey report on its appearance. It was argued, for example, that people will not answer questions of this nature honestly; either they will conceal important facts or lie about their sexual prowess. Kinsey and his fellow interviewers took great precautions to avoid such pitfalls. Other critics observe that the study's emphasis is too exclusively on the physical and mechanistic aspects of sexual activity, largely ignoring the influence of affection, tenderness, and human sentiment in sex behavior. The word "love" is scarcely mentioned. Similar in character is a point stressed by Lionel Trilling in a lengthy critique appearing in the *Partisan Review*, that is, Kinsey's equating of *much* sexuality with *good* sexuality; Trilling maintains that there is almost no relationship between sexual frequency and sexual satisfaction. On the contrary, an unusually high frequency may be a symptom of deep sexual disturbance.

Kinsey's sample of 5,300 males has been criticized, also, as unrepresentative of the total population: too high proportions of college students, professional psychologists and psychiatrists, and male prostitutes; too small a percentage of men over thirty and of residents of rural areas; and too limited geographic distribution.

A hostile comment on *Sexual Behavior in the Human Male*, heard not infrequently, is that it only proves what everyone already knows. The statement is misleading, for it is quite evident that the Kinsey report contains material that surprised everyone when it was revealed. Previous impressions and suspicions were confirmed or disproved with a mass of detailed facts useful to parents, teachers, psychiatrists, ministers, jurists, and legislators. The broad findings of the study present a picture of a people endowed with sexual drives of various intensities, whose sexual activities begin early in life and are often conditioned and modified by society. For a large proportion of the population, sexual activity is not limited to the institution of marriage, and there is a higher degree of homosexuality than was previously realized. Finally, strong and insistent sexual drives are a basic biological element in everyday life.

Complementing the original Kinsey report, *Sexual Behavior in the Human Female* was published in 1953, followed by a series of more specialized studies. The path blazed by Kinsey was taken later by scores of other writers, popular and scientific. Probably most original and constructive, because it was based on extensive laboratory research, was William H. Masters and Virginia E. Johnson's *Human Sexual Response* (1966), the work of a gynecologist and a psychologist on the staff of the Reproductive Biology Research Foundation of St. Louis, supported by the Washington University School of Medicine.

74

Upsetting the Balance of Nature
Rachel Carson (1907-1964)

Silent Spring

Comparable in its impact on public consciousness, and demand for instant action, to Tom Paine's *Common Sense*, Harriet Beecher Stowe's *Uncle Tom's Cabin*, and Upton Sinclair's *The Jungle* was Rachel Carson's *Silent Spring* (1962), describing the disastrous effects on the balance of nature caused by the irresponsible use of insecticides and other pest controls.

Actually, the dark picture painted by Miss Carson, an eminent marine biologist, was part of a larger canvas — the overwhelming problem of pollution of the air, water, and land which was increasingly disturbing the conscience of the American people. Public-spirited citizens everywhere were realizing with alarm that man was ruining his environment by fouling the air he breathes, the water he drinks, the soil that produces his food, and the food itself. Automobiles were filling the cities with lethal fumes; smog was settling down in choking volume on virtually all large urban centers; human and industrial wastes were being dumped into lakes, rivers, and streams, killing fish and steadily reducing potable water resources; oil wastes dumped in the sea were killing millions of seabirds and ruining beaches, and further pollution of the ocean was resulting from the dumping of industrial atomic wastes. Beginning with World War II, the dangerous fallout from nuclear bomb explosions had posed an even more serious dilemma for the world at large.

This was the background against which Rachel Carson wrote. She begins her shocking story with a fable, in which she tells of a small American town, set in the heart of prosperous farmland, with its wildflowers, numerous songbirds, and well-stocked trout streams. "Then a strange blight crept over the area and everything began to change. Some evil spell had settled on the community: mysterious maladies swept the flocks of chickens; the cattle and sheep sickened and died. Everywhere was a shadow of death." Doctors discovered new kinds of sickness appearing among their patients. "There was a strange stillness. The birds, for example, where had they gone?... On the mornings that had once throbbed with the dawn chorus of robins, catbirds, doves, jays, wrens, and scores of other bird voices there was now no sound; only silence lay over the fields and woods and marsh."

The town described does not actually exist. "I know of no community that has experienced all the misfortunes," writes Miss Carson, "yet every one of these disasters has actually happened somewhere, and many real communities have already suffered a substantial number of them.

What has silenced the voice of spring in countless places, Miss Carson contends, is indiscriminate blanket spraying of vast areas from airplanes with potent chemicals, and similar misuses of insecticides and herbicides.

The beginnings of the devastation so graphically condemned by Miss Carson were a by-product of World War II. In experiments with agents intended for chemical warfare, it was found that some of the compounds were deadly to insects. After the war, chemical manufacturers, drug companies, agricultural schools, and government agencies started actively to develop and to promote the use of killers designed to exterminate various types of insects and undesirable plant growths. Handed these new weapons, the forester sprayed to protect his trees, the cranberry picker to protect his bogs, the cotton planter to save his cotton from the boll weevil, and so on down a long procession of farmers and gardeners — with little or no understanding of or concern for the consequences.

For thousands of years, man had fought to control pests — insects, rodents, weeds, bacteria, and other forms. Until World War II, the chief pesticides were arsenic, nicotine, and vegetable derivatives lethal to cold-blooded animals. The organic chemicals added to the plant growers' arsenal in the postwar period included the chlorinated hydrocarbons, such as DDT, and the organo-phosphorus substances, of which parathion is a common example. As a direct result, states Miss Carson:

> For the first time in the history of the world, every human being is now subjected to contact with dangerous chemicals, from the moment of conception until death. In the less than two decades of their use, the synthetic pesticides have been so thoroughly distributed throughout the animate and inanimate world that they occur virtually everywhere. They have been recovered from most of the major river systems and even from streams of groundwater flowing unseen through the earth. Residues of these chemicals linger in soil to which they may have been applied a dozen years before. They have entered and lodged in the bodies of fish, birds, reptiles, and domestic and wild animals so universally that scientists carrying on animal experiments find it almost impossible to locate subjects free from such contamination. They have been found in fish in remote mountain lakes, in earthworms burrowing in the soil, in the eggs of birds — and in man himself. For these chemicals are now stored in the bodies of the vast majority of human beings, regardless of age. They occur in the mother's milk, and probably in the tissues of the unborn child.

The sprays, dusts, and aerosols have the power to kill all insects, good and bad, Miss Carson points out, as well as the birds and the fish, and to poison the soil, perhaps permanently — all to get rid of a few weeds and insects. The poisons are insoluble in water and therefore pollute the surfaces of fruits, vegetables, grasses, and grains. Aiming at a troublesome beetle, the chemists have wiped out the bird life of whole regions; aiming at a weevil, they have exterminated the race of bald eagles; aiming to save man from malaria, they have put several known cancer-causing agents into permanent circulation; aiming at an insect which was destroying commercial spruce plantations, the Canadians killed off all the salmon of three generations in four large rivers.

Miss Carson builds a damning and persuasive case with innumerable other specific instances of the destruction being wrought by pesticides. In the mid-1950s, the City of East Lansing, Michigan began a massive spraying of the Michigan State University campus to kill beetles which carry Dutch elm disease. The sprayed leaves fell to the ground in the autumn, and were eaten by the worms. In the spring, robins ate the worms, and within a week nearly all the robins were dead. In eastern Canada, where budworms were gradually killing off the balsams, there was extensive spraying of the forests. "Soon after the spraying had ended," reports Miss Carson, "there were unmistakable signs that all was not well. Within two days dead and dying fish, including many young salmon, were found along the banks of the stream. Brook trout also appeared among the dead fish, and along the roads and in the woods birds were dying. All the life of the stream was stilled."

As a result of the spraying of Clear Lake, California with DDT, to rid it of gnats for the comfort of fishermen, the swan-like western grebes began dying, until they had dwindled from one thousand to thirty pairs. In the National Wildlife refuges at Tule Lake and the Lower Namath, also in California, herons, pelicans, grebes, and gulls died in great numbers—the victims of insecticide residue which had been building up to lethal strength in the water flowing from heavily sprayed agricultural lands. In the Midwest, indiscriminate spraying for the Japanese beetle virtually annihilated robins, meadowlarks, brown thrashers, and pheasants in Blue Island and Sheldon, Illinois.

In "A Postscript to Rachel Carson," Clark C. Van Fleet, California sportsman, author, and conservationist, commented on the increasing use of sodium fluoroacetate, known as 1080. "Used in conjunction with grain as a rodent bait," he observed, "a single kernel will immediately kill a mouse, a rat, or squirrel or a rabbit.... Over a hundred deer carcasses were found within a small compass where state agents had carelessly scattered poison grain.... Some three thousand ducks and geese in Siskiyou County, California, died as the result of improper spread of grain containing 1080 as a poison for ground squirrels. Hawks and eagles were also found dead."

Two years after the publication of *Silent Spring*, the U.S. Public Health Service had positive proof that the pesticide endrin was responsible for the deaths of 10 million fish in the lower Mississippi River and the Gulf of Mexico; the poison had reached the river through runoff from farms.

In July 1968, *Newsweek* reported, "In Borneo, health officials recently launched a campaign to rid rural villages of flies. DDT did the job quickly, but the cure turned out to be worse than the disease. Lizards who ate the flies accumulated the poison in their bodies. Cats ate the lizards and died. Soon the rat population started to proliferate, and plague threatened the entire region."

Miss Carson continually stresses the perils to man himself from the widespread use or misuse of pesticides. If the chemicals are deadly to animal and plant life, can man with impunity eat contaminated meats and vegetables? A few human victims had already died in convulsions from exposure to certain highly concentrated pesticides, the author points out, and she fears that many others will eventually die of cancer, leukemia, hepatitis, or other dread diseases possibly caused by the pesticides. Lethal poisons spread across the land, are blown into farm homes, settle on food, and pollute tanks and ponds. Emphysema, a serious lung disorder unheard of until recent years, is becoming common in country areas, and respiratory illnesses are increasing by leaps and bounds in orchard and berry country. Because of birth-to-death exposure to dangerous chemicals, there is a progressive buildup of poison in our bodies, and the cumulative effect may well be disastrous. Many common insecticides for household use are highly toxic.

An exclamation point was added to Miss Carson's warnings when, two years after the appearance of *Silent Spring*, she herself died of cancer.

The basic fallacy overlooked by those who make extensive use of pesticides, Rachel Carson holds, is that they are upsetting the balance of nature. A vital fact which they ignore is that all life is one life, that the countless species of animals and plants and the soil, water, and air they live on are all intimately interconnected and interdependent. The ancient network of living things, in which each animal and plant depended upon every other one, has been upset by man, who is continually engaged in molding the environment to his own advantage. He must be supreme in nature, the human egotist believes, and the changes he makes are often sudden and profound—and frequently irreversible. Too often, man has looked upon himself as opposed to nature, not as a part of her, and in his efforts to subdue, he has ravished and destroyed.

One of the frightening ways in which nature fights back is to produce new and more dangerous pests. Chemicals have quickly killed off the weak and feeble among the creatures attacked, but permanent control over the survivors is not gained. A thorough spraying may kill 90% of a particular species. The hardier members, however, are resistant to the spray and survive; when they reproduce, most of their offspring inherit immunity. Furthermore, the survivors often produce in fantastic numbers. To combat the new superpests, the chemists develop ever more poisonous sprays, thereby increasing the danger to all living things, including man. Thus, Miss Carson concludes, in upsetting the balance of nature we are fighting a losing battle: "As crude a weapon as the cave man's club, the chemical barrage has been hurled against the fabric of life—a fabric on one hand delicate and destructible, on the other miraculously tough and resilient, and capable of striking back in unexpected ways."

As the author of two best-sellers, *The Sea around Us* and *The Edge of the Sea*, Miss Carson was already famous before *Silent Spring* was published. Readers had a foretaste of her newest book through partial serialization in *The New Yorker*. When *Silent Spring* came off the press, therefore, it was an instant best-seller; it remained on the *New York Times* list for thirty-one weeks, and sold 500,000 copies in hardcover before being brought out in paperback. The book had an immediate and profound effect on American opinion. The potential dangers of pesticides became known to all, and popular pressure speeded up industry and government research.

After *Silent Spring* was published, the federal government began an investigation of its pesticide control programs to find an answer to how to use chemical pesticides more safely. A world conference, called the United Nations Food and Agriculture Organization, met in Rome to study how pesticides can be used effectively without harming people. The British Ministry of Agriculture, Fisheries, and Food placed severe restrictions on the use of three widely used insecticides related to DDT—aldrin, dieldrin, and heptachlor. The U.S. Congress closed a loophole in the machinery for control by ending the "protest registration" system, under which a manufacturer whose product was disapproved by the Department of Agriculture could continue to make and sell it. Legislatures in a number of states also tightened controls.

As could have been anticipated, the multi-billion-dollar chemical industry, so vigorously attacked by Miss Carson, reacted violently. She had claimed that the industry's introduction of more and more chemicals was often based on profit rather than need. The Carson campaign was characterized by one commentator as "the most massive indictment of an entire industrial complex since the days of Ida Tarbell." The great corporations involved — mainly the major oil companies and their affiliates, the petro-chemical companies — the economic entomologists, officials of the U.S. Department of Agriculture, and agricultural research workers generally quite predictably did not submit tamely to the scathing criticism aimed at them.

A spokesman for the chemical industry, Dr. Robert White-Stevens of the American Cyanamid Company, issued a blast stating that the "book's major claims ... are gross distortions of the actual facts, completely unsupported by scientific, experimental evidence, and general practical experience in the field." Miss Carson was accused of unfairness, prejudice, and hysteria, and the image of a crackpot was built up by her enemies, who chose to ignore her long career as a professional biologist, her sixteen years' experience with the Fish and Wildlife Service, and other accomplishments.

Departing from personalities, the critics asserted that chemical herbicides and insecticides have become necessary to man's survival. Without them, in a short time there would be no more marketable fruit or vegetable crops. If chemical pesticides were discontinued, they added, the agricultural areas of the world would soon be ravaged by hordes of grasshoppers, weevils, and other insect invaders. Chemical sprays make possible the huge food crops that farmers can now grow. Lacking them, surplus food would vanish, whole populations would starve, rivers and fields would be choked with weeds, and certain diseases would get out of control. Thus, the commercial interests and their spokesmen among the scientists presented a picture as one-sided and frightening as anything in *Silent Spring*.

A telling argument used by pesticide supporters is that such chemicals have virtually eradicated many diseases. Mosquitoes, lice, ticks, fleas, and other insects are carriers of malaria, yellow fever, sleeping sickness, typhus, and other scourges. Malaria, which was formerly widely prevalent, has been practically stamped out in the United States and a number of other countries through the use of insecticides. In short, maintain the proponents of pesticides, man has no choice except to upset the balance of nature. Otherwise, the insects will eventually inherit the earth.

Propaganda is not expected to give both sides of an argument, and *Silent Spring* is a fiercely passionate tract — emotional, dramatic, sensational in many respects. Nevertheless, Miss Carson concedes that farm chemicals have a place. "It is not my contention," she writes, "that chemical insecticides must never be used. I do contend that we have put poisonous and biologically potent chemicals indiscriminately into the hands of persons largely or wholly ignorant of their potentials for harm."

Miss Carson offers various constructive alternatives to the use of chemical pesticides. She feels that in many cases biological controls would be safer than chemical controls. The use of such natural controls has been limited; only about one hundred insect predators have been successfully introduced into the United States. Other alternatives to insecticides are parasites, resistant crop varieties, sterilization of male insects by radiation, chemical sterilants, sex lures and physical attractants, such as light, to draw insects into traps. The potentialities of these approaches were shown by an English science writer, Edward Hyams, in an article for *The New Statesman*:

> Where biologists and not commercially-interested chemists, have been in charge, methods used to control troublesome insects, and even weeds, have been ecologically sound: there have been some astonishing successes, for example, in inoculating communities of troublesome creatures with the parasites natural to them, often brought from overseas, and in establishing these parasites permanently so that the control is stable and continuous. It is also and invariably enormously cheaper than the chemical methods. Very little work has been done in this field; but there is no doubt at all that it can be done by biologists and naturalists who understand the whole picture—and not, like the entomologists, only one small piece of it—biological control of most and perhaps all "pests" can be achieved.

This is Miss Carson's vital solution: that insects, pests, and undesirable growths may be controlled by encouraging their enemies—a proposal offered at the beginning of the nineteenth century by Charles Darwin's grandfather, Erasmus. Ragweed causing hay fever can be fought, writes Miss Carson, by maintining the dense shrubs and ferns that help to crowd it out; fight crabgrass by providing better soil for high-quality lawn grass; "fight insects by seeking to turn the strength of the species against itself," instead of by the careless, unrestrained use of chemicals. "As matters stand now," asserts Miss Carson, "we are in little better position than the guests of the Borgias."

The chief problem in applying biological controls appears to be a lack of research. According to a recent report, only about one hundred biologists are actively engaged in such research, a majority of them in California. The reason is financial: the universities depend upon industry for research grants, and the chemical industry provides 98% of the funds for pest-control research. Moreover, the lucrative positions are in chemical research, while biologists must be satisfied with lower-paid jobs as teachers, government workers, or with growers' associations.

Objective appraisals of the situation by scientists with no particular axes to grind have concluded that there is a middle ground where chemistry, biology, wildlife, and mankind can coexist. The complex problems, they say, must be attacked by ecologists and biologists qualified to assess all factors in the environment; specialists in the medical profession must evaluate and control dangers to public health; and more federal and state funds must be provided for basic research.

In a front-page obituary, the *New York Times* called Rachel Carson "one of the most influential women of her time." Senator Abraham Ribicoff, former U.S. Secretary of Health, Education, and Welfare, summed up her career by stating: "This gentle lady, more than any other person of her time, aroused people everywhere to be concerned with one of the most significant problems of mid-20th century life—man's contamination of the environment." Stewart L. Udall, former Secretary of the Interior, one of Miss Carson's admirers and supporters, added: "In the success of *Silent Spring* was the hope that those who truly care about the land have a fighting chance to 'inherit' the earth. That the pen of one so unassuming should have such an impact on national events was remarkable, and a heartening sign to conservationists everywhere."

Sources of Quotations

[1]Duane H. D. Roller, personal letter to author.

[2]Harold C. Urey, in *Nicolas Copernicus*, ed. S. P. Mizwa (New York: Kosciuszko Foundation, 1945), p. 80.

[3]Florian Cajori, in *Scientific Monthly* 20 (January 1925): 91.

[4]Friedrich Dessauer, in *Spirit and Nature*, Bollingen Foundation (New York: Pantheon Books, 1954), p. 300.

[5]J. R. Mayer, *Seven Seals of Science* (New York: Century, 1927), p. 77.

[6]W. P. D. Wightman, *Growth of Scientific Ideas* (New Haven: Yale University Press, 1951), p. 174.

[7]E. B. Matzke, in *Science* 98 (July 2, 1943): 14.

[8]Constance Rourke, *Audubon* (New York: Harcourt, Brace, 1936), p. 316.

[9]Lloyd Morris, *William James* (New York: Scribner's, 1950), p. 15.

[10]George Bernard Shaw, *Black Girl in Search of God* (London: Constable, 1947), p. 1.

[11]Karl Menninger, in *Nation* 149 (July 22, 1939): 103.

[12]Alan Gregg, Preface to Alfred C. Kinsey's *Sexual Behavior in the Human Male* (Philadelphia: Saunders, 1948), p. v.

Bibliographical Notes

One of the most comprehensive and scholarly series of English translations of Greek and Latin literature is the Loeb Classical Library, distributed by the Harvard University Press. The series was founded in 1912 by James Loeb, who planned "to publish everything of real importance from Homer to the fall of Constantinople." A well-edited original text and a translation by a leading authority face each other page by page. Of authors discussed in the present work, Loeb editions are available for the following:

Aristotle	Lucretius
Celsus	Pliny the Elder
Galen	Theophrastus
Hippocrates	

Another standard series of translations, comprehensive in scope, is Everyman's Library, issued by E. P. Dutton & Company, which lists, among others, editions of the following classical works:

Aristotle
Euclid
Lucretius

A series widely distributed in recent years is Great Books of the Western World (Chicago: Encyclopaedia Britannica), which contains translations of the works of the following writers:

Archimedes	Galileo
Aristotle	Gilbert
Francis Bacon	Harvey
Copernicus	Hippocrates
Darwin	Huygens
Descartes	James
Euclid	Kepler
Faraday	Lucretius
Freud	Newton
Galen	Ptolemy

Scholarly editions of the original texts only are contained in the Oxford Classical Texts (published by the Oxford University Press), limited mainly to literary works. Aristotle and Lucretius are included. A guide to other editions and translations is *The Reader's Adviser* (Twelfth edition. New York: R. R. Bowker, 1977. 3v.).

All works included in the present volume up to about 1500 were written prior to the invention of printing. The earliest texts are therefore in manuscript form, frequently in scattered versions and in fragments. Following is a record, believed to be reasonably accurate, of the first appearance in printed form—the so-called *editio princeps*—of each title, together with occasional notes on other editions. The classical forms of personal names have been used throughout.

AGASSIZ, JEAN LOUIS RODOLPHE (1807-1873)
Études sur les Glaciers. Neuchâtel: Jent et Gassmann, 1840. 2 vols.

AGRICOLA, GEORGIUS (1490-1555)
De Re Metallica. Basil, 1556. English translation by Herbert and Lou Henry Hoover, 1912.

ARCHIMEDES (287?-212 B.C.)
Opera Omnia (Greek). Basle: Joannes Hervagius, 1544.

ARISTOTLE (384-322 B.C.)
Opera. Augsburg: Ambrosius Keller, 1479. First Greek edition: Venice: Aldus Manutius, 1493-98. *Historia Animalium.* Venice: Aldus Manutius, 1497.

AUDUBON, JOHN JAMES (1785-1851)
The Birds of America from Original Drawings. London: Published by the author, 1827-38. 4 vols.

AVICENNA (980-1037)
Liber Canonis. Nuremburg: Adolf Rusch, c.1473.

BACON, SIR FRANCIS, BARON VERULAM, VISCOUNT ST. ALBANS (1561-1626)
The Twoo Bookes *Of the Proficience and Aduancement of Learning, Diuine and Humane.* London: H. Tomes, 1605. 2 pts. in 1 vol.

The *Advancement of Learning* was intended as an introduction to *Instauratio Magna*, an encyclopedia of all knowledge—a project never completed—but was revised and expanded in a Latin version, *De Augmentis Scientiarum* (1623). In *Novum Organum* (1620), Bacon discussed the uselessness of the older philosophies and the traditional errors of mankind and held out science as the hope of the future. The *New Atlantis*, published posthumously (1627), is a fragmentary sketch of a utopian community of scientists engaged in research for the betterment of mankind.

BACON, ROGER (1214?-1294)
Opera Majus. London, 1733. Parts IV-V issued in Frankfurt, 1614.

BEAUMONT, WILLIAM (1785-1853)
Experiments and Observations on the Gastric Juice and the Physiology of Digestion. Plattsburgh, NY: Printed by F. P. Allen, 1833.

BOWDITCH, NATHANIEL (1773-1838)
The New American Practical Navigator: Being an Epitome of Navigation. Newburyport, MA: Edmund M. Blunt, 1802.

BOYLE, ROBERT (1627-1691)
The Sceptical Chymist: or Chymico-Physical Doubts & Paradoxes. London: J. Crooke, 1661.

BRAHE, TYCHO (1546-1601)
Astronomiae Instauratae Progymnasmata. Prague, 1602. Followed by *Astronomiae Instauratae Mechanica.* 1602. Early correspondence in *Epistolarum Astronomicarum.* Uraniburg, 1596.

CARSON, RACHEL (1907-1964)
Silent Spring. Boston: Houghton Mifflin, 1962.

CAVENDISH, HENRY (1731-1810)
Experiments on Air. London, 1784. (*Transactions of the Royal Society,* v. 74-75).

CELSUS, AULUS CORNELIUS (c.25 B.C.-A.D. 50)
De Medicina. Florence: Nicolaus Laurentii, 1478.

COPERNICUS, NICOLAUS (1473-1543)
De Revolutionibus Orbium Coelestium. Nuremberg: Johann Petrus, 1543. 196ff. The first accurate and complete edition was published in 1873 at Thorn (Torun), Poland, by the Copernicus-Verein für Wissenschaft und Kunst.
The first written account of his theories, entitled *Commentariolus,* "Little Commentary," was circulated by Copernicus among students of astronomy perhaps as early as 1510, but was not published in the author's lifetime. The first printed account, *Narratio Prima,* written by a fervent admirer, George Joachim Rheticus, appeared in 1540.

CURIE, MARIE (1867-1934)
Recherches sur les Substances Radioactives. Paris, 1903.

CUVIER, GEORGES LÉOPOLD (1760-1832)
Le Règne Animal Distribué D'Après Son Organisation. Paris, 1817.

DAGUERRE, LOUIS J. M. (1789-1851)
Historique et Description des Procédés du Daguerrêotype et du Diorama. Paris, 1839.

DALTON, JOHN (1766-1844)
A New System of Chemical Philosophy. Manchester, 1808-1827. v. 1, pt. 1, 1808; v. 1, pt. 2, 1810; v. 2, pt. 1, 1827; v. 2, pt. 2, not published.

DARWIN, CHARLES ROBERT (1809-1882)
On the Origin of Species by Means of Natural Selection, or the Preservation of Favoured Races in the Struggle for Life. London: J. Murray, 1859.
Darwin's *Journal of a Naturalist* (1839), later expanded into a *Naturalist's Voyage round the World in H.M.S. Beagle* (1860), describes the beginning of his life work. The theme of the *Origin of Species* was subsequently developed in detail in *The Descent of Man, and Selection in Relation to Sex* (1871), *The Variation of Animals and Plants under Domestication* (1868), *Expression of the Emotions* (1872), *The Effects of Cross- and Self-Fertilization in the Vegetable Kingdom* (1876), *The Power of Movement in Plants* (1880), and other specialized works.

DESCARTES, RENÉ (1596-1650)
Discours de la Méthode pour Bien Conduire sa Raison et Chercher la Verité dans les Sciences. Leyden: J. Maire, 1637.

DIDEROT, DENIS (1713-1784), Editor
Encyclopédie ou Dictionnaire Raisonné des Sciences, des Arts et des Métiers. Paris: Briasson [etc.], 1751-72. 28 vols.

DIOSCORIDES, PEDACIUS (c.40-80)
De Materia Medica. Colle: Johannes de Medemblick, 1478. First Greek edition: Venice: Aldus Manutius, 1499.

EINSTEIN, ALBERT (1879-1955)
Über die Spezielle und die Allgemeine Relativitätstheorie. Braunschweig: Vieweg, 1917.
　　The Special Theory of Relativity was first set forth by Einstein in an article, "On the Electrodynamics of Moving Bodies," in *Annalen der Physik* in 1905. Shortly afterward, the same journal published a second article, "Does the Inertia of a Body Depend on Its Energy?," stating the basic principle for the release of atomic energy. The General Theory of Relativity was presented in Einstein's *Die Grundlagen der Allgemeinen Relativitätstheorie* (1916).

ELLIS, HENRY HAVELOCK (1859-1939)
Studies in the Psychology of Sex. Philadelphia: F. A. Davis, 1900-1928. 7 vols.
　　Volume I originally published in London, 1897, and suppressed.

EUCLIDES (c.330-c.275 B.C.)
Elementorum Euclidis in Artem Geometrie. Venice, 1482.
　　First of over a thousand printed editions of Euclid's *Elements*.

FARADAY, MICHAEL (1791-1867)
Experimental Researches in Electricity. London: R. and J. E. Taylor, 1839-55. 3 vols. Reprinted from the *Philosophical Transactions*, 1831-52.
　　James Clerk Maxwell's *Electricity and Magnetism* (1873), based on Faraday's experimentation and research, developed the theory of the electromagnetic field on a mathematical basis and made possible a greater understanding of the newly discovered phenomena.

FRANKLIN, BENJAMIN (1706-1790)
Experiments and Observations on Electricity, Made at Philadelphia, ... Communicated in Several Letters to P. Collinson. London, 1751.

FREUD, SIGMUND (1856-1939)
Das Unbehagen in der Kultur. Vienna: Internationaler Psychoanalytischer Verlag, 1930.
　　Freud advanced and developed his theories in a long series of publications, of which the most important are *The Interpretation of Dreams* (1900), *Three Contributions to the Theory of Sex* (1905), *Introductory Lectures on Psychoanalysis* (1916), and *The Ego and the Id* (1923). He was indebted to the French neurologist, Jean Martin Charcot's *Lessons on the Maladies of the Nervous System* (1880); to the writings of Pierre Janet, French physician and psychologist; and to James Braid, nineteenth-centry English writer on hypnotism and magic.

FUCHS, LEONHARD (1501-1566)
De Historia Stirpium Commentarii Insignes. Basil, 1543.

GALENUS, CLAUDIUS (130-200)
Opera. Venice: Philippus Pincius, 1490. First Greek edition: *Therapeutica.* Venice: Nicolaus Blastus, 1500.

GALILEI, GALILEO (1564-1642)
Dialogo ... sopra i Due Massimi Sistemi del Mondo Tolemaico, e Copernicano. Florence: G. B. Landini, 1632.

Galileo's second major work, *Dialoghi delle Nuove Scienze,* "Dialogues of the New Sciences," was issued in 1638, four years before his death, by the Elzevirs at Leyden. Generally considered his most valuable work, the *Dialogues* reviews the results of Galileo's earlier experiments and his meditations on the principles of mechanics.

GESNER, CONRAD (1516-1565)
Historiae Animalium. Zurich, 1551-87. 5 vols.

GIBBS, JOSIAH WILLARD (1839-1903)
"On the Equilibrium of Heterogeneous Substances." Connecticut Academy of Arts and Sciences, *Transactions* (New Haven, 1874-78), pp. 108-248, 343-524.

GILBERT, WILLIAM (1540-1603)
De Magnete, Magneticisque Corporibus, et De Magno Magnete Tellure; Physiologia Nova. London: P. Short, 1600.

GRAY, ASA (1810-1888)
Elements of Botany. New York: Carroll, 1836.

GREW, NEHEMIAH (1641-1712)
The Anatomy of Vegetables Begun. London, 1672.

HALES, STEPHEN (1677-1761)
Vegetable Staticks. London, 1727.

HARVEY, WILLIAM (1578-1657)
Exercitatio Anatomica de Motu Cordis et Sanguinis in Animalibus. Frankfort: William Fitzer, 1628.

Harvey had predecessors: Vesalius in *De Humani Corporis Fabrica* (1543) noted that the septum between the right and left ventricles is complete; Servetus, in his *Christianismi Restitutio* (1553), stated his belief that the blood circulates through the lungs, but did not recognize the heart as the pumping organ; Realdo Colombo, anatomy professor at Rome, author of *De Re Anatomica* (1559), correctly taught that blood passes from the right to the left ventricle through the lungs; Fabricius of Padua, Harvey's teacher, author of *De Venarum Ostiolis* (1603), discovered and described the valves of the veins.

HELMHOLTZ, HERMANN VON (1821-1894)
Über die Erhaltung der Kraft. Berlin: G. Reimer, 1847.

HIPPOCRATES (c.460-377 B.C.)
Aphorismi. Venice: [Bartolomaeus de Cremona?], 1473. First Greek edition: *Omnia Opera.* Venice: Aldus Manutius, 1526.

HOLMES, OLIVER WENDELL (1809-1894)
The Contagiousness of Puerperal Fever. Boston, 1843. 28p. (Reprinted from
The New England Quarterly Journal of Medicine and Surgery, April 1843.)

HOOKE, ROBERT (1635-1703)
*Micrographia: or Some Physiological Descriptions of Minute Bodies Made by
Magnifying Glasses with Observations and Inquiries Thereupon*. London:
J. Martyn and J. Allestry, 1665.

HUMBOLDT, FRIEDRICH HEINRICH ALEXANDER VON (1769-1859)
Kosmos. Stuttgart and Tübingen: J. G. Cotta, 1845-62. 5 vols.
Humboldt shares with Karl Ritter the title of founder of modern scientific
geography. The latter's monumental *Die Erdkunde im Verhältnis zur Natur und
zur Geschichte des Menschen* (10 vols., 1822-59) emphasized the relationship
between man and the physical features of the earth and the influence of these
features on history. The seventeenth-century German geographer, Bernhardus
Varenius, in his *Geographia Generalis* (1650), had paved the way for Humboldt
and Ritter and for such later writers on geopolitics as Friedrich Ratzel and Sir
Halford Mackinder.

HUTTON, JAMES (1726-1797)
*Theory of the Earth; or An Investigation of the Laws Observable in the Com-
position, Dissolution, and Restoration of Land upon the Globe*. Edinburgh
and London, 1795-1899. 3 vols. Original paper read 1785 and printed in
Transactions of the Royal Society of Edinburgh. Edinburgh, 1788, vol. 1,
pt. 2, pp. 209-304.

HUYGENS, CHRISTIAN (1629-1695)
Horologium Oscillatorium. Paris, 1673, and *Traité de la Lumière*. Leide, 1690.

JAMES, WILLIAM (1842-1910)
The Principles of Psychology. New York: Holt, 1890. 2 vols.

JENNER, EDWARD (1749-1823)
*An Inquiry into the Causes and Effects of the Variolae Vaccinae, a Disease
Discovered in Some of the Western Counties of England, Particularly
Gloucestershire, and Known by the Name of the Cow Pox*. London: S. Low,
1798.

KEPLER, JOHANNES (1571-1630)
Astronomia Nova. Prague, 1609.
Harmonices Mundi. Linz, 1619.
Kepler's laws were based chiefly on the mass of observations made over a
twenty-year period by the Danish astronomer Tycho Brahe, whose works
included *Astronomiae Instauratae Progymnasmata* (Prague, 1602-1603) and
Epistolae Astronomicae (Uraniborg, 1596).

KINSEY, ALFRED CHARLES (1894-1956)
Sexual Behavior in the Human Male. Philadelphia: W. B. Saunders, 1948.

KOCH, ROBERT (1843-1910)
"Die Aetiologie der Tuberculose." *Berliner Klinische Wochenschrift* (Berlin),
XIX (1882), pp. 221-30.

LAMARCK, JEAN BAPTISTE PIERRE ANTOINE DE MONET (1744-1829)
Système des Animaux Sans Vertèbres. Paris, 1801.

LAPLACE, PIERRE SIMON, MARQUIS DE (1749-1827)
Traité de Mécanique Céleste. Paris, 1798-1805. 3 vols; supplements, 1823-25.
2 vols.

LAVOISIER, ANTOINE LAURENT (1743-1794)
Traité Elémentaire de Chimie. Paris: Cuchet, 1789. 2 vols.

LEEUWENHOEK, ANTON VAN (1632-1723)
Epistolae ad Societatem Regiam Anglicam. Leyden: J. A. Langerak, 1719.

LEONARDO DA VINCI (1452-1519)
Notebooks. London: Duckworth, 1906. One of the numerous editions in English,
Italian, etc.

LINNAEUS, CAROLUS (1707-1778) (Swedish form: Carl Von Linné)
Systema Naturae. Leyden: T. Haak, 1735. Definitive edition (10th): Stockholm:
L. Salvii, 1758-59. 2 vols.

LISTER, JOSEPH, 1st BARON (1827-1912)
"On the Antiseptic Principle in the Practice of Surgery." *The Lancet* (London,
1867), pp. 741-45.

LUCRETIUS CARUS TITUS (99-55 B.C.)
De Rerum Natura. Brescia: Fernandus, c.1473.

LYELL, CHARLES (1797-1875)
*Principles of Geology, Being an Attempt to Explain the Former Changes of the
Earth's Surface, by Reference to Causes Now in Operation.* London:
J. Murray, 1830-33. 3 vols.

MALPIGHI, MARCELLO (1628-1694)
Anatome Plantarum. London, 1675.

MAURY, MATTHEW FONTAINE (1806-1873)
The Physical Geography of the Sea. New York: Harper, 1855.

MENDEL, GREGOR JOHANN (1822-1884)
"Versuche über Pflanzen-Hybriden." *Verhandlungen des Naturforschenden
Vereines in Brünn* (Brünn), IV (1866), pp. 3-47.

NEWTON, SIR ISAAC (1642-1727)
Philosophiae Naturalis Principia Mathematica. London: Printed by Joseph
Streater for the Royal Society, 1687.
    Newton's researches on light—the composition of light, the nature of color
and of white light—which occupied his early years, were summed up in his
Opticks (1704).

PARACELSUS, PHILIPPUS THEOPHRASTUS (1493-1541)
Opera Omnia Medico-Chemico-Chirugica. Geneva, 1658. 3 vols.

PASTEUR, LOUIS (1822-1895)
"Mémoire sur la Fermentation Appelée Lactique." Académie des Sciences,
Comptes Rendus (Paris), XLV (1857), pp. 913-16.

PAVLOV, IVAN PETROVICH (1849-1936)
Conditioned Reflexes; an Investigation of the Physiological Activity of the Cerebral Cortex. London: Oxford University Press, 1927. First published in Russian, 1926.

Nearly a century before Pavlov's experiments, a Scottish physiologist, Sir Charles Bell, had pioneered in research dealing with the anatomy and physiology of the nervous system. His findings were reported in *New Ideas of the Anatomy of the Brain* (1811) and *The Nervous System of the Human Body* (1830). Bell's discoveries have been compared in historical importance with those made by William Harvey on the circulatory system.

PLINIUS SECUNDUS, GAIUS (23-79)
Historia Naturalis. Venice: Johannes de Spira, 1469.

PTOLEMAEUS, CLAUDIUS (c.100-170)
Geographia. Vicenza: Hermannus Liechenstein, 1475.

RAY, JOHN (1627-1705)
Historiae Plantarum. London, 1686-1705.

SMITH, WILLIAM (1769-1839)
Geological Atlas of England and Wales. London: J. Cary, 1815.

Smith furnished irrefutable proof of Hutton's theories on the age of the earth by his study of fossils in rocks, the beginning of the science of paleontology. Smith's findings were reported in *Order of the Strata and Their Imbedded Organic Remains, Examined and Proved Prior to 1799* (1799) and in his renowned *Geological Map of England and Wales, with Part of Scotland* (1815).

THEOPHRASTUS (c.370-287 B.C.)
De Historia et Causis Plantarum. Treviso: Bartholomaeus Confalonerius, 1483. First Greek edition: Venice: Aldus Manutius, 1495-98.

VESALIUS, ANDREAS (1514-1564)
De Humani Corporis Fabrica. Basle: Johannis Oporinus, 1543.

The universal genius Leonardo da Vinci (1452-1519) preceded Vesalius in scientific studies of human and animal anatomy and muscular movement, but Leonardo's notebooks containing his anatomical, physiological, and embryological drawings were not published until modern times and therefore may be presumed to have had little contemporary influence.

Secondary Works

Among many general histories of science, the following titles are particularly recommended:

Bell, Eric. *Men of Mathematics.* 1937.

Butterfield, Herbert. *The Origins of Modern Science.* 1949.

Crombie, Alistair. *Augustine to Galileo.* 1952.

Dampier, William. *A History of Science.* 1949.

Grant, Edward. *Physical Science in the Middle Ages.* 1971.

Hall, Alfred. *The Scientific Revolution.* 1966.

Harvey-Gibson, Robert. *Two Thousand Years of Science.* 1929.

Lenard, Phillip. *Great Men of Science.* 1933.

Needham, Joseph. *The Great Tradition.* 1970.

Pledge, Humphry. *Science since 1500.* 1966.

Sarton, George. *A History of Science.* 1952-59.

Singer, Charles. *A Short History of Scientific Ideas to 1900.* 1959.

Trattner, Ernest. *Architects of Ideas.* 1942.

Wightman, William. *The Growth of Scientific Ideas.* 1951.

Williams, Henry. *A History of Science.* 1904-1910.

Index